PENGUIN B[OOKS]

ASKING FOR T[ROUBLE]

A fifth-generation South African, Do[nald Woods was born in the] Transkei in 1933 and studied law [at Cape] Town before becoming a journalist. At the age of thirty-one he was appointed editor of the *Daily Dispatch*, a leading anti-apartheid newspaper in South Africa. Until he was silenced by government banning orders in October 1977, he wrote the most widely read syndicated column in the country. He and his wife and their five children escaped to Britain in 1978 and now live in London, where he works as a writer, broadcaster and lecturer on South African affairs. His books *Biko* and *South African Dispatches* are also published in Penguin.

Donald Woods

ASKING
FOR TROUBLE

AUTOBIOGRAPHY
OF A
BANNED JOURNALIST

PENGUIN BOOKS

For my wife
Wendy

and our children
Jane, Dillon, Duncan,
Gavin, Lindsay and Mary

Penguin Books Ltd, 27 Wrights Lane, London w8 5tz (Publishing and Editorial)
and Harmondsworth, Middlesex, England (Distribution and Warehouse)
Viking Penguin Inc., 40 West 23rd Street, New York 10010, USA
Penguin Books Australia Ltd, Ringwood, Victoria, Australia
Penguin Books Canada Ltd, 2801 John Street, Markham, Ontario, Canada l3r 1b4
Penguin Books (N.Z.) Ltd, 182–190 Wairau Road, Auckland 10, New Zealand

First published by Gollancz 1980
Published in Penguin Books 1987
Reprinted with a new Preface 1987

Copyright © Donald Woods, 1980, 1987
All rights reserved

Made and printed in Great Britain by
Richard Clay Ltd, Bungay, Suffolk
Typeset in Baskerville

Education consists mainly in what we have unlearned.

Mark Twain

ILLUSTRATIONS

PREFACE TO 1987 EDITION

THIS BOOK, first published in 1980, is being reissued because a film based on it has been scheduled for release in November 1987. The film is produced and directed by Sir Richard Attenborough and its distributors are Universal Pictures of Los Angeles.

Provisionally titled *Asking for Trouble* during its production stages, the film is being released under another title because it is based also on a previous book of mine, *Biko* (1978), and because a broader title seemed appropriate to encompass the subject-matter of both books. The title of the film is *Cry Freedom*.

The screenplay, by John Briley, tells of my friendship with Steve Biko, the leader of the Black Consciousness Movement in South Africa, who was killed by South African Security Police in 1977. It recounts how Biko's family, and my own, were subjected to increasing harassment by the Security Police as our friendship developed; how Biko was imprisoned without trial and died; how I was arrested and banned for challenging the official explanation of his death; and of how I escaped with my family from South Africa to reach Botswana in 1978.

While events concerning both families are the foreground of the script, they are set against a background of major incidents of public record in South Africa during the time frame of 1975 to 1978 – the Soweto massacre, raids on black townships and a major trial in Pretoria – and the general theme is the effect of apartheid on the black victims of it, as well as on the whites who challenge it. The screenwriter uses factual material to reveal the apartheid policy in a manner not previously seen in a major feature film.

Filming was on location in Zimbabwe from July to October 1986, in Kenya, briefly, in October, and at Shepperton Studios, London, until completion of shooting in November. Post-production editing, sound synchronization and recording were completed at Twickenham Studios, London, in June 1987, when the finished film was handed over to Universal Pictures for promotion and distribution.

Because of the time lapse since the publication of *Asking for*

Trouble in 1980, the scriptwriter has been able to go beyond some of the details contained at the end of this book in dealing with how I escaped from South Africa. For example, it is no longer necessary to protect the identity of Robin Walker, as he has since left South Africa. He is therefore identified in the film as Bruce Haigh of Canberra, who is now First Secretary at the Australian Embassy in Pakistan.

In 1977 Bruce was with the Australian Embassy in South Africa, and his role in my escape was to drive me from Telle Bridge, on the Lesotho border, to Maseru, the Lesotho capital, in time for me to telephone my wife, Wendy, to tell her that all was set for her and our five children to cross the border later that day and join me in Lesotho. In the film he is portrayed as a journalist because, for the purposes of compacting the story into a two-hour account on the screen, the part is a composite of two characters, one of whom is still practising journalism in South Africa and therefore cannot be identified. Readers of this book will notice that Bruce Haigh is mentioned as having been with me the day I was arrested and banned at Johannesburg airport, an incident also included in the film.

As for Drew Court, he is accurately depicted in the film as a priest, although, for obvious reasons, his real name is not used and he is identified as Father Kani.

Other information that came to light, or was able to be revealed, since *Asking for Trouble* was published concerned the bright light that seemed to probe the area I was hiding in near the Lesotho border during my escape. For years I assumed it had been an uncommonly bright car headlight, but then, in 1983, I learned that it had in fact been a police searchlight and was part of a man-hunt for two bank robbers who had killed a guard in the small town of Sterkspruit near the Telle Bridge border post. I had chosen this area for my crossing into Lesotho because it was so remote, and it was well for my already scant peace of mind that night that I was unaware that the bank robbers had made it their target at precisely the same time!

The searchlight incident is one of four real incidents which occurred during my escape but which were not included in the film because of the question of cinematic credibility. Sir Richard Attenborough explained that translating true stories into film involved not only the transmitting of true facts to the screen but facts that, no matter how true, would not strain the credulity of the audience.

He had had an illustration of this when filming *A Bridge Too Far*. Although the story was absolutely true, audiences in America had refused to believe that Ryan O'Neal could have been a real colonel – he seemed too young. The fact that the real-life colonel he played had actually been two years younger than O'Neal hadn't mattered. The audiences were simply not used to young colonels, and therefore, according to pollsters, rejected other true elements of the film as "hyped".

Consequently our four incidents, true though they were, were left out of the film because audiences would probably have thought that they were put in by the screenwriter to heighten the drama. A brief description of the other three incidents might show why this decision was made.

The first of these incidents – the missal incident, described in the Prologue – was recalled by Wendy and me only when we were being interviewed by the BBC for a television programme. However, both Attenborough and screenwriter John Briley felt it would look to much like "hype" in the movie.

The second real incident, which I recalled only after writing the book, occurred at the Telle Bridge border post. One of the officials was about to stamp my "passport" and hand it back, when his telephone started to ring. He answered it and looked up at me immediately, and I imagined he was being told to watch out for me; that the Security Police had discovered I had left the house and would try to cross some border. Then, still looking at me, he assured his wife over the telephone that he would bring two loaves of bread home! He then complained irritably about his wife's calls about groceries as he completed stamping my "passport". This, too, was considered too much for cinema audiences to accept as actually having happened, though the film does have a phone ringing as my passport is about to be stamped.

Finally, a fact only briefly alluded to in the book was the car trouble Wendy had on the way to Umtata. This was extraordinary in that the car was a new Mercedes which hadn't given any trouble and had recently been serviced. But for some reason related to the distributor or diaphragm, it suddenly lost power on the uphills barely half-way to Umtata, so that what should have been a journey of little more than two hours had taken her more than four, and she and the children had arrived at her parents' house only moments before my crucial phone call from Maseru which was a vital element of our escape plan. This, too, would have looked too coincidental and too much like an exaggeration.

Real life is often more dramatic than what we see on the screen! However, Wendy and I were in complete agreement with Sir Richard and John Briley about omitting or playing down these four incidents, because we concurred in the conclusion that anything which detracted from the credibility of the real story would be counter-productive, and because we agreed that much of the power of the film derived from the fact that it tells a true story.

Readers of this book who see the film will realize that the film accurately depicts key incidents described herein, and I am grateful to Sir Richard for his determination to preserve the authenticity of the true story in cinematic terms. In the film, Steve Biko and I are played by two gifted American actors, Denzel Washington and Kevin Kline, and my wife, Wendy, by one of Britain's leading actresses, Penelope Wilton. Wendy and I were among a number of South African specialists retained as consultants during the production, in earnest of Sir Richard Attenborough's determination to tell the true story and to check details for authenticity in regard to the basic theme of the narrative. We were impressed by the lengths to which he and his unit went to ensure the correctness of even such minutiae as the number of buttons on a police uniform and the types of vehicles and expressions used in South Africa in 1977.

It is my hope, and the hope of all of us who were involved in the production, that the film will inform a wide audience throughout the world of the excesses of the apartheid system, thus moving many to require their political representatives and governments to support stronger economic and diplomatic pressures from the international community against the South African government until the scourge of apartheid is abolished.

Donald Woods
London
19 October 1987

AUTHOR'S NOTE

THIS AUTOBIOGRAPHY WAS written during 1978 and 1979, largely in London but partly in Boston where I had a visiting fellowship at Harvard by award of the Nieman Foundation. Fragments were also written during more than a hundred and fifty air trips in various parts of the world, and in such geographically scattered places as Oslo, Norway; Lubbock, Texas; Portland, Oregon; Halifax, Nova Scotia; and Cologne, Germany—and towns as disparate in size as Denver and Laramie; Sydney and Walla Walla; New York and Oshkosh. This cannot be claimed as an excuse for any disjointedness in the narrative, because the evocation of South Africa in all these exotic places seemed, for me, all the more vivid because of the far perspective.

Where detailed conversations are given in direct quotes—for example, with South African cabinet ministers such as ex-Premier Vorster, Premier Botha, Mulder, Koornhof and others —they are from notes and records made at the time or shortly after, as well as from memory, and the political developments mentioned, such as the apartheid statutes, are matters of record. For details of the statutes mentioned I am indebted to Jan Marsh of the research section of the International Defence and Aid Fund for making IDAF records available, and to the South African Institute of Race Relations publications for their comprehensive indexes of apartheid laws.

For obvious reasons the names of three persons mentioned in the concluding chapters dealing with the escape from South Africa—Drew Court, Robin Walker and Tami Vundla—are fictitious, but all are real people who did the deeds ascribed to them in this book, and the help they rendered is recounted as fully and in as much detail as discretion allows.

Special thanks are due to my wife Wendy for editing the first draft of the manuscript; to her, Deborah Morgan and my daughter Jane for typing and constructive criticism of it; and to Sheila Hodges and John Bush of Victor Gollancz for editorship and preparation of the final copy for publication.

London, March 1980

PROLOGUE

IT WAS SIX o'clock in the evening, the time to go. The house was quiet, the children playing next door. Upstairs in the bathroom I looked out of the narrow window to see if the Security Police observer was in sight. He wasn't in that arc of view, but he was somewhere on that opposite sidewalk—always there watching the house, as he had been for months.

I kept looking at my watch and at my face in the mirror. My disguise seemed effective—in a dark clerical suit with a priest's collar and with my hair dyed black I was a stranger to myself. I had the thought that I wouldn't be seeing the bathroom again. In the dressing-room I had a last look down at the garden, at the palm tree, the msintsi trees, with the children's rope ladder hanging from one of them, and the shrubs round the big lawn of overgrown kikuyu grass. It was a wet summer in the last few days of 1977.

The final thing I packed was the Beretta automatic from its hiding-place above Wendy's coats and dresses, under the spring-clips which held the Winchester riot-gun we had bought after the Security Police fired five bullets into the house.

Wendy made a final check downstairs to be sure there was nobody else in the house, then came into the bedroom to call me, mouthing the words because of the hidden microphones. We knew they were all over the place, and had stopped discussing anything confidential inside the house, rather talking in whispers out on the lawn or behind the house at the poolside.

I picked up my dark coat and a missal I was taking as part of my priest's outfit. Through some instinct Wendy reached for the missal, flipped through it and saw on the flyleaf my name and the date of my first communion. She held it up ironically to show me, then ripped out the page and handed the missal back.

We hurried down the stairs, through the hall, the dining-room, the kitchen, and into the garage. There were no last looks now at anything—I was too tense. Behind the closed doors of the garage stood our Mercedes, and more quietly than was necessary I opened the trunk and put in my carrybag, then crouched on the floor of the car as Wendy spread my coat over me. She slid open the garage door, and reversed the car out past the Security Police observer. He had grown used to seeing her driving about on her own, yet as the car went past him I crouched even lower to be sure of staying below his line of vision.

You are seldom so close to the carpet of your own car or the texture of its upholstery, and it seemed unreal to me to be furtive in such familiar surroundings as we drove down Chamberlain Road, pausing at the traffic lights before turning into Devereux Avenue. Though I couldn't see I knew by the twists and turns we took exactly where we were at any point. I knew the pause at the Frere Road intersection, and how after the junction with Western Avenue the route lay under a subway and right past police headquarters where I had been interrogated before my banning. We were now in more danger. It was dangerous enough to escape from my home, to which the State had restricted me, but it was even more dangerous to risk being caught with the contents of that airline bag. It contained, among other things, a bulky manuscript I had written in defiance of the State ban on my writing, and the text of the manuscript could mean the death penalty for me in terms of the State's security laws.

As we drove through our suburb of Vincent, it seemed hard to believe how drastically our lives had changed. Within four months our world had been turned upside down. Our friend Steve Biko had been beaten to death by Security Police, and after we had helped raise an outcry over the killing I had been banned by the State. By order of the Minister of Police I was forbidden to write or speak in public; forbidden to speak privately with more than one person; forbidden to be in a room with more than one person, even inside my house, and kept under constant surveillance, physical and electronic, with all phone calls and incoming mail monitored by the Security Police. Members of my family had been harassed, and Wendy and the children had been subjected to threats, abuse and attacks by the police.

Now we were escaping, and our escape plan was for me to cross the border into Lesotho, Wendy and the children following by a different route. Her first task was to get me beyond the city limits, then to go back to the house and create the impression, through bugged telephone calls and conversations, that I was still there, to give me the twelve hours I needed to get across the border. She and the children were to follow the next morning. It was an imperfect plan, thrown together in the last few days. We'd had to keep it from friends, for fear of implicating them, and from the smaller children, in case they said the wrong thing near one of the microphones. But now the first stage was over. I was beyond the city limits, and after a tense farewell Wendy went back to the house while I joined the other hitch-hikers on the busy road to the north. It had started to drizzle again and I pulled my coat-collar up, worried that the rain might wash out the hair-dye.

The airline bag felt heavy, and I hoped I'd get a lift soon. I had a journey of hundreds of miles ahead, and all sorts of things were going through my mind. Why was I, a fifth-generation white South African, editor for twelve years of one of the country's longest-established newspapers, escaping in disguise in fear of political police?

The answer fills a book, and this is that book.

CHAPTER ONE

FAR FROM THE big cities of South Africa are the tribal reservations, and it was in one of these, the Transkei Territory, that I grew up among the Bomvana tribesmen of the Wild Coast. The Bomvanas wore red-ochred loincloths and blankets, lived in round mud huts with thatched roofs and believed in sorcery and witchcraft. Their young men settled arguments by fighting to the finish with battle-axes, and as a child I grew accustomed to the fact, if not the spectacle, of human beings literally being chopped to death. The axe-fights took place every Sunday in our district, and it was safe to watch them from fairly close because the fighters never turned on anyone with whom they had no quarrel. The clashes were usually between rival groups of up to twenty, and bystanders were attacked only if they gave an impression of favouring one side or the other.

Although for years I was the only white child among tens of thousands of Bomvanas, I never felt in any danger among them; I could walk anywhere in the area and go into any of their huts. Apart from the axe-fights, violence was not among their chief characteristics. They had a disciplined society with rigid social rules. Tall, well-built people, they spoke with elaborate courtesy, and their code was based on generosity and communal sharing.

Their language was Xhosa, which has a variety of distinctive click-sounds, and as a white child living on a trading-post in Bomvanaland I spoke it as naturally as I spoke English. In fact, up to the age of five I expressed myself better in Xhosa than in English because it was spoken by all my Bomvana playmates and my nursemaid, Maggie Mzondo. My parents and my brother and sister also spoke it fluently.

Maggie was a *gqirakazi*, a witchdoctress, and we kids used to get her to *vumisa* for us, to go into a trance and wail her incantations to the spirits as she sagged to the floor with her eyes rolling back in her head. We loved it, although it was often scary. Maggie could "smell out" evil-doers and cast spells on them—a valuable aid in imposing discipline on kids, especially at bedtime. My brother Harland and I would show her our Superman comics, explaining the stories to her in Xhosa, but her own bedtime stories were far more vivid.

One in particular used to send chills down our spines. It was about the *sigebenga*—the monstrous Xhosa spook who was all things terrible—who entered a hut where children were sleeping and decided aloud in which order he would eat them up. "*Ndizaku qala nga le* . . ." he would begin. ("I'll start with *this* one . . .") "*Ndi ze nga le* . . ." ("Then I'll come to *this* one . . .") "*Ndi ze nga le* . . . *ndi ze nga le* . . . *ndi ze nga le* . . ." ("Then *this* one . . . then *this* one . . . then *this* one.")

Maggie's impassive face was ominous in the dim nightlight as she intoned the singsong litany of ghastly inevitability. She told many frightening stories of the loathsome *sigebenga*, but that was the scariest. And though her stories were hardly conducive to lulling us into calm slumber we always pestered her for more—especially "*leya*" ("*that* one") in anticipation of which we would shudder and burrow deeper into the blankets while she composed her features to begin the tale.

Bomvana lore was full of bogeymen and sprites. The best-known was Tikoloshe, the water-sprite who was only two feet tall and whose whole body was covered in grey hair. He had a long grey beard down to his knees and lived in the eroded banks of rivers. Tikoloshe would get you if you didn't behave. He could walk through walls, run like a horse and even fly. He could destroy entire herds of cattle, inflicting mysterious diseases on man and beast or causing people to act peculiarly against their better inclinations. He could also be blamed for anything that went wrong, so he was a scapegoat as well as a bogeyman. Another sprite was Ichanti, the watersnake, one of Tikoloshe's submarine minions, and a third was Impundulu, the lightning-bird. Knowledge of the ways and powers of these sprites was part of the qualification of the witchdoctors. It was believed that the most powerful witchdoctors rode about on baboons at night, dragging one leg and leaving a swathe through the underbrush and tall dobo grass. I was once shown such a swathe by my playmates, who gave a superior laugh when I said it was only the mark of a lightning strike. They were condescending—what could a *mlungwana*, a little white boy, know of such things?

Apart from her sorcery Maggie was a woman of substance. She and her husband cultivated several fields and had herds of cattle, sheep and goats. In view of this and her "practice", it was never clear why she worked all her life as a domestic servant, unless it was because of the close bond between her and my mother. She worked for my mother for forty years, and it was often a stormy arrangement. My mother sacked her at least a dozen times, usually after they had traded insults and imprecations in Xhosa, Mom at the top of her voice and Maggie in a barely audible undertone. But Maggie would ignore these dismissals and turn up the next morning for work, busying herself about the kitchen as if nothing had happened. Mom would heave a sigh of relief and uphold the truce.

When my sister Joan was a baby Maggie saved her life. Workmen were moving a heavy wardrobe in a bedroom and it toppled over and was falling on the child when Maggie flung herself over her on all fours and took the weight of it on her back. Sometimes when Mom was feeling sheepish about allowing "that cheeky devil Maggie" to resume work after a sacking she would mutter: "After all, she *did* save Joanie's life . . ."

Mom and Maggie were the same age, although from the time they were in their fifties Mom would often call her "the old devil" as if there were a vast age-gap. At other times they were the closest confidants and would murmur away for hours in Xhosa, Mom in a kind of monologue punctuated by Maggie's regularly spaced moans of assent and grunts of comprehension. Then the roles would be reversed and the monologue would be Maggie's, with the moans of assent and grunts of comprehension coming from my mother.

These sounds were necessary in any protracted conversation in Xhosa. It was considered inattentive to hear a speaker out in silence for any length of time, so the listener had to come in regularly with "awwww" or "ehhhh" or simply a noise in the throat.

Much of Dad's social life was with local elders of the Bomvanas. At sundown he would often have a drink with five or six of his favourite acquaintances among them, but never inside the house or in any of their huts—usually out in the yard. A servant would bring out a chair for him, and the elders would sit on the ground around him, smoking long-stemmed pipes as they chatted about crops or local events. The servant would bring a bottle of Cape brandy, a water jug and two glasses, one glass for Dad and the other for the tribesmen. Dad would pour out his measure, exactly up to a pattern on the glass, then add water. Then the bottle and the other glass would be handed round the circle and each would pour his own measure, again up to the pattern on the glass, constituting about a triple-shot of neat brandy. The Bomvanas never added water, always gulping the neat brandy down in one draught, followed by a loud "Aaahh!" to cool their burning throats, smacking their lips in exaggerated appreciation. Sometimes I would lean against my father's chair, being four or five years old, or sit on the ground to listen to the talk. Then the old tribesmen would engage me in some conversation, always solemnly, as if I were an adult, never like the old tribeswomen who clucked and made baby-talk noises like "*Mah-na-seh*!" ("Isn't he cute?").

Joan, Harland and I were all given Xhosa names at birth by the tribesmen, as a mark of friendship. Mine was "Zweliyanyikima", "the world shakes". Such names were quite arbitrarily given and were not connected to any event, there having been no earthquakes or tremors anywhere in Bomvanaland in living memory. Given at birth, Xhosa names were always complimentary. Given to adults, they would be more specific in reference to a characteristic or physical feature of the person named. As I grew older I was given additional names and could be hailed by any of them by members of different black communities, but in Bomvanaland I was always known as Zweliyanyikima. My father, who as a trader loaned money at interest, was called "Masumpa", "He who makes a gift then takes back a part of it". His assistant, Glenn Turner, was called "Ginyizembe", "He swallowed an axe", because of his quick temper.

Adults, and especially elders, conversed with strict formality when children were around, and never joked about sex or other natural functions in their presence. When I leant against my father's chair as he drank brandy in the yard with the elders, one of them would address me formally: "Greetings, Zweliyanyikima. Are you well?" I would reply: "*Molo, Mekene. Hayi, ndisahleli.*" "Greetings, Mekene: No, I am well." Mekene might then inquire after a sheep which the headman had given me for my birthday. Was the sheep well? No, the sheep was well. Then I would ask if he was well and he would reply that no, he was well, and thus the niceties of etiquette would be observed.

The Bomvanas loved practical jokes or straight-faced leg-pulling, and when a tribesman noted in the district for his big feet was persuaded by my father that there was going to be a new tax according to the area of ground a man's feet covered, they laughed about it for months and never let the big-footed one forget his gullibility.

The only Bomvana whose hut my father ever visited socially was a venerable elder for whom he had enormous respect. He was Belwana, and he was in his nineties. When Belwana saw Dad's black Buick pull up by the roadside near his kraal he would walk all the way down to the road to accompany him to the hut. The vigorous old man, bareheaded, barefoot and wearing only a loincloth, would utter a formal welcome and he and Dad would walk together as they talked. They sent each other gifts from time to time—a bag of tobacco, a goat, a blanket or a carved stick.

In South Africa the Bomvanas were regarded as the most primitive of all the tribespeople and Bomvanaland as the most remote area of the country. It was part of the Transkei Territory, set aside by the white government a hundred years before as a reservation for Xhosa tribes such as the Pondos, the Tembus and the Bomvanas. The Bomvanas were so called because in Xhosa the word Bomvu means red, and the reference was to the red ochre they used to stain their blankets and loincloths. It wasn't simply that they liked the colour—it kept away lice and ticks.

A Bomvana in full dress looked magnificent, especially the young men and the old women. In addition to the loincloth and the blanket worn as a cloak over one shoulder, the young men wore intricately patterned bead necklaces, amulets, anklets and waist-bands in the brightest colours, made by their girl-friends to traditional designs. The old women dressed even more splendidly. Their basic garment was the *mbaco*, an ankle-length skirt with the hem ornately patterned in rows of braid, and a braided bodice—both a light orange colour—over which the blanket was worn like a cloak. Scarves and bead necklaces of many colours adorned the neck, and surmounting all this was the magnificent head-dress. This was like a flared turban of coloured cloths extending outward and upward, contributing to the regal appearance of the old women. They looked stately as they walked along the road in all this gear, often with a long-stemmed beaded pipe clenched in their teeth and sometimes with a bucket of water or shopping bundle balanced on top of their turbaned heads.

The Bomvanas went barefoot at all times, and from early youth developed a thick sole as hard as horn which trod thorns and pebbles without any pain. Quite often while talking to you they'd stand on one foot and lift the other sole to pick out thorns and burrs as impersonally as if out of a strip of leather.

Bomvanaland stretches along the south-eastern coast of South Africa between the Kei and Umtata rivers, extending inland from thirty to fifty miles. Where we lived, near the mouth of the Bashee River, was the heartland of it. Every five miles there was a trading-post in which a white trader was licensed to trade with the tribespeople; the trading concession of each station extended in a circle for a five-mile radius. If blacks wanted to establish trading-stations they could trade within a two-mile radius, but there were few black traders. Throughout the Transkei Territory, about the size of Wales, there were about seven hundred white traders. Whites from outside the territory looked on our white trading community in the Transkei as strangely different because we spoke the complex Xhosa language which they couldn't understand and because, as they saw it, we lived "among the savages".

Traders sold basic commodities to the tribespeople— blankets, axes, buckets, hoes, sickles, spades, medicines, mirrors, beads and so forth. They sold grain on credit during times of famine, after a drought for instance, and when harvests were good they bought produce from the tribesmen—hides, skins and wool for bigger markets. Traders were also recruiting agents for the gold mines and functioned as postal agents, money-lenders, pension officers and scribes for illiterates.

The first white settlers in South Africa had been Dutch, who colonized the Cape of Good Hope in 1652 and whose descendants, later known as the Boers and later still as the Afrikaners, had trekked inland and evolved their own culture and language—Afrikaans, an offshoot of Dutch. Later the British Empire had annexed South Africa, and after the Napoleonic Wars the British government encouraged young Britons to settle in the country. The 1820 Settlers, as the first wave of these immigrants were called, were given land grants as farmers in the Eastern Cape area between the places now known as Port Elizabeth and Grahamstown.

One of these settlers was twenty-one-year-old Frederick Woods, my great-great-grandfather. Little is known of the first two generations of Dad's family in South Africa, apart from the fact that Frederick was said to have come from Cornwall, but his grandson, James Woods, my grandfather, became a wealthy ostrich-farmer in the days when ostrich-feathers were the fashion in Paris and London. When the designers dropped the ostrich-feather as a means of adornment, grandfather James was ruined. He became a transport-rider, leading ox-wagon supply teams inland to the diamond fields of Kimberley. He later settled in Peddie, a small town between Grahamstown and the port of East London, and became a cattle-dealer and butcher.

It was in Peddie that Dad was born, one of sixteen children, and he had little schooling. His first job, at the age of twelve, was as a butcher-boy, and at fourteen he became a postal clerk. His family were strict Wesleyan Methodists, and while still in his teens Dad became a lay preacher of some local renown. At the age of nineteen he walked two hundred miles to the Transkei coast with the ambition of becoming a trader and owning his own trading-station. He worked for several traders as an assistant, then began to look around for his own trading-site. He found it near the banks of the Bashee River, within a few miles of where the river runs into the ocean. It was called Hobeni, place of doves, and consisted of a couple of run-down mud huts—one for living in and one functioning as the trading-shop. It was owned by a man of Irish descent named Frank Lawlor, from whom Dad at first leased it. After a few months he felt he could convert Hobeni into a profitable station and bought it. Frank Lawlor lived ten miles away on a large station called Madwaleni. He took a liking to my father, who thereafter often saddled his horse and rode to Madwaleni to visit the family. Then in his mid-twenties, Dad was regarded as one of the leading sportsmen in the white community.

Christened Walter John Woods, he was always called Jack, and during his visits to the Lawlor place four of Frank Lawlor's daughters used to scramble to the window to "get a look at Jack Woods". He was tall and good-looking, and the Lawlor girls were impressed with his elegant riding-coat and boots. He, in turn, was impressed with one of the youngest, Edna, and after several years of formal courtship they were married when she was twenty. Dad was twenty-six and by now fairly wealthy, having paid Frank Lawlor the last instalment for Hobeni.

Mom's ancestors had come from Ireland after one of the potato famines of the middle 1800s. Originally from County Cork and parts of Wicklow, they were tenant farmers and at least some of them had been involved in rebellion against British rule; my uncle Fintan Lawlor was almost certainly called after the Irish revolutionary, Fintan Lalor.

Grandmother Alice Lawlor, a second-generation South African, had as a child been taught phrases like "Erin Go Bragh!" and "Up the rebels!", which she uttered with feeling from time to time throughout her life. Her mother had been one of the "Kennaway girls", a shipload of Irish girls brought to South Africa on the sailing ship *Kennaway* to provide wives for the German Legionaries hired by the British government to police the frontier between the settler farmers and the Xhosa warriors—the colonial authorities fearing the mercenaries might take black wives and dilute the white race. The *Kennaway* missed its anchorage point at the port of East London and was wrecked on a beach, but all the girls were rescued. However, after her arrival great-grandmother Warren rejected the Germans and fell in love with an Irishman named Kelly. She was fifteen, he was forty-two, and for some years after they married he was still buying dolls for her. She would sit on his lap, fascinated by his pocket watch, and he would chuckle to friends: "She's only a child!"

They had several children and one of their daughters was my grandmother, Alice Kelly, who met, married and bore thirteen children to Frank Lawlor. Edna Lawlor, my mother, was the sixth of them, born at Madwaleni. A governess was engaged for the primary education of the children, then they were sent to boarding-school at the convent in Umtata, sixty miles away, by ox-wagon. It used to take them three days to get to school, crossing river drifts and going up and down hills with no roads of any kind, through forests, and across wide maize-fields.

Granny Lawlor was a formidable woman. She was sturdily built and wore her waist-length grey hair in a plaited bun. She had handsome Irish features, and many years later when I paid my first visit to Ireland I saw counterparts of her and my mother in the features of the women in a Tipperary market-place. One of my earliest memories of her was seeing her swing a shotgun up to her shoulder to blast a treesnake which then slithered down headless in a grove of trees at Madwaleni. Wild Coast treesnakes are bright green, but they blend so well into foliage that it takes a keen eye to spot them if they keep still. They are called boomslangs—in Afrikaans "boom" means "tree" and "slang" means "snake"—and are one of the most poisonous snakes in the world. Their venom dissolves the walls of blood-vessels, and a badly bitten victim oozes blood from the eyes, the nose, the mouth and the ears. The venom also attacks the nervous system and death results from this and from rapid destruction of the blood cells. Unlike most snakes, which withdraw their fangs after striking, the boom-slang keeps chewing at the wound to inject more venom because its biggest fangs are at the back of the upper jaw, deeply grooved to carry the poison as far into the wound as possible.

The boomslang Granny Lawlor shot was about four feet long, but often they grow to six feet. They are fast-moving, especially in trees, and because of this and their brilliant green colour they are often mistaken for another deadly snake, the green mamba. But the mamba has a flat head and is usually found further up the coast in Natal. The boomslang has a round head and big round eyes, and when angry it inflates a hood behind its head like a cobra. It also rears up off the ground to strike, like a cobra, but herpetologists have estab-lished that its venom, drop for drop, is more poisonous than that of any cobra or viper. Boomslangs usually avoid human beings and only attack if they feel cornered or threatened. They eat chameleons, birds, mice and frogs, and especially like birds' eggs. The speed of their strike against a bird on a branch is like a blur.

Things went well for my parents in the first few years of their marriage. They added on to the house and shop at Hobeni, and trade was good. As a trader's daughter Mom was a help in the business, and at weekends they went to dances and gymkhanas all over the district. The dances held at the trading-stations were formal affairs, with dance-cards to be filled in by the ladies. They danced reels, schottisches, mazurkas, waltzes and barn-dances, and bands of musicians were hired from Umtata by whichever trader was the host for the occasion. Between dances there would be musical events by talented amateurs, and officers of the Cape Mounted Riflemen and the Transkei Mounted Rifles would often attend.

Returning from one of these dances my parents saw their home in flames. Hobeni and everything they had was destroyed. What started the fire was never known. There was no insurance, and they had to start from the beginning again. They were living in a tent, still clearing away the rubble, when a representative of the wholesale suppliers arrived to take an order for goods. Dad explained that they had no money, apart from some pieces of gold coin that had fused together in the blaze, and couldn't place an order. The representative, a Mr Neuper, said he had instructions from his managing director to extend credit for a complete re-stocking of all the goods lost in the fire, to help Hobeni back on to its feet. Dad placed the order, and when he was finished Neuper said: "Now I have instructions that when you have completed your order I am to double it, and to tell you the company will defer payment for whatever length of time you require." Dad asked why. "I asked that myself," said Mr Neuper. "All the boss would reply was that he liked young Woods's face."

Then came help from another quarter. Dad's ledgers and account books had all been destroyed in the fire and there were no records of amounts owed by the local tribesmen, but one after another they came forward to acknowledge or pay off their debts in grain or goats or cattle or money. Those who couldn't pay anything at that time brought relatives who took their debts over, because Bomvanas believe that settlement of debt involves the honour of a whole family. With all this support, and working at first out of tents, then mud huts, Mom and Dad earned good profits, and by the time their first child was born Hobeni was rebuilt on a larger scale than before. The new buildings were solid brick and mortar and the homestead, shop and outbuildings were spaciously laid out.

From the approach over the hills above the Bashee River Hobeni comes into view below as a fenced rectangle of ten acres enclosing white walls, red roofs, trees, vegetable gardens, banana plantations and orange groves. Its background, four miles beyond, is the ocean. There is neatness and balance in the relationships of the buildings and spaces and in the vivid colours coming together—blue sea, green grass, red roofs, white walls. Coming home to Hobeni was always a special pleasure. Even the tussocks of grass by the roadside had an individual familiarity and some of the trees had grown up with me. One, a small Mtombe tree planted when I was four years old, was later to tower over all the others and measure fifteen feet round the trunk. At that time the grownups were talking a lot about places called Czechoslovakia and Munich. All I knew about it was that Dad had added three new harrier hounds to his hunting-pack, and their names were Hitler, Mussolini and Chamberlain. Hitler was the friendliest of the three—he had long tan ears, a white-and-tan snout and big platelike paws.

After my parents had recovered from the fire they were to endure ten years of tragedy after tragedy. Their first six children were all born dead, and a seventh child, Patricia, lived for only a few months. The local doctors were baffled. Then a young black doctor named Soga came to Elliotdale. Black doctors were rare in South Africa and only attended black patients, because it was generally unthinkable for whites to seek any kind of treatment from a black man. Dr Lex Soga was descended from a family of Xhosa chiefs who believed in education and sent their children overseas to develop free of anti-black prejudice in South Africa, since white South Africans resented blacks who sought to be educated "above their station". Dr Soga, having graduated from Edinburgh University, was more highly qualified than any white doctor in the Transkei Territory, and Dad, whose regard for expertise of any kind outweighed his own racial prejudice on this occasion, took Mom to him for an opinion. Eyebrows were raised in the white community, but my parents were given new hope when he diagnosed a thyroid condition and vitamin deficiency which could be remedied through a course of injections and careful ante-natal supervision.

Thanks to his treatment my sister Joan was born. For months after her birth Mom and Dad kept her in the room with them at night and took turns staying awake in case anything went wrong. Four years later, after the same careful treatment by Dr Soga, my brother Harland was born. Two years after that my parents decided to have another child, and as Dr Soga was returning to Edinburgh for a year of further specialization he prescribed the course of injections and ante-natal treatment for the white doctors to follow in his absence, but while he was away Mom miscarried again. After his return Dr Soga resumed personal supervision and treatment of her next pregnancy, although he was by now practising in the town of Idutywa and had to travel seventy miles by car or forty miles on horseback to Hobeni. He would stay the weekend and go bushbuck-hunting with my father, or play a few holes of golf with him at a seaside resort a few miles away called The Haven.

I was born on December 15th, 1933, and as Dr Soga could not be contacted through the erratic Transkei telephone service Dr Leon, one of the local white doctors, was called. My parents were worried that I appeared to be a thin, weak baby, and several days later when I was circumcised by Dr Leon he couldn't stop the bleeding. My mother applied diaper after diaper but each became soaked with blood, and Dr Leon was so upset that he went out of the room. Then Mom heard what she often said later was the most comforting sound in the world, the voice of Dr Soga. He cauterized the wound and the bleeding stopped. He had ridden on horseback across the country from Idutywa on an impulsive visit to Hobeni, and when I fell asleep he stayed with Mom and me while Dad sat with Dr Leon in the living-room, until I woke up and started crying with hunger. "There you are, Edna!" Dr Soga shouted. "Your *nkunzana* is all right!" (*Nkunzana* is Xhosa for a young bull.) Then he went into the living-room and asked Dr Leon why he hadn't cauterized to stop the bleeding. He shook Dr Leon by the shoulders and shouted: "You should be struck off the roll!" Dr Leon shouted back, but Dad calmed things down and it was agreed that no word of the incident should reach the community, because if it had got out that a black man had shaken a white man there would have been uproar among the whites in Bomvanaland.

One of my earliest memories is of a total eclipse of the sun. I must have been four or five, and Dad did his best to explain what would happen and why. He had read of it in the newspaper and there had been broadcasts about it on the radio, which the grownups called "the wireless". We were advised to hold bits of glass over a candle-flame to smoke them so we could look at the sun without hurting our eyes. The Bomvanas were mystified at our preparations, and the more we told them the sun would be extinguished in the middle of the day and would then come to light again the more they laughed at us. Such things didn't happen. Dad relished telling them exactly when the phenomenon would occur, anticipating the pleasure it would be when *izinto zabelungu* (the things of the white man) would prove to have been accurately forecast. *Hayi*, no, such things couldn't happen, they said as they congregated outside the shop watching us hold the fragments of glass over the candle flames.

We prepared lots of these fragments so that the Bomvanas could also watch the eclipse, and Dad gave a final warning to them not to look directly at what they would see as it could damage their eyes. They each took a fragment of the smoked glass, holding it gingerly and joking unsurely at all this foolishness, then started going still as the sky began to darken. "*Yu! Yu!*" they shouted in astonishment. "*Yini!* The night is coming, as Masumpa said." Some of the women started wailing as it grew darker, but Dad called out that all was well, it wouldn't last an hour. Cocks began to crow and dogs to whine, but by now the Bomvanas were looking through their smoked glass at the orb of the moon shutting off the light of the sun by degrees, and it was not only the Bomvanas who were now exclaiming "*Tyini! Yu!*"

Then it became totally dark and we stood in the blackness, all silent. The sky was full of stars. As the sunlight began to come back, the Bomvanas broke out chattering in excitement and relief. The cocks crowed again, and all the sounds of daylight returned.

When I was born Mom was forty and Dad forty-six, so I never knew them as young parents. Both were affectionate, and because we lived far from the nearest town and were seldom near shops they indulged all three children with plentiful spending money when we did go to town. If I asked for something I got it, and was certainly spoilt in many ways. I had toys of all kinds, and a young Bomvana was assigned to me as I played with them. He picked them up after me and put them away, and when we rode donkeys he saddled mine and off-saddled it afterwards. When Harland was home from boarding school the two of us would go shooting birds with air-rifles, riding—bikes, donkeys or horses—making swings in the trees or working at the carpenter's bench behind the shop. In the evenings we had our parents to ourselves, because visitors seldom called then. Mom would play the piano or show us a card game while Dad lay down to read the paper. Sometimes we'd interrupt his reading for a story, and he usually complied. He was a good storyteller, and used to make up tales about farmers and animals, hens and chickens.

He always lay down to read the paper. He would fold the broadsheet laterally into one column-width at a time and hold it in one hand while smoking with the other. He smoked heavily all his life. He also ate a lot and drank at least half a bottle of whisky a day; sometimes a whole bottle, although I never saw him drunk.

He was a stern disciplinarian, and in this role he was a figure of awe to us. One look from him was enough to enforce order and obedience, and though he never struck any of us it was unthinkable to defy his authority. Generous to a fault, he was noted throughout the Transkei for his hospitality at Hobeni, and one fund raiser for charities told me years later that his donations were always much bigger than those of other wealthy traders in the territory. But he could be a relentless enemy. He would hold a grudge for years, and was obsessed with hitting back at those who had wronged him. He hated meanness too, and seemed to consider it his duty to get back at those guilty of this. A trader named Brussau once wrote him a letter proposing collusion to double the profit margin on maize at a time of near-famine for the Bomvanas. The letter ended: "What do you say, Jack? Let's make these blighters pay for our new cars!" Dad's response was to reduce the selling price on his own maize and take no profit at all that season, and to buy in enough to sell at cost price to all Brussau's customers, who came to get the cheaper maize from Hobeni while Brussau's stockpile of maize rotted in storage. Brussau's loss delighted Dad, who said: "The bastard's new car cost him double".

He maintained some non-speaking feuds for a lifetime, and once foreclosed on a mortgage because a man he had helped out of a financial jam spoke disparagingly of a relative of ours.

Dad was tall and stout, and physically he became remarkably lazy from about the age of fifty. He gave up all sport except for golf, and even in his golf he began to adopt energy-saving practices which astonished the general community. He took to driving round the golf course in his car, to avoid walking. He would hit the ball, climb into his car, then drive to where the ball was so that he could hit it again. Later he decided that driving the car himself was unnecessary effort, so he would be driven around the course by his chauffeur, Budge Gabada. Budge, and later Harland, developed the knack of driving the car to a point practically touching the ball, but not so close as to impede Dad's swing. He would then get reluctantly out of the car, choose a club, hit the ball to the green, and climb back into the car to be driven to the green for his putt. One year the Elliotdale Golf Club recorded a committee resolution "that Mr Jack Woods be requested to cause himself to be driven along the *edge* of the fairway rather than *on* it". After making this extra effort for a while he concluded that the game had become too strenuous, and retired from what he regarded as active participation. His main hobby was poker. He would travel hundreds of miles for a big poker game, which could take two or three days. Returning from these games he always reported his wins to Mom, but never his losses.

Rejected for military service in the war because of his age, he followed the progress of hostilities with frustrated impatience. "Damn it. I'm exactly the same age as Hitler," he would say. Lazy as he was, he could move quickly when roused to anger, and once when a trader of German descent made a pro-Hitler remark in the Elliotdale bar, Dad knocked him to the floor, without removing his hat or cigarette to do so.

Mom was a different character entirely. We children could

do no wrong in her eyes, and she was automatically on our side, against the whole world if necessary. Apart from her periodic outbursts against the servants she was the soul of good nature, and whenever I recollect her face it is smiling or laughing. Even in adult life my brother and sister and I used to joke that if it were ever reported to Mom that one of us had murdered a roomful of sleeping infants she would have concluded that it must have been in self-defence.

Practically a sixth member of the family was Glenn Turner. He came to work as an assistant trader to Dad when he was a young man, and by early 1980 he had been there fifty-five years, being still with my brother Harland at Hobeni. He was a sort of Transkei hillbilly. Always more fluent in Xhosa than in English, he spoke the language so perfectly that sometimes the Bomvana headmen would rely on him to settle points of argument about the complex grammar. His facial expressions when he spoke Xhosa were exactly those of the Bomvanas, and after many years among them he was referred to by the tribesmen as "the White Bomvana". He knew all their customs and beliefs, and to show their affection for him they would often vary his Xhosa name *Ginyizembe* (swallowed an axe) to *Ginyigusha* (swallowed a sheep) or *Ginyinkomo* (swallowed an ox) or sometimes just *Zembe* (axe). They did the same to me, sometimes varying my Xhosa name *Zweliyanyikima* to *Zweliyashukuma* (the world shudders) or *Zweliyaduduma* (the world thunders) or sometimes simply *Nyikima* (shakes).

Glenn knew all about *hlonipha*, the different words used to get around taboos. It was disrespectful in certain circumstances for young people to use the names of their elders directly. A young married woman couldn't utter her father-in-law's name or any other words that sounded like any syllable of his name. If her father-in-law's name was Sonkweni, when buying bread at the shop she couldn't use the normal word for bread, *sonka*, so in *hlonipha* language she would ask for *siqusheka*, which is *hlonipha* for *sonka*. There were a lot of these substitute words, and unless you knew them you could hardly converse with a Bomvana who was "in *hlonipha*" without going into elaborate roundabout language like "the substance which we eat, which is baked and comes in loaves".

Bomvana customs were complex, covering a whole range of

situations, like requiring a young man to carry his fighting-stick pointed down at the ground when addressing his mother-in-law. A Bomvana male always carried a fighting stick, and often two. The main one was about four feet long, often with ornamentation carved in a pattern near the two ends, and about three-quarters of an inch in diameter. The other was a *bunguza*—the same dimensions as the first but with a round knob on one end about the size of a golf ball, to add weight to any argument with a blow to the opponent's head. A bigger knob was illegal, and in some districts the magistrates ruled that if the owner couldn't fit the knob into his mouth his *bunguza* was confiscated and he was fined for carrying a danger-ous weapon. Most Bomvanas carried sticks for defence rather than aggression, and the young men often used them for the game of stick-fighting. Not dangerous like axe-fighting, stick-fighting was more an art than a form of combat, and usually the object was to spar, to feint and to strike mock blows rather than hurt the opponent. Each of the two fighters would be stripped to a loincloth, and each would be armed with a parrying stick (knobless) and a *bunguza*, the knobbed stick, for attack. The left fist clutched the parrying stick in the middle, the knuckles protected with a small blanket wound round the fist, and the right hand held the *bunguza*. The object was to land blows on the blanketed fist of the defender, or near-blows on his shoulders and head, while the defender would try to parry these blows with the parrying stick rather than the blanketed fist. Skilfully done it was a speedy art, with all four sticks flash-ing and clashing, having much of the appeal of swift swordplay. The thwacks across the blanketed knuckles were loud, and sometimes hard enough to make the recipient wince, but there was seldom serious injury.

Then there was the throwing-stick, which could be deadly. I once saw a boy with his brain split open at thirty yards when the throwing-stick entered his head as if it had been a sharpened arrow.

Axe-fighting was no game either. Every week there would be an axe-fight in which several boys would be chopped to death. The battle-axe was a stick about four feet long by an inch thick, with an iron blade at the end. The blade was between five and seven inches long, about two inches deep, and perhaps an eighth of an inch thick, the metal highly polished to glint in the sun. These battle-axes were lethal, designed to "pick" deep into the brain. More than one young playmate of mine was to die in an axe-fight. The fights were between factions from different hillsides. Combatants would dress up in their best loincloths and blankets, with *mangomanzis*—rubber anklets six inches deep cut from inner tubing—and ornate bead necklaces and amulets made by their girl-friends. One strict rule was that axe-fighting was only for uncircumcised youths. Once a youth was initiated into manhood, a six-month ceremonial process which included ritual circumcision, it was taboo for him to engage in what was regarded as juvenile irresponsibility. This rule was so strict that a youth tried in the criminal courts for axe-fighting could gain immediate acquittal by proving he was circumcised.

Entering the six-month initiation to become an adult member of the community, the youth and others in his group would be secluded from everyone but their instructor, the *Kankata*. They would be painted all over their bodies with white clay as a mark of their seclusion, and live throughout the six months in a grass hut, speaking in *hlonipha* substitute words. Afterwards the hut would be burnt, together with all the cooking utensils they had used.

I was once allowed to watch a ritual circumcision ceremony. All the initiates sat on the ground naked, with their legs wide apart. The "surgeon", called the *Incibi*, knelt before each with a razor-sharp spear-head, pulling the foreskin forward with one hand and slashing it off with the other. Each initiate, at the moment of circumcision, would shout "*Ndiyi ndoda!*" ("I'm a man!"). During the ceremony one of the youths flinched and refused to go through with the circumcision. His father, near to disgrace, stepped forward with several elders and urged him to be resolute. He changed his mind, prepared for the cutting (he clutched tussocks of grass on either side to steel himself) and his triumphant shout "*Ndiyi ndoda!*" was augmented by that of his father and the other elders: "*Uyi ndoda!*" ("You're a man!"). After the circumcisions all the foreskins were buried in an ant-heap so that witchdoctors couldn't find them to make be-witching-medicine.

After the six months there was a ceremonial dance by the

initiates, in which they were painted all over in an intricate set of patterns in many colours of clay. Each would be dressed in a grass skirt laterally about twenty feet in length, which when wound round the waist in layers gave a flared effect, and would wear a mask of reeds extending two feet above the head. Then all the initiates would go through a set pattern of dance long-established in ritual tradition, balletic, with stylized toe-pointing and arm and head movements. The uniformity of the dancers was the product of hours of training by the instructor. With this dance ended the initiation period. The paint was washed off at sundown and there was a feast of roasted ox-meat and fermented maize beer.

As a family we sometimes attended ceremonies, and in this way we were involved in the tribal community, but Glenn was the expert, and his knowledge of Bomvana ritual was later so complete that the tribesmen insisted he should plan and supervise their rituals.

One night before he went off to the war Glenn put on a hideous mask at midnight and knocked on the door of a Bom-vana hut near Hobeni. Dragging his leg, he told the Bomvanas by sign language that he had fallen from an aircraft and hurt his leg. They, keeping a distance from him, decided to lead him to "the white people at Hobeni", and in the belief that he did not understand Xhosa they discussed him freely as they walked with him. Was he a *sigebenga*? Were people in a *baloni* (aircraft) all *sigebengas*? One remarked that "*Tixo!*" ("By God!") this creature surely had the ugliest face ever seen. All laughed delightedly when Glenn whipped off the mask to reveal his identity.

In those pre-war days life seemed a bustle of social activity, for the grownups and families did a lot of visiting. We often went to Madwaleni and stayed overnight where my playmates were my cousins. We kids would be put to bed early, and from our bedroom we would hear the conversation at the big Lawlor dinner-table. It was always a babble. The Lawlors all spoke at once, and no one seemed to listen to anyone else.

But as war came closer, we sensed the growing seriousness of the grownup talk. Then Britain declared war on Germany and within days our government had declared war in support— but it was a near thing, General Smuts winning the vote in

35

Parliament by only a handful of votes. Our family were automatically in favour of the Allied cause, as we were English-speaking and among the forty per cent of white South Africans who were of British descent, the other sixty per cent of whites being mainly of Dutch descent. Most of the latter, the Afrikaners, were known as Nationalists because they supported the Afrikaner Nationalist Party, whereas we, like most of the British-descended, joined with a small percentage of anti-Nationalist Afrikaners in loyalty to the United Party. Both these parties shared one basic belief—that the white minority of between four and five million should have total political control over the twenty million blacks.

When I was a child "our" party was in power, the United Party led by General Jan Smuts. The Transkei whites must have been solidly for Smuts because almost every white adult of military age was in uniform. In other parts of the country, Afrikaner Nationalist strongholds, uniforms were scarce, because Afrikaner Nationalists were pro-German, anti-British and inclined towards the totalitarian ideas of Hitler. The extreme Nationalists formed an organization called the Ossewa-Brandwag (Ox-Wagon Sentinels) whose members committed acts of sabotage and beat up anyone in uniform whom they outnumbered. One of the leaders of the organization was Balthazar Johannes Vorster, later to become Prime Minister of South Africa.

We often listened to the war news on "Daventry", the BBC, and to the solemn tones of Winston Churchill, rallying Allied morale. Without understanding the full meaning of his words I could tell they were stirring things he was saying, things that moved the listening adults emotionally.

The anti-Afrikaner prejudice in our district must have been offset by the fact that some of our leading generals, including Smuts himself and General Dan Pienaar, were also Afrikaners, as was the ace fighter pilot, Group-Captain Adolphus "Sailor" Malan. It was part of the complexity of white politics in South Africa that those Afrikaners who fought in the war against Hitler were regarded as traitors by most of their fellow Afrikaners. Afrikaners as a whole were still bitterly anti-British because of the Boer War, in which their ancestors had had moral and material support from Germany against the

British; their sympathies weren't entirely due to ideological attachment to Nazi principles, although many of their political leaders had strong leanings in that direction, being anti-Jewish and pro-fascist.

As I was only five years old when World War II started, I knew nothing of these things and was aware of only some of their surface effects—that in South Africa "we" whites of British descent were part of a worldwide family of English-speaking peoples, the British, the Americans, the Canadians, the Australians and the New Zealanders; that all of "us" except for the Americans were in this fight against evil people named Hitler, Himmler, Goering, Goebbels and so forth; that it was purely a matter of time before our American brothers joined in the fight, and that there was no doubt that we would win eventually.

Because we lived so far from the nearest town of any size, Umtata, I had to go to boarding-school there at the age of six, and just as the little village of Elliotdale, twenty-four miles from Hobeni, seemed a town to us, so the little town of Umtata, seventy miles away, seemed a city. You came to Umtata by a tarred highway through an avenue of trees, then you had to slow down because of the speed limit. For years the town had only one traffic cop, Officer Keith Oates, and if a motorist was trapped exceeding the speed limit he wasn't a victim of some anonymous department, he was "caught by Keith".

Umtata Town Hall was a dignified mass of stone overlooking ornamental gardens. For years the town gardener was Sir Patrick Wauchope, a British nobleman whose family paid him a remittance to stay out of Britain because of his boozing, and when a stroke paralysed half his face he kept the drooping side of his lip up with a hook suspended from a headband. Everyone called him Sir Pat and he was a genius with flowers, tending the municipal gardens with loving care in between visits to the bars at the Imperial, the Grosvenor, the Royal and the Savoy.

In Umtata I saw my first Greek tearoom—in fact, two of them, the Grand and the Lounge. The South African Greek tearoom has no exact counterpart anywhere in the world. It is an everything shop which stays open all day and much of the night, serves meals at all hours and sells books, papers, periodicals, groceries, hardware, novelties, fruit, candy, tobacco, medicines, sun-glasses, and most other conceivable types of merchandise. How people in the rest of the world manage without South African Greek tearooms is a mystery. The South African Greeks, mostly descended from shipbuilders in the old country, learnt rudimentary forms of English, Afrikaans and the black languages and ran family businesses apparently without sleep and certainly without Sundays off.

York Road, Umtata's main street, was jampacked with humanity on Saturday mornings. The tribesmen would surge into town, many of them riding in on horseback to tether their horses at the hitching rail by the post office, and the pavements outside sedate English-looking shops would be a compact mass of red-blankets. White ladies escaping for a hair-do into "Maison Charlotte" would fan their faces and say: "My dear, you can't *move* in town this morning for nigs on the pavement." They would tell each other how they had been jostled and compare complaints, ". . . and, my *dear*, the smell!" But their husbands, who ran the shops and businesses, didn't complain. Money never smelt.

The tribesmen got their money by selling cattle and sheep and wool to the traders, and by sending their young men off to the gold mines in Johannesburg. Young Xhosas hated working underground, but the wages seemed high to them, and after a year at the mines they were able to bring back more than enough to buy a bride and to maintain the family until the next recruiting. Some of the banknotes they brought into the shop at Hobeni were unbelievably dirty and sometimes could hardly be recognized as currency. Before Dad banked any money Mom would wash and iron all the notes. Coins they often carried in their mouths, and whoever was serving at the counter would plunge the proffered money, hand and all, into a nearby bucket of disinfectant. The Bomvanas would grin, thinking this a strange white ritual.

In the shop at Hobeni the young men always congregated at the corner counter near the medicine shelves and blanket stocks, exchanging gossip and calling out suggestive remarks as the bare-breasted young girls walked by to buy food for the kraal. Superbly muscled, the males pranced and showed off like young stallions, their fighting-sticks wrapped into their shoulder-blankets and protruding up past their ears, and their teeth and eyes flashing white in their dark faces as they spoke *to* each other but *at* the girls. The girls and old women did more serious shopping, eking out each purchase to wring the utmost from the social occasion. "*Irali ngepeni*" would send you off to the far end of the counter for a penny-worth of cotton, and on bringing this you'd be told "*Pinda ngepeni*" ("again, for a penny"). It was no use trying to consolidate the order—that would have spoilt the ritual.

At the medicine counter an old man would be telling Glenn where his teeth hurt, frowning at the giggles of the listening youths. "*Ewe, kehle*," ("Yes, old sir,") Glenn would say. "Open wide and point to the tooth that hurts." The old man would gape and Glenn would note it down while the young men called: "Ginyizembe, take all his teeth out, he is too old for meat." This, far from irritating the old man, would half-please him. Age has status in Bomvanaland. He would frown and smile, calling them "*kwenkwes*" and "*kwedinis*" (little boys). Glenn would get out his tooth-pulling pliers and several of the young men would hold the old one's head, clattering their fighting-sticks down to do so while Glenn yanked out the sore tooth. Then a cheer would go up, Glenn would exhibit the tooth and the old man would nod with satisfaction. Glenn with his pliers yanked out hundreds of teeth over the years, but usually for old people. Bomvana teeth were generally strong, white and healthy. Appendicitis was also virtually unknown to the Bomvanas. Their main scourge was tuberculosis.

Dad built a clinic at Hobeni, and once a week Dr Leon would come and hold a surgery there, but for the rest of the week it was Glenn who examined, prescribed and sewed up axe-wounds with ordinary thread until the doctor's arrival. Once a boy was brought in to Glenn unconscious with his head split open by a battle-axe. All Glenn could do was to bind his head firmly and shrug his shoulders, yet two months later the youth came running up to him in the yard, grinning and pointing proudly to the scar.

Before I was six years old Dad nearly died after being bitten by a button-spider. He had leant against a fence-post and felt a sting on his elbow. The spider jumped away into the grass and Dad was soon battling for his life. The doctor had to cut deep into the inside of his arm to remove the poison, and the fever and large scar which resulted seemed out of all proportion to the minute size of the creature which caused the injury.

The button-spider is the most dreaded of all South African spiders. Almost identical to the Black Widow spider of America, it has a velvety black body only half-an-inch in diameter, and its poison is as virulent as that of the cobra. The victim's chest and abdominal muscles become paralysed, and death is caused by cardiac and respiratory failure. The button-spider is physically feeble, with poor vision and dull senses, which is why it has had to develop such deadly poison as a defence. It attacks only when it feels trapped, and when Dad leant on the fence-post it must have been right under his elbow. Even after medical treatment he was seriously ill, and it was weeks before he fully recovered.

Bushbuck hunting was one of Dad's favourite diversions. He and several other traders kept hounds. The hounds were harriers, which are like big beagles, and the hunting was in and around the coastal forest. The forest was full of bushbuck, which were prized for their tasty venison. Harland and I were initiated with elaborate care into the handling of firearms, being forbidden even to point toy pistols at people, and allowed to graduate only with grudging slowness through air-rifles and small-calibre weapons up to the big shotguns and ·303 rifles. Ironically, by the time I was allowed to fire the big guns, and after only one or two shots at the buck, I lost all interest in hunting. The enjoyment for me ended one afternoon when I was trying to sleep. My room at our seaside cottage was a thatched roundhut or rondavel, and a swallow flew in and circled frantically round and round. I chased it out with a tennis racquet and tried to get back to sleep, but it flew in again. Again I chased it out and was falling asleep when it flew in a third time, so I took my ·22 rifle and as it settled on a cross-beam near the top of the thatch I shot it. The way it disintegrated into a few pathetic feathers ended all my relish for shooting at anything live.

Anyway, there was plenty to do at Hobeni beside hunting. We did a lot of riding, and the only real hazard was the way horses, even at full speed, would suddenly shy to one side on sensing a snake in the grass. But riding, swimming, and all the enjoyments Hobeni had to offer became relatively rare for us from the time we started at boarding-school. Although the vacations were long, they also seemed to be a long time coming round.

My first boarding-school was the Holy Cross Convent in Umtata, where I had five years of preparatory education. Most of the other boys were also traders' sons. While I did well in class I was a poor performer at sports, especially athletics. I was never in any race in which I didn't come last. I was also known as "cheeky", and got into trouble during one mealtime for calling one of the nuns a "bloody German" when she ordered me to eat something which looked awful. I was taken to Mother Superior for my insolence, and when she demanded to know why I had referred to Sister Eugenius in this way, I offered the imaginative explanation that what I had said was that the food had "bloody germs" in it. Mother Superior, an Irish woman, wasn't able to keep a straight face.

Unlike most of the boys I avoided physical conflict whenever possible, preferring to apologize my way out of trouble. Our arch-rivals were the boys of the bigger Umtata High School, who were mostly Protestant, while most of us were Catholic, and this added an extra dimension to the tension. My brother, sister and I inherited our Catholicism from my mother, who inherited it from her Irish ancestors. Dad, nominally a Methodist, entered churches only for weddings and funerals.

In Umtata I first saw non-red-blanketed blacks. I was now out of Bomvanaland, Umtata being in Tembuland, and many of the blacks there wore western clothes. Tembus who wore blankets wore white ones, and Pondos from Pondoland blue ones. At the school those of us from Bomvanaland were teased for coming from such a primitive region, for traders' sons from Tembuland and Pondoland regarded themselves as more sophisticated than the likes of us "*qabhas*" (heathen). In Umtata, too, I first saw black schoolchildren. They were pupils of St John's College, an Anglican mission school. One day the St John's pupils were allowed to stage their athletics championships on the whites' recreation ground, which had a proper cinder track, hurdles and finishing tape. We white kids were highly amused when a black hurdler, winning easily but not knowing how to breast the tape, hurdled the tape as well.

The only blacks at our school were servants. In fact the only blacks I was aware of up to that stage were either servants or "raw tribesmen", and the sight of those black pupils of St John's was tempered with the prevailing cliché in our white community that education wasn't a good thing for blacks; that it made them "uppity"; that they preferred to stay ignorant, and that it was silly of foreign missionaries to spoil them with knowledge they couldn't handle. Adult whites often said: "These educated niggers are the worst—give me a raw old kaffir in his blanket every time."

In our society an argument between a black and a white was unthinkable. If a black customer in a shop disputed the price of an item it was considered mandatory for the white to "clout him immediately" if a warning not to be "cheeky" did not succeed. Blacks were either "cheeky" or "civil"—the word "civil" was applied only to blacks. Once I heard a white man order a black pedestrian not to rest on "his" pavement. The black pointed out that it wasn't the white man's pavement. The white advanced threateningly on the black. The black, astonishingly, held up his fists. The white man said with shock, several times: "What? You'd hit a white man!" He said this over and over again, threatening to call the police, until the black man went away.

That was one of the incidents I recall among my first impressions of Umtata. Elliotdale, being smaller, seemed less impersonal, and I have no early recollections of racial unpleasantness there, although my later experiences in the village showed that the Elliotdale people were every bit as bigoted as the Umtata people. In Elliotdale the village hall was the social hub of the district, and the magical place where touring English theatrical companies made an occasional one-night stand, which traders and their families would drive twenty or thirty miles to attend. These groups toured incessantly, presenting the same performance to small villages all over the Transkei. Then there were touring movie projectionists, whose impending arrival would create great anticipation in the community, and few would miss the "bioscope", as movies were still called in South Africa. It was in the Elliotdale village hall that I saw most of the early Shirley Temple films and first heard the strange American accent with the slurred "r" sounds.

The Transkei being less racist than the rest of South Africa, blacks were permitted into the hall for these films, provided they sat at the back. Coloureds sat in the few rows in front of them, and we whites had the best seats at the front. In Umtata the segregation was more official, with blacks and coloureds sitting upstairs in the projection room.

For the Bomvanas the movie was a miracle. A large lorry would arrive at Hobeni bearing the banner of the Ambrosia Tea Company and loudspeakers would blare in Xhosa that there would be "*i banyaskopu*" ("a bioscope") shown against the wall of the Hobeni shop that evening. The tribesmen from miles around would start arriving with their families in the early afternoon, and the largesse of the Ambrosia Tea Company would begin. Every man, woman and child would be given a cap with the inscription "Tea is good for you—always drink tea —AMBROSIA". Then, when a big crowd had gathered, the promoter would open a barrel of "motto" candy and hurl handfuls of it to the children. These sweets were in the shapes of hearts, diamonds and spades in various colours, and each bore an endorsement of Ambrosia tea. Then the movie would begin —a full bill of cartoons, shorts and feature films and an occasional reel showing how a wretched man could be transformed into a prosperous, happy, successful individual through the simple infusion of Ambrosia Tea.

Before these shows the tea merchants would seek the cooperation of my father, and this necessitated use of the unreliable Transkei telephone service. The phone at Hobeni was a hand-crank instrument. We were on a party line, and each subscriber had a distinctive code of ringing. If you made an outside call much cranking was needed to gain the attention of the switchboard operator in Elliotdale, a friendly but often inattentive lady who usually wanted to chat with the caller before putting the call through. Quite often the phone didn't function at all, if a cow had flattened a telephone pole or a storm had damaged the line. And often, even if the line was intact, there would be delays of several hours in calls spanning only a few miles. Dad once booked a call to Mqanduli, about forty miles away, and in frustration over the delay he got into his car, made the eighty mile round-trip and returned before the call came through.

Another place which loomed large in my childhood was The Haven, a seaside boarding-place known for its fishing. One of the bait-getters for the fishermen, Alec, was killed by a shark and his mutilated body was borne in on the tide into the mouth of the Bashee River in a strangely upright posture like a figure on the prow of an old sailing ship. Local tribesmen fled in fear, shouting that Alec's ghost was walking on the water.

We children were strangely unafraid of sharks, of which several deadly species inhabited our waters. We often swam in the surf in front of our seaside cottages as well as in front of The Haven, and also in the wide mouth of the Bashee River, although we occasionally saw shark fins in all three places. Between The Haven beach and ours was Shark Island, more a peninsula that the tide occasionally turned into an island, from which shark-fishermen fished by kite in the deep waters on the horizon. From our cottage we would see a distant kite swoop down from the sky and know that a shark had taken the big hooks. Sometimes we went to the island to see the shark landed, and the awful rows of teeth always gave us the shivers —but never enough to stop us running into the sea again for a swim the same day.

One menace of our tidal pools was the seasnake, which we called by its Xhosa name, *kwatuma*. Although we rarely saw seasnakes we knew they were highly poisonous, and when they did appear on the scene we got out of the water fast. Once one swam over my foot, actually brushing over my instep.

Although the Wild Coast had such dangerous creatures as *kwatumas*, boomslangs, puff-adders, button-spiders and sharks, their existence touched only a tiny part of our consciousness as children, and we seldom thought of them. For us Bomvanaland was a safe place—a lovely, sunny region of green hills and valleys, rivers, forests and beaches, and all the indelible memories of childhood.

During my last year in Umtata all the adult talk was about the Allied landings in Europe—the Invasion. Sometimes the young Bomvanas back at Hobeni asked about this war among the whites, and it wasn't easy to explain even the little I knew about it. One could talk of the *Ama-Jamani* (the Germans) and the *Ama-Ngesi* (the English) but it seemed hard to get across the idea that all this fighting was taking place so far away. They thought Germany was otherside Umtata, or somewhere beyond the Kei River. And the fact that *baloni* (aircraft) were taking part in the fighting was incomprehensible to many of them.

One day I lay on a hillside with several young Bomvana boys as a plane went by overhead, going from Durban to East London. Some refused to believe there were people in it. "No, Zweliyanyikima," they said. "It's too small. A *baloni* is no bigger than a big bird. People couldn't fit into it." One of them turned on the others. "Don't be stupid," he said. "It's because it's far away that it looks small. Look at your own hut over on that hill—doesn't that look small from here?" "Awwwwww!" they said, understanding.

It was a wrench when the time came for me to go to boarding-school outside the Transkei. At the Umtata convent boys couldn't go beyond the third grade, and when I was eleven I was sent to join Harland at De La Salle College in East London, a seaport and South Africa's only river harbour. I had first seen it as a toddler and remembered it mostly for a childish misconception. To hold my interest during the long car journey Mom had told me to watch out for the white lions near East London, and for a long time I kept my eyes peeled to see these wondrous beasts before realizing that she was referring to the white lines painted along the middle of the tarred highway approaching the city.

East London looked large and lovely. The houses seemed like mansions, and the college itself was in fact a former mansion, with a marble hall, curving stairways and several large dormitories. Harland, who was now a senior at the school, was unfailingly kind to me, but I was a sore trial to him because I seemed unable to make friends in my age group and was forever hanging around him, to the irritation of his own friends. One evening the school showed a Lon Chaney film, *The Mummy's Hand*, and I was so scared that night that I sneaked out of my junior dormitory and climbed into his bed. Although his fellow-seniors jeered at him for mollycoddling his little brother, he let me stay.

As in Umtata I was still good in the classroom and bad at sports, and it was only during that year in East London that I began to lose my scrawniness. This was in 1945, and one day I

45

noticed a commotion outside the school grounds. Newsboys were shouting excitedly, people were rushing to buy copies of the newspaper and I went and bought one myself—the *Daily Dispatch*, of which I was to become editor twenty years later. The paper proclaimed in big banner headlines: "END OF WAR IN EUROPE". Bells rang, bands paraded, and months later most of the shop windows displayed pictures of the Belsen and Buchenwald concentration-camp victims of Nazism. The soldiers started coming back, including Glenn and his fellow prisoners-of-war and there was a general feeling among the returning soldiers that they wanted to settle accounts with the Afrikaner Nationalists who had been pro-Nazi during the war.

In the triumph of General Smuts's return to the country after he had played a major role in the formation of the United Nations, it seemed that he would be in power in South Africa for many years. The Afrikaner Nationalists did not seem to be a threat any more, and few could have guessed then that within three years they would take over the country and begin more than thirty years of rule under a system that would earn the hatred of the world—Apartheid.

CHAPTER TWO

IT WAS A LONG journey from Hobeni to Kimberley—by car to Umtata, then two days by train. Dad chose Kimberley for our secondary schooling because of the reputation of the Christian Brothers College there. Run by an order of Irishmen, it achieved high academic standards through a formula of stricter discipline and longer classroom hours than most schools. It also produced sportsmen of national standing in rugby, cricket and tennis, so the choice of school also reflected Dad's hopes for us in these spheres. In fact he had more than hopes, he had expectations. Having had little schooling himself he wanted us to have the best available—and left us in no doubt that he wanted results. Harland was to have his final two years there before matriculation, and I was to have six.

Kimberley, the diamond capital of the world, is on the northern plateau of the Cape Province, which stretches to the edge of the Kalahari desert. It is flat country with only an occasional isolated hill sticking out above the plain. It seldom rains there, and when it does it pounds down in big drops, in short, intense showers. The town is incongruously urban in the middle of this arid scrubland. Victorian mansions of the old diamond magnates stand in lush lawns kept green with sprinklers, and the streets follow irregular patterns because Kimberley was once a collection of prospectors' claims, and the winding tracks between them later became paved avenues. The shopping areas have a cramped "old English" look reflecting the tastes of the turn-of-the-century merchants who flocked to the diamond fields for trade.

Whatever Rhodes's image was elsewhere in the world or in history, empire-builder or rogue, in Kimberley he was a hero. His statue stood in various parts of the town and Kimberley people spoke of him as if he were still alive. They never called him "Rhodes" or "Cecil Rhodes"—always "Cecil-John-Rhodes". During the siege of Kimberley in the Boer War he virtually assumed leadership over the military defenders and directed proceedings from his suburban mansion. His reply to the giant artillery-gun of the Boers, the German-made "Long Tom", was an equally big British-made gun which the townspeople called "Long Cecil". At Christian Brothers College we often dug up siege relics in our playground, bullets the Boers had fired a half-century before, and once we found a rusty old Martini-Henry rifle. Like Mafeking and Ladysmith, Kimberley had withstood its siege.

Harland and I arrived in Kimberley on an exceptionally hot day early in 1946. The heat was a haze above the streets, softening the tarred surface enough to leave our shoe-prints. We settled in at the college and were soon off to see Kimberley's main phenomenon—the Big Hole. This, said to be the deepest man-made hole in the world, was the largest of the old De Beers opencast diamond mines. Right in the middle of the town, it was now mined out and enclosed as a tourist attraction. It was an awe-inspiring sight. From the observation platform you looked across the mouth of the funnel-shaped excavation, perhaps a quarter of a mile across, then down into the ominous depths where the "stem" of the "funnel" plunged in a vertical drop to the bottom. It was hard to imagine how human beings could have dug down that far without modern machinery, and harder still to imagine how they could have overcome fear of that awful vertical shaft on the way down to dig further.

You couldn't see to the bottom of the Big Hole; you could only see down as far as the angle of observation from the platform allowed, to the surface of the dark green water which filled two-thirds of the shaft. Even to the surface of the water seemed a dreadful distance. When I visited the place thirty years later the water had risen a long way, but back in 1946 the rocky walls of the funnel-stem seemed to go on and on down to unimaginable depths. It was round, and about seventy yards in diameter, although it looked less because distances were distorted down that vast crater. We realized this when we saw what looked at first like a rock-rabbit moving towards a shrub on the lip of the shaft, down the incline to the edge of the "stem"—then realized it was a *goat*, and that it was *running* towards a *tree*. The guide rolled a boulder down the slope to illustrate the deceptive dimensions of the place, and we watched it grow smaller until it seemed the size of a tennis ball as it went over the lip of the "stem". Then we waited to hear it hit the

48

surface of the water far below, and several seconds went by before the splash echoed up off the rocky walls of the shaft. I was fascinated by the place—and terrified by it. I kept imagining the nearby streets and buildings of Kimberley sliding down into it if the edges started eroding, and was glad to come off the observation platform itself in spite of the strong steel fence surrounding it. Yet human beings had dug this awesome pit, and during the siege of Kimberley whole families had taken refuge down in its side-shafts and tunnels, being lowered over the edge with ropes and pulleys. It was a ghastly thought. I would rather have faced the Boer guns.

All the Kimberley people were diamond-minded, and although the De Beers Consolidated company now had a monopoly of the big workings there were still individual prospectors in the region. On a Saturday morning we watched one at work on his small claim on the banks of the Modder River. His son was at the college with us, and we joined him in helping his father to wash through the gravel from the river bed. In the first hour we found about seven bright stones in the shaking-pan, but the prospector laughed and shook his head. "Worthless, only bright stones. Not diamonds." We stayed on all morning and were beginning to lose interest when he picked out a stone and held it up excitedly. "*There's* a diamond, boys! And it's a good one." He held it out to his son. "That'll pay your school fees for the whole year," he said. We crowded round, then felt disappointed. It wasn't bright at all, it was a dull, soapy colour. The prospector laughed again. "It's still got to be cut and polished," he said. "Then it'll be brighter than all those little bits of glass you boys found earlier." In the next hour he found two more diamonds, but wasn't too excited about them. "Not worth much. They're small and not good—maybe worth about ten pounds for the two. But they'll help pay my expenses."

At Christian Brothers College Harland and I found our days were full. The academic level was high and much of the day was taken up with classes or study, and the rest with organized sport. The main sport was rugby. CBC was proud of having produced a number of international players, Springboks, as we called them in South Africa, and the school had dozens of teams for all ages and weights of pupils. It was in inter-school rugby that I first encountered Afrikaner hatred for English-speaking South Africans. When we played other English-speaking schools the games were clean, but when we played the Afrikaner schools it was like the Boer War all over again. Usually bigger and stronger and often older than we were, they would line up before the game to threaten in Afrikaans to *fok op* us *Engelse*. However, quite often, to our surprise, on the field of play they weren't as tough as they had sounded. Good in attack, they were poor in defence and seemed to lose heart easily.

Pressed into rugby under compulsion, I began to enjoy the game. I was twelve, and starting to put on weight and grow taller. I also began to be interested in cricket and tennis, and although I wasn't able to run fast I developed some ability in ball games and eventually managed to do quite well in all three sports, in my final year getting my first team colours for tennis and cricket.

In the classroom things went more turbulently, and it took me several years at CBC to be disciplined into discretion. At first I couldn't resist the temptation to answer teachers back, and I had occasional clashes with individual Brothers. Brother Elliffe, who had a hot temper, used to await his subscription copy of *Time* magazine impatiently each week, and he had just collected it from the mailbox one day when he saw me reading a comic. "I've told you not to read that trash," he said, and tore it across. So I grabbed his *Time* magazine and did the same. Then the chase was on, and I managed half a block before he caught me, but although he let me go because, as he said, he had "started it", he gave me a lecture on the folly of equating *Time* magazine with a comic. In the sixth grade we had a tyrant of a teacher, Brother Byrne, who was so immoderate in using the strap that the class started keeping corporal punishment statistics. The dullest boy in the class averaged twenty-one cuts a day and I, who led the class in marks, averaged six. Sometimes Brother Byrne would lose his temper completely and the strap wasn't enough—he'd throw it aside and slap, punch or kick one of us for an error.

In that year we did two subjects in the Afrikaans language, and one of these was American geography. To this day I think of *Noord en Suid Carolina, Alabama en Georgia* as the *katoen-*

produseerende states, and know that *Fresno, California, is beroemd vir rosyntjies* (is famous for raisins). We had our own project books dealing with the USA state by state, and one day Brother Byrne snapped his fingers for mine, wanting to check an answer. Because I didn't hand it to him quickly enough he hurled it out of the window to flutter two storeys to the ground in tatters. In a rage I went to his desk, took all his books and hurled them out of the same window. He rushed at me, cuffing me about, and gave me six cuts on each hand. Then he ordered me to fetch the books, and when I refused he hit at my shoulders and arms with the strap, shouting at me to fetch them. I still refused, and felt ready to hit back if he hit me again. He might have sensed this, because he went and fetched them all himself. The other Brothers disapproved of his methods and eventually he left the order, but academically Brother Byrne was a good teacher, and that year I came first in the country in my grade, getting a hundred per cent for Latin. It was the hardest I ever worked at school, and in the next few years under more humane teachers I never achieved such high marks.

After Harland had matriculated and returned to work at Hobeni I had four years on my own at CBC, and had to make the long train journey there and back alone each term. It was during one of these trips that I saw how intense interest in rugby really was in South Africa. It was the day of the first post-war clash between our Springboks and the New Zealand team. Passengers in the dining car were clustered round a radio to hear the commentary from Cape Town. As we were passing through mountainous territory radio reception kept fading, but this seemed only to add to the drama. Most of the passengers were English-speaking, but an old Afrikaner was there, occasionally raising his voice to say: "I yuss hopes they let Okkie Geffin take the kicks." New Zealand went into an early lead and the old chap was near to tears. Van der Schyff was taking the kicks for the Springboks and missing, and the old man kept saying: "Yuss give the ball to Okkie Geffin!" As time passed and the game appeared increasingly to be going New Zealand's way, the old man actually stood up at one point and shouted at the radio: "GEFFIN MUSS TAKE THE BLADDY KICKS!" Then, the Springbok captain called up Geffin to take the next kick at the post, and the old Afrikaner

51

suddenly relaxed: "Now the game iss ours," he predicted. Geffin put the kick over, and went on to total five successful kicks, setting a world rugby record to give South Africa a last-minute win. The old man stood up with tears running down his face and roared: "I mos *told* you all, *didn't* I? I mos told you. Geffin should have taken the kicks from the *beginning*. I tell you, that Jew can *kick*!"

At many of the stops and small sidings little black boys in ragged clothes would rush to the trainside begging for candy and coins, and some passengers found it amusing to heat pennies over a cigarette-lighter before throwing them down and watching the scramble. Through bitter experience the kids knew the trick of the burning coin, yet they still scrabbled for it through sheer need.

At CBC I took up music again, having given it up at De La Salle. I had been put off by the music teacher in East London, an eccentric German named Franz Moeller, who taught in his house. It had a piano in every room including the kitchen and bathroom, and his idea of a lesson was to lock you in to "practise ze scale of C", then unlock the door after an hour and send you back to the school. After a few days I climbed out of a window and never went back, and there was no indication that he ever noticed my absence. It was only when I got to Kimberley that I became interested in the piano again. My teacher there was a stout old lady, Mrs Horwitz, and we got on fine. She wore glasses on a chain, drank tea incessantly, chain-smoked and played stride piano like Fats Waller. She wore many rings, and her left hand was a dazzle of diamonds as she flashed out backward tenths and riffs.

Apart from sport, my other interest outside class was reading. The college library had a wide variety of books, and in my six years there I went through many of them, especially those on travel and exploration.

The ambition of all schoolboy cricketers in South Africa was to make the Nuffield Tournament team, to be chosen from all the schools in your state to play against teams from the other states, and Dad had been overwhelmed with pride when Harland achieved this. When I also managed it in my final year he was doubly delighted. He had never seen me bat, and when I came home on vacation and was included in the Elliotdale team with Harland he came to the ground to watch. Fortunately Harland and I batted together and scored more than a hundred runs between us, but when we came out Dad was strangely silent at first, looking away from us. Then we realized why: he was too moved to speak, and had tears running down his face. He could be very emotional at such moments and would weep freely. He cried when the Nazis bombed London; he cried when Tobruk fell. But he also cried, with pleasure, when Churchill threatened vengeance on Hitler and when the Allies won the war.

There was a politically minded group at the CBC, but most of us had no interest in politics. We knew there was an election on in 1948 but had no idea what it was about. I was in the seventh grade then, and one of the seniors was going about after the election with a long face saying: "The Nats have got in. The Nats have got in." I asked him who the Nats were. "Are they for Smuts?" He looked at me as if I were mad. "No, they're the other side, the Afrikaner Nationalists." It didn't mean anything to me, except a vague perception that it didn't sound good because my parents were Smuts admirers. It was a narrow victory, by only five seats, and it surprised the Afrikaner Nationalists themselves. They had consolidated Afrikaner support by promising complete segregation of the races, coining the word apartheid (separateness) and accusing Smuts's United Party of not being segregationist enough.

Soon after the election the Afrikaner Nationalists entrenched their power further by adding six seats, representing South West Africa (Namibia), which they won to increase their parliamentary majority. They took over control of all radio broadcasting, put party men in charge of the police and armed forces, and began to pass statute laws to subject every area of the country and every facet of the lives of South Africans to apartheid. At the time these developments were over my head. I was hardly conscious of them, and all I noticed was that park benches, public toilets and entrances to buildings had new signs up: "Whites only". This seemed sensible—a logical extension of the less formal segregation we had had under the Smuts government. Being white, I couldn't see anything disadvantageous to me in any of it, and when it came under discussion at school I was too bored to take any interest in it.

Dad's comment on the election was that although he was disappointed the other side had won, it might be a good thing in some ways. "The Smuts government didn't know how to deal with blacks," he said. "It would *consult* them, then *suggest* they should do certain things, and of course they wouldn't do them. But the Nationalists don't consult. They *tell* the blacks what to do and *make* them do it, and that's what the blacks understand." Yet he continued to support Smuts's United Party when it went into opposition—largely because it had been on the "right side" in the Hitler war.

In my final years at CBC I had to start taking some note of political developments because I was entered in the college debating series, and when I had to opt for political positions in these debates they tended to be on the conservative side. The principal of the college, Brother McManus, used to preside as chairman. He was a revered figure with a national reputation as a headmaster, and his air of dignified calm was seldom disturbed, but sometimes his irritation over my debating tactics showed through. The use of humour and emotional appeal often resulted in a winning vote by a show of hands for arguments which had no logical basis, and Brother McManus would rebuke the other boys for falling for this. Once he actually lost control of himself and stood up red-faced in front of the debating society to say: "Woods, it disturbs me profoundly that you so misuse your natural eloquence to manipulate the opinions of others. If you go on like this you will end up either in parliament or in jail!" If he had been able to look into the future he would have seen me nominated to the first, sentenced to the second, and kept out of both.

One of our topics for debate was whether blacks in South Africa were treated fairly. I was drawn to speak for the proposition that blacks *were* treated fairly, and won the vote by emphasising what we boys regarded as the inherent inferiority of blacks, the inadvisability of racial equality and the need to preserve white control. I made little attempt at logical argument, playing instead on the emotional views on race we all shared. This time Brother McManus thundered at the others: "Don't you boys ever think for yourselves?"

The Brothers seldom spoke politics to us. Parents would soon have objected, disapproving of the "impractical view" of foreigners on the race question. But we boys knew they dis-approved of segregation, and also ascribed this to their foreign-ness and their lack of knowledge of "our blacks".

Foreigners or not, we liked the Brothers. They were in-volved with all our activities, and were as friendly on the playing-fields as they were strict in the classrooms. You could get a bawling-out from your mathematics teacher in the morn-ing and play three sets of tennis with him in the afternoon, and many of them were young enough to give as good as they got in a rugby practice. Their Irish ebullience made them outgoing and spontaneous, so grudges between masters and pupils never lasted—you had your differences out then and there. Their lives were devoted to teaching, and they had to earn advanced academic qualifications to be taken into the Order, so the standard was high.

Half the boys at the school weren't Catholics, in fact one year the head boy was Jewish, and we all liked the idea of a school with a name like Christian Brothers College having a Jewish head-prefect. All the boys were required to study re-ligion, and every day a period was set aside for each denomina-tion. The rabbi and the various Protestant ministers conducted their own classes in this period. My six years at CBC were an intense blend of school-work and sport, with strong emphasis on religion. Catholics were required to attend Mass at least once a week, although attendance every day was encouraged. Most of us went about three times a week. There were also daily discussion periods on theology and dogma. Questions on sex were dealt with through the anonymity of a question-box, and the college chaplain was available for individual guidance. He was an elderly English priest with a ripe Cockney accent, which sounded strange in that cloister of Irish brogues.

Career guidance discussions were a feature of our final year, especially for those who hadn't yet decided what they wanted to do after matriculating. For some time it had been under-stood in the family that I would go on to university. I enjoyed writing, and might well have studied journalism, but at that time there was no journalism degree course available at any South African university, so I opted for law. Dad and I sought the advice of his lawyer, Jack Starke, who practised in Elliotdale. He explained that in South Africa there was rigid separation of capacities between the Bar and the Side-Bar. The Bar referred to barristers, or advocates, who practised in the Supreme Court; the Side-Bar referred to solicitors, or attorneys, who practised in the Magistrates Court, a lower court with limited jurisdiction. Mr Starke said that, while the Bar was more glamorous, it was also more risky, because some advocates never got important briefs or appeared in major cases, whereas attorneys like himself made a good living through drawing up wills, conveyancing property and collecting debts. He concluded by advising me to go for the Side-Bar and become an attorney, adding that the studies were less onerous. An advocate had to get two degrees, whereas an attorney had only to pass the Attorneys' Admission exam and do five years' articles of clerkship—apprenticeship to a qualified attorney. My father left the choice to me, and I opted for the Bar.

It was now a question of which university. Mr Starke recommended the University of Cape Town law faculty, and said that he would arrange for me to do articles of clerkship at the same time with his old Cape Town firm of Fairbridge, Arderne and Lawton, so that on graduation I could decide whether I still wanted to go to the Bar, with the option then of the Side-Bar if my views changed. We agreed on this arrangement towards the end of 1951, and I sailed on the *Pretoria Castle* from East London to Cape Town in time for the start of the academic year of 1952.

I was eighteen, and still untouched by the new Government's growing list of apartheid laws. They had passed a number in their first three years. First was the Prohibition of Mixed Marriages Act, making it a crime to marry a person of another race. Then came the Immorality Act, making it a crime to have any sexual contact with a person of another race. Then came the Population Registration Act, requiring all citizens to be classified racially as white, black, coloured or Asiatic. Then came the Group Areas Act, making it a crime for a person to live in the same suburb as a person of another race. Then came the Suppression of Communism Act, giving the State power to declare any citizen a communist, and to define as a communist any person seeking to change the race laws. Then came the Bantu Authorities Act, to force blacks back to tribalism and prevent them from seeking participation in national politics.

These statutes were the foundation-stones of apartheid. Over the next three decades a massive wall of further laws was to be erected, more than three hundred racial laws, to ensure the domination of five million whites over more than twenty million blacks, reserving to the whites all the political power, all the wealth in industry and mining, all the best jobs and professions, all the best land and housing, and all the advantages and privileges of an opulent society.

The first response by the blacks to the new Government's laws was a wave of riots in the black townships. I read about the riots in the papers, but not about the causes. All that came across was that troublemakers in the black community were stirring up the masses into pointless violence. In the townships outside East London angry crowds of blacks threw stones at whites. They overturned a car and dragged out a white nun, a doctor who ran a clinic for blacks in the township. They stoned her, cut her throat and burned her body. Afterwards two men cut pieces of flesh from her body and ate them. What we read and heard on the State-run radio was that rioting hordes of blacks had turned cannibal and were killing and eating whites. The new Government suppressed the riots and warned all whites that this sort of violence would be unleashed against them by the blacks unless whites united behind the apartheid policy to put blacks more firmly "in their place". Only a strong, white-supremacy government could keep the country stable and the white man safe.

It all seemed to me to make sense, and I began my law studies in Cape Town in that frame of mind.

CHAPTER THREE

IT WAS EXCITING to stand at the rail of the ship as we sailed into Table Bay, and hard to imagine a more beautiful city than Cape Town. Table Mountain had its own tablecloth of clouds over it and at its feet the city spread out to the bay and around Devil's Peak and Lion's Head. Earlier we had rounded Cape Point, where the Atlantic meets the Indian Ocean, admiring what Sir Francis Drake called "the fairest cape in all the circumference of the earth".

Cape Town was full of preparations for the celebrations marking the three hundredth anniversary of the landing of white settlers in 1652, but my own excitement at arriving in the midst of all this festivity was spoilt by the discovery that the Registrar of the University of Cape Town knew nothing of my enrolment and had had no communications from Mr Starke. Nor had Messrs Fairbridge, Arderne and Lawton any knowledge of my serving articles of clerkship with them. One of their representatives pointed out that "old Mr Starke" was "very forgetful these days . . ." and Cape Town suddenly seemed an intimidating place.

One thing Mr Starke had remembered to do was to arrange for me to lodge with his daughter and son-in-law, Edith and Charles Feldwick-Davis. They lived in the pretty suburb of Pinelands, with its thatched roofs and shady walks, and across the street lived Edith's sister Barbara and her husband, Mervyn Howard, with whom I also stayed for a while. Barbara was a qualified attorney, working for a legal aid bureau, and she helped me look for a law firm which would take me on as an articled clerk. We talked about the recent riots, and Edith and Barbara seemed dismayed at my views on race. I was somewhat shocked at their liberalism, and put it down to their long absence from the realities of the tribal Transkei. It seemed to me that they had come under the influence of the sentimental sophistication of scholarship in the big city. I had seen this in my sister Joan. She was now arguing with Dad on race, and whereas he would talk of blacks as "natives" she would use the new term then in vogue, "Africans", and use other nomenclature that suggested she had gone in for the fashionable leftism of students. I was sure I wasn't going to be taken in by this kind of sentimentality. But my first concern was to find a firm of attorneys so that I could become articled, and after a long interview MacCallum and Company took me on. They were a small firm but had good standing in the legal community. The head of it was Charles Smit, and he became the "principal" to whom I was articled.

The system of articles of clerkship was Dickensian. In theory it was a form of apprenticeship in which the principal instructed the clerk in the practical aspects of the law, while the clerk studied theoretical law under lecturers to pass the required exams. In practice few principals had the time to do much instruction, and the clerk, without the necessary initiative to learn practical procedure for himself, functioned mostly as an office-boy for negligible pay. In earlier times the apprentice had to pay for the privilege of being articled, but we received at least a token wage, referred to as an honorarium. My honorarium was seven pounds a month for the first year, ten for the second and fifteen for the third. I moved in and began the search for a lecturer. Other articled clerks spoke highly of a lecturer named Harold Levy, and I joined his class. Advocate Levy, a godlike figure to us because he was an actual barrister, lectured us in Roman Law, Roman-Dutch Law, South African Common Law, and Criminal Law. He had a tough manner but the more we grew to know him the more we realized his concern for each student to learn to think for himself.

One day in the class during a discussion on politics, Levy said: "Woods, you're from the Transkei, you've lived among the blacks there—what do you think is the best policy?" I said: "They should all be sent back to the reserves, where they belong. They're happier there. It's no good educating them and bringing them to the towns. It's either send them back to the reserves or shoot them—it's them or us." There was a shocked silence. Levy looked at me silently for a long time. "Do you really believe that?" he asked. "Is that really how you feel?" I said it was, and that ended the discussion, but in the days that followed I felt increasingly uneasy about my answer,

59

increasingly unsure of whether it was partly a form of posturing to project an air of knowledge of the black man which these city slickers with their liberal sentimentality did not have, or partly a crude over-simplification masking rustic ignorance. Levy's silence on the subject was unnerving. He made no effort to reopen the discussion. Often I hung back after classes to reopen the topic myself, but he said little, simply letting me talk myself out each time, watching me put dents in my own armour of prejudice.

Other dents came from study of Roman Law. I was impressed with the concept of codified fairness that ran through it, and particularly through the Institutes of Justinian, and became more and more attracted to the ideal of the principle of perfect justice—the concept that mankind, no matter how imperfectly, should strive to codify a fair set of rules to govern the behaviour of people. Human nature might not be perfectible, but human behaviour could effectively be controlled and regulated by an agreed consensus based on sound law. These ideas were obviously at variance with racial discrimination, because sound law was ultimately a refined statement of fairness, and there could be no fairness in laws based on skin-pigmentation. Yet, it was hard for me to reject apartheid, and I still tried to defend it, justifying the contradiction on the basis that South Africa's situation was unique, and that in this unique situation apartheid was a practical political necessity for whites.

Then I read one sentence by Abraham Lincoln which knocked that crutch of justification away: "What is morally wrong can never be politically right".

I kept raising the subject with the reticent Levy, who ventured no more than a constant stare of his dark eyes and an occasional word to prod me into all manner of verbal ramblings around, over and through all these contradictions. I started buying newspapers—the *Cape Times*, the *Cape Argus* and the organ of the Afrikaner Nationalist Party, *Die Burger*. What I read in these inclined me towards the Nationalists, although the first two were strongly anti-Nationalist and pro-United Party. What attracted me were the reported speeches of Dr Malan, the Afrikaner Nationalist Prime Minister, arguing the case for more rigid segregation, including sending blacks back to the reserves. Yet at the same time that I was drifting closer to the arguments for more segregation, two further things set me questioning it all again. One was a sermon during Mass which criticized apartheid as un-Christian, and a contravention of the religious ethics of Judaism and Islam as well, and another was meeting a black American. English-language universities were not yet segregated, and this man attended a couple of classes as a student visitor. I was struck by the fact that his accent was as American as those of white Americans on the movie screens, and reasoned that, if accent was a matter of environment, so might racial culture be. And as he was the first black foreigner I had encountered, I began to consider that the assumption of black inferiority in South Africa might be a result of the environmental circumstances forced on South African blacks. I thought that if a black baby born in the Transkei were brought up in Buckingham Palace, it would grow up to attend Oxford or Cambridge and would speak, think and react like a member of the British royalty. For me this was a startling concept, because it challenged all my racial prejudice.

It was a period of inner turmoil, because I was having to make major adjustments not only in my thinking but also in my studies. I came to realize that being confined to the Attorneys' Admission course meant that I was destined solely for the Side-Bar, without the options Mr Starke had mentioned in Elliot-dale; and the more I saw of the legal profession the more I wanted to be a barrister rather than an attorney—specifically, a barrister like Harold Levy. Yet I liked Mr Smit as a boss. He was one of two senior partners in the firm, the other being a courtly old Afrikaner named Johannes Jacobus de Villiers.

My first prescribed task for the firm was to amend their copy of the Companies Act, which was figuratively like digging a mile-long trench with a teaspoon, because it involved cutting each single clause out of a pile of government gazettes and pasting amending sections on to practically every page. This took weeks, the Companies Act being a thick volume, and it was interrupted only by having to run errands with documents for the Deeds Registry, the Master's Office, the courts and other law firms. At such places, and at the morning and afternoon Levy lectures, I met other articled clerks and we formed a sort of apprentices' guild characterized by long complaint sessions.

"We're nothing but messenger-boys." "Do you have to stamp all the letters?" "My principal teaches me nothing." "Are you amending the bloody Companies Act?" We would spend half-an-hour at the Koffiehuis Restaurant on the way to the Deeds Registry, longer at the Roxy café-cinema on the way to the Magistrates Court and at other familiar ports of call for bored errand-clerks. I often thought back to *H.M.S. Pinafore*:

> "When I was a lad I served a term
> As office-boy to an attorneys' firm,
> I cleaned the windows and I swept the floor,
> And I polished up the handle of the big front door."

Officially the office-boy tasks were performed by Andrew Hartzenberg, a genial gap-toothed Cape coloured man often high on marijuana and full of entertaining stories of District Six, the notorious coloured quarter. Andrew and I shared a back office down a dark corridor and took a long time to make the ritual tea. He was fascinated that I could speak Xhosa, and spoke disparagingly of blacks. He would say: "So Master lived among the savages, Master?" One day he noticed that I was becoming attracted to a girl from the next office. "Does Master fancy that girl, Master?" he said. "Yes, Andrew, I'm going to ask her for a date." Andrew laughed, hitting himself on the knee: "No, Master. She jail-bait, Master! She from District Six, coloured!" I was astonished: "No, she's white," I said. "*Nee, nee, nee*, Master! She a coloured pass-for-white. You date her you go to jail. She classified last month under ra Population Registration Ack. I know ra family, Master!"

The wording of the classification law was that the race-classification officials, in cases where a person suspected of being coloured had a very light complexion, had to examine the complexion of the person's relatives, and had to take into account the area where the person lived and the complexion and living-habits of associates and friends. This meant that if a light-skinned coloured girl wanted to "pass for white" she had to sever all ties with her parents and darker friends and go to live in a white area. But if her deception was discovered by the tracing of her birth certificate or by someone else's testimony, she faced criminal charges for deceiving the State. One of the physical characteristics which some of the officials were testing thoroughly was the thickness of hair, and they had a standard steel comb in their offices. If the person "passing for white" couldn't pass the comb through his hair he was graded non-white, and referred for more specific classification in one of the non-white ethnic groups. This practice was stopped after an uproar when a person subjected to the comb test was able to prove that he was an Afrikaner with white credentials, and that he had been reported to the Race Classification Board out of personal malice.

The dominant personality in our small firm was a formidable old woman, Miss Templeman. She intimidated us all—including the three senior lawyers. She ran the office as a captain runs a ship, and her desk in the general office was the "bridge". Her stout form crouched over a typewriter which she pounded as she called out instructions to other typists. She drew up all summonses, handled most of the correspondence, received all callers and despatched them to the lawyer of her choice. She berated debtors, lectured husbands behind with alimony payments and sent forth a stream of documentation all over the city via Andrew and me. She was rude to most, deferred to nobody and was respected throughout Cape Town's legal fraternity. She was seventy, she was ugly and she was offensive, yet she was competent at her work and she often showed me kindness when she sensed I needed it.

Her one indulgence was the opera. When the opera season began Violet Templeman would be in her reserved seat in a fur wrap of huge proportions, and she knew her librettos with encyclopaedic thoroughness. "One of the best Bohèmes I've seen," she would say the following day. Every morning she would feed the pigeons on the window ledge beside her desk. Generations of Cape Town pigeons owed their nutrition to Violet Templeman. Both the other senior typists tended to mother me and protect me from the wrath of Miss Templeman, and their protection was often necessary. Miss Templeman seemed to know exactly where I'd been playing truant when required. I would come into the office from the Roxy cinema. "Where've you been?" she would glare. "The Deeds Registry," I'd say. "What film was showing?" she'd snarl.

After a month or so of the articled clerk routine, I realized I would have to do something extra to break out of a rut leading straight to the Side-Bar. I had seen enough to know that an attorney's life was drab compared with the riskier but more exciting career of a barrister. Only occasionally did an attorney handle a case in court, and then he could argue it only in the lower court. Too much of the work consisted of drawing up wills, registering deeds, notarizing documents, collecting debts and applying for licences of various kinds for clients. Especially depressing were the debtors' courts, where wretched defendants were dunned for accounts they could never pay and the dregs of humanity waited with listless eyes to be called before the magistrate.

I went to the head of the Law Faculty of the University of Cape Town, Professor Beinart, and told him how I'd been sidetracked by default of Mr Starke. After some hesitation he agreed to allow me to do the Attorneys' Admission course and the university law course at the same time. From then on I led an academic double-life, attending both the Levy lectures and the B.A. (Law) lectures before and after the day's duties for MacCallum and Co. My fellow students in both streams thought I was crazy, and if I'd gone in thoroughly for both sets of courses and studied each diligently I would probably have had some sort of breakdown, but I skipped the classes I didn't need for a first-year pass, and a stroke of luck led me to unexpected success at the end of the year. Most Attorneys' Admission students failed Roman Law in the first year, but fortunately the Roman Law paper in the university course was largely a mass of solid Latin comprehension, and as I had been good at Latin at school I was happy with the translations and got my Roman Law credit. This, allied with high marks in Criminal Law and a scraping pass in Roman-Dutch Law, actually put me through my first-year examinations. It was coincidental good fortune, because I had done little hard study except for the two weeks preceding the exams.

What kept me from my studies was a blend of politics, sport and social activity. I had met a girl who was a student at a teachers' training college in Mowbray, and we spent many evenings together. This involved a regular eight-mile walk because we often parted too late for me to get the last bus or train, and I had moved to student digs in Sea Point. Sea Point was an exciting suburb for a young student in the early 1950's. It had a cosmopolitan atmosphere and was where the artists and non-conformists lived. The only snag was that the long walk from Mowbray, practically on the other side of the city, meant passing through some of the toughest suburbs in the Cape late at night. The first time I had walked several miles and found myself in a forbidding area with little street-lighting. Buildings were old, grim and battered; hallways were mysterious and gloomy. I walked in the middle of the street, not trusting the dark pavements. Then I saw the blue glow of a police station light and asked the officer on duty where I was. He looked at me with shock: "My god, you're lucky to be alive here at this hour —don't you know this is District Six?" That scared me. District Six was notorious for murders, attacks and muggings of sailors and other foreigners unaware of its reputation. The policeman, who was armed, walked with me until I was out of the danger zone.

One night I had an even worse scare. I had completed most of my long walk, this time avoiding District Six, and had reached Green Point, only a mile or so from Sea Point. It was between two and three o'clock in the morning, and at one point there was a high wall extending over part of the pavement. I had passed this wall when three black men stepped out from behind it and stopped me. Two stood behind me and one stood in front—the one in front holding a long-bladed knife. Through some instinct I spoke sharply in Xhosa: "*Nifuna ntoni?*" ("What do you want?") "*Yu!*" one of them said. "A white who speaks Xhosa!" They made sounds of surprise, and the one with the knife said: "Young white man, how is that you can speak Xhosa?" I told them that I was from the Transkei, and they excitedly said they were also from the Transkei, and pushing my luck I asked indignantly why I was being confronted with a knife. The knife-wielder looked at the knife as if he had forgotten about it, then said: "No, we were just wanting tobacco." I feigned concern: "*Aw—niya nqanqateka!*" ("Oh, you crave to smoke!") They burst out laughing at the colloquialism of "*nqanqateka*"—typical Xhosa slang referring to tobacco-craving—and I pulled out a packet of cigarettes and gave it to them, saying goodbye as casually as I could and walking on. When I was out of sight around the first bend I ran as fast as I could, never stopping until I reached the safety of my digs, where I was physically ill. After that experience I made a point of always catching the last bus from Mowbray.

It was in the early days of bus-segregation, with blacks on the upper deck and whites below, but many Cape Town people ignored this at the time and I enjoyed the way black passengers responded to insult. The conductors and ticket examiners were often offensively rude when speaking to blacks, whose reaction was to smile politely at the white conductor while remarking in Xhosa: "Have you ever seen such big ears?" or: "Now here's a really ugly white man—look at that nose." Sometimes I couldn't resist smiling, to show the blacks that I understood. This would set them talking and asking where I was from, and the result was often a long conversation involving many passengers, with the white passengers glaring at me or staring curiously at this fellow-white talking the black man's language. Once an old Coloured passenger muttered something in Afrikaans, and the Afrikaner conductor, who certainly looked coloured himself, wheeled on him shouting: "Wie's *nie wit nie?* Wie's *nie wit nie?* ("*Who's* not white? *Who's* not white?"). I had never seen such rage. His eyes were dilated, his mouth distorted with fury. The old man said nothing, and only looked at the floor with a knowing little smile on his face. Enraged further, the conductor stopped the bus and put him out.

At the office I started handling *in forma pauperis* divorce cases, in which the litigants had no funds and law firms would act free for them on a roster basis. I handled about a dozen of these, making some awful mistakes and inadvertently prolonging several marriages by months in the process. My worst experience was in the first of these cases. I had briefed an equally inexperienced barrister, Advocate McKenzie, and we drew the most crotchety judge in Cape Town, Mr Justice Joseph Herbstein.

That day I prepared my file neatly, stapling all the documents together, and when our case was called Judge Herbstein asked my barrister where a certain document was. Advocate McKenzie relayed the question to me, and in my nervousness I responded directly to the judge: "Oh, sorry, I've got it right here in my file." Judge Herbstein exploded: "Who are you? You're not an advocate of this court! How dare you address the Bench? This is outrageous!" "I'm sorry," I said. "Don't address me, sir! Don't address me! Be silent!" the judge howled.

I fumbled for the document, saw it was stapled to the others and tugged to get it free. It tore in a wide curve from the corner, leaving nearly a quarter of it stapled to the other documents in the file. In my confusion I walked up and handed the jagged remnant to the judge. "What are you doing?" he shouted, involuntarily taking the torn paper from me. "You can't hand documents in to this court—you have no standing!" He handed it back to me, I took it and handed it to the mortified McKenzie, who had by now advanced dazedly to the front of the court, and he handed it back to the angry judge. Judge Herbstein looked at it again. "It's torn," he said. "And it has no revenue stamp." He handed it back to Advocate McKenzie who handed it back to me, repeating superfluously: "No revenue stamp!"

I snatched it and ran from the court, telling McKenzie: "I'll get one right now." Arriving breathless at the office of the Supreme Court Registrar, Mr Hitchcock, I said: "Please, Mr Hitchcock, give me a three-shilling revenue stamp. I'll pay you later. I haven't time to explain now." The usually talkative Mr Hitchcock gave me the stamp quickly and I stuck it on and ran back to the court, where some of my fellow articled clerks stood about at the back, smiling nervously. Again I extended the document to the judge but this time Advocate McKenzie intercepted it, snatching it from my frightened fingers to hand it himself to His Lordship. Herbstein accepted the mutilated document, muttering: "Most irregular. Most irregular."

Shortly after this our firm had an unusually interesting case. A wealthy young publisher was charged with raping a teenaged coloured girl, and we were engaged to defend him. The prosecution led evidence that he had driven to Simondium, a village near Cape Town, to hire the young girl as a nursemaid for his two small children, had stopped on the way back to Cape Town to buy a bottle of brandy and some chloroform, and had spread a blanket in a remote spot, chloroformed her and raped her. The trial lasted nine days and our client was acquitted through lack of evidence, but he was ostracized from Cape Town society, his wife divorced him and he went to live in the Seychelles Islands.

67

There were a growing number of prosecutions under the Immorality Act, the law forbidding sexual acts between persons of different race, and many whites prosecuted under it committed suicide to avoid the public stigma. A number of the whites charged were Dutch Reformed Church ministers—men who were usually loudest in condemning inter-race sex.

At this time I was becoming interested in politics, ducking lectures to sneak into the public gallery at Parliament to listen to the debates. Parliament fascinated me, and at that stage I could think of nothing more exciting than to be an MP. What first sparked my interest in the doings of MPs had nothing to do with Parliament at all. It was a newspaper report of vandalism committed by young Afrikaner Nationalists on a war memorial, and this so angered me that I felt I should do something to help oppose them. I was by now fairly certain that their apartheid policy was morally wrong, although I couldn't think of any practical alternatives. However, the obvious place to look for such alternatives was in the opposition United Party, and I began to attend some of their meetings and to question their spokesmen. Morale was high in the Party: it was the eve of the 1953 general election, which they expected to win.

The Party had a checkered history. When the British handed the new Union of South Africa back to the Afrikaners after the Boer War the two main Boer heroes, Louis Botha and Jan Smuts, emerged as the champions of reconciliation between Afrikaans- and English-speaking whites, and their moderate South African Party won power in the first Union parliament in 1910. But another Boer War general, James Hertzog, wanted a narrower nationalism, basically for Afrikaners only, and he founded the Afrikaner Nationalist movement. Hertzog believed he would eventually come to power because two-thirds of whites in South Africa were Afrikaners, and he played on their wish to re-establish an Afrikaner republic with strong emphasis on the Afrikaans language and culture. He also exploited Afrikaner hatred of the British, and denigrated Botha and Smuts for helping their former foes to fight Germany in World War I. Botha and Smuts had honoured their Government's alliance with Britain, and when war broke out Botha led an army to capture German South West Africa (Namibia)

68

and Smuts led one to capture German East Africa (Tanzania). For these blows against the German Empire South Africa's reward was to be given the League of Nations mandate to administer South West Africa.

The Hertzogites had violently opposed South Africa's participation in the war, and an Afrikaner Nationalist rebellion had broken out which Botha and Smuts put down by force of arms, further raising national tension. Then in 1924 Hertzog's Afrikaner Nationalists, in a pact with the segregationist Labour Party, came to power and ruled until they were toppled by the economic crisis following the world-wide depression and the failure of the gold standard in the early 1930s. By now Botha was dead, and Smuts formed a coalition with Hertzog, serving under his continuing premiership. Their two parties fused, becoming the United Party, and Hertzog's more extreme followers broke away to found the "purified" Afrikaner Nationalist Party—the party of Malan, Strydom, Verwoerd, Vorster and P. W. Botha, which was later to introduce apartheid.

Then came a major rift between Smuts and Hertzog over World War II. When Britain declared war on Germany Hertzog wanted South Africa to remain neutral, but Smuts forced a vote which he narrowly won; he became Premier and declared war on Germany. Hertzog and his co-neutralists abandoned the United Party and rejoined the "purified" Afrikaner Nationalists, who were pro-Nazi. They formed the Afrikaner Nationalist Party and started drawing up their apartheid blueprints.

They were not taken seriously, even in the months leading up to the 1948 general election, although some of Smuts's advisers begged him not to underestimate them. Their "apartheid" slogan was winning them support, and their exploitation of white prejudice and fear of the blacks was filling halls at their election meetings. Moreover, some of Smuts's deputies had been seeking liberalization of United Party policy on the colour issue, and Afrikaner Nationalists responded by calling the United Party leaders *Kaffirboeties* (nigger-lovers) and *linksgeneigde liberaliste* (leftist-inclined liberalists). Smuts's party was anything but liberal, having co-operated with Hertzog to take away voting rights from even the few blacks who had the vote under British colonial rule and having passed a number of racial laws. However, in the white political climate of the time it was considerably less segregationist than the Afrikaner Nationalists, and opposed the excesses of segregation proposed in the apartheid blueprints.

Smuts knew that delimitation, the drawing of voting districts to favour rural areas, would help the Afrikaner Nationalists, but he didn't think their apartheid call would put them into power. He reckoned without a significant block of his own supporters, the returned soldiers from the war, many of whom still seethed over his broken campaign pledges to provide generous housing and other rewards for war veterans. In protest they voted Afrikaner Nationalist, most of them never thinking this would put the party into power. But it did—by that small margin of five seats, and that was enough. The country was stunned. Many of the victors were as surprised as the Smuts people were. There was a surge of Afrikaner Nationalist celebration, and one old Afrikaner said: "Even the trees look different."

Yet although one of their first measures to consolidate power had been to redraw the voting districts to make one pro-Nationalist vote worth almost two anti-Nationalist votes, and although they spent five years entrenching themselves by passing laws to gain increasingly totalitarian control of the country, their opponents in the United Party believed they had a good chance of winning the 1953 election, calculating that a small percentage swing their way in the rural districts could bring back up to thirty seats.

It was during this election campaign that I attended a big United Party rally in the Cape Town City Hall. Thousands were there to hear the new party leader, J. G. N. Strauss, who had taken over leadership after Smuts's death. Emotions were high and the crowd sang wartime songs like *So long Sarie* and *We are marching to Pretoria*. A pipe-organ led the singing and the crowd was ready for an inspiring message from their new leader. What they got was a damp squib. Strauss, in his thin, reedy voice, made a painfully dull ninety-minute speech which bored the crowd to silence and apathy, and they filed out in disappointed silence.

There was clearly no inspiration to be had from him, so I went to newspaper files and senior United Party officials to find out all I could about his young deputy, who was being spoken of as the next leader, Sir De Villiers Graaff. Party members and officials described him as brilliant, and full of what would later be called charisma. The only baronet in South Africa, he was in his middle thirties. A big, swarthily-handsome man, he looked like Clark Gable and was a barrister with degrees from Cape Town University, Oxford and Leyden; he had been a heavyweight boxing champion, a provincial cricketer and a distinguished soldier. I went to the House of Parliament and asked to see him, but was told he was too busy to see anyone, so I simply kept calling to leave messages for him, and meanwhile undertook my own political researches. Having rejected the Afrikaner Nationalists and their excesses, I went through all the United Party policy statements and literature obtainable. All conveyed the right condemnations of apartheid, but seemed to have no dynamic alternatives to offer. There was little point in opposing apartheid only to support a watered-down version of it.

I started spending a lot of time in libraries, making notes on Constitutional Law and in particular on the governmental system that seemed to offer the best framework within which apartheid could be dismantled—the federal system. I read in particular everything I could about the federations of Canada, the United States, Australia and Switzerland, and began writing what turned into a long theory about the kind of federation which would best suit South Africa. The overall concept was that of a geographic federation of the whole of Southern and Central Africa, from the Cape to the Copperbelt of Zambia, with a US-type Bill of Rights for all and a phased programme going over a twenty-five-year period from a qualified franchise to a full franchise for all citizens. What seemed clear from every single book on all the countries concerned was the obvious economic integrity of this vast region, and also the fact that cotton and other agricultural crops could powerfully complement mining and make the "Federated States of Southern Africa" one of the wealthiest countries in the world.

Eventually Sir De Villiers Graaff, possibly intrigued by the persistence of a student, agreed to see me. Like many who met him in those days I was soon charmed, and could see why men would follow him into battle. I was also flattered that he spent some hours in conversation with me and then invited me to dinner, where the conversation continued. The scene was like something from the Victorian age—the tuxedoed statesman, his moustached lip curling to a large cigar in the candlelight; messengers bringing him notes from the debate; the liqueur glasses gleaming in the private parliamentary dining-room. In effect he said: "Follow me!" He was indulgently critical of my federal ideas, remarking with a raised eyebrow that an uncle of his was the constitutional lawyer who had drafted the constitutions of "half those South American republics" and that federalism was a discredited system. Flattered as I was by his attention, I somehow knew at the end of that evening, though my head was spinning from wine and liqueurs, that this was not the leader for me and that his was not the party for me. There was no spark; no dynamic ideal that could fire the followers of his party with enthusiasm. Apparently a number of voters felt the same way, because the United Party lost the 1953 election by a wider margin than in 1948.

After this two new opposition parties were formed in a breakaway from the United Party. The first was the Liberal Party, but when it adopted a policy of universal franchise, one-man-one-vote, I rejected it, not favouring a system which would amount to immediate black majority rule. I still believed in a qualified franchise with the vote going initially to all who had educational and financial qualifications within a federal system. It seemed important to maintain white control for a long time, although it also seemed important to remove all unfair obstacles preventing blacks from participating increasingly in the political process.

Then two United Party senators broke away to form the Federal Party. The name excited me, keen as I now was on federalism, and I went to the Senate to inquire about it. Within minutes of talking to Senator Edward Browne of Natal I joined the party, because it seemed to embody the very ideas taking shape in my mind. The leader, Senator Heaton Nicholls, was the most distinguished member of the Senate. Formerly High Commissioner to London for the Smuts Government, he was a tall old man with long silver hair, whose earlier record of conservatism was now offset by a relative liberalism. In the view of members of the new Liberal Party, such as Alan Paton, he was still too conservative, but I liked his statesmanlike concept of the Federated States of Southern Africa, so close to the thoughts I had had in my own library researches.

While I was looking into these two new parties, my boss Mr Smit arranged for his father to take me to lunch at Parliament. Dr D. L. Smit was the Member of Parliament for East London City; he was very deaf, and like many deaf people he spoke loudly. Our lunch table was next to that of the Afrikaner Nationalist cabinet ministers—Malan, Strydom, Louw, Swart and Verwoerd. Dr Smit said piercingly: "My boy, do you see that bunch at the next table? A rotten lot! They were pro-Nazi during the war, specially Malan and Verwoerd. Smuts could have had them hanged. And that little swine Louw was just like Goebbels." Malan, Verwoerd and Louw heard every word of this diatribe and their necks puffed up red, but they did nothing about it. Still new to power, they were unsure how to react, not yet having reached the heights of arrogance they would later attain. Louw did have a physical resemblance to Goebbels, and Strydom resembled Rudolf Hess.

I enjoyed hanging around Parliament listening to debates. The House of Assembly with its green leather benches had atmosphere, and debate was often bitter. Usually the Afrikaner Nationalist speakers spoke in Afrikaans and the opposition speakers in English. One of the most frequent interjectors was Gerhardt Bekker, the Afrikaner Nationalist MP for Cradock, who seemed to believe that all opponents of apartheid were communists. Whenever one of the more liberal spokesmen on the Opposition side, Dr Bernard Friedman, spoke, Bekker chanted: "MOSCOW! MOSCOW!" Eventually Friedman appealed to the Speaker for a ruling, and the Speaker ruled that in this context "MOSCOW" was unparliamentary language. As Dr Friedman resumed his speech, Bekker leant forward and said distinctly: "Vladivostok!" But Dr Friedman had his revenge. After one of Bekker's shrill interjections, he said: "Mr Speaker, will the Honourable Member with the double chin and the treble voice now be silent?" Another witty speaker was Mr Harry Lawrence of the United Party, who during a debate on snake extermination referred to "the honourable Mamba for Zululand". Lawrence had been Smuts's Minister of Justice during the war, when pro-German members of the Afrikaner Ossewa-Brandwag organization had rushed the platform during a speech of his and beaten him up, kicking him so severely in the kidneys that he never fully regained his health.

I spent much time in the public galleries, time that should have been passed at law lectures, but in a way the debates were more educational. It seemed to make little sense studying law at the university when legislators down in the Assembly were busy tearing up South Africa's legal system.

After the first batch of statutes to found apartheid, the Afrikaner Nationalists pushed through several more to tighten their hold on the country. One was the Public Safety Act, allowing the Government to proclaim a state of emergency at any time without giving reasons; to suspend habeas corpus; to jail anyone without trial during the proclaimed period and to prevent any legal proceedings being taken against the Government for any actions against citizens during such a period. Then came the Criminal Law Amendment Act, which made it a crime to oppose any law by campaigning for its withdrawal. Next came the Reservation of Separate Amenities Act, making it a crime for blacks to use white amenities such as park benches, toilets, entrances to buildings, elevators or ambulances. And after that came the Bantu Education Act, which made it illegal for blacks to get the same education as whites and set lower educational standards for blacks to prevent them from aspiring to the same standards of living as whites.

The black response to these new laws was a campaign of defiance led by the African National Congress. The ANC, founded in 1912, had consistently sought the abolition of segregation by peaceful negotiation, and forty-two years later it was still committed to peaceful methods. The 1953 campaign was supported by masses of blacks, and the Government imprisoned more than eight thousand people for defying segregation laws and curfew regulations and for responding to police action with passive resistance methods—lying down or standing still when ordered to disperse. Again these campaigns were represented in the media, especially the state-controlled radio service, as Communist-led attempts to undermine national stability, and that was how I saw them at the time. The only militant opposition to the Afrikaner Nationalists that I felt I could support was the Torch Commando, an organization led by white anti-fascist ex-servicemen whose chief was "Sailor" Malan, formerly one of the fighter-pilot heroes of the Battle of Britain.

His movement spread like wildfire, with some rallies of over forty thousand militants, and once they nearly brought down the Afrikaner Nationalist Government by intimidation when a multitude started pushing over the railings at Parliament to get into the House of Assembly. Premier Malan, "Sailor's" uncle and bitter foe, was locked white-faced in his office. But the United Party, fearing the Torch Commando would compete with it for parliamentary seats and possibly replace it as the official opposition, urged its members not to support it. Without United Party support the Torch Commando gradually lost influence and faded away—the last mass white movement militantly opposed to apartheid and totalitarianism.

When my three years were up in Cape Town my articles of clerkship were ceded by Mr Smit to Mr Starke of Elliotdale as arranged. By now I had about two-thirds of the examination credits I needed to qualify at the end of the five years, which meant preparing for the rest of the subjects by correspondence while working in Mr Starke's Transkei law firm, without a Harold Levy or the University of Cape Town lecturers to help. Before leaving Cape Town I tried to pull off a minor academic miracle, doing the final-year practical exam two years ahead of time. The exam consisted of a series of tough written papers followed by verbal questioning by a panel of three judges. Surprisingly I passed the written part, but then failed the oral section hopelessly. The judges' questions on procedure tripped me up completely, and the panel advised me to try again "at the proper time, and after adequate preparation". Their Lordships did pass one compliment, however, saying that a certain section of my written paper had been "good literature"—a Supreme Court petition "De Lunatico Inquirendo" to have someone committed to a mental institution. The spokesman of the panel said the clauses of the petition were "elegant", and the imaginary behaviour of my imaginary lunatic so "inventive" that both he and his brother judges had been "considerably amused". He added: "Perhaps, Mr Woods, you are meant to become a journalist rather than a lawyer." It was a barbed compliment, unaccompanied by pass marks.

Before leaving Cape Town I was urged by Senators Heaton Nicholls and Browne to help their representative in the Eastern Cape to start branches of the Federal Party there. And so, aged twenty-one and with two years of articles left to serve in the legal profession under Mr Starke, I returned to the Transkei determined to complete my degree and articles—but far more determined to get into Federalist politics and campaign against the Afrikaner Nationalists.

CHAPTER FOUR

AFTER CAPE TOWN, Elliotdale came as a shock, although I had known the village all my life and had grown up in the district. The houses straggled down a hillside at random like pins pushed hurriedly into a pincushion. There was one street, apart from a tributary road near the end of the village which veered round the only hotel. Each passing car threw up a cloud of white dust that infiltrated every building in the village. In the Gordon Hotel bar-drinkers adding water to their whisky routinely sloshed some out of the neck of the water-bottle to get rid of the dust-coating.

Elliotdale was essentially a trading village, the market centre for the twenty-six trading stations in the district. Apart from the Gordon Hotel the only amenities other than dwellings were five shops, the jail, the village hall, the courthouse, the police station, two little churches and a school.

There were, however, a golf club and a cricket club, which lay on the other side of the Xhora stream from the village, across a little bridge. The small number of members was made up for by diversity of styles. Viv Whitfield, a trader with a big paunch and a moustache like a western villain, had a controlled slice of huge lateral dimensions. Buster Dreyer, the barman, used to converse with each of his Henry Cotton irons: "Talk to me, Henry, talk to me . . ." Dick Langheim, the stock-inspector, kept his pipe in his mouth throughout his swing, removing it only to guide his caddy with the despairing shout: "*E-dipini!*" ("Towards the dipping-tank!").

There were two lawyers in the village, Jack Starke and Percy Rose. Percy was careful with his money. The privy he built at his seaside shack was so small, for reasons of economy, that he had to lower his trousers outside and reverse into it. There were few Afrikaners in Elliotdale, a couple of policemen, the jailer and the local doctor, but there were some people of German descent. Among them was Mrs Bauer, the only white witchdoctress in the district. She had a big black clientèle who

77

were always impressed when she covered her head and shoulders with a shawl to intone: "*Ndiyavuma! Ndiyavuma!*" ("I yield to the spirits!").

I checked in at the Gordon Hotel, and on the first morning reported for duty at Jack Starke's office. It was a far cry from the sophistication of MacCallum and Co. in Cape Town. Facing on to the village square, the reception structure was a boxlike two-room building of brick with an overhanging verandah, as in the cow towns of the cinematic wild west. The front room was where the clients came, in their blankets and loincloths, to sit on benches along the walls and tell their story to Kwezi Gabada, the interpreter and general-purpose clerk. The room behind this was my office. It also had a bench for clients, a wall-safe for their fees, and a rickety desk, chair and book-shelf. Behind this was an unkempt yard with two rondavels, or thatched round huts. These were in appalling condition and seemed, like Mr Starke's practice, about to collapse at any moment. The far rondavel was Mr Starke's office, and the near one was the office of Kathleen Wild, for many years his secretary, typist, clerk and book-keeper. Nominally Mr Starke, a widower, owned the practice, but Kathleen was the effective head of it and Kwezi Gabada ran it.

When I arrived on the first morning dressed in a suit, by Cape Town habit, I had the first of many surprises at the firm. It concerned a ragged old man outside the office who sat on an upturned bucket on the dusty sidewalk intercepting passers-by and exhorting them to step into Starke's for legal advice. Horsemen would arrive and tether their horses to thorn trees in the square, heading for the office of Percy Rose, and the old man, Tubeni, would lope up to intercept them and lead them to Starke's instead. Shocked, I said to Kwezi Gabada: "That old man is touting! We can be struck off the roll for that!" Mr Starke came in, heard me, and was appalled: "Kwezi!" he said. "How many times must I order you to stop Tubeni? This is disgraceful! Tell him again!" Kwezi went and spoke earnestly to Tubeni out in the square, but day after day he continued touting until I confronted Kwezi again, whereupon Kwezi thought for a while, then seemed to come to a decision before telling me: "Ah, sir, the fact of the matter is, ah, that Mr Starke pays Tubeni two pounds a week to, ah, guide the clients here. Mr Rose also has a guide out there for clients who are, ah, looking for him."

It certainly was a long way from Cape Town . . .

And Transkei law practice was an even longer way from law practice in Cape Town. Most of the cases were over seduction of tribal wives or stock-recovery (civil) and rape, assault and axe-fighting (criminal). These accounted for most of the clientèle. The remainder, the white clients, were so much a rarity that they paid no fees. Traders usually rewarded legal services with gifts of sheep or vegetables—which helped everyone's tax position.

One of my earliest tasks was for a white trader, Bertie Kelly of Mdwaka. I had to collect twelve thousand pounds in outstanding debts from his tribal customers, and much of this debt dated back many years, which made it a problem to trace the debtors' whereabouts, as there were no street numbers in Bomvanaland. The tribespeople lived on hills and in valleys, sometimes moving from grazing land to grazing land and from district to district. But Kwezi Gabada, who knew all things, told me exactly how to go about it. He handed me hundreds of official-looking warrants printed on blue paper in impressive italic script, which were letters of demand from Starke's, and all we had to do was to fill in the names of the debtors and the amounts of the debts as discovered from the Mdwaka ledger. It all seemed pointless to me, as most of the debts were prescribed by lapse of time, but Kwezi only smiled. "You'll see," he said. When the documents had been filled in, he presented to me a group of horsemen, the district's professional debtor-trackers. Each was given a supply of the demand-forms and a list of names of the debtors, and they cantered away in a cloud of dust.

Within a couple of weeks the lost debtors began to stream into my office, strangely eager to pay off their debts. I couldn't understand this and sought out Kwezi. "What the hell is this all about, Kwezi?" He said, "Oh, well, sir, the next thing is to get their thumb-prints on to this document," indicating another file of impressive-looking forms. I saw the point: their fresh acknowledgment of debt would undo the prescription by lapse of time and would convert the new forms into liquid documents on which they could now be legally sued. I felt this was unfair, and protested to Kwezi: "Don't they realize their debts are out of date? Don't they realize the law no longer requires them to pay?" Kwezi said: "You can point that out to them, sir. You can explain it all. But they will insist on paying."

Of course it was true, according to Bomvana custom. Although I took them into my office in batches, explaining that the debts were time-prescribed and no longer binding, they all dismissed such legalistics. "How can you say these things, son of Woods, child of Hobeni? Don't you know that a debt is a thing of family honour? A debt never dies until it is paid, even after generations have passed." One by one they inked their thumbs on an inking-pad and pressed them at the foot of the documents acknowledging debt. Several paid on the spot in notes, having sold cattle to do so, and most of them settled the Mdwaka debt within six months. Each one, after making his thumb-print, would rub his thumb on the back of his head to remove the ink against his thick stubby hair. Bertie Kelly was grateful, and I was also thanked by Mr Starke, who explained that my salary was to be fifteen pounds a month plus ten per cent of the annual profits. It was all academic, because there were never any detectable profits in my two years there and seldom enough for my monthly salary either, so that I had to live on an allowance from home.

Within days of arriving at the office in a suit and tie I began to realize I was the only person in the village so dressed. Even the magistrate functioned in a worn alpaca jacket, so I started coming to work in shirt-sleeves, then tieless. Then it seemed easier to shave only every second day, and after some weeks I was beginning to look like a hobo and had to get back into some sort of Cape Town discipline again—especially after an unnerving experience.

I had passed enough subjects to be allowed to appear in minor matters in court, and one day I was chatting, jacketless, to Mr Starke in continuation of a conversation of the previous day. He had told me that as a youth he had done sentry duty in the Boer War, and our talk had drifted to the clothing of that time. He still had a suit of the period, and promised to bring it to the office to show me. "They knew how to make cloth in those days," he said.

When he showed me the jacket I found it hard to keep a

straight face, because it was one of those ancient high-buttoned jackets Cecil Rhodes and his contemporaries wore in yellowed prints of the time. At that moment Kwezi said I was urgently needed in court to apply for a postponement, and I got up to run to the hotel for my jacket, but Mr Starke stopped me. "No time," he said. "Just wear this one." I thought he was joking, and laughed, but he was serious, and agitated. "That matter must be postponed, or we'll lose it, and I can't get up there because I'm waiting for an important phone call from Johannesburg." I pulled on the ancient jacket and ran to the court, looking like someone from the last century. The jacket had many buttons and narrow sleeves and, Mr Starke being a small man, I bulged from it like John L. Sullivan. A handlebar moustache would have completed the picture. As I rose to make the application the magistrate looked up, the prosecutor and he exchanged glances, and the application was made to their suppressed chokes and snorts of amusement. It was a long time before the officers of the court let me forget my "Boer War" jacket.

Small as it was, Elliotdale was noted for high jinks, and on one occasion the magistrate, the prosecutor, the police chief and the clerk of the court were all prosecuted for illicit liquor selling. A special prosecutor and magistrate had to be sent out from Umtata, but all the Elliotdale officials were acquitted for lack of evidence, none of the loyal locals being prepared to testify effectively against them. It was really a technical charge, anyway, as the illicit booze was being sold to raise money for the golf club, but it was a singular experience for the men in the dock to be prosecuted in the very court in which they usually officiated. One of the unsatisfactory witnesses was Bill Thompson, the local hobo, who lived in an abandoned car on the edge of the village. The car was a wreck, with all its wheels missing and weeds growing up through the floor. Villagers used to say: "Bill, you should weed your car some time," but the radio worked and Bill said the front seat was his lounge and the back seat his bedroom. He had no visible means of support, but was in the pub most evenings and always offered others drinks. The only time he emerged from his car-dwelling well-dressed was to play for the village cricket team. It was rumoured that Bill slept with black girls, and other members of the team always avoided using the "box" he used when going out to bat.

Dad had by now given up trading, having turned Hobeni over to Harland so that he and Mom could retire to Umtata. Whenever I could get a lift I would visit them for a weekend, and often the whole family—Harland, Joan, their spouses and children and I—would gather at the Umtata house. Harland had married a girl of Afrikaans descent, Dawn Siebert, and Joan's husband, Jim Inglis, was a Scotsman who had met her in her student days in Cape Town when he was in the RAF and had been sent to South Africa for training. Then Dad gave me a car, a Chevrolet coupé, and after that I never needed to ask others for lifts to get to Umtata.

One day Jack Starke and Kathleen Wild got married without telling anyone beforehand, and the sudden matrimonials took everyone by surprise, not least Dad. He and Mr Starke had been friends for many years, and Dad had accompanied him as a United Party delegate to Transkei congresses of the party. Not that Dad was much interested in politics, but in his time one was either U.P. or Nat, and he used to make large and regular donations to the U.P. out of a sense of duty. The donations stopped after the Afrikaner Nationalists took the vote away from the coloureds and the U.P. leader, Mr Strauss, refused to commit the party to restoring it if he was returned to power. Dad felt it was a breach of faith, and despised Strauss for his expediency in trying to salvage racial votes by saying the matter would only be considered when the U.P. was back in power. Conservative as he was, and supportive of the idea that whites should retain control of all power in the country, he felt strongly about what he regarded as unfairness toward coloureds and blacks. "We've got to give them a square deal," he would repeat on such occasions—although he never equated a "square deal" with integration.

Generally, however, he took little interest in politics, especially in the last year of his life when his health was deteriorating. His death in 1955 followed his hospitalization of several weeks, and wasn't a surprise because the doctors had warned us that he was in a serious condition after a coronary attack at the age of sixty-seven. But it was a major shock to me because he had been such a strong personality as head of the family and such an influence on us all. He died in the Umtata hospital with all of us present, and my strongest memories of him then were of the stories he used to make up for Harland and me when we were children, as we lay with our heads on his shoulders, one on each side, and how we used to wrestle across his chest. His funeral was a moving ceremony—especially for me, when I saw so many Bomvana tribesmen arriving on horseback and on foot to pay their last respects.

The Umtata house was sold and Mom came to live with me in Elliotdale. We bought a rambling old house near the top of the village and rebuilt it, and this was the first of two disastrous ventures of mine into ambitious architecture and extravagant building. I designed what looked something like an antebellum Alabama plantation house, and duly transformed the place we had bought into this multi-pillared vision—at about double what it should have cost, because the builder inflated the price of the materials and I never bothered to check his accounts. But at least the result was a house big enough for full family weekends, and we would all gather there on Friday evenings.

Leisure times in Elliotdale were filled with golf and cricket and parties, but the work at Starke's was becoming depressingly monotonous—axe-fight trials, rape or seduction cases again and again. The stories were the same and only the parties to the litigation varied. The routine became grindingly familiar. A dozen or so axe-fighters would sidle into the outer office asking to be defended, and Kwezi would take two pounds from each man "for taking instruction". Then Mr Starke would sidle in to preside over the taking of the statements, with me at his side. (Kwezi, unaided, could have done it all more effectively.) Mr Starke would ask endless repetitive questions, which Kwezi would translate into Xhosa. He would then receive the answer in Xhosa, and translate it back into English. Kwezi often did some efficient editing in the process, especially when Mr Starke's mind wandered. In his old age Mr Starke often confused terms, referring for example to "the accused" as "the deceased". One day he said: "Kwezi, tell them to bring in the deceased to see me. I want to ask him some questions." Kwezi (stolidly): "The deceased is dead, sir." Mr Starke: "What? What?" Kwezi (patiently): "The deceased is dead, sir." Mr Starke: "Dead. Yes, of course he is dead."

In court, too, Mr Starke's mind often wandered during his cross-examination of a witness. He would stray right away from the point, losing all relevance to the case being tried. At first I thought the old man had some clever trick up his sleeve, and assumed his obscure questioning was a circuitous tactic to trap the witness, until I realized what was happening. Sometimes his cross-examination was from a case tried many years before, and he was re-conducting it in his mind, not conscious of the time lapse. This used to puzzle the prosecutor and exasperate the magistrate, who had to write all the evidence down in longhand because Elliotdale couldn't afford a shorthand writer or a recording machine. Mr Starke lost several cases that initially seemed impossible to lose, and managed to convict some of his clients in spite of the magistrate's gallant attempts to rescue them.

Yet often the Bomvanas didn't seem to mind losing cases. They loved litigation, and got a kick out of being parties to court proceedings. As long as they could refer to "my lawyer" up front, this gave them standing in the tribal community. And they were less interested in the substance of their lawyer's address than in the duration of it. A lawyer could make a brief, telling speech to the magistrate, winning his client's case, and still draw a scowl of discontent from the client. On the other hand, if he made a long, oratorical speech, the client was happy whether he won or lost. He was, after all, paying the "talker" to "talk" for him. That was why many Bomvanas thought Jack Starke was a good attorney—he made very long speeches.

One of the characters of Elliotdale was a girl called Mary Putzier. When the Hungarian Revolution of 1956 occurred, Mary decided that Elliotdale should raise funds for the gallant Hungarians, and organized a concert in the village hall. Her pamphlets were boldly headed: "Hungry Relief Fund". It was decided that one of the early items on the programme should be the Second Hungarian Rhapsody by Liszt, performed on two pianos by Mrs Thelma Gray and me. In the weeks preceding the concert Mrs Gray was driven nearly to distraction by my failure to practise my half of the music. She practised her part faithfully, and I kept intending to set aside several evenings for the same purpose, but my social life obtruded and suddenly the concert was upon us with me almost totally unprepared. To keep her from getting the jitters I pretended to know the part and said the performance would have more "spontaneity" if we didn't practise together beforehand. It certainly did. Poor Thelma, a mass of nerves, swallowed her apprehension, and quite a lot of gin, before we emerged on to the stage for the actual performance. I had managed to learn the first four pages at least, and for the rest had simply scrawled in pencil what key we should be in. The first four pages sounded fine, and Thelma hissed "Very good, very good" in an encouraging tone. Then the whole thing deteriorated into a shambles, bearing little relation to what Liszt had in mind at the time. I heard little groans coming from Thelma, but these only spurred me on to ever-bolder improvisations. And astonishingly, because we carried the entire travesty off with straight faces—hers stiff with shock, mine with concentration—and some pianistic panache, the audience assumed the whole thing was going according to plan. After the final improbable chord they exploded into applause, completely enthusiastic in their innocence. Thelma tottered from the stage in grim search of the gin bottle, muttering: "Never again. Jesus. Never again."

My brother Harland decided to expand the small bus service for tribesmen that Dad had inaugurated between two coastal parts of the district and Elliotdale. He bought a third bus, a Mercedes, or rather he bought the cab and had the body built in Umtata by one Piet Venter, who didn't follow the required design. The result was that grafted on to the beautiful cab was a rectangular, boxlike body bearing a regrettable resemblance to the trucks in which the Nazis conveyed their prisoners. Each side had only one small window, which couldn't be opened, and the only ventilation was through a small door at the back. On our dusty roads this meant that the interior was a vacuum which sucked up white dust through the rear door. When Harland objected Venter insisted that the body was all right, and prevailed on him to try it out with passengers on an actual trip. On the day of the test run, Harland phoned to tell me what time the bus was due at the Elliotdale square, and asked me to report my observations.

I saw the vehicle arrive, and as it came to a stop I noticed that its light-green colour was thickly coated over with white Bomvanaland dust. I went to the small side-window, and saw passengers staring out with stoic Xhosa resignation on their faces, along with much dust—especially about their eyebrows and beards. The opening of the rear doors was like the switching on of a blizzard. Clouds of white dust billowed out as the first passengers alighted, their normally red blankets or brown *dhlamini* coats likewise white, and as they smacked and smote at these, to send fresh dust-clouds issuing from them, they said only a mild: "*Kweku!*" (The nearest English equivalent is "Good heavens," or, depending on intonation, "Darn" or "Drat".)

Reflecting on what long-suffering people the Bomvanas were, I asked how they liked the bus. "It's a lovely bus," they chorused. "Look at that fine bus!" "No, that is a splendid bus." "Very comfortable to ride in, doesn't bump badly like other buses." They stood around it, looking at it with admiration. Then a couple of them addressed me as if in after-thought. "*Zweliyanyikima,*" they said, "you must tell *Dumekude* (Harland) that the dust coming into the bus is very great. Tell him that it's a fine bus, a magnificent bus that he has provided for us, and we like it very much, but that the dust—*yu!*" I reported to Harland that his passengers had emerged resembling a detachment of snowtroops from Siberia, and he promptly sent the bus back to Venter to be rebuilt to proper specifications.

During my two years in Elliotdale I became increasingly involved in politics. Having been commissioned in Cape Town by Senators Browne and Heaton Nicholls to team up with their representative in the Eastern Cape, Malcolm Kettles, and particularly to get the Federal Party launched in the Transkei, I wrote to Kettles and we held a number of successful inaugural meetings of the new party in the area. I was then invited to address a big anti-Government rally in East London. I was not too confident of the wisdom of speaking at a large rally in a big city with established speakers, but as it happened the meeting went off well. As we approached the hall we saw the crowd was so large that it overflowed the auditorium. The other speakers made factual, sober speeches, and when my turn came I sensed that the restless audience shared my own impatience with cold logic, so I made an emotional speech, and the response was enthusiastic. It was 1955, and there were still large numbers of whites angrily opposed to the Afrikaner Nationalists. These numbers were to dwindle in the years ahead.

The Federal Party started having a real impact in the Eastern Cape after this rally, although we had few members compared to the old-established United Party. I felt we needed a newspaper in the Transkei to promote our ideals there, and made an offer to buy the *Territorial News*, which was owned by a close-fisted Scot named Hutcheson. He named a price he thought would scare me off, and when I agreed to it he summoned up some panicky excuses—just as well, as I hadn't yet worked out how to raise the money. Since he owned the only available press I then asked him for an estimate to print a weekly paper for me, and again accepted his high quote without argument. I made arrangements to take wire service copy from Reuters and the South African Press Association, and was geared to deliver the copy for the first issue when Hutcheson again reneged on the deal, saying that he feared my paper would damage his own paper's circulation. So I resolved to acquire my own press, and to teach myself the rudiments of printing I ordered from England a small hand-platen Adana press at a cost, including shipping, of only £35. It was a well-made little machine, and at first I printed letterheads for traders and village businesses, then started setting more complicated copy. But when I discovered its limitations I lost interest in it and began looking around for a bigger press, capable of printing a tabloid.

But suddenly this became unnecessary. The *Daily Dispatch* in East London started using my letters and articles about the Federal Party, and as the *Dispatch* was the major paper of the region and covered the Transkei extensively it was a better vehicle for explaining our policies and ideals than any fledgling paper would be. I began travelling to promote the Federal Party, going all over the region, and increasingly to East London, to spread the party creed of firmer opposition to apartheid and a non-racial federal system of government.

The United Party in the Transkei, and particularly the incumbent Member of Parliament, Thomas Gray Hughes, became increasingly concerned at our challenge, and Hughes came to Elliotdale to address a special meeting to recover his lost supporters. Through a combination of mishaps, the meeting was a failure. Hughes was a nice man but not a subtle one, and he lacked local knowledge. He didn't know that the lighting plant engine in the village hall needed at least two bottles of fuel to last out a full meeting. In the past such matters had been left to Boyce Nelson, a "coloured" man whom everyone liked, and who was drowned in 1956 when he went to the aid of a swimmer in difficulty, and was swept out to sea by the backwash current. By the time of Hughes's meeting, Boyce and the whole coloured population of Elliotdale were secret Federalists, and as the coloureds took their seats at the back of the hall nothing further was said on the matter of fuel. Accordingly, after the introductory speeches Hughes rose to begin his talk just as the engine sputtered out and the hall was plunged into darkness. Nobody had thought to bring candles, so a party member was sent to get some from his house. Mr Hughes's voice, issuing from the darkness, was heard to mutter that I was trying to sabotage the meeting.

When light was restored by the setting up of several candles, giving the meeting a clandestine character, Mr Hughes launched into his belated speech, and was in full cry when the hall suddenly emptied of all the men in the audience. The hotel proprietor, Derek Hards, had gone outside to urinate, and all the men thought he had gone to reopen the bar so they followed him out. Rather than disappoint them he provided two quick rounds for the thirsty ones, who then returned to the meeting in a cheerful state. One of the more cheerful among them was my uncle, Pat Lawlor, who was a loyal supporter of Hughes. I suggested a question or two for Uncle Pat to put to Hughes, and the result of this was a heated argument between them, Hughes's anger fuelled by resentment and Uncle Pat's by beer. This led to uproar in the hall, and I crept to Derek Hards's seat asking if I could see him outside for a moment. Derek, who had been half-dozing, complied, and as I had hoped the men again thought he was going out to open the bar. This time the exodus brought an effective end to the meeting, and it was a long time before Hughes ventured into our district again.

One of the most dangerous political meetings I attended was

an Afrikaner Nationalist meeting in Umtata. I went there to put challenging questions, and found I was the only dissident present among hundreds of avid pro-apartheidists. My questions, put in Afrikaans because it seemed appropriate to challenge the speakers in their own language, so angered the crowd that several railway workers among them moved towards me threateningly. The chief speaker, an Afrikaner Nationalist Member of Parliament, shouted to them to stop, telling them that such a beating-up was exactly what "left-wingers" like me wanted to provoke. But the way the railway gangers kept eyeing me and muttering that they would deal with me after the meeting kept me in a tense state, and as the meeting ended I sauntered casually to the door, then as they made a run for me in the street I tore for my car. Not being a fast runner, I was glad I had parked close to the hall, but they were within feet of the car as I accelerated away, blessing the House of Chevrolet for the reliable ignition system and their six big cylinders. The gangers gave chase, and it was only when I was about twelve miles from Umtata that I managed to leave them behind. It was the uphill stretches that beat them, but my palpitating heart only calmed down near the turn-off road to Elliotdale.

We were provoking the Afrikaner Nationalists considerably at the time. Some Federalists had started a clandestine radio station called "Freedom Radio" which broadcast from a different place each week, branding the Nats as neo-Nazis. The Government spent a lot of time and money tracking down "Freedom Radio", and finally did so. The main culprits were caught and heavily sentenced, but the rest of us carried on a kind of leaflet war.

An interesting experience for me during these early Federal Party days was the first national convention of the Party, held in Durban, which I attended as a delegate from the Eastern Cape. I was asked whether I wanted to stay at a hotel in Durban or with a party member at his home. Although I would have preferred the privacy of a hotel, I thought it would be more in the party spirit if I stayed with one of the members in what I imagined would be a crummy little flat. I was in for a surprise. The party member to whom I was assigned met me at Durban airport and drove me to his home. We turned between two big gateposts into what looked like an extensive park, before sweeping up to stop in front of a mansion. I was given a suite of rooms in the top storey of the left wing, and told when dinner would be ready. It was served in a large room with a high ceiling and rich, dark-red drapes. There were only three of us to dine—my host, his father and me. We sat in high-backed chairs and behind each chair, against the wall, stood a Zulu manservant. The manservants, uniformed, did not serve the meal—that was done by a sort of head-manservant—but only stirred to fill up our water glasses or pick up table napkins that had fallen to the floor. It seemed a strange life-style for people demanding social change. I was later to meet other liberals in Johannesburg, Cape Town and Durban who lived like this, and whose uniformed black manservants wore sashes and white gloves while attending them at dinner.

Back in Elliotdale I found an invitation to go to East London to discuss with the editor of the *Daily Dispatch* an article on the franchise proposals of the Federal Party. I liked the look of the *Dispatch* building from the minute I saw it. It was old, with massive walls, and had the architectural character of the previous century with arched windows and ornate masonry. The editor, Vernon Barber, was a legendary character in the Eastern Cape. He was editor of the *Dispatch* for twenty-seven years, and many colourful stories were told about him. Born in Yorkshire, he had come to South Africa as a young journalist, but had never lost his north-country accent. We soon completed our discussion about the projected article, then he looked at me sharply over the top of his glasses and said: "Son, have you ever thought of going into journalism?" I told him there was nothing I'd like better, but that I didn't know how to get a start. "Well, you get a job as a cub reporter on a newspaper," he said. "I'll have a vacancy for a cub reporter in three months, and if you want it I'm prepared to give you a trial. I like the way you write, and I think you might make a journalist." Overwhelmed, I thanked him and accepted. "The pay will be twenty-seven pounds a month," he said as we shook hands. "You'll be welcome on the staff of the *Dispatch*, son."

Leaving his office I peeped into the newsroom where the reporters were clattering on typewriters. A radio was blaring out the news that South Africa had beaten England by seventeen runs to win the fifth Test and square the 1957 series.

I had explained to Barber that I couldn't simply abandon law overnight, because I still had two months of my five-year articles of clerkship to serve out by contract, and I felt I should also consult my family. We had a conference the following weekend in the Elliotdale house. Most of the family were basically opposed to the idea, pointing out the uncertainty of what I was contemplating, the poor salary and the vagueness of the prospects compared to a solid career in a country law practice. Dawn alone spoke in favour of the move; she felt I was stagnating in Elliotdale and should be tested in deeper waters. But all of them made it clear they would support my decision.

This decision was to join the *Dispatch*, because the idea of journalism excited me, and because the practice of law was boring me beyond further endurance. My financial position was good, on paper. I had inherited ten thousand pounds from Dad's estate, but it was in property, mainly the Elliotdale house and some stands in the south part of the village. This meant I had little actual cash—especially when I realized at the final meeting with Mr Starke that my wages for two full years with him would remain nil. Yet I couldn't feel anger against him because I liked him too much and realized how muddled he had become.

As I drove to East London I had moments of doubt that I was doing the right thing, but they didn't last long, especially when I recalled Mr Starke's kindly parting words, uttered with great sadness, that he felt I was making a terrible mistake. My experience of Mr Starke's judgement was such that I found comfort in his words, and reassurance that I had made the right decision. My articles of clerkship had expired two hours before I left Elliotdale, ending my five years of indenture to the law. I may not have learned much law, but I had learned a lot about that portion of it most relevant to journalism in South Africa— criminal law, statute law and the law of defamation. I knew I should miss living in the Transkei, being near Hobeni, the family seaside cottage at Bashee Mouth, Elliotdale, Umtata and all the friends I had made and the whole easy Transkei life style.

91

During my two years in Elliotdale a long constitutional struggle between the Government and opposition had come to a head over the question of voting rights for Cape coloureds. One of the entrenched clauses of the 1910 Constitution on which the Union of South Africa was founded guaranteed the coloured people of the Cape Province the right to vote. The Afrikaner Nationalists passed the Separate Representation of Voters Act to take away this vote, and when the opposition had this law tested in the Supreme Court the judges ruled the law invalid because the entrenched clauses of the constitution could only be changed by a two-thirds vote of both houses of Parliament, the Senate and the Assembly. There were still vestiges of judicial law surviving from the Smuts era. The Government tried for this two-thirds majority and failed, then passed the High Court of Parliament Act, which purported to turn the parliamentarians into judges for the duration of a vote overruling the Supreme Court decision—in effect, making Parliament a higher court than the Supreme Court for an hour or two to nullify the Supreme Court's ruling.

This Act was also declared unlawful by the Supreme Court, and when even the central court of appeal, the Appellate Court in Bloemfontein, refused to condone such cavalier tinkering with the constitution the Government appointed party members as additional judges to this ultimate court of appeal. They passed the Senate Act, enabling them to appoint any number of party members to enlarge the Senate sufficiently to get the two-thirds vote, and their party appointees to the appeal court bench ensured that this was "legal".

The first sitting of the artificially enlarged Senate was extraordinary. The original Senate chamber with its crimson leather benches couldn't seat all the extra new "senators"— mostly farmers and other rural party members obviously unaccustomed to wearing suits and ties, and so ignorant of senatorial procedure that the party whips had to give group lessons on how to vote. Many of them were as baffled by the proceedings as the watchers in the public gallery. But not all the spectators were unaware of the significance of it all. Some observing the farce were coloured men with degrees—university professors, doctors and lawyers—looking on as the white "senators", several of them barely literate, went through the final cynical process of stripping away their remaining civil rights. From now on, only whites could vote for representation in the South African Parliament.

The final irony was that more than a few of the "senators" were considerably darker in complexion than some of the coloured spectators whose rights were being taken away "to preserve white purity". One of them was a certain Van Staden, whose swarthiness of complexion was so noticeable that his nickname, behind his back, was *Witbooi* (White Boy), and he let it be known that he would sue for defamation anyone calling him this in public. Van Staden was so zealous a champion of white racial purity that he was later given a safe seat in the House of Assembly when the enlarged senate was shrunk back to normal size after doing its work. His constituency was Malmesbury, and it was of him that opposition MP Harry Lawrence once observed during a debate: "Mr Speaker, the honourable Member for Malmesbury is almost white with rage . . ."

When the dust of the constitutional clash had settled it was obvious that more than coloured voting rights had been removed. Entrenched clauses in the constitution were now meaningless, the Senate was enlargeable whenever the Government wanted its approval, and the tradition of judicial independence for all Supreme Court judges was now a thing of the past. The Afrikaner Nationalist Government had tightened its grip on the country further, and was preparing to impose a new batch of apartheid laws on the blacks. It announced that it would now begin to take action against the "disloyal, un-South African" English-language press. It was hardly a propitious time to join one of those very newspapers, as I was about to do. On the other hand, it was also a stimulating prospect. To become a journalist on an anti-Government newspaper in South Africa in 1957 was to begin an experience that promised to be anything but dull.

It was dark by the time I reached East London. After Elliotdale it seemed a vast metropolis as I drove through the suburbs to my apartment near the *Dispatch* building. The city had street names and areas called after places in the real London in

England, such as Oxford Street and Argyll Street, and that first night I fell asleep with neon lights from Fleet Street flashing through the windows.

At the *Dispatch* the next morning I was shown around, welcomed by Vernon Barber and his deputy, Murray McPherson, a professorial figure, and introduced to everyone in the editorial department. The news editor, Jock McFall, was a clean-cut pleasant-faced man with a tidy desk and a businesslike manner, and the sports editor, Sandy Johnston, had a booming voice and the build of a rugby player. The chief sub-editor, George Farr, was dapper and bustling, and his deputy, Ken Courage, had the air of a military adjutant. I was handed over to chief reporter Ted Holliday, who introduced me to the other reporters. One of these was John Ryan, like me a cub reporter on trial. He was also a Transkeian, and we were to become close friends and share many adventures. He was slim, fair-haired and lantern-jawed, and his quiet manner hid a subtle sense of humour.

After following Ted Holliday around for a week I was allowed to turn in odd paragraphs like the daily sea temperatures and the register of ships in the harbour, graduating by degrees to slightly better assignments. At the end of three months as a cub reporter I was called into the editor's office and told that my trial period was over, and that I was now on the permanent staff at a salary of thirty-two pounds a month.

But the first phase of my career as a journalist ended abruptly within days of this promotion. The United Party Member of Parliament for the East London North constituency dropped dead at a public meeting, and this necessitated a parliamentary by-election. Shortly after this was announced, the editor called me to his office to tell me that he had had a visit from a delegation of businessmen representing the Federal Party; that the Party had decided to contest the seat, wished to nominate me for the parliamentary vacancy, and had asked him to release me from my job for the purpose. Barber said he was prepared to do this for the duration of the three-month campaign, and to take me back on to the staff in the event of my losing—which seemed probable. It was the first of several surprises I was to experience in Barber's office, and I thanked him in a kind of daze. I loved the idea of going to Parliament, although I had no illusions about the near-impossibility of wresting the seat from the United Party. East London was about the safest U.P. stronghold in the country, and other parties seldom bothered to contest the seat. However, our potential as a new party was untested in national politics—we had polled heavily in provincial elections in Natal—and the national leadership clearly saw this as an opportunity to challenge the old order of parliamentary politics in South Africa.

A second surprise came two days later—the United Party also wanted to nominate me for the seat. This was flattering and tempting from two points of view: if I accepted the U.P. nomination I should go straight into Parliament at the age of twenty-three without having to go through an election, since I should be unopposed; and the parliamentary salary was enormous by my standards. But ultimately there could be no question of accepting the offer; I disagreed so fundamentally with what the Party stood for. The difference between the Federal Party and the United Party on the race issue was basically that the F.P. rejected apartheid totally, whereas the U.P. offered merely a tamer variation of race discrimination. The U.P. offer had been conveyed by the party's Member of Parliament for the City seat, Dr D. L. Smit, the father of the Cape Town attorney to whom I had been articled for three years. Dr Smit was a highly-regarded senior official of the U.P. and a revered figure in East London, which he had represented in Parliament for many years. He was particularly respected for his integrity.

After my rejection of the U.P. offer I was cleaning out my desk at the *Dispatch* on my last day before leaving the staff to start the election campaign when I was again called to the editor's office. With Barber were several senior officials of the U.P., including Dr Smit, and I noticed that Barber's normally ruddy face was white. With tension in his voice he said he wanted to tell me in the presence of these "distinguished gentlemen" that they had asked him not to release me from the staff for the election, and make it a condition of my employment at the *Dispatch* that I should be barred from anti-U.P. politics, and that the *Dispatch* should take note that most of its biggest advertisers were U.P. supporters. He added in his Yorkshire accent: "I also want to tell you, son, in their presence, that I know you'll give them a fight to remember, and that I hope in the process you'll fuck them up." He nodded dismissal to me, and as I went out of the office I saw Dr Smit open-mouthed and speechless.

But the United Party wasn't finished with me yet. I got a message from Mr Starke that it was understood from Dr Smit that unless I withdrew from anti-U.P. politics his son would be prevailed on to withhold his signature from my certificate of service for the three years' articles of clerkship I had served with him. I guessed Charles Smit knew nothing about this, and flew to Cape Town, went to his office and got the signed certificate without any difficulty—which confirmed my conviction that Charles had no knowledge of the threat.

And so the campaign began. It was to be one of the toughest by-elections fought in South Africa, partly because it was the last in which coloured voters had the right to vote directly in a parliamentary contest; the law removing their voting rights had not yet been promulgated by gazette. There were only about three hundred coloured voters in the constituency, but the symbolism was important to them, and they voted almost to capacity of their numbers. The poll percentage from the coloured area of Parkside was nearly a hundred per cent, and according to Federal Party canvass figures I should get all but three of these votes. With the whites it was the opposite story. There were about fourteen thousand voters in the constituency, and at first our canvassers gained the impression they must all be habitual, knee-jerk U.P. supporters. We were to hear over and over again: "Oh, we don't understand politics, but we're staunch U.P.!" My opponent, the U.P. candidate, was South Africa's popular cricket captain, Clive van Ryneveld, former Rhodes Scholar and international rugby player for England during his days at Oxford. A barrister by profession, van Ryneveld was a likeable man temperamentally unsuited to politics.

Both parties threw considerable resources into the campaign. The U.P. leaders came from all over the country to speak in the constituency, and the party spent a fortune in pamphlets and campaign literature. So did our party, sending from Natal a special official to disburse the contributions of the rich sugar-planters who financed my campaign, although they preferred our Federalist constitutional plans and stronger brand of anti-Nationalism to our liberal race policies. The U.P. tried to brand us as *kaffirboeties* and as Union Jack wavers and largely succeeded, aided by the image of our own ultra-British types from Natal. One man, Steve King, who owned an asbestos mine, made a generous donation to our campaign fund and then offered to accompany me on my door-to-door visits. But the old boy was a disaster. To the first woman who opened the door to us, saying: "The Federal Party? That is . . .?" He replied loudly: "British to the backbone, madam!" I winced and got him out of there, after repairing the damage as best I could. That sort of thing might have gone down well in Natal, but in the Eastern Cape, in 1957, it was too sectional to compete with the U.P.'s call for "white unity" between English-speakers and Afrikaners. At the next house Mr King told the occupant: "You can't vote for Clive van Ryneveld because he's a *kaffirboetie*! He likes the blacks!" I discovered I had a head-ache and drove the old man back to the campaign office to lick stamps and address envelopes, where he could do less harm.

Only one incident during the campaign gave me a slight twinge of conscience. A woman said that she was voting for me because my opponent had an Afrikaans name, and instead of protesting at such bigotry I replied: "Will you need transport on polling day?"

By the closing stages of the election campaign we had, according to canvass estimates, three and a half thousand supporters, which suggested perhaps four or five thousand votes; but the U.P. sent its biggest gun in for the last public meeting. Marais Steyn, a brilliant orator in both English and Afrikaans who was later to join the Afrikaner Nationalist cabinet, destroyed us with innuendo, insinuation and every kind of debating trick short of actual defamation, and convinced many of our would-be supporters that if they deserted the U.P. this would shatter "white unity" and let in hordes of blacks to destroy "white civilization". We polled seven hundred and twenty-eight votes, losing by over six thousand . . .

It was the end of my parliamentary ambitions, but I had learnt some interesting things, such as that the rich were the most selfish politically, that the most opulent houses were generally the most conservative bastions of ignorance and indifference, and that far more was known in the small, crowded coloured houses about the actual terms of statute laws. The degree of general white ignorance of the practical effects of apartheid laws was astonishing. I realized in that election the futility of trying to convert most whites from racism by oratory or individual argument, and decided that from now on I would have to try to achieve through journalism what I had failed to achieve as a politician.

So Clive van Ryneveld went to Parliament for the U.P.; and it was at least some satisfaction to me two years later when he defected to join the newly-formed Progressive Party, which was founded on the ruins of our by then defunct Federal Party. At that time the formation of the Progressive Party was a step forward because it placed more effective emphasis on the progressive elements of Federal Party policy, such as opposition to apartheid and commitment to federalism, and did not have reactionary aspects of Federal policy such as the Natal emphasis on extreme pro-British sentiments which were a throwback to the old colonial days. The Progressives took our anti-racist cause further while shedding our jingoes, and for the first time, through the remarkable Helen Suzman, gained white parliamentary representation for rejection of racial discrimination. But that development was in a future I couldn't foresee as I returned to my *Dispatch* job after the election campaign. There was much good-natured chaffing in the newsroom, and above my desk hung a large sign: "His Head is Bloodied but Unbowed". There had been general amusement the night before the election when news editor Jock McFall had put me on the assignments diary for the next day.

Vernon Barber welcomed me back with a smile and a handshake. "Bloody good scrap, son. You gave the bastards something to think about. Now settle down to learn your trade, and if you try as hard in journalism as you did in your campaign, you'll make the grade!" It was August 1957. Contemplating the wreckage of my attempted careers in law and politics, I hoped I'd have better luck in journalism.

CHAPTER FIVE

FOR A YEAR I learnt the basics of journalism on the *Dispatch*, first as a junior reporter writing and rewriting every paragraph of a routine news item, then as a junior sub-editor trying to condense every report into as few words as possible. At the end of the year John Ryan and I decided to go overseas to gain wider experience, if possible on hallowed Fleet Street itself, because we realized that from a salary point of view we had some catching-up to do with younger journalists who had gone straight from high school on to newspapers. I was now twenty-four, and there were nineteen- and twenty-year-olds on the paper earning more than I was.

To finance the trip I sold my car and got Harland to sell all my Elliotdale property except the house Mom lived in. We sailed from East London on the *Arundel Castle* bound for Southampton—a voyage lasting nearly three weeks, and made memorable by the fact that the girls aboard outnumbered the boys by about three to one.

We docked on a sunny day in June 1958. England seemed at once so foreign and yet so familiar. It seemed foreign in the sense that the scenery was gentler, neater and more ordered than at home in South Africa, with tidy hedgerows dividing the green fields and no wide-open countryside such as we were used to. The sense of familiarity came from an inherited culture —we saw shop signs with our surnames on them, houses with chimney-pots that reminded us of children's storybooks, and words like "borough" that were somehow old to us in their newness. And when we came into London we didn't see the foggy city of Sherlock Holmes or the drab city of Charles Dickens, but a colourful place in which the red buses and green parks, and the trees and flowers, made it seem bright and welcoming. We were to get to know a very different London over the next two years during the bleak winters, but it couldn't have looked better on that first day.

In one respect my first impressions had more impact than my first impressions of most large cities. The New York, Vienna and

Paris of the movies always have a musical sound-track accompanying the visual image, so there is invariably some disappointment in the first real encounter with somewhere like Broadway at night without that large unseen orchestra playing jazzy rhythms. But it wasn't so with London, thanks to the buskers. In the summer of 1958 there were always buskers at places like Earl's Court station playing accordions, trumpets, violins and saxophones.

Our first unusual experience was seeing white men sweeping streets and digging ditches. Then came the sight of "mixed" couples—black men with white women or white men with black women—without heads turning or police closing in . . .

One Sunday morning we went with Johan Jerling, a young Afrikaner who had travelled with us, to Hyde Park Corner and heard a black orator berating South Africa. Although John and I were against apartheid, we resented his extreme criticism. But Johan Jerling wanted to fight him, muttering: "*As ek net daardie kaffir in die hande kon kry . . .*" ("If I could just get my hands on that nigger!"). But there were policemen about, one of them standing by to protect the rights of an Irish speaker who was referring to the Queen of England as "a bloody whore". This, to us, was a surprisingly generous manifestation of the right of free speech.

In spite of Johan's vehement racism John and I liked him and also his friend and fellow-Afrikaner, Danie Burger. Although we had some hot political arguments with these two Afrikaner Nationalists over apartheid, there was a good deal of compatibility in other spheres of interest. Johan and Danie were contrasting characters. Both were big and powerful but Danie was the intellectual—the science teacher, the university graduate, the magistrate's son—while Johan was a farmer's boy whose trade was welding. Johan became more broadminded about race the longer he stayed in England, whereas Danie left London still committed to apartheid. But at first neither would concede anything on the issue. We had arguments which must have mystified the patrons in English pubs, because Johan and Danie would argue only in Afrikaans and John and I would reply only in English. Sometimes, in the heat of such a four-way argument in the two languages, we would become aware of the looks of astonishment around us and would end up laughing at what the bilingual slanging-match must have sounded like. At other times the argument grew violent; once Danie threw a typewriter at John, and on another occasion he heaved a chair at me. But most of the time we got along well and shared some entertaining adventures together.

It all started with the flat. All four of us wanted to get away from the Earl's Court area after a scrape or two there. We called at several real estate offices until we agreed on a place which was so attractive that we couldn't resist it, although we couldn't really afford it. It was crazy, because the rent was above what the four of us combined could sustain for more than a few months, yet John—who was standing nearest the counter at the time—signed the lease for a year, and we moved in.

Soon afterwards we invited three Fleet Street journalists in for drinks and they asked us about apartheid, which they pronounced "appetite", and John and I told them all about it. Johan and Danie stirred uneasily, feeling that John and I were making too much of what they called the "negative" side, and eventually it was too much for Johan, who said: "Lissen, I'll tell you a side to South Africa you don't hear over here. We had a pet Hotnot on our farm!" One of the British journalists looked shocked. "A what?" he asked. "*Ja*, a pet Hotnot," said Johan. "A Hottentot, a little coloured boy! We used to let him sleep near the stove, in the kitchen!" "Good God!" said the journalist. "*Ja*, that shakes you, hey?" said Johan. "*Ja*, that's the side of South Africa you don't know! You don't hear much about the nice side here, do you?" "Good God!" said the journalist again. "A pet Hottentot!" "You see!" said Johan to John and Danie and me. "That shakes them!" By this time even Danie was hiding his head in his hands with mortification. "Do you know how we kept him clean?" said Johan, warming to his theme. "We told him that if he washed every day he would be white like us. He used to wash like hell, man!" When the journalists left Danie told Johan he feared the story had "made things worse" for South Africa—which stopped Johan in the middle of yet another triumphant claim that "That shook them, man!"

One night the four of us were returning from a party given

by some Canadian girls, and while walking down Kensington High Street we saw a large metal sign in the street: "Metropolitan Police—No parking". Deciding in our party mood that it would look good in the flat, we picked it up and carried it the rest of the way home. As we neared home—Danie and I were carrying the heavy sign at the time—Johan and John suddenly fled into the night and a striped sleeve fell on my arm. We were under arrest. "*O, Hemel—dis die polisie!*" Danie muttered. He was particularly concerned, being due to run for South Africa against England later that month and knowing that a Russian athlete named Nina Ponomareva had been kicked out of the Olympics for stealing five hats from Harrods.

The policeman said: "Now, then, gentlemen—where were you taking that sign?" Danie babbled: "No, man, we were just carrying it a short way." The policeman said: "A short way, sir? I've been following you lot for nearly a mile since you picked that sign up." He took out his notebook and entered our names and addresses, Danie almost incoherently pleading for leniency as he envisaged lifetime expulsion from international athletics for larceny. "At least a week in jail for this, sir," said the policeman. "But first we're going to put the sign back where we found it, aren't we?"

We were, and Danie and I again took up our heavy load and trudged all the way to its original position, with the bobby at our heels. We replaced it, then walked back to the apartment, the policeman holding Danie's elbow. Danie was feeling worse and worse about it, and matters weren't improved when Johan and John strolled by without so much as a glance of recognition. Back at the entrance to the flat, with Danie now literally in tears, the policeman said: "All right, gentlemen, if you go quietly up to bed now we'll forget the whole thing—after all, you are visitors from the Commonwealth." Danie flung his arms around him and hugged him, thanking him repeatedly and saying he'd always heard how good the British police were but now, by God, he knew it from experience. We parted with many expressions of mutual goodwill, but when Danie's elation subsided he lapsed into a curious mood of resentment against Johan for deserting him and pretending not to know him. "Why pick on Johan?" I said. "John also deserted us. They ran off together. Besides, what could they have done?" But Danie's special resentment against Johan was that he was a *mede-Afrikaner*, a fellow-Afrikaner, and that no Afrikaner should desert another.

After some months Johan moved to a welding job in Dorset, and several weeks later Danie had to return to South Africa for family reasons. John and I had very little money left, and without Danie and Johan we found the rent for the flat even further beyond our means. Since our arrival in London we had been trying to get newspaper jobs and had written scores of letters without even getting to the interview stage. The national newspapers of Fleet Street were regarded as the pinnacle of journalism, and there were literally hundreds of applicants already on the waiting lists for whatever jobs were occasionally available. Those on the waiting lists were often top journalists already in executive posts on major provincial newspapers, with many years of experience in British journalism, so a pair of freshmen South Africans stood little chance. The advice we kept getting was to start on a local paper, then graduate to a provincial paper, then get in the waiting line for the nationals.

Up to now John and I had both been living on what was left of his money. Funds were yet to come from the sale of the Elliotdale property, and I felt the onus was on me to earn something to keep us eating. Our leanest time followed, when for a full week we did not have one square meal. All we had in the apartment was a tin of Horlicks, and we were sick of the taste of it. Then I saw an advertisement in the window of a hotel in the neighbourhood. They wanted a pianist for the cocktail hour, and I applied and was told to return that afternoon for an audition. When I did I found there were six of us auditioning and my heart sank. I was the fifth to play, and I already knew that two of the others were better, but fortunately the manager had seen a recent musical and liked the tunes, and I was the only one among the candidates who had heard them and could play them, so I got the job. Pay was two guineas a night and a full dinner. This warded off hunger for the next few weeks, then John and I had a lucky break into journalism.

Allister Sparks, formerly of the *Dispatch*, was leaving a local London paper to join Reuters in Fleet Street, and he asked if the little paper he was leaving would take us on. I got the job Allister was vacating because I had subbing experience and

John had none, but the paper took John on as well out of compassion because we were together and they planned to expand. It was an extraordinary outfit. Called *Weekly Post Newspapers* and based at Ickenham, West London, it was run by two enterprising brothers named Richards. It was basically a local weekly with several different titles and a few paragraphs to match each area in which it was sold. Thus in Uxbridge it had Uxbridge items and its masthead was *Uxbridge Post*. It was also the *Harrow Post*, the *Southall Post*, the *Airport Post* (circulating around the Heathrow area) and several other *Posts*. In each area it had only a couple of thousand circulation, but looked convincing enough to draw some advertising revenue. The Richards brothers were unconventional journalists. Ronald was big, beefy and aggressive and Derek slim, quiet and aggressive. Both were tireless workers and exacting bosses. In the office about seven of us generated enough local copy, subbing and headlining it as well, to fill all the local editions.

Shortly before getting this job I had at last had an interview for a possible Fleet Street job with Associated Press. It was a harrowing interview with a Mr McNicoll. I found him at an angular desk in a roomful of busy-looking journalists typing at speed, and stood for almost a minute before he looked up. He seemed to be doing several things at once, mentally sub-editing running copy from a teletype machine on to his typewriter while answering questions from a succession of journalists about lead points in various reports. Three or four of the journalists waited in line for such guidance, which McNicoll gave out of the side of his mouth without looking up from his typing or his reading of the telex. It was impressive to watch.

Presently he looked up and noticed me, then said he had no vacancies but would "try me out" for possible future reference. He looked sharply at me and asked how old I was. I told him I was twenty-four, and he threw up his hands and said in a loud voice to the whole room, in a Scots accent: "Gentlemen, gentlemen, we have a *genius* here! This *genius* is newly arrived from some far-flung corner of the earth. Journalistic experience in Britain—nil. Age—twenty-four. And, if ye please, he considers himself ready to join Associated Press!" The other journalists looked at me, then down at their typewriters again.

One winked as if to tell me not to pay any attention to their eccentric chief. This was easier said than done—McNicoll was raising his voice even higher. "Well! Perhaps he *is* a genius!" He looked at me fiercely: "*Are* you a genius?" I said: "That's not for *me* to say." He laughed. "Ah!" he said delightedly. "I'll soon find out!" He reached behind him, plucked from a used-copy spike a thick handful of cables and thrust them at me. "You've exactly an hour to sub those. Tight, mind! Not one unnecessary word! One hour, exactly!"

He couldn't have been serious—there were more than fifty cable stories in the pile. So when he wasn't looking I re-spiked half of them and got down to work on the rest. They were a mixture—one was about President Sukarno of Indonesia, one was about a new David Niven film and some were on sport. I did the tightest subbing job I could, going over each item to reduce the number of words without sacrificing hard news facts, and at the end of the hour I had worked through the reduced pile. What happened then was unnerving. He took my subbed cables, picked up a red pencil, and while continuing to answer queries from various staff men who advanced to his desk went through my copy with the red pencil flying over the pages, leaving savage gashes here, fresh paragraph marks there, tearing out and rewriting great swatches of words and working through the entire pile in barely fifteen minutes. He handed the mutilated cables back to me wordlessly and turned back to his work, and as I went over each one I saw that I was out of my depth. McNicoll had taken what I thought was rack-tight subbing and effortlessly tightened it by more than half, leaving out no essential element of any story and vastly improving the wording—in particular, re-structuring introduction paragraphs with fresh news angles. It was an impressive display and I was awed by it.

He said in quite a kind way: "You see, my boy, you're nowhere near ready for such a job, even if there was a vacancy. You'd have to learn a lot before you could come here." He advised me, as so many others had done, to get a job first on a local, then on a major provincial—then to try for Fleet Street. "It'll take you *years* to get here," he added.

I resolved to try no more short cuts. If I had to start on a local, that's what I would do. So when John and I presented ourselves at Ickenham to join the *Weekly Post* we saw it as stepping on the first rung of the ladder to Fleet Street. At first merely staying on that lowly rung took some doing. We'd never worked so hard in our lives. We covered everything from municipal meetings to magistrates' courts to soccer and rugby games, and the hours were long and frenzied. I was simultaneously political correspondent, sub-editor for one of the editions, religious editor for another, part-time sports reporter, court reporter at Wembley, page designer for the airport edition and stone-sub for the whole group.

As political correspondent I had a particularly interesting assignment. The Member of Parliament for Harrow East had died, and there was a by-election contested by six candidates. It was a safe Conservative seat and the Conservative was the predictable winner—but the rest of the candidates were colourful. One was Sir Alan Herbert, the famous satirist, who was standing as an independent. Another was a dancing master, Henry Cooper, whose chief claim to fame was that he had taught King Edward VIII to dance. Another was a West Indian named Heldsinger whose platform was state-aided prostitution, and another who announced his candidacy early maintained until nomination day a coy refusal to disclose his name to anyone—which didn't matter because he withdrew in a fit of pique, complaining that "the media" were denying him publicity . . .

The most serious challenger to the Conservatives was the Labour Party candidate, a young schoolteacher who knew he stood little chance but fought an uphill battle with tenacity. I liked him the most, and spent a couple of evenings with him in his small house learning about socialist policy in Britain. His name was Merlyn Rees, and many years later he became Britain's Home Secretary.

The most entertaining of the candidates was A. P. Herbert. He was by now an old man with overgrown eyebrows and he blinked a lot. He planned to draw up his election manifesto in verse, and at one stage he suddenly asked me to be his election agent. Then he asked for directions on how to reach the constituency by tube, and it felt unreal to explain to this most distinguished of Londoners how to use the local transport system. The West Indian, Heldsinger, was a pathetic figure. I found him in a garret in Brixton, coughing sepulchrally as he consumed a ghastly bowl of gruel, and he turned his large brown eyes on me and asked for "a pound or two" for his campaign.

I enjoyed covering the election, and was commended by Richards for my reports. However, our relationship wasn't all smooth sailing, and I was nearly fired for a strange headline in the airport edition. I had become friendly with a Barbadian compositor on the paper—the first black man I got to know on equal terms. We used to go drinking in a pub called the Soldier's Arms during the late break between editions, and one night we celebrated too well and stumbled back to do the airport edition in a mood of frivolity. Most of the page was in place when Vernon drew my attention to a strangely-shaped hole in it, about mid-page. It was in the shape of a profile of steps going upwards to the right—and I thought I had just the story for it. A plane at Heathrow had had some difficulty gaining altitude after take-off, and I said: "Vernon, tonight we make history—the world's first-ever ascending headline." He seemed doubtful but I insisted, so what went in the page was a headline reading:

. . . and up!

. . . and up!

Aircraft struggled up

The editor told me the next day that if such a crazy thing happened again I should be fired.

Those were icy days. John and I had never known such bitter cold in South Africa as the cold of that British winter of 1958. At night we slept in outer garments worn over our pyjamas, and put newspaper pages between the blankets. On our daily return from work we would race to determine who got the first hot bath, and one day I reached the bathroom before John and turned on the hot tap. Then I went to my room and heard him dash into the bathroom and slam the door shut. I also thought I heard him locking the door. "Ryan, are you using my bath water?" I asked, enraged. "Yes—what are you going to do about it?" he replied. "Get out of there, dammit!" I shouted. "Go to hell!" he yelled back. "I'm going to count up to three, then smash this door down if you don't come out!" I shouted. "Go ahead!" he taunted.

I took a long run down the passage and thumped into the expensive door, which smashed open. He wasn't in the bath at all, but on the toilet seat. I was shocked at the structural damage I had done, and as my anger faded John's indignation grew. He rose, clutching his trousers. "Who-do-you-think-you-are? Who *are* you, man!" I said: "Well, I thought you were stealing my bath water . . ." He advanced on me, holding his trousers up with one hand and making threatening passes at me with the other. "Yes, but who *are* you, man?" he shouted.

I had never seen the quiet Ryan so angry, and backed away down the passage, wondering what it would cost to repair the door.

John stormed into his room, and some time later after I had taken my bath I went to clear the matter up with him. The sight that met my eyes made it hard to keep a straight face. John was in bed with the blankets heaped up as high as his ears, and he was reading *Time* magazine. Because he had to turn the pages he had one hand protruding from the blankets in a thick woollen glove, and because the thin pages of *Time* magazine are not easy to turn with gloved fingers he was having difficulty. I mumbled an apology. "Okay," he said grudgingly. "Well, I suppose I was also to blame, so let's just forget it." Then, as his gloved hand made another botch of turning over a page, he suddenly dashed the magazine aside angrily and shouted: "But who *ARE* you, man?"

When a draft of money arrived from Harland I was able to settle up with him and have the bathroom door repaired, and we decided to get out of the apartment before more of its valuable fixtures were destroyed. Increasingly, John wanted to move on from the *Post* to a bigger paper. He felt that four months on a local weekly was enough, and told the Richards brothers he was leaving. They called me in and said that as John was going I should also leave. I said I would prefer to stay for a few more months, and was expanding on this when I saw from the expression on Derek Richards's face that this was not an option. He explained that they didn't consider me worth keeping if John was leaving. It was a blow to my ego, and meant I would have to look urgently for another job, so back I went to Mr McNicoll at Associated Press. He was surprised that I should be back after such a short time when he had suggested an apprenticeship of several years, and he tested me and savaged my copy again, repeating that I should get on with "learning the trade".

I managed to get a job on the Cardiff *Western Mail* and here my real journalistic education in re-writing, condensation and headlining began in earnest. I was one of fourteen subs, and started on the local desk working with the copy of regional correspondents. We had seven major edition changes nightly, with radical page-design alterations from edition to edition. I was put through the mill by my immediate superiors, especially by one named Glyn Williams who had McNicoll's ability to whip a pen through copy and shrink verbiage to tight information at speed. At first he was ruthless in revising my subbing efforts and threw out almost every headline I wrote. Then as the months went by the stories I handled were revised less and less, the headlines I got in were bigger and bigger, and after six months on the *Western Mail* I knew I'd learnt a lot.

There were some mortifying setbacks, like the night I burnt the front-page lead story. The stone-sub, Charlie Rudy, was leaning across my desk dangling the long roll of telex copy when part of it touched my cigarette, and in seconds it had gone up in flames. That cost us a twenty-minute delay while he got a re-run from London, and I had some dark looks from the dreaded Glyn Williams. But the worst experience came on the night I graduated from the local desk. The chief subeditor, Bob Lee, told me with quiet ceremony that I could now go into the international basket for copy. I felt I had won my spurs and could have burst with pride. But pride went before a fall. I saw a wad of copy plopping into the international basket and rose with outward casualness to get my hands on it. As I walked around to fetch it I sensed a tension among all the subs, an atmosphere of suspended concentration, and when I picked up the copy I saw why. It was the front page lead, the "splash", which was handled only by the "splash sub", and I froze with this holy material in my crass hand. Bob Lee coughed and said: "Ah, not that copy, you see. Wait for another story." I felt myself blushing, and, not knowing how to walk back to my desk with any dignity, I went to the washroom and stayed there until the ten o'clock break, pacing the floor with embarrassment.

John Ryan had meanwhile got a job with a paper in Plymouth, and occasionally he came to Cardiff for a weekend. By the summer of 1959 we both felt we'd learnt enough after eight months to try crashing Fleet Street again. But first we decided to take a vacation round Europe. Before we set out I went to McNicoll and got another "trial", although there were still no vacancies. I wanted to find out how much I had improved. This time McNicoll made only a few marks with his pen, and as he handed the cables back he was positively genial: "A grand improvement, you've been working with real journalists at last. I'll keep an eye out for a suitable vacancy, because you're almost ready and I could round off the edges here." I went off smiling at his arrogance and pleased with his approval.

We pooled our money, bought a van and travelled through Belgium, France, Germany, Austria and Italy, staying in youth hostels or pitching tents in camping grounds. Since I knew a few words in some languages I functioned as the linguist, with amusing results. Belgium was no problem because Flemish is similar to Afrikaans, but when we got into Germany one of the first things we needed to find was a toilet. I couldn't think of the German word, and eventually in some desperation I asked a dignified-looking businessman: "*Verzeihen sie, mein lieber Herr, können sie mir sagen wo ist der Scheisshaus?*" He kept a straight face and gave the necessary directions.

In Venice we met a South African couple and planned to meet up with them later in Florence and Rome. In Florence we couldn't find them, and when we linked up with them in Rome we asked what had happened. "We couldn't find Florence at all," they said. "We must have taken the wrong road. The biggest city we passed through was a place called Firenze."

The old van took us thousands of miles across Europe, only giving up the ghost in the last stages of the journey near Rheims. We got back to London by train and ferry, and I resumed my campaign to get on to Fleet Street. John didn't feel inclined for this yet, and after he met an old schoolmate of his from Umtata, Snookie Langley, the two of them got a job as fur-packers in a Hudson's Bay company's London warehouse. They had rooms adjoining mine and often worked overtime, but I always knew when they returned in the late hours because I would hear cries of "*Voertsek! Voertsek!*" down in the street. An expression understood by all South African dogs as a dismissive order, it was never so understood by British dogs, and they always followed John and Snookie all the way home, sniffing at their heels for the smell of the furs they had been packing.

At last I had a lucky break into the great citadel of Fleet Street, getting a subbing chance on the *Daily Herald*; and within days of that I got a second break, landing a job as assistant editor of a trade journal.

This meant I now had two jobs, one with the magazine from 8.30 to 5 p.m. and the other at the *Herald* from 6 p.m. to 1.30 a.m. As the Fleet Street minimum was then twenty-five pounds a week I was earning at least a hundred pounds a month from the *Herald* and seventy-nine pounds a month from the magazine. At that time a monthly income of that size in London for a single male in his mid-twenties was abundant wealth and I lived extravagantly, taking cabs everywhere and enjoying the best restaurants and theatres on the occasional night off. Then came promotion to editorship of the magazine, with a secretary to do all the hackwork, and after two months an increase in salary, so that by the end of the year my monthly income was over two hundred pounds. London seemed more marvellous than ever.

Subbing on the *Herald* meant heady experience of life among the gods of Fleet Street, but the actual subbing pressure was less than it had been on the Cardiff *Western Mail*. Being a national newspaper, the *Herald* produced only three editions a night instead of the *Western Mail*'s seven, so we had more time to consider headlines and rewrites. But there were chill reminders of the precariousness of life on Fleet Street; on my first night I was given a front page "top" to sub, and whispered to the sub next to me that there must be some mistake, but he told me shortly to get on with it; that Fleet Street papers didn't take time to ease new subs into their ways as provincial papers did, and that if I didn't do the story pretty quickly I'd be thrown out and replaced in a flash. I got down to the task. It was a three-column headline about an eccentric ex-army man, and it was exciting to think that the headline and story would be read by more than two million readers—if I did it properly. The result was: "The Galloping Captain of Stableford Tawnay"—I rather fancied the equestrian rhythm of it—and it survived intact and went into all editions. Just as I was basking in this achievement I was given a tiny filler which I botched up and was told off shortly by the chief sub-editor.

I had set myself a time limit of two years overseas, and as there were only a few months left and I still wanted to see America I negotiated an interesting assignment with the *Herald*, to look round the Southern states there and compare Dixieland segregation with South African apartheid. I sailed from Southampton to New York on the *Queen Mary*, then travelled south by Greyhound bus through Philadelphia and Washington, allowing time in the major cities for sightseeing, and spending some weeks in Alabama, Mississippi, Georgia, Tennessee and Arkansas. My main destination was Little Rock, Arkansas, then the symbolic headquarters of diehard resistance to integration because of the segregationist stand of Governor Orval Faubus.

There I checked into a hotel and went into the bar where several customers were standing drinking Busch beer. I was ordering one for myself when the door clattered open and a state trooper came in with a wild look in his eye, yelling in a high-pitched whine: "They dynamited a nigger's house on the edge of town!" There were whoops of approval by the bar customers, who ordered more drinks to celebrate. I slipped out to phone the police for details, and within half-an-hour I was interviewing the victim. His name was Cartelyou Walls, and his was one of the few black families in that part of town. He told me that nobody had been hurt in the blast as the family had been out when it happened. They had had repeated threats of violence through anonymous phone calls, presumably from members of the Ku Klux Klan. Walls spoke with quiet resignation, dismissing all thought of moving out of the area. He felt the dynamiters represented only a vicious minority, and he wasn't going to move for the likes of them. He was a modest man, because I found on checking with the *Arkansas Gazette* that he had a war decoration, a fact he hadn't mentioned during our interview.

As a journalist I was glad of the timing and filed a long account to the *Herald* in London. At first the Little Rock cable office was reluctant to transmit the report. The clerk queried my cabling card, then his superior challenged my credentials in view of the high cost of transmitting the message to London, then said bluntly that it was "newspapermen like you who give Lilruck a bad name with your sensational reports". Coming from South Africa I knew all about this ploy, and especially the use of the word "sensational", and went on the offensive. I said stories of blacks being victimized in the South were a dime a dozen, but the sensational story I was really after was whether Southern telegraph officials were trying to censor reports, because this would give me a far better story to file from Washington. Before I had even finished speaking they were denying this and making placatory noises, and they filed the original report.

During my stay in Little Rock and other parts of the South I noticed some interesting differences between Southern segregation and South African apartheid, although there were basic points of similarity. One had to do with the cable officials. In Little Rock they still had the American reluctance to be cast in the role of scorners of the law. In South Africa in a comparable case the cable officials would not have been sensitive about thwarting or delaying transmission of the report. The reason was that in America such action would be in conflict with officials in their federal capital, whereas South African officials always knew they had the backing of their central government.

Another difference had to do with personal expression of race hatred. In the South whites were more vocally vicious about blacks, more ready to give public utterance to their bigotry. In South Africa it was in only a few rural districts of the Transvaal and Orange Free State that I could imagine customers in a bar openly applauding the dynamiting of a black man's house. There was also the matter of the absence in South Africa of a lynching mentality or a Ku Klux Klan approach to violence against blacks. Perhaps it was because South African whites were so much more outnumbered by blacks than whites in the American South, or because South African racism, being more comprehensively entrenched by statute law at all levels, had less need of reinforcement with personal or group violence by ordinary citizens.

Some of the characters in Little Rock conformed remarkably to reputed stereotype. The head bartender at the hotel was Homer P. Hurd. Stockily-built, he had a craggy face with grey hair tumbling thickly over it and wore a hearing aid, the battery of which bulged in the left breast-pocket of his shirt. Whenever he used the phone he would speak into the mouthpiece, then clap the receiver to his left breast-pocket to hear the reply. The battery must have had an amplifier of some sort, because when the receiver was clapped to his pocket he would stare into the distance in concentration. It looked strangely military, as if he were presenting arms with the instrument in acknowledgement of telephonic orders, though at other times it was as if he was punctuating his statements with passionate gestures of sincerity. The first time he did it I thought he was having a heart attack.

It became known at the bar that I was from "Sowth Afrikuh", and the general assumption was that I was one of them in spirit regarding the white man's burden. I neither confirmed nor denied this, so that they would speak freely in my presence. Homer Hurd said: "Hey, son, that Sowth Afrikuh—aint that a seg'gated country?" I confirmed that it was. "Wouldn't yawl like to meet our great Governah, Orval Faubus?" he asked, pronouncing it "Oval Fobus". I said I would, and he phoned Faubus's secretary, who, he told me, was a personal friend. He spoke at length into the mouthpiece, saying I wasn't like those other lying journalists who just wanted to smear the state of Arkansas; that I was from a seg'gated country and saw things the right way. He then clapped the receiver to his breast-pocket and stared ahead to listen, then spoke again into the mouthpiece, saying that if I could see "Oval" it would "he'p" the people elsewhere to understand the special problems of the South. Then he clapped the receiver to his breast again to listen. At the end of the conversation he turned sadly to me. "Son," he said, "ole Oval is in bed on doctor's odours—too sick to see innabody. He's just tuckered out from fightin for the rights of us white folks. He's a great mayan, and he's give his life for states' rights."

That was another thing I noticed in the South. Although

there was open talk of "niggers" and overt applause of the dynamiting of the Walls house, when it came to discussion of actually withholding voting rights from blacks there was a prim avoidance of the issue, and refuge was sought in code language and euphemisms like "states' rights". There was also much talk, familiar to a South African, of how "strangers" did not understand the black man and his ways.

Another colourful character regularly in the bar was a tall man in his eighties, dressed in a black topcoat and wearing a string tie. He was State Senator Blackwell, who punctuated every phrase by slapping the counter and emitting a high-pitched: "Heh!" When he heard me telling Homer I was based in London he slapped the counter a glancing downward blow and said: "London! England! Winston Churchill! Chaaaaarles Dickens! Oliver Twist! Please, suh, ah want some mo! Heh!" I had several talks with Senator Blackwell, and one day he said: "I've taken a liking to you, son. Ah'm going to do you a favour. Come with me." We were soon walking down Markham Street and after persistent questioning from me as to where we were headed he said: "Son, wheah ah'm taking you has the *cleanest* women in Little Rock." I thought of my grey-haired mother back in the Transkei and had visions of being fatally stabbed in a bordello; of the story going via Associated Press to Reuters to the South African Press Association and then to the pages of the *Daily Dispatch*, where she would read of her son's sordid demise. I quickly invented an excuse that I had an appointment with the editor of the *Arkansas Gazette*. Senator Blackwell was deeply disappointed, and kept talking of the cleanliness of the women he had intended me to meet. "Ah'm not sayin' they are the most *beautiful*," he stressed. "But they are the *cleanest* women in Little Rock." Eventually he accepted my excuse but pressed me to have a cup of coffee with him in a favourite café nearby before leaving for the appointment. A waitress greeted him warmly as she arrived to take our orders, and the Senator, giggling, grasped her left breast with his ancient mottled hand. "Blackie!" she said angrily, stepping back out of reach. "Ah've told you *befoah* not to do that!" We were joined by a friend of his, a man from Kansas City, and I left the two of them happily discussing clean women.

I left Little Rock with a lot of material for my *Daily Herald* articles on apartheid and segregation, and travelled back to New York, where I met by chance and became friendly with a young engineer named Sy Glist. One night we were walking in Greenwich Village when a drunk black man asked me for "a dime for a cup of coffee". The smallest coin I had was a quarter, which I gave him. Sy said to the man as he was walking away: "My friend is from South Africa." The drunk stared at me furiously, hurled the coin into the gutter at my feet and walked away. Sy felt badly about it. "I don't know what made me say it," he said. "Maybe I wanted him to know that not all South African whites are anti-black."

That weekend Sy invited me to go skiing with him in the Catskill mountains. I had never even seen a ski before, in fact I had seen snow for the first time only the previous year, in Britain, but I was curious to try it out. When we arrived at the resort and headed for the ski run we found it had been closed to beginners because the snow was starting to granulate, so we turned back. Not used to handling skis, I turned without checking who was behind me and my skis struck a woman full in the face. I apologized repeatedly but this only seemed to anger her more, and she and her friends closed round me talking loudly. Sy rescued me from this angry circle, muttering that I was a foreigner, then when we were some distance away he said: "Listen, what's all this *apology* stuff? This isn't England. Here if you apologize you immediately put yourself in the wrong—you're admitting your guilt. If that happens again, you must go on to the offensive—bawl the woman out. Say: 'You dumb broad—why'dya stand in the way?' What the hell, this *apology* stuff!"

After staying with Sy in New York I wanted to see something of Canada and travelled to Toronto, getting a job for a couple of months on the Toronto *Daily Star*. During my stay I wrote several articles on South Africa which were used by the paper. There was an Overseas Visitors Club there, and I met a number of South Africans and Rhodesians. A black South African medical graduate doing his housemanship in Toronto applied to join the club, and the only member who objected was an Afrikaner Nationalist. His objection was overruled, and barely a week later, during the screening of a film at the club, he had an epileptic seizure, and the only doctor in the house was the man he had tried to keep out. He treated his would-be excluder and earned his thanks and subsequent apology.

The biggest newsbreak during my time in Toronto was the Sharpeville tragedy in South Africa on March 21, 1960. As an event in itself, Sharpeville had been inevitable. The law requiring black citizens of South Africa to carry passes at all times was the most hated of all the apartheid laws. The pass, or "reference book", was a bulky booklet like a passport, containing the bearer's ethnic origin, fingerprints, tax payments, salary, and many other details enabling the police to regulate the movement and employment of blacks from place to place. In terms of the "influx control" laws blacks couldn't stay in the main cities, and could only visit them for a specified number of hours. They had to get special permission to go to any specific area to seek work, and to do so they needed a "work-seeker's" permit. Since the idea was to keep them away from white-owned areas, which meant 87 per cent of the country, unless they were needed for work, it was made hard for them to comply with all these regulations. The administrative offices issuing the many kinds of permits were scattered all over the big cities, so that it was physically and financially difficult to get to them. The pass-book was also a convenient way for white employers to keep a hold on black workers. If a white housewife refused to sign the pass-book once a week the domestic servant could be arrested because technically the book wasn't in order, so at the least sign of provocation white employers often threatened to withhold this signature.

The pass laws empowered the police to arrest any black who didn't have the pass-book on his or her person at any time. If a black was challenged in the street by a policeman to produce the pass, and it had been left at home in the township, no time was allowed to produce it—the black went straight to jail. From 1948, when the Afrikaner Nationalist government came to power, to 1980, when the pass laws were still being enforced, yearly arrests under the laws averaged 368,000, more than a thousand a day.

The African National Congress and its breakaway youth wing, which formed the Pan Africanist Congress, had launched passive resistance campaigns against the pass laws throughout the late 1950s, and in early 1960 these demonstrations became bigger and bigger, culminating in the demonstration at Sharpeville, where an unarmed but angry crowd of several thousand blacks demonstrated against the pass laws, chanting their defiance outside Sharpeville police station. The white policemen inside the building lost their nerve and opened fire on the crowd, killing and wounding 186, and maintaining their fire even while the demonstrators were trying to run away. Most of the victims were shot in the back, and the impact on world opinion was stupendous. As a result of the Sharpeville massacre whole groups of nations adopted a more critical attitude towards apartheid.

Sharpeville was a microcosm of the minority white fear of black numbers in South Africa, and of inordinate response to this fear. It was inevitable because there was by now a discernible pattern in the periodic eruption of mass black anger against the race laws in South Africa, and because white South Africans lived under such tensions created by their racial fear that they were constantly on the edge of over-reaction to any black challenge. But though there had been similar manifestations of black anger before, and consequent shooting of black demonstrators by white police, Sharpeville was the best-publicized and the biggest up to that time; and though similar tragedies occurred during the next decade it wasn't to be eclipsed in scale or impact on world opinion until the Soweto uprising of 1976. For years to come, after March 1960, apartheid repression was summed up in the view of the world by the single word "Sharpeville".

From my Canadian perspective I felt a sense of urgency to go back to South Africa and somehow through journalism help to warn my fellow whites of the need to dismantle apartheid, not only for moral reasons but also in their own interests. I sailed from New York to Southampton on the *Queen Elizabeth*, spending the last of my money on the voyage so that I had less than a pound left on my arrival in London. I took my articles on apartheid and segregation to Mr Pinnington at the *Daily Herald*, and to my relief he found the copy acceptable. Then I thought he said: "We'll give you fifteen pounds now and fifteen on publication." I nodded gladly, only too pleased to be getting some money as I had by now only about two shillings on me. Mr Pinnington opened a drawer and counted out what looked like a lot of notes, which was when I realized he had said not "fifteen" but "fifty", and I took from him my first wad of fifty pounds and walked out of the *Herald* building elated. I went to Simpsons in the Strand and had a sumptuous lunch, with a bottle of champagne. Then I went to my lodgings and typed out a short humorous piece called *Springbok in Little Rock*, about Homer P. Hurd, Blackie Blackwell and the others, and sent it to *Punch*. Within two days I had a letter of acceptance from one of the assistant editors, Patrick Skene Catling, whose own writing I admired, and an invitation to meet him at El Vino's in Fleet Street. He had a good knowledge of the South himself, having worked on the *Baltimore Sun* and travelled about the United States, and he was generous in his comments on the article. I was disappointed to learn that the fee would be fifteen guineas, but he observed dryly that the financial people at *Punch* considered that having an article published in that highly-regarded journal was honour enough, beyond what mere money could approximate. But I was so thrilled to have an article published in the magazine that I would have waived any payment if this was a condition of publication.

One day I went with a South African architect, Bernie Belonsky, to see the South African cricket team play against an England team at Lords. Outside the ground I saw picket lines and demonstrators urging boycott of the game because the all-white Springboks were playing. In a rage I tore into the demonstrators, asking why they blamed innocent cricketers for the policies of politicians. "No member of this team is an Afrikaner Nationalist supporter of the South African government," I argued. "Why don't you go and demonstrate outside the Russian Embassy instead—they do worse things!"

On my last day in Britain I went again to see Mr McNicoll at Associated Press. "Come for another try-out, have you?" he said. "Well, if you pass muster I actually have a vacancy soon." He handed me the customary fistful of cables and I went at them for the customary hour, after which he reached for the customary red pen and poised it above the first cable. He didn't change anything on the first one, or the second. When he came to the third he shot me a sharp look. "Where've you been working since the *Western Mail?*" he growled. "Oh, I've done a bit of subbing here and there—the *Daily Herald* and elsewhere," I replied. He put the pen aside. "Well, you've come a long way in how long is it, two years? I think I may be able to give you a job now." I couldn't stop grinning. "I can't," I said. "I go back to South Africa tomorrow." He stared at me. "Then why go through all this? Why apply here today?" Then he smiled: "I see, I see. You had to show me and you had to show yourself. Well, that's understandable. Good luck to you!" We shook hands and I left. After McNicoll I felt I could face anyone in the newspaper world.

My friend Allister Sparks, after a spell with Reuters, had returned to South Africa to join the *Rand Daily Mail*, and suggested I should also go to Johannesburg to join the *Mail*, but I was more interested in the Eastern Cape, and of the four main newspapers in the Eastern Cape I was most attracted back to the *Daily Dispatch*. I admired Barber as an editor, I liked the paper's aggressive anti-Government policy and all the people on the staff, and I assumed that in later years the editorship would pass either to Ted Holliday or to George Farr, both men I enjoyed working with. I saw my future career as that of a senior sub-editor writing occasional articles and perhaps, eventually, a novel or two.

Shortly before I left London came the news that an English-speaking South African farmer, David Pratt, had shot Premier Verwoerd in the head. But the pistol was only a ·25 and the wounds had not proved fatal. At Southampton, in June 1960, I sailed on the *Carnarvon Castle*, calling at Madeira, Cape Town, Port Elizabeth and East London.

John Ryan was now in Canada. Originally he had intended to join me in Toronto, but he was delayed in leaving England, and had waited for Snookie Langley to accompany him. John and Snookie had had an adventurous Atlantic crossing. Wanting to save money on the fare they sailed on a tiny cargo ship, but it took nearly two weeks to reach Canada, and they spent so much time and money in the ship's bar that they were broke on arrival. At first they couldn't get work in Toronto, so they answered an advertisement calling for golf-course worm-gatherers. Earthworms wrecked the fairways with their casts if they were allowed to proliferate, and the club paid worm-gatherers a dollar per hundred worms gathered. The worm-gatherers worked by night. They were each issued with a miner's helmet-lamp and two cans—one strapped on each leg—to fill with worms, but John and Snookie were no match for the skilled gatherers of Toronto. Although the fairways were crawling with worms they earned only about two dollars each. John said Snookie cut a few of his worms in two but the worm-counters were on the lookout for this, and weren't fooled in the payout.

I had my first sight of South Africa for two years as Table Mountain appeared on the horizon, and it was good to get home again and see the streets of Cape Town take form as the ship sailed into Table Bay. The ship was due to sail the following morning for the coastal ports, so I had a day to spend visiting friends. First I took a taxi ride direct from the docks to the main post office, where I sent a telegram to my mother saying I had arrived safely. As I came out of the post office an old black man in ragged clothing stopped in front of me. I thought he was a beggar and offered him some coins, but he took no notice and seemed to want to talk. I tried to walk round him, but he held my jacket and started saying in an intense near-whisper: "Young master, you are travelling on a big ship. The ship has come from far away, from the other side of the world."

I was embarrassed. People were turning their heads to stare at us. I had the thought that the old man couldn't have seen me get off the ship because I had come straight to the post office by taxi, and couldn't be going by the clothes I wore because they weren't different in style or appearance from those of the other whites in the street. I started to feel uneasy and decided to walk on, but he still had hold of my jacket and began to speak again: "The ship has come from England, but you are not from there. You are from here. You are coming home, but your home is not here in Cape Town, it is far away along the coast."

I hadn't said a word to him, I was so astonished, and he began to speak more quickly: "You were born in the Transkei. You are leaving the ship at East London. You have been away for two years. You have one brother and one sister. You went to school in Kimberley. When you get off the ship in East London your family will meet you, your mother, your brother, your brother's wife——"

I wanted to get away from him. I shook my jacket free and hurried off, but he raised his voice and called out some more facts about me which I couldn't remember later but which were startlingly accurate. Before I vanished into the crowd on the corner of Adderley Street I heard him call: "Young master, don't be afraid. God loves you very much." Thinking back later I often regretted not staying to talk with him, but recalling how weird the experience was at the time I knew I couldn't have done so.

When the ship docked in East London I was met by Mom and Harland and Dawn, and their accents sounded so strongly Eastern Cape—Dawn saying: "Wee've got yaw rewm all riddy for yew at Hobeni!"—that I just burst out laughing with pleasure at the sound of it. But I had two items of business to attend to before I could relax with the family. First I went to see the editor of the *Dispatch*, who told me he had two applicants for one senior reporting vacancy, and that the other applicant had the advantage of being married, which meant he was more likely to be a settled employee. However, he said he was prepared to take both of us provided I could assure him I intended to stay on the paper for at least a couple of years. I told him I wanted to stay in the area, and he offered me a salary of £110 a month. It was generous—far more than a single man in his mid-twenties needed—which delighted me, because I had in mind some years of unfettered bachelorhood in which to function as a downtable sub-editor and writer, while getting in a lot of golf and night life.

My next visit was to the Standard Bank, where I asked to see the manager. He was "Jacko" Reed, a former rugby star who had recently taken over as manager of the bank's main branch in the city. I was broke again after spending freely during the three-week voyage home, and asked him for a fifty-pound overdraft. "Well, that's a lot of money," said Mr Reed. "What do you want it for?" "To spend," I replied. "To maintain me for the next month until I start a job on the *Dispatch*." Mr Reed looked disapproving. "That's a lot of money simply for spending. What sort of things will you buy with it?" "Things like beer," I told him. "Cigarettes, golf balls, green-fees—that kind of thing." Mr Reed shook his head. "Nobody's ever asked me for an overdraft to buy beer and golf balls," he said. "We're not supposed to authorize overdrafts for that kind of thing. How could I write that on your file?"

I told him the money would be paid back in six months. "Six months!" he exclaimed. "With the salary you mentioned you ought to be able to pay it back in one month!" "Yes," I said. "But I'm planning to spend a lot of my salary on frivolous things, so I'd rather pay the overdraft back over six months." "Jesus Christ," he said. "I've never had a customer say such things to me before. You want a fifty-pound overdraft to, well, just to spend on beer and golf—and I suppose girls . . ."

"Yes, definitely on girls too," I said. "But, Mr Reed, surely it's a business transaction. You'll get the money back with interest. What do you care what I spend it on?" "Christ Almighty, you don't know our head office," he said. "I must say you've got a lot of cheek, coming in here and asking for a fifty-pound overdraft . . . Well, at least you're honest about why you want the money. You should hear the fancy stories some of these bastards come out with. Now that remark was off the record, understand? I know you journalists!" He laughed nervously. "Well, all right," he went on. "I'm buggered if I know why, but I'll okay this overdraft. I'm quite new here, so I better put some more serious reason why you want the money."

He pulled a form towards him and picked up a pen. "Now," he asked. "How long have you been a customer of this bank?" "I'm not," I said. "I've only this morning got off a ship in the harbour and I'm now opening an account." "Jesus Christ Almighty!" exploded Mr Reed. "You mean you're not even a customer!" "Well, I'm about to become one," I replied. "Shit!" he exclaimed, throwing down his pen. "I've never come across anything like this. You're not a *customer*, and you walk in here and ask for a fifty-pound *overdraft* to *squander*. You don't even have an *account* here! Shit!"

I said that if I could open my account starting with a fifty-pound overdraft, that surely made me a customer, if he could let me have the fifty. Mr Reed gave a sort of abandoned laugh and picked up his pen. "I'm going to bloody do it," he said. "I'm giving you the overdraft. I've never heard of such a thing but I'm going to bloody do it." During the rest of the interview he was chuckling as he filled in various forms, pausing occasionally to shake his head and say shit.

He ushered me to the door and wished me a happy vacation. "Now try not to squander it all," he added. "And you will pay it back, hey—you're not bullshitting me?" I assured him I wasn't and that I realized it wouldn't be in my interests to deceive him since I planned to deal with his bank for many years. Mr Reed raised his eyes to the ceiling. "Jesus—this is going to be a hell of an account," he said. In view of what was to happen over the next seventeen years, his concluding remark was prophetic.

CHAPTER SIX

BACK ON THE *Dispatch*, where I did some reporting before settling down to my main interest, sub-editing, my first major assignment was to cover a large-scale insurrection of tribesmen in Pondoland. The tribesmen were rebelling against the Government's new Bantu Authorities Act, a law designed to keep them permanently subjected to Government-paid chiefs and headmen. The rebellion was widespread and armoured cars, helicopters and armed forces were being used to try to suppress it. Ostensibly the Government claimed to be trying through the Act to "preserve the cultural heritage and traditional system of administration of the Pondo people", but it was a transparent attempt to reinforce one of the pillars of apartheid policy—fragmentation of black political groups through imposition of defined ethnicity. The Government aim was to drive wedges between the main groups, such as the Zulus and Xhosas, although their languages and cultures were almost identical, and then to drive wedges between the sub-groups of the main groups, the sub-groups of the Xhosas being the Pondos, Tembus and Bomvanas.

The Government was underestimating the intelligence of these "simple people" and mistaking lack of formal education for lack of wisdom. The Pondo tribesmen weren't fooled by the Government's fine-sounding edicts for them, and their leaders took to hideouts in the Pondoland hills and directed coordinated campaigns by thousands of the peasants to burn down the huts of chiefs collaborating with the Government. The tribesmen were on the march not only against collaborators but also against the police, the troops sent to subdue them —and any whites who got in the way. Cars were being stoned and fired on, so I took a pistol with me on the assignment. My base was Bizana, in Eastern Pondoland, a little white village like Elliotdale, where at the height of the rebellion the Pondos staged an impressive display by riding on horseback at walking pace right through the village in their thousands. They rode past the armed police station without turning their heads even to look at it, and the small garrison of police and the white villagers virtually held their breath until the disdainful parade was over. It had been staged not only as a warning but also as an indication that their fight wasn't with whites as such, and the whites of Bizana got the message. Drinking nervously in the bar at night the villagers kept repeating that the Government should "leave the Pondos alone and take the Afrikaner generals and captains back to Pretoria to mind their own business."

The officer commanding the government forces was a man destined later to be armed with awesome powers by the Afrikaner Nationalist Government as head of the Bureau of State Security, General Hendrik van den Bergh, but in Pondoland his forces never succeeded in subduing the tribesmen. The rebellion was ended by a young policeman who was born in the Transkei, Donald Card. Card, one of the few non-Afrikaner policemen in South Africa, was a fluent Xhosa linguist, and he walked alone and unarmed into the hills and talked the Pondo leaders into ending the uprising. Many years later both these men, Van Den Bergh and Card, were in strange and different ways to have a major impact on my own future.

After the Pondoland story I was assigned to sub-editing, and it felt good to be back in the *Dispatch* subs' room again with George Farr and the others. The working hours suited me well. We went on duty at six in the evening and worked until 2 a.m. Then I would get back to my apartment, type out one editorial, one column item and one feature article, and read until falling asleep at about four. I would be up at ten and off to golf, stopping on the way to lodge the submitted items in the editor's letter box at the *Dispatch*. After golf I would return to the flat to bathe and change for work. My articles and other items began to appear regularly in the paper, bringing me considerable extra income. For an accepted editorial the fixed payment was two pounds and for a column item or feature half-a-crown per column inch, and in this way I averaged an extra forty to fifty pounds a month. Combined with my salary, it meant an abundance of money for my bachelor lifestyle, with champagne dinners on my two nights off each week. East London had four good night-clubs with cabaret and several good restaurants, and it also had a high ratio of young single girls to young single men. This known statistic, and the city's beaches, attracted a number of journalists to the *Dispatch* from the inland cities.

After several months during which my byline grew to be a regular feature of the editorial page, it became known that one of the paper's directors, possibly disliking the anti-apartheid emphasis in them, had asked the editor if I was being given preferential treatment, and that Barber's reply had been that I had more articles rejected than accepted, but that in submitting at least one article a day I was bound to get one or two accepted in a week. Barber had a novel way of rejecting an article—he'd tear it up in front of you and drop the pieces in the waste-basket. I started keeping an alternative article in my pocket for such occasions, to hand him after his tearing up the rejected one. Sometimes he'd chuckle and accept the new one; sometimes he'd look over it quickly, shrug, and tear that up too.

Barber was a man of strong views and strong prejudices. He didn't like the Pope, the Catholic Church or the Irish, and if I wrote anything sympathetic on any of these subjects he would give a kind of smirk and say: "Oh yes, you're one of them, aren't you?" If I wrote attacking anti-semitic remarks by a cabinet minister he would say: "Christ, son, what is it you like about the Yids?" But generally he used the articles, muttering that he'd "let it go this time". Like all newspapers the *Dispatch* had a style-book prescribing how organizations, officials and countries should be referred to, and I objected to the fact that the *Dispatch* required Catholics to be called Roman Catholics. I used to put in regular memo notes to him saying that Roman Catholics lived in Rome, but Barber never yielded the point. He was particularly touchy about Irish republicanism and the Ulster question, and he and the chairman of the board, Denis Ross-Thompson, whose family were Ulster Protestants, thought my articles were too favourable to the cause of Irish reunification. Yet he occasionally allowed such articles to be published, sometimes attacking the point made in an editorial he would write himself.

I infinitely preferred Barber to his deputy, Murray Mc-Pherson, an intellectual but over-cautious man who when Barber was away accepted nothing in the least bit controversial for publication and was especially negative about my submitted articles and editorials. McPherson's general attitude suggested that he regarded me as a young upstart, though he was always strictly polite. I hoped Barber would be around for many years, because McPherson was his obvious successor, although I had the hope that Ted Holliday or George Farr might get the editorship after Barber if he hung on long enough, as he and McPherson were about the same age.

Barber had a mixed reputation. As a journalist he was highly regarded, but he was a notorious boozer. Once he passed out so rigidly in his second-floor office that he couldn't be carried into the elevator or down the stairs, and had to be strapped in a stretcher and taken by fireman's crane through the window and lowered to the sidewalk. Occasionally reporters on late night duty would see him crawling on all fours to the toilet, unable to walk upright. There were many stories of his drinking-bouts, and at one formal banquet both he and his wife had collapsed forward—he with his head on the table and she with her head against his shoulder. How he had kept his job for more than a quarter-century in spite of his drinking was something of a mystery, though at least part of the reason was the loyalty of his staff, who protected and covered-up for him as much as they could. There was a myth that he wrote his best editorials when drunk, but he was often so drunk he couldn't write a word. Sometimes at about midnight we would hear the printing foreman, Joe Keeley, banging on his locked office door and calling out that there was no editorial. There would either be no reply, or a slurred Yorkshire growl: "Fook off, Keeley!" Often in these circumstances Barber would phone Ted Holliday at his home and ask him to come in to do an editorial, and Holliday never let him down. As a night reporter I often saw him at his typewriter in his bedroom slippers and with a jacket over his pyjamas, pipe clenched in his mouth, typing an emergency editorial. Once I noticed he was keeping a carbon copy of the editorial and I asked him why, and he took his pipe out of his mouth and said in his pedantic way: "Because, young Woods, it has been my experience that when shown the original the editor invariably pukes on it."

But in spite of his boozing we all had great affection for Barber as a man and respect for his ability and integrity as a journalist. He was a rough diamond like our chief process engraver, Ossie Kershaw, who seemed incapable of a single sentence without several copulatory adjectives and verbs. *Dispatch* legend was that when World War II began Ossie became a drill instructor and balked at having to drill a squad of rookie privates which included Denis Ross-Thompson. "But that's my fuckin boss at the fuckin *Dispatch*," he was reputed to have said. "How can I fuckin drill my fuckin managing fuckin director?"

Ossie had featured in at least one remarkable coincidence during the war. George Farr had been wounded in action in the Sahara, in an engagement for which he was awarded the Military Cross for conspicuous gallantry in combat. Picked up by Rommel's staff car, he had been personally interrogated by the Field Marshal, and because he had refused to disclose troop numbers and names of units Rommel had had him thrown out to bleed to death. He was found later by Italian ambulance men, and spent four years in Italian and then German prisoner-of-war camps. Towards the end of the war, as General Patton's troops were liberating these camps, the Germans moved George and his fellow-prisoners to a camp nearer Berlin with meagre provisions for the day-long train trip. The train was so often bombed or strafed by Allied aircraft that it had to spend long hours in mountain tunnels until the raids were over, and the journey eventually lasted nine days. The P.O.W.s were literally starving to death when they arrived at the new camp, and George was crawling along a perimeter fence, too weak to walk, begging some French prisoners for food, when he heard: "Fuck me, George fuckin Farr, what the fuck are you doing here?" It was Ossie Kershaw, and he gave George bread, chocolate and a tin of condensed milk from his own Red Cross parcel. Years later I often heard them arguing over a late picture, Ossie claiming he would miss the last bus to Amalinda if he engraved the plate and George saying: "It's for the front page, Oz! The front page!" Ossie would storm out, saying: "Fuck the front page—I should've let the fucker starve."

One thing about Ossie was that if he wasn't in his process department you always knew where to find him—in the bar across the street from the *Dispatch*. Another good customer of the bar was my friend Ian Farquharson, a reporter with a prodigious capacity for beer. He had a shock early one morning, after several of us had spent the night celebrating a win at cricket. We were eating hamburgers at an all-night kiosk, Ian was in an advanced stage of beery benevolence, and the trainers from a nearby circus decided to exercise their elephants at about two a.m. by walking them along the deserted street. Ian looked up blearily from his hamburger to see several elephants walking by and he broke down quietly, swearing he was giving up liquor.

Most of us on the *Dispatch* got along pretty well, and my group of drinking friends and golf friends were from the reporters' group as well as the sub-editors' group. George Farr was an amiable chief sub-editor, and we younger ones took full advantage of his good nature. When he gathered up his papers to attend the editorial conference on the floor above he would usually leave his large horn-rimmed spectacles on his desk, and while he was away I would get green paper and paste tiny green dots all over the lenses so that he'd come back, slam on his glasses and think he had kidney trouble. He was a bit of a hypochondriac, and sometimes by blanking out one of the lenses with ordinary white copy-paper you could fool him for an instant into beating the air in front of him in fear that one eye was failing him. While he was away at the editorial conference we had a full twenty minutes to sabotage him, and would load his cigarettes with match-heads. The consequent mini-explosion used to cause him to snap back in his swivel-chair.

I used to join up all his steel paper-clips in a long chain attached to several bizarre objects, and when he darted his fingers into the paper-clip container without looking up from the copy it was quite a sight to see him wrestling with the long chain that emerged. His pipe was very sabotageable, and we'd empty out the tobacco, put back a thin layer, pack about twenty match-heads in, then cover them with another layer of tobacco. George would light up, puff away for a while, then the lot would detonate in quite a spectacular display. Eventually, in self-defence, he took all his accoutrements with him to the daily conference.

He was capable of total preoccupation. When he was working on a page he would get a glazed look and it would be hard to catch his attention for anything else. Once he was working on the shipping page and had a query for the waterfront reporter, Mel Godfrey. He phoned the reporters' room on the floor above to ask for him, and at that moment Mel himself walked into the subs' office and sat on the end of George's desk. "Hello, George," said Mel. "Hello, Mel," said George into the receiver. He started asking Mel some questions, and Mel was replying to about the third one when George realized what was happening, brought his eyes back into focus and slowly replaced the receiver.

He used to get into an awful state as edition deadlines approached. He would steal upward glances at the wall-clock and hunch his shoulders lower over his work, calling out: "Gentlemen, gentlemen—it's a race against time!" At such moments he would lose his pen under a mass of copy spread all over his desk, and beat a frantic tattoo with his hands all over the copy to feel where the pen was. If he went out to see the printing foreman we would advance the hands of the wall-clock by half-an-hour, which would drive him to paroxysms of endeavour on his return. That was usually the time to slip in the odd phoney headline containing an obscenity, and when he recoiled we'd hand him the right headline already done. More than once he probably indulged us by exaggerating his reaction.

One Saturday morning I was in the reporters' room, having written an article headed "Open Letter to Dr Verwoerd"—a no-holds-barred attack on the Prime Minister, reminding him of his record of Nazi sympathies and accusing him of embodying Hitler's master-race theories in his apartheid policy. A big man in shorts and a rugby blazer, speaking in an Afrikaans accent, came up to me and asked to speak to "this Donald Woods who wrote this article". He had the clipping with him. For a second I toyed with the idea of pointing out someone else, and then with hammering heart I admitted my identity. He gave me a long look, then said heavily: "I've driven all the way from Kei Road to find you—and to shake your hand." We shook hands vigorously and he went off, leaving me to recover on my own.

Another morning in my flat I was shaving and wondering whether I'd get into trouble with the Government over an article of mine that had appeared in the *Dispatch* that day. It was one of my "Open Letters" to a cabinet member, Eric

Louw, and it quoted pro-Nazi statements he had made during the Hitler era and compared Afrikaner Nationalist institutions like the Jeugbond (Youth League) to their Nazi counterparts. There was a knock on the door and, half-shaved, I opened the door to find two policemen there. "We have a warrant for your arrest—you are to come with us," they said. They stood at the door while I finished shaving and put on a tie and jacket. I was scared but stimulated, having half-expected such a moment. They took me by the arm and, with one on each side of me, I walked down the corridor. "What is the charge?" I asked, wondering which of the many security laws they would use against me. "Failing to appear in court for a traffic charge," one said. "You parked in a no-parking space, then ignored the summons." I felt somewhat deflated. At the charge office I saw my parish priest, who was reporting the theft of the luggage roofrack from his car. He was Father McLoughlin, an Irishman. "What are ye doing here?" he asked. "I've been arrested," I said. "Get away with ye!" he laughed. The police took my watch and pen. "Great God, ye *have* been arrested!" said Father McLoughlin, then as they moved away to find a charge form, he added: "Mind ye, ye've been sailing close to the wind lately."

The police said I'd have to go to jail until the following morning, then appear before the magistrate. "But the traffic court is still in session, let me appear now," I protested. They said it wasn't possible, I'd been summoned for nine o'clock and it was now eleven. I could have kicked myself for ignoring the summons, which I had completely forgotten about, and asked if I could phone my lawyer, Kingsley Kingon. They agreed, and Kingsley spoke with the prosecutor and arranged for the police to bring me straight to court. I was led into the prisoner's dock and saw with relief that the magistrate on duty was Mr Bezuidenhout, not one of the more fanatical party men. The reason for my relief was that on the previous Saturday at the West Bank Golf Club I had been drawn to play in a foursome with Magistrate Bezuidenhout and had hit a nine-iron shot which landed on his ball and knocked it to within a foot of the pin, giving him an easy birdie putt which he was delighted to sink, thanking me repeatedly in the bar afterwards for that lucky bounce. In court he kept his face stern and delivered a long lecture about the dangers of treating court summonses with contempt, at the end of which he let me off with a reprimand. I just knew that birdie putt had got me off the hook.

Our *Dispatch* staff golfing forays were keenly contested — we had a tournament every month — and as the betting money rose so we all started to take the game more seriously. Most of us consulted books by Gary Player or Bobby Locke for tips on basic technique, but Ted Holliday, typically, did his golf research in the *Encyclopaedia Britannica*. He had a pontifical swing, full of dignity. He never hit the ball very far, but invariably hit it straight, whereas Dudley Dickin and I tended to get considerable distance but disastrous direction. Dudley had a hook and I had a slice, and as we improved Dudley's hook became a draw and my slice became a fade — but we seldom had straight hits. The worse Dudley's game got the more his stomach ached, and he would rub it morosely while muttering that he was sure he had "carcinoma of the colon".

The seventeenth hole at West Bank was spectacular. Ideally one drove from an elevated tee across a valley and a pond to land the ball on the small plateau green with enough backspin to stop it skidding through into a nest of sand-traps or down the other side towards the ocean. We lost a lot of balls on that hole. Dudley and I usually swatted them out of bounds and Ted tended to land his with a sad splash in the heart of the pond. After one such shot he said morosely: "Golf is the only game in which an error results in attrition of the actual playing equipment." But his most notable achievement on a golf course was to hit a ball into his shirt. The ball was on springy turf and Ted took a number two iron and swung for the distant green. The clubhead passed right under the ball, flipping it gently up past his right ear, and as he held his follow-through pose, as advised in the *Encyclopaedia Britannica*, the ball dropped down past his ear and into the neck of his shirt. Ted groped confusedly about his person, and there were hysterical suggestions that he should walk to the green and unbutton his shirt over the hole, but he took it very well, although Dudley and I noticed a whiteness about his lips as he bit on the stem of his pipe.

We played golf at least twice a week, and it was on my way to one of these games that I stopped by the *Dispatch* building for a minute to leave my overnight articles. I ran in, dropped the material into Barber's letterbox and was turning to run back to the car when I saw Barber beckoning to me. "Come into my office, son," he said. Staff members were seldom invited into the editor's office unless they had done something pretty good or something pretty bad, and as I hadn't done anything pretty good I wondered if I had botched a headline the night before. Ruefully I realized I was dressed for golf in open-necked shirt and shorts, and hadn't shaved because I had overslept.

Barber's manner was strange. "Lock that door," he said, then he reached into his bookcase and took out a Bible. "Swear on this that you won't disclose to a single person until the proper time what I am about to tell you," he said. I did so, wondering if the editor could possibly be drunk so early in the day. "Now sit down," he said. "It has been decided by the Board of Directors that you are to be groomed for this job—for the post of editor of this newspaper."

I was shocked speechless. There was a dreamlike quality to the scene, and not even Barber's solid oak desk looked real. "I've been authorized by the Board to tell you—but to charge you strictly to say nothing about it until your appointment." "But surely you'll carry on as editor?" I asked. "Then there's Mr McPherson after you." "Yes, son," he said. "All this isn't going to happen overnight. When I finally retire in a few years —and that will depend on the Board—Murray McPherson will succeed me, but he's not a young man, and the Board felt a young man should be chosen now and groomed for the future."

"But what about all the others?" I asked. "There are plenty of others senior to me—George Farr, Jock McFall, and surely Ted Holliday, especially Ted Holliday who . . . er . . . often . . . carries responsibility . . ." Barber smiled: "You mean Ted Holliday writes the editorials when I'm drunk." "No," I lied. "Yes, you do," said Barber. "Well, son, I'll be honest with you, you weren't my choice, not that I'm against you, far from it, but my first choice was Holliday, and I don't mind telling you that I argued strongly for him to the Board. He's older than you, has more experience, and I have a lot of confidence in him —but I was outvoted. But I know you and Holliday are friends, and so I'm happy to tell you they agreed to my suggestion to groom him to be your deputy when the time comes."

I was amazed that the Board should choose me—not one of them really knew me, and I hardly knew what some of them looked like. It seemed an illogical choice in view of the candidates for the job, all of whom wanted it, whereas I'd never thought of it because it was so far outside my range of expectations. Yet within a few moments I had adjusted to the idea and it felt terrific, although the shock of it kept hitting me afresh. In our small world of the *Daily Dispatch* it was the equivalent, in American political terms, of a Senate page being told he is to be nominated for the Presidency.

Barber said: "Your salary will be increased with immediate effect, and over the next few years you will be set three tests. First you'll be appointed Political Correspondent and sent to the parliamentary press gallery for two sessions, then you'll write all editorials for a prescribed time, then you'll be entrusted with the daily column for a year. If you come through these tests without landing in trouble or committing serious errors of judgement, you'll succeed to this job after Murray McPherson's retirement. If you fail in any of them, Holliday will succeed Murray McPherson—but this arrangement is to be kept strictly confidential, and the Board is emphatic about this because your discretion and confidentiality are also on trial." He gave me no chance to reply to this but got up abruptly, shook hands, and said: "Now go and play golf—and get over the shock of what I've told you this morning!"

I left the office still stunned, not least by all the drama over the Bible, which I suspected Barber had used for sheer theatricality because it was probably the first time he'd touched a Bible in years. On the way out I saw Jack McFall, who gave his usual cheery wave, and I thought: "My God—if he only knew what I've just been told!"

Being very late for my golf date with Ted and Dudley I drove at great speed to West Bank, my mind spinning with all the ideas I could introduce to improve the paper as editor. Unable to stop grinning to myself, I was already into a mental format redesign as I swept to a stop near my two friends, and had to caution myself to wipe the grin off my face and act as normally as possible, not only for the sake of discretion but because Ted had often told me he hoped to be editor of the

Dispatch one day and that Barber had said he would recommend him. It was going to be awkward keeping my news from Ted, but I knew I'd have to.

CHAPTER SEVEN

Dr Verwoerd, the Prime Minister, had led the Afrikaner Nationalist Party Government to a narrow victory in a referendum among the all-white electorate designed to turn South Africa into a republic, and the new republic was expelled from the British Commonwealth of Nations because of the apartheid policy. The parliamentary session of 1961, therefore, promised to be a particularly interesting one—South Africa's first as a republic. On the eve of my departure for Cape Town Barber reminded me that I was on trial, and that while he wanted me to write freely in criticism of whatever I wished to criticize, within the maze of publication law already in force in South Africa, it would count heavily against me if I got myself or the *Dispatch* into trouble with the authorities.

My career as a parliamentary correspondent nearly ended on the first day. South Africa had not only more than twenty strict laws governing what could or could not be published, but extremely strict rules to uphold what was regarded as the dignity of parliament. The Speaker of the lower house, the House of Assembly, could impose heavy penalties on anyone whom he deemed to have written or spoken disrespectfully about any of the appurtenances of parliament, including the pictures on the walls, the furniture, and particularly the symbols of authority in the Assembly or Senate. The new republican mace had not yet been coated with the gold that was being prepared for it, and was still no more than an intricately carved mass of dull-looking wood. Not knowing much about the rules of parliamentary reportage, I wrote in my descriptive article in the *Dispatch* about the inaugural proceedings that the new mace resembled a piece of chewed biltong, or dried meat, and that the State President's sash of office was broad and garish. I also wrote about how his limousine had broken down short of the red-carpeted entrance to the Senate, belching clouds of smoke before coughing to an ignominious stop, and suggested that such an omen might be symbolic of the new republic's ultimate fate . . . Luckily the parliamentary officials were too preoccupied with the protocol and organization of the initial days of the session to react to it.

There was considerable tension in the press gallery between Afrikaans-language and English-language pressmen. We were separated by a central corridor, and there was little social mingling either in the press offices or in the bar. We had our own toilets and telex facilities and they had theirs. We criticized the Afrikaner Nationalist Government and they never found fault with it. We regarded the Afrikaans newspapers less as newspapers than as party organs, and their correspondents less as journalists than as party officials.

The two outstanding personalities among the English-language journalists in the parliamentary press gallery were Anthony Delius of the *Cape Times* and Stanley Uys of the Johannesburg *Sunday Times*. Delius, recognized nationally as a poet and prose writer, produced a daily item called "Notes in the House" in which he gave cameos of debates with exquisite touches of irony and satire. He was so brilliant and often so subtle that much of his stuff was over the heads of the authorities, which enabled him to get away with certain observations that would have landed him in jail if the Afrikaner Nationalists had understood what he was really saying. Some, including the MPs themselves, got away with less subtlety. Front-bench opposition debater, Harry Lawrence, sharply rebuked by the Speaker for calling government MPs "lackeys" of the cabinet, amended the word to "sycophants" and got away with it because the Speaker wasn't sure what the English word meant.

Delius, then in his early forties, had jet-black hair and an impassive expression which gave him the appearance of a Cherokee brave. In the manner of an absent-minded poet he seemed to spend more time with his inward thoughts than in observing the debates. Wearing the same shapeless jacket throughout almost two sessions of parliament, he would shamble in from the corridors with his distinctive walk, a kind of shuffle in which he scarcely bothered to lift his feet, and slump into his seat to observe the legislators down below. Educated by Jesuit priests, he had a wealth of theological diagnoses to chew on in his assessments of members of the cabinet. One day, as the Prime Minister, Dr Verwoerd, was implying a direct relationship between his cabinet and divine guidance, Delius muttered: "Christ, now I realize what this bastard is—he's a bloody Gnost!"

Stanley Uys was a totally different character. Acknowledged as one of the ablest journalists in South African history, he had cornered the national and international correspondence market, and now wrote on South African developments for literally hundreds of publications all over the globe, including all the leading newspapers in the Western World. Unlike Delius he seldom bothered to visit the actual debating chamber, preferring to stay at his desk in his gallery office listening to the relayed debate over the intercom system. He knew by voice which Member was talking, and often knew what he would be saying next. Yet he got all the big scoops for his main paper, the *Sunday Times*. He drove the Afrikaner Nationalists crazy week after week by splashing details of their secret caucus deliberations, and his reports were so accurate that they once came to his office to see if he had rigged up a listening device from his desk to their distant caucus room. But Uys's methods were more prosaic than that. He supplied a veteran leg-man named Solly Belfort with generous drinking-money, and Solly, who spoke good Afrikaans, haunted all the Sea Point and Rondebosch bars where the Members got drunk in the pubs and discussed their caucus secrets rather louder than they realized. The Afrikaner Nationalists hated Stanley Uys with a terrible loathing, especially because he had an Afrikaans surname and was therefore seen by them to be a "traitor to the Volk".

My friends in the press gallery were Allister Sparks of the *Rand Daily Mail*, Tony Heard of the *Cape Times*, Stewart Carlyle of the *Natal Mercury*, Don Prosser of the *Eastern Province Herald*, Harvey Tyson of the Durban *Daily News*, Bob Steyn and Max Leigh of the Cape *Argus*, Tertius Myburgh of the Johannesburg *Star* and Brian Stuart of the *Natal Witness*. All the major papers but mine belonged to one of the two big newspaper combines—the Morning Group and the Argus (evening) Group. The *Dispatch* alone was totally independent. The two big groups were in strong competition and worked in isolation from each other in case a member of the rival camp might spot a story or news angle they hadn't thought of. The morning squad worked in a corner office and the Argus boys several doors down the corridor. Because I was neutral in the conflict I was a welcome visitor in both camps and managed to capitalize on this. Each group readily passed on their carbon copies of every story they had done during the day, provided I didn't disclose these to the other camp. This meant that without doing any work I had half-a-dozen good parliamentary reports a day, so I would do two of my own, pass one on to each group, rewrite the intro paragraphs of the "acquired" stories and send the lot off to the *Dispatch*.

To ensure early transmission I asked the parliamentary telex operator if he could get my stories off first each evening before the big groups started transmitting, and he obliged. His name was Van der Merwe, and because of the speed of his hands over the keys while transmitting I nicknamed him "Fingers", a name which stuck. With his help and that of my friends in the Morning Group and Argus Group I was daily sending the *Dispatch* so many stories that I got a note from Barber commending me for my hard work and comprehensive coverage. I didn't reply with the truth, which was that I covered much of that first session of parliament on the fairways of Mowbray Golf Club.

At the end of the parliamentary session Barber assigned me to fly to South West Africa—later to be called Namibia—for some scene-setting articles on the eve of an inspection tour there by a United Nations Commission. Since World War I the territory had been administered by South Africa with the aim of guiding it to self-government and independence. When the United Nations supplanted the League of Nations, and Malan's Afrikaner Nationalist Government replaced the Smuts government, trouble began in earnest over the country. For many years the Nationalists wanted to incorporate it into South Africa as a fifth province, but United Nations opposition was so vehement and internal resistance by the black population through SWAPO, the South West Africa People's Organization, so determined that Pretoria adopted the tactic of stalling —of using the issue as a red herring to divert international attention from the apartheid state itself while appearing ready to negotiate with the world community over the territory. As the result of an invitation from Pretoria, the United Nations

Commission was due to travel all over the territory, and Barber wanted me to acquaint our readers more fully with the place and the issues.

I flew from Cape Town and spent ten days travelling all over Windhoek and the territory, primarily in search of SWAPO members. It was frustrating. I interviewed many locals, black and white, and researched a lot of background material, enough to send the *Dispatch* six features on the issue, but I couldn't find a single SWAPO member. Whenever I mentioned this to whites in the territory they would scoff. "There's no SWAPO," they would say. "SWAPO's an invention by the foreign press and interfering clerics. The blacks want nothing to do with SWAPO."

One afternoon near the end of my stay, after a totally negative day in search of SWAPO members, I returned to my hotel and got into the lift to go to my room. I was alone with the attendant, a dull-looking Ovambo tribesman, and burst out irritably to him: "Where's SWAPO? Where the hell is SWAPO? Is there such a thing?" He ignored me, letting me out at my floor without even turning his head. About twenty minutes later I was typing in my room when an Ovambo hotel cleaner entered carrying a bucket and mop. I nodded, and was about to continue typing when the thought struck me that the room had been cleaned earlier, so why was this man here? He was making mopping movements on the floor and I was about to ask him what was going on when he said: "Master wants SWAPO?" I stared at him and merely nodded. He told me to wait another half-hour then go to the lift and accompany the same attendant I had spoken to earlier, who would guide me to "SWAPO people".

I did as he said and the attendant, still without looking at me or speaking, took the lift right down to the basement of the hotel. He beckoned me to follow him and led me by various turns to the living quarters of the black hotel staff, knocked on a door and left me, returning to the lift. The door opened and I was led into a big dormitory with multi-tiered bunks on which sat more than forty of the hotel staff. I recognized several waiters and a bartender. The "cleaner" was a sort of secretary, and he and a spokesman sat at a packing-case serving as a desk, beside which was a chair for me. The spokesman explained that they would all be off-duty for the next ninety minutes, and began by questioning me closely about my newspaper and myself. When he seemed satisfied by my replies, there followed some forty minutes of explanation for me about the case for Namibia. It was the most enlightening political experience I had had, and after it the discussion was thrown open to all present and one of the hotel workers asked me to "tell the world what is happening to us in our country". Several of them, sitting high up on one of the top bunks, murmured their support.

When I asked if it could be arranged for me to meet one of the national leaders, the spokesman said I was to be at a certain place in the Kaiserstrasse at 3 p.m. the following day, and to get immediately into a big black car which would stop there. At precisely the appointed time the following day a big car stopped and a tall, handsome black man in an elegant dark suit got out, holding the door open for me. I climbed into the back seat next to another tall black man in a suit, and the first man also got in, so I was sitting between the two of them. In the front seat there was another man beside the driver. The car pulled off. "Where are we going?" I asked brightly. None of them replied, the man on my left holding his hand up for silence. I felt a bit apprehensive about the whole operation— especially the silence of it all. We drove out of Windhoek towards the airport, and several miles out of the town turned right on to a dusty track, then accelerated for several miles. At first both men beside me kept looking out of the rear window, and when I asked what they were looking for the first man said: "Security Police—Special Branch." But he seemed satisfied that nobody had followed us, and as we were now trailing a stream of dust he no longer bothered to look out of the window because he couldn't have seen anything anyway.

Then the tall man on my left who had opened the door for me to get into the car introduced himself. "I am Chief Clemens Kapuuo," he said. I was excited: this was the charismatic Herero leader, and I now realized that all the other men in the car were Hereros. They didn't look negroid, like the more numerous Ovambos, but had Arabic features. About twenty miles after turning off into the veld we came to a dry riverbed in which I saw a strange scene: on the riverbed were three dining-room chairs, and on one of them sat a very old man dressed in formal clothes of another time, with an old-fashioned watch-chain across his waistcoat. He was introduced as Chief Hosea Kotako, King of the Hereros, whom Kapuuo would succeed on his death. Chief Kapuuo and I sat in the other two chairs, and on both banks of the river-bed sat between twenty and thirty councillors. We talked for more than an hour about the issues dealt with by the SWAPO "cell" in the hotel the previous evening, Chief Kotako speaking first. He was then ninety-two years old, and he set out the main points of the case for Namibia that he said he and his people wanted to be made known to the world. Then Chief Kapuuo spoke at length along similar lines, but in more detail. Their main complaint was that their country had been illegally occupied for many years and that the whole world acknowledged this, but that the South African overlords were not being punished in any significant way by the world community for such occupation.

The old man spoke again, about how his people had been slaughtered by the Germans and how, when the Germans were driven out by the South Africans, the Herero people had hoped this would lead to their liberation, but that the South African enslavement had increased with the apartheid laws since 1948. He added simply: "I knew Botha—but Botha is long dead." He was referring to the first South African Prime Minister, Louis Botha. He said: "We helped Botha beat the Germans, and we are still waiting for our reward." I was allowed to ask questions and to take all the notes I wished, and when the discussion was over I was driven back to the hotel. That night the orchestra was playing a selection of tunes from Lehar's *Merry Widow* as I went in to dinner, and a man sitting at my table said to me: "Well, have you found your SWAPO yet? Ha—you won't either. I've told you already there is no SWAPO." I noticed that the waiter serving us was one of the men who had been at the basement meeting. We acted as if we had never set eyes on each other.

Chief Kotako died a year after my visit to Namibia and Chief Kapuuo was assassinated in March 1978, after favouring a compromise deal with anti-SWAPO elements in the territory. At the time of his death the Western powers were still refusing to vote for the United Nations sanctions the old king was pleading for at that river-bed meeting in 1961, and the world community was still allowing the illegal occupation of the territory by South Africa.

Before leaving South West Africa I decided to take a look at Swakopmund and Walfish Bay on the Atlantic coast. As a boy I had read the book *Skeleton Coast* about that dreaded graveyard of ships, and wanted to see the stark black rocks and deserted beaches where no man could live. I arrived at the airport for the regular flight to Swakopmund, by five-seater Piper Cub, and we flew over the Namib Desert, which was a riot of pastel colours. As we landed the pilot's radio caught a message that a ship was lost in the fog off the Skeleton Coast, and after the other passengers had left I asked the pilot if I could charter the plane to look for the lost ship. I had visions of a front page lead story. The pilot was hesitant, but I talked him into it for ten pounds an hour, and after refuelling we took off. I asked him to fly low over the beach to the north, and it was a memorable flight. Below us was a godforsaken coast of smooth dark sand and the sharpest, most jagged black rocks I had ever seen, gleaming darkly from the breaking waves and as multiform in their spikiness as coral. Every now and then we would be in thick fog from the cold Atlantic meeting the hot air of the Namib Desert. The engine droned on and on as we flew northward, feeling far away from mankind. I imagined this lunar beach stretching all the way up past the Kunene River into Angola and up to the Gulf of Guinea, and thought of Captain Scott's impression of the South Pole: "My God—this is an awful place", and of all the shipwrecked mariners who had died along this coast. A spectacular sight was a flock of flamingos turning and suddenly revealing a mass of red feathers, and this was the only sign of life we saw.

After flying over this weird desolation for perhaps a hundred miles we turned away from land and headed out to sea, flying above thick fog. The lost ship could have been anywhere within hundreds of miles of us, as its last reported position was quite far away and its radio wasn't functioning, but after turning back towards land and starting a wide circle we suddenly saw a vessel through a gap in the fog and went down low. The name stood out clearly, and the deckhands waved frenziedly. It was the lost ship. The pilot hit his knees with excitement and put out a radio message giving the exact position. Within minutes of this a rescue ship was heading towards the spot from twenty miles south, and we flew low over the "lost" ship, giving encouraging thumbs-up signs and waggling our wings as we turned back for Swakopmund before the fuel ran out.

After landing I gave the pilot his twenty pounds and a five-pound bonus and reached the nearest telephone in Walfish Bay to call the *Dispatch*. Senior man on duty was George Farr, who seemed upset, as a *Dispatch* shareholder, that I was proposing to dictate a story by telephone from two thousand miles away, but when he heard the essence of it he took it down himself and led the front page with it. How the *Daily Dispatch* had chartered a plane to find a lost ship off the Skeleton Coast made good reading back in the Eastern Cape, and the story finished off my Namibian stay with a flourish—especially after the exclusive interview with the SWAPO and Herero spokesmen and the series of background articles from Windhoek.

CHAPTER EIGHT

THE NEXT SESSION of parliament was a dramatic one. Reporting rules had been tightened further, and before the session was over Tony Delius and Stanley Uys had both been expelled from the precincts—Tony for life. He had written a facetious article about the removal of royal portraits from the walls of parliament, and this was deemed to detract from the dignity of the republic, and he had not been respectful enough when describing certain parliamentarians and their procedures, and so incurred the ire of the authorities that he was marched from the grounds by Serjeant-at-Arms Retief with drawn sword. First, however, he was taken to the office of the Speaker, Mr Henning Klopper, who said sadly that he regretted the necessity to order Delius's expulsion. Tony remarked: "And on my birthday, too." "Is it your birthday today?" asked the Speaker. "Yes," said Tony. The Speaker leapt up, came round the desk and shook Tony warmly by the hand. "Many happy returns of the day!" he said. Then he returned to his desk, gave a lecture on the dignity of parliament, and nodded to Retief, who marched Tony from the premises for the rest of his days. Before he went out he said to Speaker Klopper: "Why is my expulsion permanent?" Klopper replied: "Well, it is for the duration of rule of South Africa by our party—and that is forever."

After Stanley Uys was also expelled a meeting of the Press Gallery Association was called, but not one member of the Afrikaans press would petition the Government for a fair hearing for both journalists. They said they didn't want to "interfere". The doyen of the Afrikaans Press, Schalk Pienaar, kept puffing on his pipe and shaking his head when asked to use his influence with the authorities for at least a review of the expulsions. They were strange men, the Afrikaans-language newspapermen. They had an unhealthy respect for cabinet ministers and didn't seem to realize that slavish reverence for politicians is incompatible with real journalism.

My turn came several days later. I was summoned to the Speaker's office, and he had an entire file on the *Dispatch* open at a certain page. He pointed at a report in which, he said, I had sailed "close to the wind", and informed me that if he found one more instance of my writing anything about the mannerisms of Members of Parliament or anything which detracted from their dignity, or anything other than what was actually said in debates, I should be expelled. He slapped the report, which was on a right-hand page, for emphasis. Then I froze, because as he glared at this page I saw that on the page opposite, in front of me as I stood on his left, was a large headline he must have missed. It was a humorous article by me on the editorial page, and the main point of it was Prime Minister Verwoerd's surreptitious addiction to peppermint candy. From where we sat above him I would see Verwoerd glance round furtively, open his desk drawer about an inch, stick two fingers down into it and withdraw a white peppermint which he would sneak into his mouth. I had described all this, adding that he was probably addicted to peppermints because they were white. I moved quickly to the Speaker's side as he went on about the report on the right-hand page, and with an attentive air I leant on the left-hand page so that my elbow and forearm covered the Verwoerd article, making it appear that I was studying the offending report more closely and with a suitable air of contrition. As the Speaker concluded his warning and stepped back I sighed and closed the file as if to signify that a new and more responsible chapter of my career as a journalist was about to begin. As the file of the *Dispatch* copies was about eight inches thick, I trusted he wasn't likely to hunt up that particular page again.

My next alarming experience at parliament came some weeks later. The new Minister of Justice and Police, Mr B. J. Vorster, later to be the longest-serving Prime Minister in South African history and to become State President in 1978, decided to hold a press conference in view of the controversy surrounding his new law to introduce imprisonment without trial. The press conference came at an awkward time for me. It had originally been scheduled for late afternoon, so some of us had seen no reason to change our usual habit of a liquid lunch of Hansa Beer—a potent brew from South West Africa which we drank in quarts, not pints. Accordingly we were in a party mood when at about 2 p.m. it was announced that Vorster would hold his conference immediately. Press conferences by cabinet ministers in South Africa were so rare they were practically unknown, and the protocol secretaries instructed us to ask questions according to seniority. As I was one of the most junior members of the press gallery, this meant I would be far down on the list of about thirty of us to ask questions.

We filed into Vorster's office and sat in a big semi-circle round his desk. My chair was directly in front of him, and on my left was Tony Heard and on my right Allister Sparks. Vorster's face was rocklike as we took our seats. Looking at the most senior member of the press gallery, government-supporter Arthur Classen, Vorster said in his heavy way: "Now—are there any questions about the Bill?" All heads swivelled to Classen, but to my own surprise I heard myself say: "Yes, I've got a question—how do you square this Bill with democracy?" A kind of shock-wave ran through the room and I had the impression that Tony and Allister, on either side of me, edged their chairs a bit further away. Vorster's head turned deliberately back from Classen and I was aware of his bushy eyebrows as he settled his gaze on me. After a long, tense silence he asked: "What is your name and what newspaper do you represent?" In a higher than normal voice I told him. Vorster looked steadily at me for some moments, then said: "What's undemocratic about the Bill?" I replied: "Well—putting people in jail without trial is undemocratic." Vorster said: "What about the British Official Secrets Act?" I had never heard of such a thing, but answered: "Well, that must have been in time of war." Vorster's eyes bored into me. He said: "We *are* at war, Mr . . . er . . . Woods. We are at war with *Communism*!"

I made no reply, but he kept on at me. "Well, Mr Woods—how would *you* fight Communism without the provisions of such a Bill?" I decided that as I was already in trouble, was unmarried and had no domestic responsibilities, I might as well go down truculently, so I replied: "I'm not prepared to disclose my tactics until the second-reading debate!" This time an even bigger shock-wave ran through the room. The tension grew, then a heavy low sound was heard. Vorster was chuckling. By some miracle the remark had amused him. Others started asking questions in the more relaxed atmosphere and the rest of the press conference passed without incident.

Afterwards Vorster asked me to stay behind, and when the others had all gone he told me to sit down, ordered coffee, and said: "Tell me—why are you so cheeky?" I quoted him Lincoln's "What is morally wrong can never be politically right", and said that he of all people should know the evils of imprisonment without trial, as he had been jailed without trial by Smuts during the war. Vorster said heavily: "*Ja*—it is precisely because I know what it's like that I won't abuse these powers I am seeking. Yes—I know what it's like. And when I was released I came to this very building, to this office, to Minister Colin Steyn to plead for the other detainees—and he ordered me out of the building in five minutes or I'd be arrested." Sensing a scoop here I said: "Sir, why don't you let me interview you about what it's like behind barbed wire— jailed without trial by the State?" Vorster gave me his hooded look, then to my surprise he nodded and agreed. He gave me a full interview describing his arrest and imprisonment, how he went on hunger strike in protest against the conditions in Port Elizabeth jail, and how his wife was forbidden to telegraph the family to tell them what had happened to him. With a wintry smile he said: "She got round that by sending a telegram reading 'John is staying at the King's Hotel for a while.' "

He described how he was moved by train to Koffiefontein detention camp up-country, and how his Ossewa-Brandwag group were separated by a high wall from German internees and Italian prisoners of war; how one of his friends made a radio from spare parts to hear the news, and how they wrote the news on a piece of paper, wrapped it round a stone and lobbed it into the next compound. "We called it rock post," said Vorster.

I asked how he felt now about the accusation that he had been pro-Nazi during the war. "I was never pro-Nazi," he said. "I was only against the involvement by South Africa in the war. To me it was Britain's war." He talked at length, and out of this interview I got a feature article which, after the *Dispatch* had used it, I sold to a number of the morning news-papers. That was my first encounter with Balthazar Johannes Vorster. There were to be many more. His detention-without-trial law was passed, and in succeeding years it was made even more severe. At first it provided for unexplained detention for ninety days. Then it was amended to allow for unexplained detention for 180 days, then finally for indefinite jailing without trial. He and his government used it ruthlessly against every effective opponent of apartheid.

In the press gallery was Hans Jurgen Kruger of the *Frankfurter Allgemeine* and the German Press Agency, who had had his own problems with the Gestapo in his native Germany. Whenever Vorster got up to speak in the Assembly Hans would say: "*Ja*, I know vot he will say next. I have heard all zis before in ze Third Reich!"

One amusing aspect of the session that most of us in the press gallery noticed was the obvious lust of the Speaker, H. J. Klopper, for the attractive lone Progressive MP, Helen Suzman. Politically they were poles apart, but the goateed old founder of the Broederbond secret society for Afrikaner dominance clearly drooled in the presence of Mrs Suzman, and she was one MP who seemed to "catch the Speaker's eye" whenever she wanted to speak. "The Honourable Member for Houghton" he would intone, and the cunning Helen took full political advantage of his beady-eyed admiration.

In spite of the anxious moments it was a stimulating session for me, made especially pleasant by the fact that my girl-friend, Wendy Bruce, was now with me. Soon we decided to get married, and wrote to tell our families. We set a wedding date following the end of the session, and the press gallery gang gave us a memorable engagement party which was attended by the few MPs we got on well with. I was seven years older than Wendy, and had known her since she was twelve. Her parents and mine had seaside shacks at Bashee Mouth, and during vacations there I had seen her grow into an attractive girl with an appealing sense of humour. By the time she was sixteen I was very interested in her, and when we found the interest was mutual we began to write to each other. While I was overseas she was in Maritzburg studying to be a librarian, and when I got back the relationship developed. It was hard for us to get together, because Maritzburg was hundreds of miles from East London, but when I was assigned to cover parliament in Cape Town Wendy got the library service to transfer her there as well.

As the long parliamentary session drew to a close I realized it would be my last in the press gallery for the *Dispatch*, because Barber had indicated in a letter that I was in for phase three of the "tests" devised by the directors to determine my suitability to be groomed for the future editorship.

Wendy and I were married in the Catholic Cathedral in Umtata, and for our honeymoon we went to Uvongo Beach in Natal—which was about as original as American newlyweds going to Niagara Falls. Back in East London we found a ground floor apartment which was roomy but sparsely furnished, as we had little money. One thing we splurged on was a grand piano, and when I was discussing the price with the salesman he said: "You can't go wrong with a grand piano. There's always a demand for them. How many grand pianos do you see around? Not many!" The same salesman said only two years later, when we wanted to trade in the grand for an upright with a better tone: "I can't give you much on the grand—no demand. How many grand pianos do you see around? Not many!"

At the office on my return I was called in by Barber and told that the directors were pleased with both assignments I had fulfilled—the two parliamentary sessions and the spell as leader-writer and editorial page director—and that I was now officially appointed assistant to the editor. The third test, which I was now given, was to produce the daily column. This had been run for many years by Murray McPherson, and I had thought it dull and unoriginal, consisting largely of items culled from magazines of all kinds, often, it seemed, just to fill space. Barber assured me I could run it as I wished, and this I did, changing the format, giving it a modern logo at the top, breaking up what used to be long slabs of grey type by using short items with lead paragraphs in bold typeface and a heading over each, and ending each column with a local limerick using a place name from the Eastern Cape. Writing a new limerick every day was an interesting challenge. I was also given my own office, and could come and go as I wished without accounting to anyone.

When Wendy became pregnant, we started to look for a house with a garden, so that our future brood of kids—we planned to have a big family—could run around freely. After looking at many properties and learning to differentiate between realtor's terms and reality, we found a large double-storey house with a garden and a view of the ocean. "It's a fine neighbourhood," the owner said. "Look, I feel I should tell you that an Afrikaans couple live in one of the opposite houses—but you hardly ever see them." He beckoned us to the window and pointed. "That house there, *see*, not a *sign* of them!"

Pending our move to the new house we moved to temporary lodgings, and during this time I had an awful shock. I was sitting in my office at about midday, having finished the column and sent all the material down to the works. I had roughed out a lead topic for the following day's column, and was leaning back in my chair and enjoying a cigarette, when the phone rang. It was Barber asking me to come to his office. I noticed he looked unusually sombre. He said: "I'm sorry to tell you this, son, but the Board have changed their opinion of you. The way in which you've run the column has distressed them, and they've decided you aren't the man for this job after all. They've decided you are not to have the editorship or the number two job, and Holliday is now going to be groomed for the editorship." With the bravado of severe shock, I said: "The Board gaveth; the Board taketh away—Blessed be the Board." But it was hollow flippancy. I was shattered. It seemed unbelievable —even more unbelievable than the day in that same office when Barber had told me I had been chosen to be groomed as editor.

Knowing it would serve no purpose, but curious even in my shock to know what had caused the turnabout, I asked the reason for the decision. Barber said it was simply my way of presenting the column that had offended. Murray McPherson had resented the changes I had made in its format and tone and, more seriously, the Chairman of the Board, Mr Ross-Thompson, felt that the column showed my lack of judgement and taste. I now recalled that Barber had once told me that "the people upstairs" were shaken by the bluntness of the column. In fact he had advised me to tone it down, but I had felt it would be false to do so, and that I would rather not write a column than produce one made artificially dull. I also remembered having written a piece in the column about a topic on which the chairman was known to be touchy. Along with numbers of other wealthy citizens, he had a fine house on the banks of the Nahoon River into which a new textile factory was now pumping its waste upstream, and I had titled the paragraph "Effluent for the Affluent". Well, I reflected, I couldn't say I hadn't been warned . . .

But Barber had something even worse to tell me. If I stayed on the staff, he said, I would not revert simply to what I had been doing before the decision to groom me for the editorship; McPherson insisted I could only stay on the paper as a junior journalist. This meant, he said unhappily, that I would have to return to junior routine chores on police and hospital calls, ships' movements and checking the sea temperatures. It all sounded so crazy that I laughed out loud, and for an instant I thought it might mean the whole interview had been a joke. But Barber looked too serious, and he wasn't a man for such a joke. He said: "I'm sorry, son, but Murray is adamant on this."

"Well, bugger Murray!" I said sharply. "It sounds as if he wants me forced right out. But you're the editor—do you agree with him about this?" "No, I don't," he replied, "but he is due to succeed me and he feels strongly about the whole thing." I realized it was useless to pursue the subject. In normal circumstances I would have resigned immediately, but now I was in no position for angry gestures. My wife was pregnant, the pregnancy was complicated, and we were committed to a house mortgage. As I got up to go Barber said: "I just want to say again how sorry I am about this whole business, Woods. As I told you originally, the choice of you by the Board was not my idea—I was for Holliday. But Frank Streek was strongly for you and Murray McPherson was as well, and Mr Ross-Thompson supported them. Now only Streek stands by you, and I can tell you he really fought for you."

As far as I was concerned such information was of academic interest only, although I appreciated Streek's advocacy. The newest and youngest director on the board, Streek was something of a mystery man to us. An accountant from Natal, he was as remote a figure as any of the other directors, although some months after my demotion we met in a corridor and he said I shouldn't let my circumstances get me down. He was obviously sympathetic over what had happened. So was Ted Holliday. The irony of it was that Ted and I were good friends, and now that Barber had made the whole position clear to him he told me he would do what he could at the right time to have me restored at least to a senior grading.

It was Ted who broke the news to me as I came in from a police call that Wendy had had to go into the nursing home prematurely, and I rushed off to the building which was to become increasingly familiar in later years—the Mater Dei Maternity Hospital. I was so glad when the gynaecologist arrived that I could have embraced him, but I practically pulled him into the labour ward. And when Jane was born and it was clear that she and Wendy were "doing well", it was the most exhilarating feeling I'd ever had. With the new baby we moved into our new house during a week of national shock caused by the murder of a white family by Transkei tribesmen. The Grobbelaars, husband, wife and several young children, were ambushed in their caravan and stabbed and hacked to death. This wasn't in character with the Xhosas, but there were reports that Grobbelaar had antagonized local tribesmen. There was also an intensification at the time of the beleaguered feeling among most whites.

The long passivity of the African National Congress had come to an end with the realization that a half-century of peaceful protest had resulted in no concessions from the whites, and the movement decided to start a campaign of graduated violence. Leadership of the ANC had passed from a great old man, Chief Albert Luthuli, a Nobel Peace Prize winner whose tireless attempts to win the compassion of whites by non-violent means had been in vain, to a younger but also remarkable man, Nelson Mandela. Mandela, a lawyer who was born near Elliotdale, led the guerilla wing of the ANC, the Um-khonto we Sizwe (Spear of the nation), on the campaign of escalating violence. First only inanimate objects were to be attacked—power-stations, electricity pylons, railway-lines and government offices which were empty. Then, if there were no concessions from the Government, guerilla attacks would be launched against the police and military barracks. Finally, if there were still no concessions, full-scale civil war would be un-leashed. The Pan-Africanist Congress, whose leader, Robert

Sobukwe, was in jail, also turned to violence through its guerilla wing, Poqo, which like the Irish Sinn Fein meant "We Alone".

For two years these movements launched increasingly effective attacks against a number of communities, but partly because of the remarkable network of informants built up by Donald Card, the young policeman who had ended the Pondoland uprising and had been transferred into the Security section of the police force, the police got the upper hand and the campaigns were frustrated. Card, an apolitical man who initially resisted his transfer to the political section, became a hero to the whites of East London when he blackened his face one night and infiltrated a column of 300 Poqo men marching on one of the outlying suburbs with guns and pangas. Carrying a two-way radio with him he directed police to their position and earned the personal commendation of Minister Vorster, who was then head of the police ministry. I interviewed Card a number of times before and after his transfer to the political section, and it was clear that he preferred criminal detection to political work. He was an unusually able detective with a sort of sixth sense for tracking down burglary suspects. He had been shot at, stabbed, clubbed and attacked with a wide variety of weapons including bicycle chains and battle-axes, and on his office wall was a collection of the fearful-looking implements he had confiscated after such attacks. At the time we were moving into our new house the Poqo scare was abating, although hundreds of white women were still attending pistol-shooting classes given by the police.

Soon another crisis occurred for me at the office. Barber wrote an uncharacteristic editorial attacking the black singer Miriam Makeba and her activities for the United Nations anti-apartheid campaign. It seemed to signal a switch in the paper's editorial policy, and before leaving the house that morning I wrote a "letter to the editor" in which I challenged the editorial, asking if the *Dispatch* was now going to commit itself to a line of attack on anti-apartheid campaigners. I read the letter over to Wendy, explaining it could well mean I would be out of work by the end of the day. We were conscious of the mortgage on the house, the baby and the fact that I was already under a cloud at the office. But Wendy was emphatic. "You must do it," she said. "You can always get a job on another paper." I said it would mean moving to another city. "It doesn't matter," she said.

I got to the office and put the letter in Barber's letterbox. Within an hour I had a note from him in his copper-plate handwriting: "Woods—your letter is impudent and it has angered me. Furthermore, it is dishonest in that if you really meant it to be published you would have concluded it by resigning. Accordingly, I assume you did not intend it to be taken seriously and I have torn it up. Realizing that you wrote it in the heat of emotion I am prepared to forget the matter." I typed the reply: "Sir—anticipating such a reaction from you, I kept a carbon copy of my letter which I now re-submit for publication, and since it appears that my resignation is necessary to get the letter published, I hereby resign." I sent this to him by messenger, and within minutes I was called to his office. His face was red and he had some difficulty in speaking, yet when he did so it was in a conciliatory tone. "Son, I don't want you to resign. Now tell me why you are so worked up over that editorial." I told him I didn't want to resign either, but that if his editorial represented a change of policy by the *Dispatch* I was no longer prepared to work for the paper. "I came to work for the *Dispatch* because of its political policy," I said. "It is more outspokenly anti-apartheid than any other paper in the country—thanks to you. But if *you* are now going to start wavering then I'm off."

"Christ, son, I'm not wavering!" he roared, losing his reasonable tone and his temper, and for a full quarter-of-an-hour we argued over the wording of the editorial. Eventually he said: "I see what you mean. Well, I'm prepared to say I was wrong. How about that? I'm prepared to give you my word there is no change in our policy. I don't see why I should have to justify to a member of the staff why—" growing angry again, he paused—"But I can tell you that *I* set policy around here and there's *no* change. Now go back to your work!"

We had been in the new house less than a year when our second child, Dillon, was born. Again I paced the familiar corridor of the Mater Dei Maternity Hospital, and again I welcomed the gynaecologist impatiently as he arrived at the labour ward too coolly for my comfort. With Dillon's birth I got into a routine for our future stays at the Mater Dei. Wendy would nudge me awake (it always seemed to happen at night) and dress while I carried the prepared suitcase to the car. Then we would drive as gently as possible to the Mater Dei, and wait in a private ward for the intervals between contractions to decrease. I would have my shaving-kit, a book to read and spare cigarettes, until Wendy indicated that it was time to head for the labour ward. While the nuns prepared her I would await the gynaecologist, then sit at the labour bed holding her hand and shushing her bad language during the worst pains.

During my period of disfavour at the *Dispatch*, which lasted about a year, I was given only junior routines to do. It seemed as if McPherson wanted me demoralized or provoked into leaving the paper, and now that Ted had the "front-runner" position McPherson started making things awkward for him too. What Ted and I didn't know in our innocence in those days was that we were both pawns in a power-play going on upstairs in the boardroom. Later, when I became a director myself, I heard the whole story.

On the day before Barber had called me into his office for the dramatic Bible-swearing ritual, some directors had raised the question of the grooming of a future editor and deputy in preparation for both Barber's and McPherson's retirement. Barber, who had no intention of retiring, had nominated Ted Holliday for the future editorship, and McPherson, who had no intention of retiring either, had suggested McFall. McFall was anathema to Barber and Holliday was anathema to McPherson, so when the new director, Frank Streek, suggested me McPherson had seen this as a way of shutting out Holliday and had backed me also, being confident that I was too "dangerous" politically and too adventurous journalistically to last the course without slipping up. But when McPherson saw, as he felt, that I was becoming a real threat to his plans and hadn't got into serious political trouble in the press gallery, he started bringing up repeated complaints about my immaturity and lack of judgement in running the daily column; and although Frank Streek had seen through this and defended me, Barber had capitulated to McPherson because he also felt I was getting too close to his job too quickly for comfort. Then when Ted got his chance McPherson turned his attention to whittling away at him, so that the final field would be clear for himself and his favourite McFall. George Farr seemed to have been left out of all these machinations entirely.

Clearly we had all underestimated the quiet, scholarly Murray McPherson. He was an enigmatic personality. Tall and distinguished-looking and in his early sixties, he had wavy grey hair and the stooped posture of Rex Harrison. While fairly liberal in his own views, he was under the influence of friends who were highly conservative in the city's business community. He wasn't a strong character, and Barber's personality overwhelmed him. Although he was on the board of directors, like Barber, he was always deferential to him and seemed intimidated by him.

One day in 1964 McPherson saw a chance to strike at Barber and he took it. Barber had gone on a monumental binge the night before and was so drunk by midday that he could barely stand. McPherson telephoned the Chairman, Denis Ross-Thompson, who had taken the afternoon off and was about to leave home for the golf course. For Ross-Thompson, who had put up with Barber's inebriate lapses for twenty-seven years, this was too much. Normally an easy-going man, he could stand disruption of almost any element of his life except his golf and trout-fishing, and while he had often turned a blind eye to Barber's nocturnal booze-ups this midday lapse was the last straw. He retired Barber on the spot, and Murray McPherson was appointed editor. .

By this time, thanks to McPherson's tactics and Barber's weakness, Ted Holliday was in a sort of limbo and it had been made clear that neither he nor George Farr would succeed McPherson. Since I was only prepared to stay on under the post-McPherson editorship of Holliday or Farr, and both were now out of the running, I made plans to leave. I had had an approach to join the staff of the *Rand Daily Mail*, and since I admired Lawrence Gandar, the crusading editor of that paper, as much as I had previously admired Barber's crusading approach in former years, I let it be known that I would be receptive to a formal offer from Gandar. I was chatting to George Farr and a couple of other friends in the subs' room when Gandar's letter arrived offering me a highly generous salary of three hundred rands a month (£150) plus entertainment allowance plus car allowance, to be the *Rand Daily Mail*'s man in the Transkei. I was excited. The Transkei was in the early stages of "self-rule" in terms of the "homelands" policy, and this would be a challenging assignment, apart from the fact that Wendy and I would both feel at home in the Transkei. I showed the others and they congratulated me as I sat down, typed out my resignation and took it in to Murray McPherson. McPherson could scarcely conceal his pleasure at my resignation. "We're sorry to lose you, but obviously it's a great step forward for you," he said. "What a salary! What an offer! You couldn't turn it down."

I went to Frank Streek's office to say goodbye and to thank him for his kind words on my behalf at the time of my demotion. I explained about Gandar's offer and said it was too good to turn down. "I don't blame you," he said grimly, shaking hands. "You've heard, I suppose, that I wanted you to be editor here eventually, but the others prevailed. Good luck to you." I returned to the subs' room and was discussing my new job with George Farr when I got a summons to the boardroom up on the top floor. I'd never been in that august chamber and wondered what was up. The Chairman, Denis Ross-Thompson, was there with Frank Streek, grim-faced, on one side and Murray McPherson, red-faced, on the other.

Ross-Thompson said: "Mr Woods, I understand you're leaving us." I told him about the *Rand Daily Mail* offer and said I had taken it on its merits, not out of any special wish to leave the *Dispatch*, and that the prospect of the assignment was exciting to me. "Well," he said, "we'd like to keep you here. What would keep you here? We wouldn't like to lose you, you know." I glanced at Murray McPherson, who was looking down at the floor with knitted brow. "But I've already resigned, and the staff know it. And Mr McPherson's accepted my resignation," I said. "Well, I thought it was irrevocable," said McPherson. "Your mind seemed made up."

Frank Streek said in a sharp voice, glaring at McPherson: "I've made it plain to the Chairman that I believe we need you here to make more of this paper," he said. "Someone's got to succeed Murray as editor, and there's been all sorts of talk of Holliday or Farr or McFall but as far as I'm concerned none of them is suitable. We need a man who can put extra vigour into the paper." He looked directly at Ross-Thompson and said: "If that man isn't Donald Woods I will reconsider my own position here." It seemed incredible. Here I was in the board-room, seeing a director of the paper putting his own job and career on the line for me, for someone he'd hardly exchanged a few dozen words with in his life. Streek's stance was doubly courageous in that he was the newest director and the youngest —he was then barely forty—although he had already won the regard of other directors with his financial acumen and his rejuvenation of several aspects of the company's operations. His gamble worked. Ross-Thompson, who obviously thought highly of him, barked half-humorously: "Now don't *you* talk about leaving!" He then turned to me, ignoring McPherson. "What if we pay you four hundred rands a month and appoint you as Murray's deputy, making it clear that you'll succeed him when he retires?"

My heart leapt at the thought, but I said with what I hoped was outward calm: "Yes, of course I'd like to stay on those conditions, but not on any further kind of trial or if there is any ambiguity about my position." Murray frowned even more deeply as I added: "There's one other thing—we'd have to agree now on a strict adherence to the *Dispatch*'s present anti-apartheid policy, with no wavering of any kind." I had in mind McPherson's conservative friends. Ross-Thompson re-plied positively: "There'll be no change in policy. It's been laid down and agreed for years and we'll stick to it. Eh, Murray?" "Of course we'll stick to our policy," said Mc-Pherson. I went on: "The next thing is does Mr McPherson feel he can work well with me? We're different characters, with different styles of approach, and there would have to be complete trust between us for consistency of approach." Mc-Pherson said: "Oh yes, I don't see why we shouldn't work well together. I've never had anything personal against you, al-though I *have* felt you lacked a certain maturity. You *are* young, you know." He smiled disarmingly. I was then thirty years old and conceded the point, accepting his olive branch.

We all shook hands on the deal, and in Frank Streek's office afterwards I thanked him for risking his neck for me. He grinned broadly and ran his finger round his collar before simulating a mopping of his brow. "Whew! That was quite a meeting! Well, now it's up to us. We'll make something of this paper, you'll see!"

Frank Streek was a complex man. Raised in Zululand, he had fought in World War II as a teenager, and seen action in Ethiopia against the Italians and in the Sahara against the Germans. Because of the war, and because his parents couldn't afford to send him to university, he had no institutional education beyond high school, but while working as a civil servant in Natal he put himself through several diploma courses, then through private study by correspondence he gained a B. Comm., and he went on to get his Master's degree and finally a doctorate—all by private study. He joined the Maritzburg newspaper, the *Natal Witness*, as an accountant, and was instrumental in modernizing its plant and methods. Then he saw an advertisement for the secretaryship of the *Daily Dispatch* and applied for and got the appointment. Within a few years of joining the company he had achieved impressive things, investigating and reforming department after department and putting younger men in charge with new ideas and bigger incentives. As head of the advertisement department he installed a young man named Terry Briceland who had intelligence and energy, and between the two of them they tripled the *Dispatch* advertising revenue within barely a year.

Terry, Frank and I became close friends, and we were to share many experiences. Shortly after my appointment as deputy to McPherson the three of us took a long trip to Central Africa. Frank felt we should get to know black-ruled Africa, and we set off in his car on the five-thousand-mile journey through Rhodesia, Malawi, Zambia and Mozambique. The strangest experience we had on the trip was in Mozambique, near Tete. We were on the way to Malawi to attend the independence celebrations there, and by nightfall I was feeling hungry and sleepy, but in spite of signs by the roadside saying that thirty miles ahead was a comfortable hotel with mosquito netting and fine food, Terry and Frank insisted on pitching a tent in the bush. I said it was crazy. We were in the wildest part of the bush, none of us spoke the local tribal language, there was a guerilla war on and we were unarmed. But Frank and Terry, keen outdoorsmen, scoffed at these fears and put up the tent as chirpy as boy scouts. I was sullen and refused to help them with it, or with the cooking, but they just laughed and went ahead. There being nothing else to do in the heart of the Mozambique bush at night, we went to bed, and I spent some time reminding them that the hard ground they were sleeping on could have been a comfortable mattress in an air-conditioned hotel an hour away.

They were both soon asleep, and I lay awake for at least an hour, then heard the beat of a tom-tom start up fairly close by. Tom-toms weren't a feature of our part of Africa down south, but we were now in Central Africa, and the sound was far more menacing in reality than in the movies. It was a monotone, steady beat which went on for ten minutes, then was joined from a different direction by a second tom-tom playing a fast two-tone beat. These went on and on for more than half-an-hour, and I wondered whether the drummers were tireless or whether they worked in shifts. Then, alarmingly, a third tom-tom burst into sound much closer to our tent and with a more complex rhythm pattern than the first two. My imagination ran riot and I visualized the signal: "I see a tent. It belongs to white men. They are asleep in the tent. They have left a fire glowing outside it. I see suitcases standing by the tent in the firelight. There is also a car." And I imagined the reply: "Ah, yes! I too see the tent of the foolish white men. They are surely asleep. Let us take the suitcases." Then the response to this: "Yes, in fact let's kill them."

I woke Frank and Terry. "Listen!" I said. They listened, then Terry said: "Tom-toms. Three of them. Wish they'd shut up," and went back to sleep. Frank grunted: "Yah," and also went back to sleep. I woke them up again. "Listen, what makes you think we're safe here? This is Central Africa, you silly buggers, and I've got a family to consider." Frank answered: "Don't worry, we've also got families. Go to sleep." I lay still for a while. Then two more tom-toms joined the first three. I said: "*Five* bloody tom-toms now—maybe they're calling up every spear-thrower in the area for a mass attack." "What?" Frank exclaimed. "Is this the fearless, crusading journalist we once knew? Are you scared of blacks?" I said: "You're bloody right I'm scared, and if you two aren't, you're crazy. This isn't my safe old Bomvanaland or your safe old

Zululand—we're thousands of miles from there now." But they were more amused than concerned, and we argued on sporadically until I fell asleep. In the morning they had a great time at my expense, giving exclamations of surprise that we were alive and unscathed, and from that time the incident was referred to in *Dispatch* circles as "the night of the five tom-toms".

We drove a long way the next day, and that part of Africa looked very different from our southern part. Even the terrain and the vegetation looked foreign. Coming out of the wildness and bush of central Mozambique into the eastern part was a contrast again, like driving into Europe, then as we neared the Malawi border the scenery became lush and spectacular. I was bowled over by the beauty of Malawi. It was as if the green hills and craggy mountains of Scotland had been transplanted into Central Africa, and Lake Malawi, formerly Lake Nyasa, 450 miles long by about 50 miles wide and one of the deepest in the world, was like a bright blue mirror in the green mountains.

We drove into Blantyre and checked into the press quarters where representatives of every major newspaper in the world had arrived to cover the Malawi independence ceremonies. Among the journalists were two Russians, one from *Pravda* and one from *Isvestia*. Driving the three miles from the press hotel to the hall where Dr Hastings Kamuzu Banda, President of Malawi, was to give a press conference, we saw these two Russians walking and offered them a lift. As they got in I said to the tall one, who spoke good English: "If our government knew we were giving a lift to Russians we'd be imprisoned." He said promptly: "Hah! If *our* government knew we were *accepting* it we'd be *executed*!"

Banda struck us as a megalomanic autocrat, with a personality unrepresentative of the national character of Malawians, who seemed to be the friendliest people in the world. There was a surrealistic air about the independence lunch, with Prince Philip sitting next to President Banda as the band of the Malawi Rifles played "Regular Royal Queen" from *The Gondoliers*. Britain was handing over yet another chunk of empire—this time to the strains of Gilbert and Sullivan played expertly by black bandsmen in white gloves in the heat of Central Africa. At midnight in the independence stadium the same musicians gave us Purcell's "Trumpet Voluntary". After the week's ceremonies were over Frank, Terry and I stayed in a beachside lodge at Salima on the lakeshore, and at night as the surf pounded from the wind it was hard to believe we were in Central Africa deep inland, rather than on the shores of the ocean at home thousands of miles to the south. The sounds were identical. The next day we swam in the lake, body-surfing in the waves, and the far shore was out of sight beyond the horizon.

At first it felt strange working closely with Murray McPherson, but we got on increasingly well after discovering we had mutual interests in cricket and music, and in all the time we worked together there was only one major clash between us. I had come in on a Saturday to find he'd gone off for the weekend, having written an editorial sympathetic to the South Africa Foundation, a pet project of his right-wing friends and neighbours. The South Africa Foundation was a whitewash operation founded to project what was called a "positive image" of South Africa to the world, which meant it sought to counteract the image of South Africa as an unjust apartheid state. It also aimed to encourage investment from abroad. The *Dispatch*, under Barber, had consistently opposed the Foundation as an ally of the Government's propaganda effort, and had maintained that its efforts helped to preserve apartheid. One of the Foundation's leading spokesmen in the city, a businessman who was friendly with Murray, had stopped me outside the building one day and said: "Now that Murray McPherson is editor we'll soon have the *Dispatch* backing the Foundation." And here was Mc-Pherson's editorial, saying that perhaps the Foundation had been unfairly judged and that perhaps it deserved support for its "more positive" aims.

I went to Denis Ross-Thompson's office, where he and I chatted about golf, then I went back to McPherson's office, tore up his editorial and wrote one attacking the Foundation. On the Monday he called me into his office. I had never seen him so angry. His face was flushed, and when he spoke his voice was hoarse with rage. "How *dare* you change my editorial! How *dare* you! I *am* the editor, you know!" I said: "Oh, I talked to Denis Ross-Thompson on Saturday morning—you weren't here so I couldn't talk to you—then I rewrote it because it

didn't accord with our policy." McPherson gaped. "You—
you talked to the *Chairman* . . ." "Yes," I said. "I talked to him
and then I changed the leader." I didn't say that only golf had
been discussed, but I knew my Murray, and he never said another word about the matter. And he never tried to write a
right-wing editorial again.

Thanks to Frank Streek's managerial skills several aspects of
the paper were considerably improved under McPherson's
editorship, especially the photographic section, and an extra
edition was introduced. Then a building committee was set up
and I was commissioned to submit ideas for a re-structuring of
all editorial accommodation. This was long overdue, because
our editorial workers were spread over three floors and it was
feasible with some rearrangement to bring them all on to one
floor. After many consultations with architects and builders
I submitted a plan which Frank described as over-ambitious
and too costly, but which he nevertheless backed, to take over
the whole of the third level of the building for the editorial
department. It meant moving the process engravers, the works
canteen and the machine-storage rooms off the floor, knocking
big windows into the wall overlooking the ocean to let in lots of
light, and completely rebuilding that floor as a modern newsroom to plans based on work-flow studies. I was also given
McPherson's approval for the plan and we went ahead. It
meant a lot of temporary inconvenience to the journalists and
other workers because it involved hammering, sawing and construction work going on about them as they typed, the idea
being to get it finished as soon as possible. The architects and
builders estimated it would take eight to ten months, but by
rigging up temporary lights for night construction work and by
throwing in different shifts of carpenters and masons round the
clock, day and night, we managed to finish the entire job in
under three months.

During this time Murray McPherson's sight had begun to
deteriorate alarmingly. He had had eye trouble for years, but
now it got so bad that he became almost totally blind. It was
pathetic to see a man to whom reading meant so much turning
to ever-stronger lenses so that he could read even normal print.
Eventually he was wearing spectacles with projection-lenses an
inch thick. His wife, Nell, took to coming into the office to read

all his correspondence to him; at other times his secretary would, or if she was busy typing I took on the job and went through all his papers for him. In the circumstances his sense of humour was amazing. One morning during our building operations he groped his way cautiously to my office and said with a smile: "You might have warned me that you switched the men's and women's toilets around last night in your building plans—a moment ago I bumped into Miss Johnston in what I recall as the men's lavatory!" I apologized, and didn't point out that there were large signs on the toilet doors proclaiming the change. Then, with a straight face, he added: "I suppose if I'd encountered her in a state of undress the tactful thing would have been for me to say—I beg your pardon, *sir!*"

Some members of the staff couldn't handle Murray's condition, hard though they tried. And sometimes we had to do some fast thinking. On one occasion Murray, conducting the editorial conference, thought the all-important conference list was a scrap of waste paper, crumpled it up and threw it into his wastebasket. Then he said: "Right—now will someone read the conference list?" It was awkward. None of us wanted to tell him he'd just thrown it away. Then the news editor, Fred Croney, tiptoed silently to the wastebasket where he retrieved the list, tiptoed back to his conference seat and coughed loudly to cover the sound of uncrumpling it.

Most of the time, however, we managed, and we could have managed indefinitely no matter how bad his sight became, because all the staff were prepared to help. He was more popular in his brave response to the onset of blindness than he had been before. But then he had a series of serious heart attacks, and was in hospital for a long time. I used to visit him in hospital, and read him the cricket reports, but his morale was low and he died soon after. I heard of his death as I was walking into the hospital one day—Monsignor John O'Keeffe, a remarkable old Irish priest whose ministry was the hospital and who had the manner of Barry Fitzgerald, stopped me and said: "I gave the last rites to your friend McPherson." I said: "Thanks, Monsignor. Actually I think Murray was Anglican or Presbyterian, I'm not sure which." "Aah sure, who cares?" said the old Monsignor, gesturing vaguely at the sky. "They can sort it all out up there."

CHAPTER NINE

I WAS APPOINTED editor of the *Daily Dispatch* at the beginning of 1965, and when the initial exhilaration waned I realized the challenges facing me were more complex than those faced by editors in most parts of the country. The *Dispatch* circulated in an area that included two of the black homelands which the Government regarded as crucial to the apartheid policy of territorial segregation, the Transkei and the Ciskei, and the Afrikaner Nationalists were ultra-sensitive about material published in this region. The homelands policy involved the creation by the Afrikaner Nationalists of nine autonomous regions based on ethnic sub-groups among the blacks, an idea the blacks didn't want and had never been polled on for their opinion. It set aside barely thirteen per cent of the nation's territory for the black majority, reserving eighty-seven per cent for the white minority. The "white" territory included the best agricultural and mineral land, the gold and diamond mines and all the major cities, and the homelands were scattered about the perimeter of the country, far from the main urban areas.

The Afrikaner Nationalist theory was based on arithmetic and wishful thinking—if they could fragment the black majority of twenty-five million into groups no bigger than five million, like the Zulus and the Xhosas, with smaller groups like the Tswanas, Vendas and Sothos, they hoped to prevent general black unity. And by assigning each group to one of these perimeter homelands they thought they had the classic formula of divide and rule. According to this theory all blacks who could be moved to the homelands would be moved, and the remainder, needed as workers in the white economy, would be regarded as foreign labourers whose civil rights, like the vote, could only be exercised in regard to the distant homeland —even if they'd never seen it. The last thing the government wanted circulating in such homelands was a newspaper like the *Dispatch*, which constantly exposed the true nature of "geographic apartheid", so I could be sure that the eyes of the

Government would be on every editorial and report in the paper.

The Government had at its disposal more than twenty statutes governing what could be published in newspapers, and several of these laws empowered them to close down any newspaper arbitrarily, without court proceedings, and to jail or ban any editor without explanation. The only protection newspapers had was the Government's reluctance to endanger its trade and diplomatic links with America and Britain, and its consequent reluctance to seem to be acting extra-legally against the press. But this meant that editors had to be sure of their law, and know all the complexities of the statutory powers of the State affecting newspaper publication. Horace Flather, retired editor of the Johannesburg *Star*, said editing a newspaper in South Africa was like "walking blindfold across a minefield", and when I took over the editorship of the *Dispatch* I pricked as many little holes in the blindfold as I could, by studying every aspect of press legislation from all conceivable angles.

Then there was the question of local white opinion. The city of East London was one of the most conservative white centres in the country, and most of its white citizens resented any criticism of apartheid. Because of my anti-apartheid articles I had gained many enemies among the local whites, particularly in business circles and among members of the local establishment who ran industrial and commercial concerns.

And there was my age. At thirty-one I was regarded by some members of our board of directors, who were also members of the city establishment, as too young for the job, as well as being politically "dangerous". And finally, I had been appointed over the heads of dozens of *Dispatch* journalists senior to me in experience or length of service with the paper. For all these reasons my performance would be closely watched from all sides, and any mistake would be used to try to get me out of the editorship.

On the credit side Frank Streek, now appointed general manager, had taken a firm grip on the management side of the newspaper and gave me a free hand on all editorial matters while assuring me of protection from boardroom pressures. His own stature on the board was enhanced by his remarkable results in increasing the company's profits. He was the most energetic man I ever met, and seemed to work round the clock, turning his attention to every detail written down on his list of priorities. He and Terry Briceland completely reorganized the paper's distribution system. Previously the *Dispatch*, like all other major South African newspapers, had been distributed by a national company called Central News Agency, but Frank and Terry dropped the Agency completely, bought us our own fleet of vans, and enabled us to reach areas as far as three hundred miles away with the paper before breakfast. To take advantage of this we introduced an earlier first edition and experienced our first major circulation increase. But to exploit the system fully I had to restructure the editorial content and methods, and I took Frank Streek's advice and did nothing in the first weeks but watch operations and fill a notebook with ideas. My main concern was simply to produce a paper without disastrous items in it. I used to have nightmares about headline errors or printing errors in prominent parts of the paper, like sub-editors slipping obscene words into headlines. All I wanted at first was that several weeks should go by without the older directors thinking they had made a ghastly mistake in appointing me.

Then I considered staff quality. Most of the editorial executives were good, but five of the senior men, three reporters and two sub-editors, were either incapable of or simply not interested in helping to make the *Dispatch* a better paper, and I persuaded them to transfer elsewhere. They were replaced by men I recruited from other papers and tested personally, with preference given to those who had had overseas experience including a spell on Fleet Street. This gave us a strong sub-editing staff and some good all-round reporters who could use a camera.

Soon after my appointment I told Frank Streek I wanted to bring my old Cardiff boss, Glyn Williams, on to the staff. I said that we would have to offer him at least double what he was getting in Cardiff, and would have to fly him out first to form a judgement on the spot. Frank agreed, saying: "If he's as good as you say he is—get him." Glyn Williams, then in his thirties, flew out to spend about ten days with us on the paper, returned to confer with his wife, and accepted the appointment as night editor. Throughout my twelve years as editor he was to prove a major asset to the paper. Before he left Cardiff I cabled him: "Bring your best design sub-editor at an appropriate salary", and he hired for us a talented page-layout man named Phil Jones, who was also to play a major part in the improvement of the paper.

My two assistant editors were George Farr and Ted Holliday, and with them, Fred Croney and Glyn Williams as the staff core we began a programme to improve the content of the paper. Like many English-language papers in South Africa at that time, the *Daily Dispatch* was patterned on the British press. This was a strength and a weakness. It was a strength in that the best British papers had fine qualities but it was a weakness in that the tone of these papers often seemed too "English", and certainly too "white", in orientation for newspapers on the continent of Africa. Although Barber's editorials had been strongly anti-racial, the *Dispatch* news and feature pages had reflected an exclusively white society most of the time. With Frank Streek's encouragement—he increased the editorial budget substantially for the purpose—we started recruiting experienced black journalists and training black cub reporters in order to turn the *Dispatch* from a "white" newspaper into a non-racial one in content as well as editorial stance. Over the next few years the staff complement changed from an all-white newsroom to one which eventually had about as many black journalists as white ones. Although other newspapers in the country tended to disparage this as "bleeding heart liberalism", especially when we became the first daily newspaper in the country to have black sub-editors and editorial executives, some of them started to emulate our programme several years later.

Changing the racial content of the newspaper columns was harder than changing the racial complexion of the staff. When we started putting pictures of blacks in the news pages there was an immediate and angry response from many white readers, especially in the rural farming community, and substantial numbers started cancelling their subscriptions. This put Terry Briceland on the spot. Terry, though staunchly liberal in his personal views, was in the hot seat as circulation man, and he and his staff caught the full force of the reaction.

We in the editorial department also felt the onslaught in telephone threats, bomb threats and complaints that we were turning the *Dispatch* into a "Kaffir paper". The protests became worse when we began to "integrate" our sports pages, but the one page we shrank for months from integrating was our "weddings" page. We were, in fact, scared stiff of putting the first black couple in among all the white couples whose fond parents used to buy extra copies to send to doting relatives elsewhere. Frank was with me on the day we first planned a black wedding picture right in the middle of the page. We hid our nervousness in jokes—Frank suggesting facetiously that the process-engravers might acid the plate more severely to lighten the skin-colour of the couple—and with cowardly cunning we began the integration of the page with a "coloured couple". As the howls of rage from the whites started dying down the faces on the page became blacker and blacker, until there were more black faces than white on it.

Then Terry started tackling a problem we hadn't thought of —the "smalls" advertisements in the classified section. Some of these advertisments were highly offensive, such as the offering for sale of "Reliable watchdogs—trained to bite Natives". The most offensive ones were easy to deal with—we just threw them out. But many advertisements at that time used words like "Natives" as a matter of course, and many advertisers, when told this had to be changed to "Africans", preferred to withdraw the advertisements rather than comply. One major advertiser phoned me to say that unless the paper stopped my editorials he would withdraw his advertisements, and as he represented one of the biggest advertising accounts it was more with bravado than conviction that I told him: "We don't want your bloody advertisements anyway." This sort of talk caused Terry to clutch his head, but Frank used to manage somehow to comfort him and encourage me at the same time.

I wrote to the United States Information Service for as many picture-features as they could let me have of black success stories in the U.S., and they responded generously. For years our editorial and feature pages ran splendid prints and articles on black Americans like Carl Stokes, Martin Luther King, Muhammed Ali, Willie Mays and Roy Wilkins, and these noticeably raised the morale of our black readers, as could be seen from our correspondence columns. The protests of the white community reached a peak in that first year of my editorship, and some of our directors grew concerned at the drop in readers and advertising revenue, but Frank Streek, Terry and I dug in our heels, and Denis Ross-Thompson as Chairman trusted Frank's judgement, so we carried on turning the *Dispatch* into a more accurate reflection of our multi-racial South African society.

Then began an interesting development. Our "lost" readers and advertisers gradually returned, their sense of shock apparently exhausted. One other paper, the Johannesburg *Rand Daily Mail* under the editorship of Lawrence Gandar, which also became more multi-racial in content as well as in ideology, was having the same experience. The *Mail* had been the first South African paper to follow the *Dispatch* in calling "Natives" Africans, and some years later, when we on the *Dispatch* changed "Africans" to the then preferred term of "blacks", the *Mail* was again first to follow suit.

Our first black reporters were hounded by the Security Police. One, Gordon Qumza, was jailed without charge for three months before being released. When I protested to the Security Police one of them said Qumza was a Communist and handed me a batch of crank pamphlets claiming that most "liberals and integrationists" were Communists. When I said: "I'm a liberal. I'm an integrationist. Does that make me a Communist?" he replied that I might not be one but that I was being "used by the Communists". When they finally released Gordon, having discovered that his attendance at what they thought was a prohibited meeting of the African National Congress was actually attendance at a black rugby association meeting, he couldn't even sue for wrongful arrest because the State was indemnified by parliament against detentions in terms of the very law Vorster had told me he wouldn't use "irresponsibly" . . .

Perhaps out of sheepishness at the stupidity of their error, they never hounded Gordon again. Not that he would have been daunted—he was the toughest reporter on the staff. In fact, Gordon and two other black reporters got us our first big scoop on "transit camps". The Government were moving "surplus" blacks, those in "white" urban areas without work or State permission to seek work, to the homelands without regard to whether there were homes or jobs for them there. We heard they were being dumped in remote areas, and that the Government, in its haste to get them out of the cities, was depositing entire families in tent towns or shantytowns far from main roads or cities so that they couldn't be seen. These places were euphemistically called "transit camps", and we learnt that at least three were in our area—Dimbaza, Sada and Ilinge. Gordon and his two colleagues sniffed out these places, wearing tribal blankets over their clothes and carrying press cameras under the blankets, and the *Dispatch* splashed an exposé which triggered off a parliamentary debate and a national controversy. We concentrated mainly on Dimbaza, using it as a symbol of the others, and it was soon known internationally as yet another apartheid affront to humanity. The infant mortality rate there was appalling, and a friend of mine from a Fleet Street newspaper, a tough reporter, was reduced to tears at the sight of the hundreds of tiny graves with dolls and feeding bottles left by the parents as their last token of identity. This was later high-lighted in the film *Last Grave at Dimbaza*, which had a worldwide showing.

The *Dispatch* started coming under attack by the state-controlled South African Broadcasting Corporation, which had an insidious daily propaganda programme called "Survey on Current Affairs". The accusation against us was that we were giving the country a bad name overseas and inciting blacks to hate the white Government. Broad hints were aired that the paper should be closed down in the national interest. This was ironical, because at about this time East London's small Afrikaans community—mostly strongly pro-Government—was commending us for being the first English-language newspaper to promote the Afrikaans language. Conscious that most English-speaking South Africans were weak in the language, we ran articles in Afrikaans in the paper, including instruction courses in it, and gave prominence to Afrikaans cultural affairs and campaigns. We promoted an "Afrikaans-speaking week" in the city and I addressed a number of meetings in Afrikaans, getting these campaigns backed by Rotary, Lions and other English-language associations.

We had taken several Afrikaners on to the staff as reporters, most notably a senior journalist by the name of Jac van Wyk whom I talked into leaving the *Oosterlig* (*Eastern Light*) newspaper. Jac told me soon afterwards that he was happy on the paper except for one thing—that the flag flying over our building was the Union Jack. I agreed with him. The Chairman, Denis Ross-Thompson, felt strongly that the Union Jack should continue to fly over the building because it had been there for a hundred years since the days of British rule and the era of his uncle, Sir Charles Crewe, who had owned the *Dispatch*. The more anti-British whites complained about it, the more stubborn Barber had become about stating in editorials that the flag would remain. Ross-Thompson wasn't as truculent as Barber about the reason for flying the flag, but he was no less determined to keep it there. He saw it as a sort of trust reposed in him by Crewe, to maintain the tradition. I felt it was a mistake, strategically and in principle. It blurred our essential message of racial reconciliation and it blurred what I wanted to be an indigenous South African image accurately reflecting our multi-racial society. To fly the British flag was therefore irrelevant as well as unwise, the latter because it gave racists an easy excuse to label us as unpatriotic and un-South African. As long as they could attack us for unpatriotically flying a foreign flag they could avoid confronting the main issue of race.

Frank Streek was away doing a course at Harvard Business School at the time, so Terry Briceland and I went to see Denis Ross-Thompson to ask him to have the Union Jack taken down. We went into his office confident we could appeal to his reason, and slunk out of it like two schoolboys chastened by the headmaster. As we sat down he greeted us warmly in his usual friendly fashion, saying: "What can I do for you?" I said: "Well, Mr Ross-Thompson, it's about the flag." His face turned dark red and he barked abruptly: "What flag?" Terry and I exchanged lightning sidelong glances. These were deep waters. I said, in a less certain voice: "The, ah, Union Jack . . ." Although he remained seated Ross-Thompson appeared to snap to attention behind his desk and said angrily: "That flag flies over this building as long as I'm here—and that's the end of the matter!" Terry and I went into an unrehearsed and craven backtrack, babbling that of course it should remain, but as there were *two* flagpoles couldn't the South African flag be flown as well . . . ? "All right," said Ross-Thompson. "As long as the Union Jack remains I don't care what you fly on the other flagpole. You can fly the Jolly Roger for all I care. But remember that the Union Jack stays! Sir Charles Crewe would turn in his grave if that ever came down."

And so the two flags flew side by side, and when Frank Streek returned he roared with laughter on hearing of our abject defeat. But he agreed with us that it would be better to have no flag over the building at all, and when he judged the time to be ripe he spoke to Ross-Thompson about it himself. Ross-Thompson's regard for Frank's judgement was so high that he consented to the removal of the flags, and I called Jac van Wyk into the office and gave him the following instructions: "I want both those bloody flags removed and both flagpoles as well. You are to cut the flagpoles down personally, and secretly, at midnight, so that the *Oosterlig* can't get a picture." Jac's eyes lit up at the thought that he, an Afrikaner, would have the honour of lowering the Union Jack.

I told him to report to me after the job was completed, no matter how late it was, and that night before setting off he called at my house for a ceremonial brandy. He was dressed in tennis shirt, khaki shorts and tennis shoes, and to reduce noise in the interests of stealth he had a handsaw instead of an electric saw. The task he thought would take him half-an-hour took nearly four hours, because although the South African flagpole yielded up the ghost easily enough he found when he got to the Union Jack that its flagpole was made of hardwood— of almost the same toughness as ironwood. And when he arrived at my house for another ceremonial brandy at 4 a.m. after he had finished the job his hands were painfully calloused and tears of fatigue mingled with tears of joy in his eyes. "*Liewe* Jesus," he said. "I never thought the British Empire would die so hard."

I knew the flag issue meant a lot to Afrikaners, who ever since the Boer War had wanted a return to the old Vierkleur (four-colour) flag of the republic. I wrote an editorial saying this should be done since it meant so much to Afrikaners and so little to the rest of us in the country, and received a flood of grateful telegrams and letters from Afrikaner Nationalists. I was being called on to make a number of speeches at the time, at universities and associations such as chambers of commerce, and to fly a debating kite I suggested that the Afrikaner Nationalists should consider a more radical extension of their homelands plan by partitioning the country to enable the predominantly English-speaking whites of Natal and the Eastern Cape to split off from the Orange Free State, Transvaal and the rest of the Cape and live in what could then be a black-ruled half of the country. This was given sensational banner treatment in the Afrikaans newspapers and regarded as an enterprising suggestion, but neither the Vierkleur idea nor the partition idea was effected by the Afrikaner Nationalists—the first because they thought most English-speaking whites would object (they wouldn't have) and the second because they *knew* most English-speaking whites would object (they certainly would have—and many wanted to lynch me for suggesting that "our" areas should come under black rule).

Although my suggestion was a kite-flyer there was a basis of seriousness to it. National debate on apartheid was sterile, and I believed such a suggestion might provoke imaginative response. The concept of the entire Eastern Cape and all of Natal being able to join up with Lesotho and Swaziland meant a much bigger slice of the territory out of Afrikaner Nationalist hands, and I thought it might appeal to them to get rid of most of the "English" whites and most of the blacks at once—while we could get rid of apartheid and seek real progress. I think what turned the Afrikaner Nationalists off the idea finally was the thought of losing three of the country's four main ports—Port Elizabeth, Durban and East London. My argument was that they would lose the lot one day anyway.

While wooing Afrikaners culturally and slamming apartheid daily in editorials, we kept expanding our coverage of matters of special interest to blacks and tried an experiment which had an interesting conclusion; we introduced a third edition specifically for the overwhelmingly black areas of the region, and this edition was nearly a hundred per cent "black" in content. But it was not well received by blacks, and we soon discovered why. We had visits from black community leaders saying they didn't want a "different paper from the whites", and would we please discontinue the daily "black" edition? They agreed there should be some heavily black supplement section in the paper occasionally for specifically black interest, but wanted the main body of the paper to continue as it had before, "integrated" the same for blacks and whites. We complied, dropping the third edition and developing instead a weekly supplement called *Indaba* (*News*), with half the material in English and half in Xhosa. This gave us what appeared to be the best formula for all concerned, and we improved the paper in a number of other ways, buying more international services and subscribing to the additional morning newspaper pool of pictures, news and features.

Then we had a real stroke of good luck. There was a sudden upsurge in advertising demand for the newly discovered "black" buyership, and the things we had done for ideological reasons began to bring us benefits in advertising revenue. Since my appointment as editor our circulation of 21,000 had slumped to below 18,000, but subsequently it picked up and was to reach and remain steady at 33,000. The increased business from the advertising agencies came because detailed circulation surveys showed we had a high and growing proportion of black readers. In time we reached a stage where we had more black readers than white, and in view of the advertising benefits our "integration" of the newspaper and increasing emphasis on coverage of the black community was no longer seen by some directors as a liability but as a commercial asset.

Frank Streek commissioned a survey from a circulation specialist, Professor James Irving of Rhodes University. A Scot who had performed the first such survey for the *Manchester Guardian*, he began a poll designed to discover at what point "readership—newspaper tension" became counter-productive. The theory was that a high degree of tension or disagreement between a newspaper and many of its readers in regard to editorial policy was a good thing for circulation, on the basis that a husband and wife who never disagreed would soon be bored with each other, but that there had to be a high level of respect for the newspaper's integrity and impartiality in hard news coverage and there was a cut-off point beyond which readers would boycott the paper in damaging numbers. The survey also showed how a newspaper in such a position could best defend itself and its unpopular editorial stance.

The results of Professor Irving's survey were illuminating.

Predictably, more than ninety per cent of our white readers resented our liberal policy on race and all our black readers approved of it, but the overwhelming majority of white readers respected the objectivity of our news columns and regarded the *Dispatch* as an honest paper which would not, for example, suppress news at the request of influential people. And a high proportion of readers, more than twelve per cent, read all the editorials, which contrasted with the national average for other newspapers of three per cent. The message was that you could get away with highly unpopular editorials attacking apartheid totally, provided no taint of comment or slanting crept into news columns. We tried to follow the dictum of the famous editor of the *Manchester Guardian*, C. P. Scott: "Comment is free; facts are sacred." We tightened up further on sub-editors' guidelines for headline-writing, banning even the faintest suggestion of comment in headlines, and for good measure we also banned direct quote phrases in headlines—not only because they carried the risk of biased emphasis but because they made for lazy headline-writing and looked typographically messy with inverted commas scattered all over the page in large type. We spent months producing an in-house handbook, an updated stylebook covering every aspect of design, grammatical style, policy and newspaper law we thought each member of the *Dispatch* staff should know. One of my first style changes was to call Catholics Catholics—removing the "Roman".

Newspaper law in South Africa was complicated enough, really a sword of Damocles hanging over every editor's head, but you learnt to live with it through experience and instinct. The question of not only *how far* to go in attacking apartheid but *when* was a matter of private judgement for editors only, and I evolved a greater "feel" for it as the years went by. Although nearly all our editorials were attacks on various aspects of apartheid and appeals to reason for a rejection of it, I often chose Saturday mornings for the most strongly worded editorials on the most delicate aspects of it, because I knew that the key members of the cabinet had farms in the country to which they liked to retire for the weekend, and instant reaction by them to such an editorial would have meant travelling all the way back to Pretoria, or summoning secretaries at great inconvenience. The theory was that by Monday their tempers would have cooled or their attention been diverted by something in the Sunday papers. Another good time for particularly strong attacks on apartheid was during national rejoicing over a Springbok victory against New Zealand or a Gary Player win in the Masters at Augusta. At such times the Afrikaner Nationalists were so exultant that they tended to be less vicious about criticism than usual. Constantly preoccupied with what they imagined the world, and in particular the Western world, thought of them, they basked in what they saw as the reflected glory of Professor Chris Barnard when he did the first successful human heart transplant, and that was a particularly good time to get in the sharpest jabs.

Not that such tactics escaped their notice. Members of the cabinet got clippings of all critical comment, and several of them threatened from time to time in speeches that I was being "watched" in the expectation that I would "go too far" sooner or later. But there was a certain margin of safety that one could perceive at that time. In spite of all their threats they weren't keen to close down an opposition newspaper because one of the few things they could boast about internationally was South Africa's relatively free press.

There were also threats against the *Dispatch* from other quarters. The Transkei and Ciskei homelands had been provided with "self-rule Governments" by Pretoria, and these Governments, heavily obligated to the Vorster government, did not relish newspaper criticism implying they were collaborators with the apartheid plan. Threats by them to ban the *Dispatch* from sale in their territories were constant down the years and were to increase as time went by. In the case of the Transkei this would have cost us nearly a fifth of our total circulation.

Yet in spite of all these threats and pressures our circulation and our profits kept rising, and Frank Streek made generous amounts of money available for overseas travel and study by staff members. More than twenty of our senior staff men were able to benefit from this, although the Government always delayed granting passports to black staff members until the week before their departure. It was a kind of war of nerves designed to let us know that the State disapproved of our sending black journalists on study trips to America or Britain where they would experience non-apartheid societies.

After his own course at Harvard, Frank Streek sent seven other staff members there, including five directors, and it was on his initiative that the company diversified into fields other than newspaper publishing, as a precaution and reinforcement of our journalism in case the government should try to stifle our political campaign by economic pressure. Frank was determined that the company should be broadly based to withstand such an economic onslaught by right-wing business circles which threatened to shut off advertising revenues. It was at this time that he brought in a brilliant young Johannesburg accountant, thirty-one-year-old Peter Eastwood, as financial director, and he was instrumental in supervising several takeover bids on behalf of the *Dispatch*. Frank, Terry and Peter were the main brains of our financial management, and through their negotiations the *Dispatch* acquired a number of other companies. Their studies revealed a consistent pattern in the history of the country's economy which showed that the construction industry complemented the newspaper industry best in terms of investment compatibility. When construction returns were down press advertising revenues were up, and vice versa, so their diversification programme was mainly into construction and allied industry. They bought control of a building company, a glass factory and paint agency and a large property-holding motor business, as well as properties in areas of probable future urban expansion.

One of our subsidiary companies was a security company, guarding factories and homes at night. We bought it because we saw a probable growth of what Frank cynically called "the fear industry", and when we talked Donald Card into leaving the Security Police to head this business he was only too glad to get out of political work. We recovered our purchase price in the first year, took two more years of profit in spite of paying higher wages than the previous owners, and sold it with him as managing director for more than three times what we had paid for it. Card's organizational know-how and personal reputation had built the business up and he became one of the highest-paid executives in the city, prospering further under the new owners—a multi-national British company. At a parliamentary reception for editors Prime Minister Vorster commented on his defection. "You've taken one of our best security police-men," he said sourly.

My main contribution to the business side of the paper was to accompany Frank to try to buy a small newspaper in Grahamstown. We had bought local weeklies in Uitenhage, Queenstown and King William's Town, and the idea of buying the Grahamstown paper was to complete the circle of local papers in the region which could then act as regional offices of the *Dispatch* for local daily news. But on this occasion we were defeated by tradition. The paper there, *Grocott's Mail*, had been published for about 150 years and had been owned by the Grocott family for generations. The building was Dickensian. You entered through nineteenth-century engraved-glass doors, and the staff looked as if they were out of central casting for an old-time movie. The two bookkeepers, one eighty-one years old and the other ninety, sat on high stools at raised desks using dipping-pens, and old Mr Grocott, himself in his seventies, felt so proprietorial about the family concern that we stood no chance of making the purchase.

During one of my trips to Grahamstown the local Security Police followed me first to a bar and then to a restaurant, so the next morning I presented myself at their offices and offered to answer any questions they might have. The two officers seemed embarrassed at such candour and couldn't think of any ques-tions, but gave me tea and sat wide-eyed while I drank it. Incredibly, their names were Sweetman and Sauerman.

At the peak of our company's diversification we had an additional ten companies, and felt this provided a prudent cushion against threats to the *Dispatch* on the economic front. The first overt threat was the decision by a group of wealthy right-wing businessmen to establish an opposition newspaper in support of apartheid. Knowing that most whites deeply re-sented the *Dispatch*, they believed that by producing an effective conservative newspaper they would enable these whites to drop the *Dispatch* both as readers and as advertisers and thus put us out of business. Terry was worried by the challenge, especially when he saw the first copy of the *East London Times*, which was well put together, but Frank and Peter were unmoved, and when we held a sweepstake in the office to guess how long our new rival would last, Peter specified its exact duration to the day. Afterwards he had the nerve to deny that his guess had been a fluke . . . The *East London Times* lasted less than a year, and its sponsors lost a lot of money.

Frank Streek had me appointed to the board of directors and proposed me as a member of the East London Club, élitist if unofficial headquarters of the city's Anglo-Saxon establishment. All the directors of the *Dispatch* were members, and Denis Ross-Thompson was a particularly highly respected one. My membership of the club came to an end when I proposed a Jewish friend and he was regarded as "unacceptable". Frank and Terry resigned in support of me, and the national newspapers made a splash of the controversy. At the time I belonged to a predominantly Jewish golf club, and although some of the members were supportive over the controversy most of them seemed embarrassed and avoided all reference to it. This reaction among leading members of the city's Jewish community was also evident when the *Dispatch* broke up a virulently anti-Jewish organization in the city by public exposure and stopped them from circulating pamphlets about the *Protocols of Zion*, the notorious forgery which kept surfacing in South Africa whenever anti-Jewish feeling arose. And when two subtly anti-Semitic letters in the paper drew an angry response from non-Jews I had a visit from a delegation of the local Jewish Board of Deputies asking if, instead of setting up such letters to be repudiated by the public, the letters themselves could be suppressed. I said I didn't believe in running the newspaper that way; that it was better to flush bigots into the open.

We conducted a number of campaigns in the paper against bigotry and racism, and asked our readers to report any incidents they witnessed, giving names where possible—especially names of shops which made blacks wait at the counter until all the whites were served. Many of our white readers were enraged at this campaign, and there was a sharp increase in telephone threats against the paper and against staff members personally and our families. But some whites and many blacks co-operated, and we were able to report enough specific instances to make shops more careful about their racial attitudes. Shops became scared of possible boycotts by blacks and revised their attitudes accordingly. One incident reported by a white schoolboy named Kaplan concerned a Greek shopowner who had called a black man a "bloody kaffir" and refused to serve him. I knew the shopowner, Jerry Sofianos, and had often bought cigarettes from him. In fact his daughter, Pepe, worked in the features department of our editorial staff. We published this report on our front page, and that evening on my way home I stopped at the Sofianos' shop. A distraught Jerry was behind the counter with his wife and daughter, and when he saw me he said: "Meester Woods—the report in the paper ees wrong!" I asked him how it was wrong, and he said agitatedly: "Look, I tell you what happened. This Kaff—I mean, er, this black man, was drunk, so I said to him very nicely that he must please leave my shop, then all of a sudden this bloody leetle Jew-boy interfered!" His wife and daughter shouted: "That's right, Papa—make it worse! Make it worse!"

We frequently had requests, always declined, to keep things out of the paper. Several came from an accident-prone undertaker in the city named Lloyd. Things often seemed to go wrong with Lloyd burials. There was the day his staff inadvertently buried an old Afrikaner near Macleantown, a rural area twenty miles out of the city, instead of in a city cemetery, and when his tearful family came to pay their last respects they shrieked that the body in the coffin wasn't theirs. It was, of course, the body of the old gentleman who should have been buried at Macleantown. Lloyd assured the family that he would produce their body the following day, giving them the impression that it was in a central mortuary in another part of the city, and that night he and his staff went furtively to Macleantown with lanterns, picks, spades and the right body to exhume the old Afrikaner and make the appropriate substitution. But a farmer's family saw the lights of the lanterns down in the fields and called the police, who charged Lloyd with "interfering with a tomb". In making the body-substitution Lloyd had found that the right body was taller than the wrong one and wouldn't fit into the coffin until he smashed the end panel so the feet could protrude. Our reporters got hold of the story, and it was going into the paper when Glyn Williams phoned me after midnight to tell me Chris Lloyd was in the office asking that it should be held out in deference to the feelings of the family. I asked him to put Lloyd on the phone and explained that we couldn't keep the story out, but that in deference to the family we would leave out the part about the feet . . .

On another occasion a Lloyd hearse took a corner too fast and crashed through a garden hedge, overturning on the lawn and depositing in a rosebush a coffin from which an arm dangled. That was a picture we didn't use, and when Lloyd came into the office in a vain attempt to have the report suppressed I urged him to consider going into another line of work.

Most requests to keep reports out of the paper were over court cases, often Immorality Act convictions under the law forbidding sexual acts of any kind between people of different race. The Afrikaner Nationalist Government didn't like such reports either, because they "gave South Africa a bad name overseas". But they never considered the obvious course of scrapping such legislation. We came under increasing pressure from Government officials who, not being able to catch us out publishing material contravening the publication laws, still managed to subject us to extra harassment under the industrial regulations. The company's tax situation was rigorously probed by revenue officials and the most severe company tax interpretations were applied. The building inspectors put us to extra cost by forcing us to comply in the strictest terms with clauses in the regulations which they interpreted more severely against us than against other enterprises.

We were classified as a factory by state officials and ordered to segregate all toilets in all departments, and also to leave a specified amount of space, and erect partitions, between workers of different race. This would have been absurd on the *Dispatch*, where we had black, white, coloured, Indian and Chinese journalists all seated together and working together, and I told the factory inspector we would defy his edict. He was enraged, especially when he saw a white woman reporter, Sylvia Haggerty, seated between Gordon Qumza (black) and Benito Phillips (coloured). He demanded that I should move her away to a partitioned area and I said: "I couldn't do that —they're very close friends." This made him even angrier. He threatened to prosecute us, and I told him to go ahead, that it

184

would look great in the overseas press, and eventually he backed down on the question of seating. But one thing he wouldn't back down on was the question of segregated toilets. Toilets were always of supreme importance to Afrikaner Nationalists, segregation in this matter being a key aspect of apartheid in many regulations because they shuddered at the thought of using toilets also used by "non-whites". The Factories Act specified that every factory built must have separate toilets for every "ethnic group", and that for every twelve or fewer persons of each sex of each ethnic group there had to be an extra toilet. I once wrote an article in which I calculated that if a small factory had one female and male worker of the African, coloured, Indian, Chinese and white groups, it would have ten toilets and ten workers, and suggested that future archaeologists digging into ruins of our time might be puzzled by the proliferation of toilets they found.

Actually the East London factory inspector had us over a barrel on the question of segregated toilets, because the factory laws prescribed a heavy fine for every day of contravention, so that if we had defied him on this question it would have cost us an infinite amount of money. What we did was to make the prescribed toilet-segregation signs—"White Males", "White Females", etcetera—and put them up only on the days when the factory inspector called. At first he called three times a month, but later, reassured, he called only once a year, and on a signal from our reception desk downstairs we would put the signs up for his inspection, then take them down until his next visit.

As the years went by we had fewer and fewer objections from members of the staff as they became conditioned to our internal integration. On the first day that I seated a black reporter next to an Afrikaner Nationalist reporter I observed them through the louvred window between my office and the newsroom. For an hour or two both were frigidly formal, then at the first coffee break I noticed they were in animated conversation. They had discovered a mutual interest in rugby football.

Frank Streek and our technical director, Len Beacom, travelled through Europe to find a good colour press, and decided, after looking at several types, to order a Halley-Aller Swedish press—a real Rolls-Royce among high-fidelity colour presses—and although the total cost was over a million rands the results were spectacular. You couldn't get more accurate high-quality colour pictures on to newsprint paper—they were superb. And from the day of our first front-page colour picture we noticed a further rise in circulation. The colour pictures were so sharp and detailed that you could see the fabric-weave in a coat, and the new press also brought us added benefits in colour advertising. Frank's assiduous researches and readiness to be an innovator gave the *Dispatch* a technical lead over all the other newspapers in the country, and we became the first paper on the continent of Africa to be automated throughout the printing process. Copy was set in type by computer and processed by the Japanese-invented Napp system, and we had no major union problems because we guaranteed all technical jobs and the union men agreed to be retrained into the new techniques.

In the editorial department we had become such a close-knit team, so alike in our thinking and in the assessment and presentation of news, that we reduced the three daily editorial conferences to two, then to one, then to none. My predecessors had had full editorial conferences chaired by the editor and attended by the assistant editors, the news editor, chief sub-editor, features editor, chief photographer, sports editor and financial editor. It seemed to me to tie up a lot of highly-paid people for hours just to talk about group decisions when any one of them could have taken the necessary decisions independently. I felt also that if after five years the senior executives didn't know how I wanted editorial matters handled I had failed in basic communication. So we just got on with things.

One of my disappointments was Ted Holliday's decision to retire prematurely, but he had often spoken of giving up journalism to live at his mountain shack in the Hogsback mountains, and when he left Glyn Williams was appointed assistant editor, third in command after George Farr, who became deputy editor. This meant I needed a new night editor, and in view of increasing threats by the Government I wanted a journalistic and political alter ego on the staff. The journalist I wanted was young, with an understanding of black politics as well as of the white parliamentarians, and well versed in the special characteristics of the Eastern Cape. He was Roger Omond, a graduate of Rhodes University, who had impressed us with his versatility on the *Dispatch* before going to London for further experience. He was then subbing on *The Times*. I phoned him and offered him a large salary to return as night editor and politico-journalistic aide, as I put it, to "guard my back". He accepted, and with him in charge at night I felt safe.

George Farr joined me on the board of directors. With Frank Streek, Terry Briceland, Len Beacom and Peter Eastwood, under the chairmanship of Denis Ross-Thompson, we had a compatible board, and in editorial policy I felt I had their full support. This was unique in South Africa, where it was virtually unknown for editorial departments to have even one representative on a newspaper's board, let alone two, and also rare to have a full board supporting an editor's independent right to formulate policy. In fact, the *Dispatch* was unique in several ways. It was the only newspaper I knew of whose board of directors consisted entirely of staff members and whose shareholders were all staff members or their families, and which paid two-thirds of all dividends to charity. This last was a provision of the Crewe Trust, formed from the estate of the founder of the company, Sir Charles Crewe. The Trust owned two-thirds of the entire shareholding, and Sir Charles's will stipulated that every penny of income should go to charity. The Trustees were Denis Ross-Thompson, Frank Streek and the Standard Bank. It was an ideal arrangement, making it virtually impossible for any outside interests to take us over or interfere in the administration of the paper.

The only major threats to the *Dispatch* were from the Government, and they were considerable. Afrikaner Nationalists hated English-language newspapers, especially liberal ones like the *Dispatch*, and their leaders always found it convenient to rally their supporters and earn acclaim by threatening the press or passing some new law against press freedom.

But we were soon to feel the effect of a new Premier with even stronger views on the press. During the 1966 session of parliament my friend Gerald Shaw of the *Cape Times* was typing away in his press gallery office minutes before a major debate was due to begin. He pressed the buzzer for a parliamentary messenger and ordered a hamburger and coffee. The messenger, a Greek immigrant named Dimitri Tsafendas, said: "I'll bring it, but I'll have to hurry—I've got something to do!"

He bustled in moments later with Gerry's order, then went down to the debating chamber and stabbed Premier Verwoerd to death with a long knife.

Afrikaner Nationalists went into mourning all over South Africa, smashing up some Greek tearooms in the process, then the party caucus chose Balthazar Johannes Vorster as Verwoerd's successor.

Right from the start of his premiership Vorster felt he should establish his toughness by threatening new press legislation, and he began early to promise his supporters that he would put the opposition press "in its place" if it continued to "betray South Africa" in its criticism of racial policies. The Vorster Government early developed the belief that it was synonymous with the country, and increasingly appeared to regard criticism of its policies as treason against the entire nation.

CHAPTER TEN

MY FIRST ENCOUNTER with Balthazar Vorster had been during his period of office in 1962 as Minister of Justice—the confrontation at his press conference over the ninety-day detention law —but from 1966, after he had become Prime Minister and I had become editor of the *Dispatch*, we were to meet often over the next ten years. Some of these encounters were stormy.

Every February when parliament opened in Cape Town it was the custom for editors to apply to the Prime Minister for a private interview with the idea of gauging the temper and immediate intentions of the Government for the forthcoming session's schedule of legislation. As Vorster's accession to the prime-ministership was fairly soon after I was appointed editor such customs were new to both of us, but considering the circumstances of our last encounter he was fairly amiable in these private meetings—at first. I was processed carefully through the security network before being taken to his office, and at the first meeting he came to the door to welcome me with a handshake. His parliamentary office was enormous, panelled in dark wood, and he ushered me to a kind of alcove with sofas and chairs. Coffee, sandwiches and biscuits were brought in and all phone calls held. I had wondered whether the conversation would be in English or Afrikaans, naturally hoping it would be in English, but left that initiative up to him. During the first meeting he spoke in English throughout, except for one anecdote. He chain-smoked cigarettes, saying in his slow, heavily accented English: "One thing my wife has given up trying to get *me* to give up is smoking."

He congratulated me on my appointment as editor of the *Dispatch*, and said I had a "great responsibility to contribute more positive journalism". He said that as he had been born in Jamestown in the Eastern Cape and had gone to school in Sterkstroom he and his family had "had to read the *Daily Dispatch*", and that its "old British imperialism" had angered his father. "My sisters spoke English most of the time—until the Second World War, when they refused to speak it again on principle," he confirmed in his grim, deliberate way. He asked what the people in the Eastern Cape were talking about, and I said they were speculating on what sort of Prime Minister he would make. Vorster suddenly got up, went to his desk and took from a drawer a letter which he showed me. It was from an old Afrikaner Nationalist, and it said that the writer noticed a relaxed mood in the country and hoped Vorster could maintain it; that Dr Verwoerd had been like a schoolmaster and had made the people feel like schoolchildren, whereas Vorster's less formal style was a welcome break from such national tension, and he hoped Vorster would continue to encourage this. Vorster seemed proud of the letter, and observed: "Well, each one has his own style in this job."

Then he fixed his eye on me and said: "So people in your part of the world are wondering what sort of Prime Minister I'll make? Tell me, Mr Woods, what sort of Prime Minister do *you* think I'll make?" I said: "Sir, quite honestly I'm afraid of what sort of Prime Minister you'll make." He looked half-annoyed and half-amused at this and asked: "How so?" I started to say that unless apartheid was abolished entirely it would lead to the destruction of the country, and he interrupted: "On the contrary, if apartheid is done away with *that* will destroy the country—but go on with what you were saying." I continued that he seemed to acknowledge that at least some of the extremest elements of apartheid should be waived, but that if he started to do this his right wing would challenge him, and my fear was that he would over-react. "To be blunt, sir, I am afraid that sooner or later you will feel that you have to prove to your party how tough you can be—as tough as Dr Verwoerd."

He closed his eyes for a moment and leant back in his chair, saying nothing, and I thought I had gone too far and that he would terminate the discussion then and there. But after a while he sat forward, opened his eyes and said with a humourless smile: "I thought I had already proved how tough I was as Minister of Justice and Police. You people in the English-language press drew cartoons of me in jackboots and Nazi uniform because I caught Communists and threw them into jail without charge. You have small children, Mr Woods, haven't you?" I said yes. He went on: "It's for them and for you and for all of us in this country that I throw Communists into jail. Do you think I do it for enjoyment? Thank God we have Security Police who are dedicated, because I tell you that without them we would have been finished in 1962." I asked: "But how do you know they are Communists? How can anyone know they've broken any law unless they're charged in court and allowed to defend themselves?" "I know," he answered. "*I* know they're guilty—as guilty as *hell*. If the public knew and if you knew what *we* know your hair would stand on end. You liberals amuse me, you think we can fight fire with little rules. But we can only fight fire with fire. The Communists aren't fighting by the rule book so why should we?" I suggested that he as a lawyer surely knew the dangers of untested allegations made by Security Police, saying that all we knew was that he'd thrown hundreds of people into jail who might not be Communists anyway. I asked: "Could you name me any such Communists?" He replied: "Rowley Arenstein of Durban, for one, and Lewis Baker of Pretoria for another. Have you heard of Lewis Baker?" I said no, and that I didn't even know that a person of that name was in jail.

Vorster poured some coffee. "Well, let me tell you the story of Mr Lewis Baker. I knew him well. We were lawyers together. We were quite friendly, but I knew he was a Communist, and when I was appointed to the cabinet I went to him and warned him. Lewis, I said, get out of the country. Take your family and get out before I have to throw you in jail. And he laughed at me and refused. Well, so I threw him in jail, and he's still there. The other night I was driving past the jail, it was late, and I went into the jail and visited him. He said: 'My God, John, what are you doing here at this hour?' He said it in Afrikaans and I replied: '*Ja, jou donder, sommige van ons moet laat werk terwyl mense soos jy hier op jou gat sit.*' ('Yes, you bugger, some of us have to work late while people like you sit here on your arse.') Baker was craving for a smoke, so I gave him a whole packet. He protested: 'John, I'm not allowed cigarettes here and it's risky having a whole packet,' and I said: 'Keep the packet—it's your risk, and if they find it and you tell them the Minister gave it to you they won't believe you and I won't admit it either.' Then I went on: 'Lewis, why didn't you act on my warning to get out of the country?' and he said: 'John, you're right, I was a fool. I should have gone when you gave me the chance.' I told him: 'Well, it's too late now,' and there he sits in that jail to this day. Once I was made Minister in the cabinet and had the facts officially put before me I had to act. He was just a bloody fool for not getting out while he could."

Vorster sighed a deep sigh, a bit theatrically. "I didn't ask for this job of Prime Minister. I hope I won't have it for long. I want to retire and enjoy my family life—I've been in politics since I was at university." He spoke at some length about the press, and especially the English-language press. "You people must realize that I would like to have a good relationship with your newspapers," he said. "But that doesn't depend on me— it depends on you. I won't hesitate to act against the press if my duty requires it. I would rather not do it, but I won't hesitate if I have to for the sake of the country."

I pointed out that he had many laws under which to act against newspapers that had put a foot wrong—more than twenty—and he said heavily: "Let me tell you, young man, and you can tell your fellow-editors I told you, and I will tell them too if I see them, that many members of my party are not satisfied with the existing press laws. They want stronger action taken against disloyal newspapers." "Disloyal to whom?" I asked. "Disloyal to the country," he replied. "Disloyal to South Africa." "Will a judge decide that?" I asked. "That is for parliament to decide," he answered. "I didn't say that I myself want more powers to act against the press, only that members of my party want me to take extra powers. I prefer to wait and see how things go. I'm new to this job, and perhaps the opposition newspapers will behave more responsibly than in the past."

He then turned the discussion to more personal matters. "You're a Roman Catholic, I believe. Well, I'm a believer in God although I don't beat my chest and call myself religious. I am a Christian." I asked how he could reconcile apartheid with Christianity, and saw the first real flash of anger from him since the start of the interview. We had quite a long argument on this point, he reiterating his claim that there was no in-compatibility between apartheid and Christianity. When I put some quotations to him on the issue he said: "I'm not one for religious quotations. I don't hold myself up as a good church-

The author with his mentor and barrister, Harold Levy, outside the
Grahamstown Supreme Court.

Steve Biko with Dr Ramphele.

Above: With Premier B. J. Vorster at a dinner for South African editors.
Below: With Helen Suzman.

Above: Biko's funeral.

Below: The Woods's house, showing the garage from which the escape began.

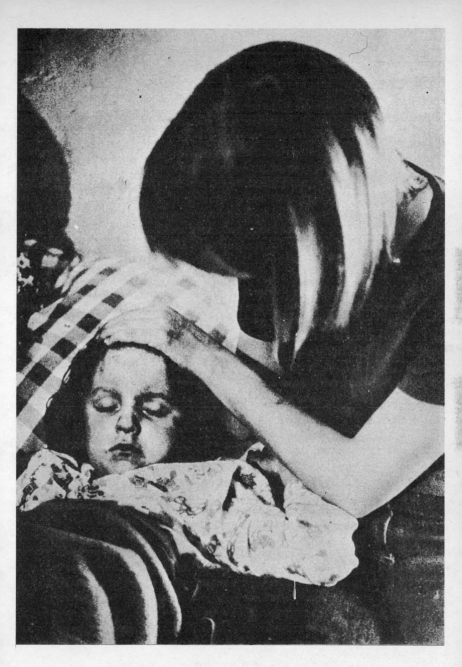

Mary sedated after the tee-shirt incident.

Warrant Officer Jan Marais, the man responsible for sending the tee-shirt and, *below*, Don Card, who assembled the evidence against him.

Right: Across the border in disguise—with glasses back on!

Below: Moments before take-off for Botswana—after official warnings not to fly.

At the White House with President Carter and Vice-president Mondale.

With Wendy at the UN, when the author became the first private citizen invited to address the Security Council.

goer." After a long series of further exchanges on the morality or immorality of apartheid I saw him glance at his watch and got to my feet, thanking him for sparing time to see me. We had spoken for an hour-and-a-half. He shook hands and said with a little smile seldom seen from him in public: "Yes, well, we have had a frank talk and I don't mind frank talks off the record like this. Good day to you." It was the first of a number of increasingly frank talks.

Vorster was facing a revolt in his party. Since taking over as Premier he had made a number of minor concessions in the apartheid policy, such as allowing Maoris chosen for the New Zealand rugby team to enter South Africa to play the Springboks, and the right wing of the party considered this a betrayal of the apartheid principle. The right wing, led by Dr Albert Hertzog, had few adherents, but Vorster feared it was becoming more influential, and that it could develop a strong appeal to the party rank-and-file by opposing all concessions of any kind. The last thing he wanted was a split in the party under his early premiership. In his first months of office he had been photographed playing golf (he was a fourteen-handicap), playing chess, and doing other more "human" things than Dr Verwoerd had appeared to do. And while this gained him some popularity among English-speaking whites it harmed his image among most Afrikaners who seemed to want a grim *volksleier* (people's leader) whose mask of solemnity never slipped into what they regarded as frivolity. In consequence Vorster suddenly stopped allowing informal photographs to be taken of him, and started to avoid smiling in public. Progressive Party member Colin Eglin told me that whereas as a freshman MP Vorster had been animated and full of jokes, and always ready to go over to the Stanley Bar with opposition MPs, he now preserved his mask of solemnity even with old acquaintances.

The next time I had a private meeting with Vorster he was faced with the decision of whether or not to allow England's cricket team to include a coloured South African, then living in England as a professional, for their tour of South Africa. Basil D'Oliveira had gone to live in England because as a coloured man he wasn't allowed to play in the official leagues in South Africa. In England he had succeeded brilliantly in county cricket, and had been chosen for England against Australia,

New Zealand, India, the West Indies and Pakistan. Vorster's dilemma now was that if he allowed D'Oliveira to tour South Africa with the England team it would enrage Dr Hertzog and the other right-wingers and make a mockery of apartheid. And if he scored well against South Africa it would emphasize the injustice which prevented him from playing for his own country. When I saw Vorster I raised the issue with him, saying what a disaster it would be for South Africa's international sport if D'Oliveira were stopped from playing against the Springboks. He was non-committal, but I formed the impression that he would allow D'Oliveira in. Urging this further I used a golf analogy. "As a golfer you know that in playing a shot the worst mistake is not to go right through with the swing," adding that by allowing in the Maori members of the New Zealand rugby team he had committed himself boldly to a "swing", and that I hoped he wouldn't quit on it just because of "a few flat-earthers" like Hertzog. Vorster gave a wintry smile and said: "You seem confident that there are only a few." What interested me was that he allowed me to get away with the insulting reference to Hertzog, who was then still a member of his Cabinet.

Unfortunately for Vorster the Hertzogites lobbied powerfully on the D'Oliveira issue and Vorster started wavering in his original intent to let the cricketer in. Shortly before the England team was to be chosen D'Oliveira had a slump in form and was considered out of the running—which was cheered by Afrikaner Nationalists who foresaw that a decision on the issue might not be necessary. Then at the eleventh hour in his final turn batting against Australia he slammed a brilliant century, and was chosen for the tour. Vorster, addressing the Orange Free State congress of the Afrikaner Nationalist Party, announced to the cheers of the delegates that D'Oliveira wouldn't be allowed in.

Shortly before Vorster made his announcement I was asked to give the main address at a public banquet attended by South Africa's international cricketers, and when I said in my speech that the cricketers themselves should speak up in favour of non-racial cricket there was an uproar in the audience. A local politician shouted: "Don't drag politics into sport!" and one of the Springbok cricketers walked out. I tried to make the point that it was the politicians who were dragging politics into sport, and that if the cricketers didn't publicly commit themselves to merit selection of teams it would actually weaken Vorster's position in his party on the D'Oliveira issue and result in the isolation of South Africa's international sport. The South African cricket captain, Trevor Goddard, said to me privately after the speech: "I agree with a lot that you said, but we can't speak up. We're in a very difficult position." I said simply: "Why?", and he gave no answer. I said: "You're not in a difficult position. You're in a very safe position. You are national heroes and you won't be thrown into jail if you speak up." But he kept muttering about being in "a very difficult position", and moved away in embarrassment.

The result of the D'Oliveira ban and the cancellation of the tour was that South African cricket, then stronger than in all the other cricket countries, was isolated from the rest of the cricket world, and the most successful national team in eighty-five years ended up with no one to play against. Moreover, it boosted the campaign against the country's participation in world sport; years afterwards there were still repercussions from Vorster's fateful decision. A couple of years later the Springbok cricketers made a public protest against apartheid by walking off Newlands Cricket Ground—but by then it was too late. Vorster's capitulation to his right wing on the issue didn't preserve his party's unity, because the split occurred anyway. Dr Hertzog led his followers into the Herstigte Nasionale Party (Reconstituted National Party), which although it never polled strongly enough to pose an electoral threat was to harass Vorster from the extreme right throughout his premiership.

I continued to see him at the start of each parliamentary session, and my fellow editors began commenting wryly on his readiness to see me when he was "too busy" to see any of them. They joked that Vorster and I had a love-hate relationship. I raised the question with him, asking him why he had agreed to see me after refusing to see the other editors of the English-language newspapers. Vorster said in his slow, ponderous way: "Do you really wish to know?" I said yes, and he looked at me balefully for a full minute. "It's because I like to know what the real enemy is thinking," he said levelly. "I know what the others are thinking, but you are younger than they are and you are more outspoken than they are. I don't like what you stand for. But we speak directly to each other. I have noticed that you do not hold back in our discussions, and that is helpful to me. I am surrounded here by *ja-broers* (yes-men) who often tell me what they think I want to hear. Why else do *you* want to talk to *me*? Is it not to know how the enemy is thinking?" I agreed and laughed. He nodded and didn't laugh.

He was beyond his laughing days, and I began to doubt a story that had been told to me about his sense of humour. The story was that Tertius Myburgh of the Johannesburg *Star* had taken a new pocket-recorder into an interview with Vorster, but after twenty minutes it started clicking in his pocket, whereupon Vorster looked him in the eye and said: "Is that yours or mine?" Certainly in our "frank" discussions I encountered less and less humour from him, apart from one or two dry observations which might have passed for humour. Having explained why he talked with me and not with most other "opposition" editors, he added: "As for Gandar of the *Rand Daily Mail*, I wouldn't see him anyway. I don't like the man." "Have you met him?" I asked. Vorster replied: "No, I can't say that I know him—but from what I know of him I dislike him intensely." I said: "Sir, Lawrence Gandar is one of the nicest men I've ever met. He's a man of total principle, and I'm sure that if you met him you would at least respect him." Vorster: "No." I said: "Mr Vorster, why not let me arrange a golf game between you and Lawrie Gandar? He's a good golfer, about a seven handicap . . ." Vorster: "No." I changed the subject.

Later in the interview he returned to the general topic of golf, and it emerged that at the time I had the same handicap as he. I said: "But of course, if you wouldn't play golf against Lawrence Gandar you wouldn't play against me either." He replied, with the merest suggestion of a smile: "Perhaps such a match could be arranged—if there were no photographers around." And thinking what my friend Helen Suzman would say if ever I were photographed playing golf with Vorster, I silently echoed his qualifying remark.

As this interview was ending Vorster said: "There's another reason why I speak to you, and I should mention it—your newspaper circulates in two important homelands, Ciskei and Transkei, and you should be careful what you publish because a lot of Bantu will read it." At the time Afrikaner Nationalists all used the word "Bantu" for blacks, and it was only ten years later that they conceded it was offensive and dropped it. It was a silly word to use, as it means "people", and blacks disliked it mostly because it was an apartheid-identified term. Vorster's comment about the *Dispatch* circulating in black areas was significant, and hoping to divert his attention from a kind of ultimatum which I would be seen to be defying I asked: "Why, in terms of your homelands policy, don't you amalgamate the Transkei and Ciskei, since both are Xhosa-speaking areas?" He replied: "That is up to the Bantu themselves to decide. It is not for us to prescribe to them what is best for them." I left his office flabbergasted at this statement.

My next private discussion with him took place a year later. He had recently been issuing ominous threats against liberals, and I brought him a copy of a book by John Fisher about Emily Hobhouse, the remarkable Englishwoman who had campaigned in England against the Boer War, then came to South Africa to help nurse the Boer women and children ravaged by disease in the concentration camps. I inscribed the book in Afrikaans: "In order that you may understand what liberalism is all about". He took the book, read the inscription with a glint in his eye, and said: "This is very kind of you. Emily Hobhouse was a great woman, and I look forward to reading it." I replied: "Well, I'm hoping you'll stop your attacks on us liberals when you realize that Emily Hobhouse was a liberal, and that we stand up for blacks for the same reasons that she stood up for Afrikaners." "Ah," he said. "There are liberals and liberals. She was a Gladstone liberal and that's a good kind of liberal." "It is the only kind of liberal," I said. He opened the book again, looked at my inscription, and said quietly but with finality: "Well, we'll just have to disagree over that."

On this occasion he tackled me about several editorials which had appeared in the *Dispatch*, saying: "Can't you write about anything other than apartheid?" I replied that if a man saw two armies preparing to clash he shouldn't be criticized for repeatedly warning of the consequences; that it would be irresponsible of him to talk about anything else while the major issue loomed. This, I went on, would be as much a dereliction of duty as if a man saw a neighbour's house burning and turned aside to discuss his flower-garden. Vorster showed genuine astonishment. "Is that really how you see South Africa? Do you really see that sort of confrontation coming?" "Most certainly," I replied. "If apartheid continues then violence is inevitable." "That is not our information," he retorted. "Certainly that is what the Communists would like to see happen. Certainly that is what the troublemakers want to bring about." I said: "Sir, I don't think your Security Police inform you accurately in their reports. I don't think, with respect, that you people know the extent of black resentment and anger against you." Vorster asked: "What makes you say that?" I said: "You never speak to black leaders. You never consult them . . ." He interrupted harshly: "You can't say that. That isn't true. I consult Bantu leaders constantly."

I remained silent, and after a moment he went on: "You want to know who I'm referring to? I meet regularly with Chief Matanzima of the Transkei, Chief Buthelezi of Zululand and the other homeland leaders." "Sir, I know both men, and both have a following, but believe me the majority of blacks don't regard them as their most important leaders. Even Chiefs Buthelezi and Matanzima will tell you what I am telling you if you ask them." He said: "Who are *you* to know who the real leaders are? Why should *you* know who the majority of blacks regard as their leaders? Who do *you* say these leaders are?" I replied: "Nelson Mandela—" A taut look appeared on his face and he spoke sharply: "God help them if that's whom they follow." ". . . and Robert Sobukwe are the main two," I finished. "If you released Mandela from Robben Island and had talks with him . . ." "That will be the day," said Vorster emphatically. "Over my dead body will Mandela be released, that I can tell you."

Once when I came into Vorster's office he said he understood I had met Senator Robert Kennedy, and I replied that I had, during his South African visit in 1966, and that my wife and I had visited him in Washington in 1967, when he was campaigning for the Presidency. Vorster wanted to know what I thought of him, and I said I had been impressed, and felt he would make a good President if elected. Vorster asked why I thought so, and I told him: "He's too rich to be bought, too idealistic to be corrupted, and he really believes in democracy. He's a shy man, but he's not scared of anything or anyone, and he's the hero of the young people, the Mexican Americans and the blacks—he won't let them down." Vorster's eyes dilated and his shoulders hunched up towards his ears. He said with heavy emphasis on each syllable: "If Robert Kennedy becomes President of America, all I can say is—God help South Africa."

Vorster's English was usually grammatically correct, but on one occasion he made a mistake that was almost endearingly pardonable, because of the difficulty of suddenly switching from Afrikaans to English. He said: "You know, the terrorists aren't only after *us* in the *government*. They're after *every* white person in this country—they're out to extermish us *all*!"

The next time I saw him a couple of years later, he made an unexpectedly kind-hearted gesture. I had taken my son with me to Cape Town, and while I went into Vorster's office Dillon sat in the waiting-room. He was then eight years old, dressed in short trousers and his school blazer, and when my interview with Vorster was over and he took me to his door and saw Dillon he asked if this was my son, then invited him in with me and sat him in a chair, speaking with grave charm to him. Dillon responded immediately, and eventually Vorster said: "Tell me, my boy—what do you want to be when you grow up?" Dillon considered this, then replied: "I don't know— maybe a priest." Vorster nodded slowly and said: "Well, I tell you this—whatever you decide to be, be it a priest or an architect or a lawyer, the important thing is to be as good at it as you can be. A good priest, or a good architect or a good lawyer. To try your best to be good at it, whatever career you choose, even"—with a sidelong glance at me—"journalism." I said: "Maybe he'll be a Prime Minister one day—in a Progressive Government." Without a glimmer of a smile Vorster stood up and replied: "That'll be the day. There'll never be such a thing." He bent down and shook hands with Dillon. "Good luck to you, my boy, and God bless you." As Dillon went out I said goodbye to Vorster and thanked him for his thoughtful gesture. He nodded stolidly: "It was my pleasure."

My next encounter with Vorster was to be in Pretoria, in his office at Union Buildings, in bizarre circumstances. Our financial director at the *Dispatch*, Peter Eastwood, had been told by Frank Streek to delegate his routine work to a deputy and devote all his time to deciding on a suitable target for our next takeover bid. We now had, in addition to two daily newspapers, four local weeklies, two printing concerns, a construction company, a glass factory, a security company and a property company. Peter's mandate now was to find the best available investment return in a further takeover target. He cloistered himself in a small corner office on the top floor and we didn't see him for weeks as he submerged himself in company reports and profiles. Then he emerged to astonish Frank, Terry and me by saying the best investment available to us was South African Associated Newspapers.

This was an audacious concept. South African Associated Newspapers, or SAAN, was a giant company compared to ours. It was, in fact, the second biggest newspaper group in the country, eclipsed only by the Argus Company. SAAN owned the Johannesburg *Sunday Times*, one of the world's twenty biggest-selling newspapers in the English language, the *Rand Daily Mail*, the Eastern Province *Herald*, the *Sunday Express*, the *Financial Mail* and the Port Elizabeth *Evening Post*. Control of SAAN would also lead to control of the *Cape Times* and the *Natal Mercury*—virtually all the country's morning papers apart from the *Dispatch* and the *Natal Witness*. It was a case of David aspiring to swallow Goliath, but Peter's calculations were compelling. He estimated that for four and a half million rands we could gain a company worth more than twenty-five million.

SAAN had been going through a lean time because, although half its papers were profitable, the other half were eating up most of these profits and the shareholders were complaining. Control of the group was a complex matter, but in the final analysis it rested in the hands of one man, an enigmatic Cape Town magnate named Clive Corder who was known to be politically conservative and unhappy with the returns on the SAAN investment. We learnt that he was on a coastal cruise aboard a ship due to dock in East London, and when it arrived the four of us, Frank, Terry, Peter and I, called on him in his stateroom and put our offer, which it had taken weeks to prepare. Our presentation, handled mostly by Frank and Peter, took over an hour, and Corder puffed on his pipe as he considered it. He expressed interest, and surprise at our audacity, and promised to let us have his reply soon.

During the next few days he decided we were too "left" to be given control of the SAAN papers, but was sufficiently impressed with our concept to turn it over to the Argus Company, which jumped at the chance and closed a share-option deal with Corder at fractionally more than our offered price. Argus chief Layton Slater knew a good deal when he saw one, and Corder preferred the Argus as buyers not only because they were more conservative than the SAAN papers and ourselves but because, the Argus being a big outfit, the deal would give him more prestige in Cape Town clubs than a sale to a small company like ours.

The deal was announced on the national radio news before we could be given a chance to top the Argus offer. Corder clearly wanted a *fait accompli*. We decided to deprive him of it, and to try to keep the benefit of what had been our idea in the first place. We moved to Johannesburg, where we phoned Layton Slater and asked for a meeting. Slater, a big, friendly man, saw Frank and me at the *Star* building in Sauer Street. We explained that Corder had peddled him our idea, but offered to let Argus keep a quarter interest in SAAN if Slater would return the deal to us. Slater laughed at the idea, asking why the Argus Company should sacrifice the bulk of such a deal. We said we believed the deal would not be allowed to go through; that the Government would block it under the Monopolies Act for political reasons, because Vorster would realize that an Argus Company owning ninety-five per cent of the English-language press could push up national advertising rates and screw the Afrikaans press into the ground. Slater told us that he had checked this out with Marius Jooste, an Afrikaans press magnate with friends in the cabinet, and it wouldn't be a problem. What Slater didn't know was that we intended to make it a problem if necessary.

The first thing we had to do was to raise about five million rands, and thanks to Peter's and Frank's financial formulae and our company's sound equity this was achieved remarkably quickly. Terry raised a million and a half in an afternoon with a multi-millionaire insurance whizz-kid, and our political friend of the Progressive Party, Max Borkum, did the rest. Max was president of the Johannesburg Stock Exchange, and in one extraordinary minute, in my presence, he phoned a friend and suggested that he should come in on a good deal. The conversation went like this: "Well, just take my word, it's a good deal. A lovely deal. You can come in for half-a-million. No, I want to know now. Look, if you're going to argue over half-a-million, forget it. That's better. Okay, you're in. You won't regret it—money's thicker than blood!"

The next step was to get Vorster to block the Argus deal, which meant I had to get to his office quickly, but preferably at his invitation. What we had to offer him was simple and attractive. Under the existing legislation he couldn't block the Argus deal unless alternative buyers existed, and these had to be (a) South African; (b) with South African money; (c) small enough not to constitute a monopoly as the Argus-SAAN merger would; (d) solvent enough to be credible buyers. But someone else would have to plant the idea in his mind, and we decided on John Robinson, editor and part-owner of the *Natal Mercury*, because Robinson was terrified of what a SAAN-Argus-backed *Daily News* would do to his morning paper in Durban, he was conservative, and he and Vorster had recently been getting along pretty well and were contemporaries. I phoned Robinson in Durban, and he was delighted to hear we were determined to block the Argus. He undertook to phone the Prime Minister, and we jumped around shaking hands and slapping each other on the back, then had a drink as we waited for my summons to Union Buildings. Within minutes it came. Vorster's secretary, Mr Weilbach, said: "Mr Woods? The Prime Minister would appreciate a visit from you at three-thirty this afternoon."

Meanwhile the South African Society of Journalists had issued a statement denouncing the Argus-SAAN deal as monopolistic, dangerous to journalists and likely to lead to a "grey uniformity" in South African English-language newspapers. It called on the Prime Minister to block the deal. The statement was issued by George Oliver, president of the journalists' union. It was about the first time the SASJ had issued a statement involving Vorster's name which wasn't condemning him for threatening the press. Our editorial friends on the SAAN newspapers were also rooting for us, as they weren't keen to be swallowed up by the giant Argus Company.

Press and radio bulletins were full of the controversy as I travelled to Pretoria. Punctually at 3.30 Vorster walked in with two bodyguards, holding his hat by the brim at about waist level like a waiter carrying a tray. He made much of holding a hat or reading-glasses, which he would fold up and bunch in his fist while talking. I suspected he didn't like wearing a hat, but that he saw it as part of his *volksleier* image, harking back to the political figures of the 1930s like the elder Hertzog and Malan. The hat did nothing for him aesthetically—with its dated turndown brim it made him look like an old-time Chicago hood—but he obviously felt it was correct attire for a Prime Minister. As he walked in he nodded gravely, and said as he went into his office: "Good day to you." It was only after I was conducted into it by Mr Weilbach that he shook hands. Usually he would motion me to an easy chair or sofa and leave his desk to sit nearby, but on this occasion he indicated that I should sit at the other side of his desk as he took his working-chair. This was no social occasion, we were there to do business.

He questioned me closely about the seriousness of our bid for SAAN, and I told him the entire history of the deal. When I reached the part about Clive Corder trying to close the deal with the Argus Company without giving us a chance to better the Argus offer he shook his head and asked: "But isn't Corder a trustee of the controlling portfolio?" and when I said yes, Vorster raised his eyebrows and said: "*Uberrima fides . . .?*" Being a lawyer he was referring to a trustee's duty to act with utmost good faith in securing the best deal for his trust. I nodded, and said that if we were allowed to top the Argus offer the return for Corder's clients would obviously be higher. "There is one question I must ask you," he said. "Is your money South African?" I said: "Mr Prime Minister, our money is so South African that it can whistle *Sarie Marais.*" This amused him, and he gave a rare chuckle. I added: "But you needn't accept my word on that. We are prepared to furnish proof." He held up his hand. "No, I accept your word unreservedly. I see that the South African Society of Journalists also wants me to block the deal between Corder and the Argus," he went on. Then he grinned widely—an even rarer sight. This was the Vorster face the public never saw, with his whole expression given up to amusement. "I never thought George Oliver and I would ever agree on anything."

Reverting to his serious expression he said he felt it his duty to block the deal, not because he liked the English-language press but because the Argus-SAAN deal would lead to a monopoly which could harm the Afrikaans press and would be against the interests of the country. "I don't blame the Argus Company for trying it," he said. "Mr Slater came to see me this morning. He seems a nice man." I said: "Well, he's from Oos-Kaapland." (Afrikaans for Eastern Cape Province.) "Is he really?" asked Vorster with interest. I pointed out that journalists were talking of the merger being an Eastern Cape Mafia deal, since we were from the Eastern Cape, Slater was from the Eastern Cape, Leycester Walton, Managing Director of SAAN, was from the Eastern Cape, and George Oliver was from the Eastern Cape, and I concluded: "Of course, you are also from the Eastern Cape." The idea seemed to intrigue him, and he repeated with some relish: "The Eastern Cape Mafia." He leant back in his chair and looked out of the window, then said: "You know what I think? You know why Corder and his colleagues don't want you fellows to get SAAN? They don't want to be shown up by the small-town boys!" It was a shrewd assessment, and probably pretty close to the truth.

I said: "Mr Vorster, there's one thing I must ask you. Do you realize that if we buy SAAN the SAAN papers will attack you more than the Argus people would?" He nodded. "Of course I realize that, but that has nothing to do with the issue. I'm stopping a monopoly, I'm not organizing your deal for you —that's up to you. I don't mind *who* buys SAAN as long as it's not the Argus Group and as long as it's not foreigners. Alan Paton can buy SAAN for all I care. I don't give a damn—Paton or Gandar or you people, whoever can raise the money. Besides, you people have never cost us an election. We keep on winning our elections."

He then said: "What would be the best way to block the Argus deal?" "A simple announcement by you over the radio," I replied. "How would one word such an announcement?"

Vorster asked. I said I would leave a suggested draft with his secretary, and sensing this would be a good note on which to end the interview I got up and took my leave. "You don't think it will be necessary to use legislation?" he said at the door. I laughed: "Corder will be so nervous he'll drop the thing like a hot potato right after your statement. He might be so scared that he'll hold off our offer too, but at least the present deal will be off, and that'll be to the advantage of everyone against it." He gave a slight smile. "The South African Society of Journalists will approve of me for a change."

Outside his door I worded a draft announcement for Vorster to release over the radio the next morning. I kept a copy, and the next morning Frank, Peter, Terry and I listened with anticipation to the radio news bulletin, following my draft, and noting that Vorster hadn't altered a single word. We wondered what the people of South Africa would say if they knew that I'd written his statement for him.

Minutes later I phoned Corder in Cape Town and the shock waves were still hitting him. He confirmed that in view of the Prime Minister's statement the Argus deal was now off, and when I restated our readiness to resume negotiations he said: "I think we'd better put everything into cold storage for a while. We must wait for the dust to settle." On that note, after celebration drinks with our journalist friends in SAAN and the SASJ, we headed home to East London. Corder being Corder, the dust was still settling years later, and as far as we were concerned it permeated the air permanently. The "small-town" boys might not have shown him up, but we certainly stomped on his double-cross, prevented what would have been an unhealthy press monopoly, and alerted SAAN to their vulnerability in a manner that was to stand them in good stead nearly a decade later, when right-wingers tried to take them over with secret Government backing.

My next encounter with Vorster was during a series of campaigns I conducted in the *Dispatch* against the pass laws, against the banning and jailing without trial of black dissidents, and illustrating the practical effects of apartheid on the daily lives of blacks. It took place in Cape Town, and it was tense from the start. He didn't meet me at the door this time. In fact, when his bodyguards opened the door to show me into his office Vorster was standing in the middle of the room and didn't offer his usual handshake. Without any sort of greeting or preamble he said sharply: "Don't you think the stuff you're writing in the *Dispatch* is stirring up the blacks to revolution?" I replied that his apartheid laws were doing that, and he glared at me for a moment, then stared down at the floor with a frown. I was nervous and wondered what would come next. He gestured at a chair and said: "Sit." I sat. He went on slowly: "You know, if you keep telling people they are being oppressed they will begin to believe you." I was speechless. There seemed to be nothing to say to someone so far off on another wavelength of comprehension.

I changed the subject and asked him why, if he was so confident that nearly all whites wanted segregation, he didn't allow at least a minority of liberals to have social contact with blacks. "Tell me," he said, "if you had a teenage daughter old enough to go out at night would you allow her to go to a multi-racial pop session?" I was so astonished at words like "pop session" coming from the mouth of B. J. Vorster that I was quiet for a moment before replying: "Yes." With a gleam of triumph in his eye, he said: "You seem hesitant to reply." I couldn't tell him my hesitation had been because of the incongruity of hearing the phrase "pop session" from him, and I replied that not having a daughter of that age I hadn't been confronted with such a question, quite apart from the fact that such a multi-racial function would be a contravention of his apartheid laws; but I did assure him that if I prevented my daughter from attending any function it would be for reasons other than the race of the participants. "I certainly wouldn't stop her for reasons of colour," I said. "I've no objection to her dancing with blacks, if that's what you mean." A look of pain or revulsion or simply distaste crossed his face. It was a drawing back of the lips which threw his cheeks into prominence just below the eyes. Leaning back in his chair as if tired, he closed his eyes. "Then all I can say is that I don't understand you," he said heavily.

My next major encounter with him was at his official residence in Pretoria, a mansion ironically named "Libertas". He had invited all the editors in the country to a private dinner and an evening of discussion. We were ushered into a large chandeliered reception lounge where whisky was served while we waited for Vorster to make his appearance. I decided tactfully to stand at the back of the group so that he could mellow as he proceeded through the Afrikaans editors and thus be in a less abrasive frame of mind when he reached me. Conversation hushed as he made his appearance, and when he reached the place where I was standing he said with an angry expression on his face: "*Man, waarom neuk jy die ding dag na dag na dag?*" (Man, why do you hammer at the subject *day* after *day* after *day*?") The atmosphere was highly charged, and all I could think of to say into the tense silence was: "But, sir, I am helping the Government to stay in touch with the feelings of the black people. Shouldn't the Government welcome such help?" He closed his eyes momentarily as if in pain, then opened them to say ironically: "My God, *met vriende soos jy wie het vyande nodig?*" ("My God, with friends like you who needs enemies?") There was general laughter at this, and as Vorster moved around the room chatting to various editors, others came to me to grin and repeat: "*Met vriende soos jy wie het vyande nodig?*"

After Vorster had circulated among his guests dinner was announced, and it was also announced that lest any favouritism in the seating arrangements might be suspected, numbers would be drawn to determine the seating plan. There was general hilarity when I drew seat number one, to be placed on Vorster's right, and he himself said with an exaggerated expression of mock dismay: "Oh, my God, I see that you are next to me!" I replied: "*I* didn't arrange it, sir!" The Minister of the Interior, Dr Connie Mulder, burst into laughter, then saw that Vorster wasn't laughing and cut his laughter off in mid-guffaw. It was an interesting insight into the real relationship between Mulder and Vorster. Mulder was regarded then as the Crown Prince, Vorster's automatic deputy and most respected confidant, but this incident suggested that he was too deferential to be that sure of his position. He was acting like an obsequious school prefect in the presence of the headmaster.

At the table Vorster acted the dutiful host, speaking to me most of the time in Afrikaans. The meal was served by his armed bodyguards. As two of them placed plates of soup before us, their jackets were sufficiently open to reveal shoulder holsters. The only time Vorster spoke English to me all evening was to say: "Have some eland", which I declined. It was a dish of minced eland, the big buck which several cabinet ministers hunted with high-powered rifles, with a kind of pastry. Then Vorster urged me again to try some. "I shot it myself," he added sombrely. In the circumstances I decided to have some.

Vorster's conversation turned to chess. He knew I was a chess enthusiast and told me of his collection of sets—a steel set, a wooden set, and sets in various designs and substances. He said he had learnt the game in detention camp during the war, being taught by a fellow-internee called Bokelmann—"a German from your city".

After dinner we went into the reception lounge and Vorster sent for Mrs Vorster's large collection of scrapbooks filled with clippings from the time of his wartime detention by Smuts. But although these were circulated none of the editors showed more than a cursory interest in them, and they ended up in a pile of neglect on the floor. Vorster was always wanting to show people his scrapbooks and boring them senseless. Ambassadors spoke of them with dismay. Vorster addressed general remarks to the gathering along the lines that as the country was entering dangerous times it was incumbent on editors to exercise what he called "self-discipline", especially in the delicate sphere of race relations. A law was soon to be introduced making it a crime to publish anything "which might have the effect of stirring up racial animosity". Obviously such a law would have such wide scope that publication of anything reflecting adversely on the apartheid policy might be construed as inciting blacks against the white Government, and editors asked a number of questions about the proposed legislation.

I didn't ask any because to me it was purely academic. The Government already had more than enough laws to do anything they wished to newspapers, and one more law would hardly matter. All I was concerned about was when the line would be crossed by the Government—the line at which they still stopped short of severe action against newspapers. Vorster was reiterating that if it became necessary he would act against any editor, and I put the question: "Before taking drastic action, would you consider first giving him a sort of final warning?" There was general laughter, and Connie Mulder said: "Well, Mr Prime Minister, just give Mr Woods his final warning now and get it over with." There was more laughter from the editors, and I had the feeling that perhaps some of them didn't realize how unfunny the real business of the evening was. As I saw it, it was a last appeal to all anti-apartheid editors to toe the Government line or suffer the consequences.

As we filed out at the end of the evening Vorster stood at the door saying goodbye in Afrikaans to each one. To those ahead of me he said formally, using the surnames of all of them: "*Tot siens, Meneer Wepener*," "*Tot siens, Meneer Myburgh*," and so on. When I got to the door, near the end of the line, he used my first name for the first and only time in all our talks. He shook hands, gave me a long look and said: "*Tot siens*, Donald." Perhaps he knew, as I didn't, that it was to be our last encounter.

CHAPTER ELEVEN

DURING 1967 Evalina Mvunelwa came to work for us as a domestic servant and nursemaid for the children. When she arrived from the Transkei she was what was known as a "raw" tribeswoman, but in the ten years she worked for us she underwent a transformation, becoming a sophisticated woman of the townships, dressed in the latest fashion and practically running the whole family with the sheer force of her personality. She was as dominant in the house as "Hazel", the American "supermaid" with the wisecracks and extrovert indomitability. Barely literate, she developed strong political views and commented freely on my editorials, which friends translated into Xhosa for her. She had a proprietorial attitude towards the children and bossed them, not to mention Wendy and me, as if she were the sole parent of us all.

While we had only two children, Jane and Dillon, our house seemed big enough, but when two more sons were born, Duncan in 1966 and Gavin in 1968, we decided to look for a bigger house. Our fourth son, Lindsay, was born in 1970, and towards the end of that year we found what we were looking for —a big double-storey house on to which we could build. We got an architect to plan additions and alterations which could be built in stages, as money became available. But soon after we moved into the house Lindsay got meningitis and died a few days before his first birthday. I took my full measure of overdue leave accumulated, nearly three months, to stay at home, and still in some shock I went into the building venture on a scale that was out of touch with reality, implementing the entire plan of the architect in one operation instead of in stages as originally conceived. I went building-crazy, and turned an already large house into an enormous one, at huge cost.

Although my bank account had fluctuated over the years, into and out of overdraft in a manner that seemed to drive my amiable bank manager to distraction, I wasn't much worried about money. Frank Streek had made it plain to Peter Eastwood, Terry Briceland and me that we would be generously looked after in the 1970s. The three of us had all been "motivated" by Frank on his return from Harvard business school. He counselled each of us about our present and future goals, and said that as the company was doing so well as a result of our combined efforts it was possible to forecast the future expectations and rewards of the three of us, as his most senior executives, and encouraged us to "send down roots" in houses that we would find adequate as permanent residences. Peter, Terry and I all bought houses within a few hundred yards of each other in the rather affluent suburb of Vincent. All had large grounds and we planned additions and alterations, mine being on a considerably more extravagant scale than theirs.

I acted as my own building contractor, ignoring the job-reservation laws by using no white artisans on the construction. These laws were vicious. Designed to reserve all the best jobs for whites, they prescribed strict penalties for builders who allowed blacks to perform certain categories of skilled work. There was a rule against a black man using the back of a hammer, the claw part, to extract a nail from a plank. He could hammer in a nail with the front but not extract it—that was graded as skilled work reserved for whites and coloureds. There were categories of building work for coloureds, Indians and blacks, and although such restrictions were later scrapped when the country experienced a manpower-shortage they were in operation for many years, and held back the earning-capacities and talents of hundreds of thousands of blacks.

By paying double rates I acquired a highly-motivated little gang of workmen. The foreman was a coloured artisan, Charlie Scheefers, who had all the self-confidence in the world. I showed him the architect's plan and he whistled. "You going to turn this place into a hotel?" he said. "Can you build it?" I asked. "Blerrie easy," he said. "I'll build any blerrie thing. All I need is a blerrie plan and the materials. I could do it on my blerrie own. You show me any other brickie in this town can lay two thousand bricks in a day . . ." Charlie chose an assistant bricklayer and mason, an Indian named Walla Naidoo, and five black labourers who soon came under the natural leadership of one of them, Bigboy Buluba. Bigboy was one of those people who go through life with a special stature for which "dignity" is an inadequate description. They seem to be equal to any situation, and have a degree of self-esteem which marks them as special. In the case of Bigboy this was to be demonstrated repeatedly. The next most notable of the labourers was an impassive man named Goliath. My main task was to keep them supplied with materials, and as there were occasionally brick shortages or cement shortages this often took a lot of negotiation with suppliers.

Within a week of starting the building we had our first raid by police over passes. Two Bantu Affairs Department vans pulled up and uniformed men swarmed on to the site. As they appeared all five of the black labourers dropped what they were doing and ran towards the back wall, four of them getting away by jumping over it and vanishing into suburbia. To my surprise Goliath seemed the slowest runner, and he was caught before he could jump over the wall. He had seemed the most athletic of them all, yet the others had outstripped him. I was being naïve. As the policemen led him back in close custody past me, he gave me a wink. And when they demanded his pass book he handed it over quite unconcernedly. The police seemed disappointed that his papers were in order, and left. Only then did the impassive Goliath break into laughter and explain that, as he was the only one of the five with a pass, it was his duty to run slower than the others and be caught while they got away. "It's done on all the building sites," he said. "The ones with passes run the slowest. The Boers still don't realize it."

When the coast was clear the other four reappeared one by one from various directions, Bigboy going straight back to the cement he had been mixing and resuming his work without a word. There was much grinning and chuckling from the other three. Clearly there was going to be a kind of campaign against this particular building project by the Bantu Department police. I had had trouble with them before. Some years previously we had had a nursemaid for the children who was in her late teens. Her name was Dolly Radebe, and she was an orphan who had been born in the Transkei. One day I returned from the office to find her being dragged out of our front gate to a police van by two uniformed Bantu Department police. When I challenged them they said she had no pass book and was under arrest. I followed them in my car as they took her to their headquarters. She was in tears, trembling with fear.

Their superior officer was aggressive when I spoke to him. "Don't think you are the important editor here," he snapped. "There's nothing you can do to help this Bantu girl, so you can forget it. You've got no influence here—here we follow the laws of the Government." He said Dolly would be "taken back to the Transkei where she belongs". I protested: "But she has no family there, no relatives, and as you know there is no work there for her." He said loudly: "The law is the law. She has no right to be here. Besides, there are lots of local Bantu girls out of work. You can easily get another." "That's not the point," I replied. "We like her, our kids are fond of her and she likes us—so it's her we want and nobody else." "No chance!" he said. "She's got to be out of the area within twenty-four hours."

He got up suddenly and took me to an outer door facing on to a backyard where more than a dozen black women stood in a line. "There!" he said. "Take your pick! You can choose any one of those. They're all legals. They've all got passes. You can get one now. Today." I retorted: "You talk as if they're cattle. I'm not here to hire anyone else. I'm here to take Dolly Radebe to my house." He put his hands on his hips in an aggressive gesture, with his head thrust forward. "You can do that—for twenty-four hours—if you pay her bail, but tomorrow we'll come for her to take her to the Transkei where she belongs."

He went on bitterly: "You liberals make me sick. You're so bloody holy about your Dollies and Annies and apartheid and the pass laws, but what about those Bantu women out there? They need work and they're in the area legally. Why must you hire someone from elsewhere? You think we have an easy job?" He walked to his desk and hit a folder on it with his open palm. "There are thousands here out of work, man. We're protecting them by keeping out others . . ." I interrupted: "Even if the others have nowhere to go? Dolly Radebe has no family in the Transkei. She doesn't know anyone there. She's practically a child herself. And there's no work for her there anyway." He sat down at his desk, saying: "That's *her* problem. It's someone *else's* problem. I have *my* duty to do *here*—to keep out illegals." Then, astonishingly, he stood up at his desk, to attention, and recited the last lines of the Afrikaans anthem:

"Ons sal antwoord op jou roepstem
Ons sal offer wat jy vra
Ons sal lewe, ons sal sterwe
Ons vir jou—Suid Afrika!"

("We will answer your call
We will sacrifice what you ask
We will live, we will die
We for you—South Africa!")

"What's all that in aid of?" I asked. "That's how I see my job," he said. "Not to question these pass laws and other State rules as people like you do, but to obey them. I do that for my country." I bailed Dolly out of her cell and she was warned by him to be ready within twenty-four hours to be taken to the Transkei.

That afternoon I spoke to one of the black reporters on the *Dispatch* who knew more about the pass laws than the people who had drafted them, and he said there was only one way to get Dolly legally registered in the area—to arrange a bogus marriage for her to a "registered male Bantu". So we arranged a bogus marriage for Dolly with a bogus parson and a bogus husband, a young man who didn't even know her but who accepted a fee for his formal services. Right after the "wedding" Dolly was taken to the pass offices and "registered" by her "husband". Here the bureaucracy defeated itself because there were so many officials and so many counters, and blacks were viewed so anonymously, that she went through the process unrecognized. After she was registered, we arranged a "divorce". When the Bantu Affairs Department police arrived to take her to the Transkei, I greeted them at the door with her pass book. They looked dumbfounded, and probably went through the registration files for weeks without realizing how it had been done, because even two years later they didn't know about the bogus marriage racket.

In view of this experience, and also because the *Dispatch* had run several campaigns against pass raids and police application of the pass laws, it was no surprise that the Bantu Affairs Department police kept a special watch on our building venture. After Goliath's stratagem we had a kind of sentry system on the building site to warn of any police van approaching the house. But on their second raid they were more cunning. They waited until I was away, negotiating for bricks at a brickyard, then posted men outside the back fence and at all points round the property before making their raid; and when I returned it was to find only Charlie, Walla and Goliath. The other four were in jail. In a rage I stormed off to the police station and got into a slanging-match with the station commander until he threatened to arrest me for "disturbing the peace, using abusive language and interfering with a police officer in the exercise of his duty". I bailed out the four, and as we were about to drive off the police sergeant warned me to produce all of them in court the following morning. Then he walked round to the front passenger seat where Bigboy sat massively puffing on a cigarette, and said to him: "You! Do you understand, hey? You've got to be in court tomorrow morning!" Bigboy drew on his cigarette, exhaled slowly into the face of the white police sergeant and said: "Fuck off." I accelerated away before the sergeant could bring himself to believe his own ears.

The next morning in court I sat near the four as they stood in the prisoners' dock, and was relieved to see that the trial magistrate was a Mr Young, who had been a friend of my father's in the Transkei. After three of the Bantu Affairs Department police had testified for the prosecution, I asked to be sworn in as a witness for the defence and said the four men were being punished for working, not for any crime or delinquency, and that as their employer I should have been charged for their non-registration as work-seekers, not they. Magistrate Young seized on this point and said he was prepared to caution and discharge the four accused provided I undertook to apply on their behalf for the "necessary registration". I spent much of the next ten days going through an incredible maze of bureaucracy and red tape negotiating these passes with the sympathetic aid of Magistrate Young, who bent a few rules in the process, and eventually all four were registered as entitled to seek the jobs they were already doing.

One afternoon when the house was finished Wendy asked me to be back early as she was giving a birthday party for Gavin. I arrived home at about five o'clock to find a police van parked at the front gate and two policemen scrambling out of it. I asked what was going on, and one said: "Two unregistered Bantu have run into your house." I said brusquely: "Right! Wait here and I'll go and look!" This was a delaying ploy. Sometimes in my dealings with South African policemen I found they could be disconcerted by a curt, authoritative tone, and although on this occasion it didn't put them off it at least bought me a few moments of hesitation from them as I ran inside and bounded up the stairs. Wendy was standing at the top. "Where are they?" I whispered. "I've hidden them in there," she said, pointing to the guest room." "Take them into the bathroom and stay in there with them," I told her.

She understood immediately. A white South African policeman could neither imagine nor believe that a white woman would ever be locked in a bathroom with a black man, and she led the two nervous blacks in there and locked the door as the two policemen, having recovered their confidence, hurried up the stairs. I said to them: "I don't see anyone up here, and I think you must be mistaken." They said they would look for themselves, and as police in South Africa don't need a search warrant to enter and search any house at any time there was no point in protesting. They started in the guestroom where the two men had hidden before going into the bathroom. They looked under both beds and behind the door, and they even looked behind the window curtains which didn't hang to the floor. Then they searched the other three bedrooms on the second floor. In the room where Gavin and his friends were having their party all the children went silent, and stared as the two uniformed policemen conducted their search. "What are they looking for, Daddy?" asked Gavin. "People!" I couldn't resist answering bitterly.

They completed the search of the bedroom, then eyed the bathroom door. I said: "You want to look in here?" and grasped the door-handle as if to open the door. Wendy called sharply: "I'm in here!" and the two policemen moved quickly away. Then they saw the balcony, and went out to look there. "They must have jumped over here and got away," one said.

When they were out of sight down the street I let the two men out of the bathroom and took them down to the garage, got them to lie low on the floor of the car and reversed into the street. I drove them several miles from the house and let them out near a township bus.

After all the bills for the house were paid we were considerably in debt, and I looked forward to my long-expected salary adjustment to get us back into credit. Meanwhile, I sold most of the *Dispatch* shares I had bought over the years to reduce the bank overdraft interest as much as possible.

As 1972 drew to a close we were approaching our *Daily Dispatch* centenary, the paper having been founded in September 1872, and my job for the planned celebrations was to find a suitable guest speaker. Knowing that many of the guests at our centenary banquet would be editors and proprietors of pro-government Afrikaans newspapers, I wanted a speaker who would be able to tell them from personal experience how the integration process had worked in the American South. My choice was Charles Morgan, the civil rights lawyer from Atlanta, whose book, *A Time to Speak*, had impressed me. We flew Morgan and his wife over from America, and his speech at the banquet was precisely what we wanted. The shockwaves it generated among the conservative Afrikaans press moguls were considerable. He spelt out for them how intransigent southern racists had been and how they had nevertheless adjusted to integration—and how the same would inevitably happen in South Africa. He told how racists had been re-educated through non-racial sport, and how for many southerners black sports stars had "brought them to their feet —and to their senses".

A major organizational chore which I undertook the following year was a multiracial conference near East London. Colin Eglin, who had been elected leader of the Progressive Party, thought of the idea and raised the money for it, but because he didn't want it to be sponsored by the party he invited me to co-ordinate and run it entirely. One of the major problems was getting black homeland leaders to attend, and especially to arrive and speak when scheduled. Most had the reputation of keeping "African time", and some invited to past conferences had simply never responded. I had chosen a resort hotel about twenty miles from East London, at Glengarriff Bay, as the venue for the conference, and had fixed the date as the day after all the homelands leaders were due to leave Umtata after a "summit" meeting of their own. After phoning and writing and securing their agreement to attend I drove 150 miles to Umtata and spoke to each one individually on the day before the conference. To Paramount Chief Kaiser Matanzima of the Transkei I said: "Please do me a personal favour. Chief Gatsha Buthelezi is notoriously unpunctual, so please arrange that your car is right behind his and that he leaves five minutes ahead of time." Matanzima assured me he would do this. Then I said to Buthelezi of Kwa Zulu: "Matanzima is notoriously unpunctual, so please arrange that your car is immediately in front of his and that he leaves five minutes ahead of time." I did the same to all seven of them, arranging to meet them a mile or two from a certain turnoff on the national road. In the event I myself was two minutes late at the appointed place, and was pleasantly surprised to see seven chiefly cars parked in line with each homeland leader standing beside his car. Chief Buthelezi said with twinkling eyes: "You see, Don—even Kaffirs can be on time!"

The theme of the conference was "Federalism as a formula for a non-racial South Africa", and after a stimulating three days of speeches from black, white, Indian and coloured spokesmen a resolution was passed endorsing geographic federation as a system best suited to a non-racial South African society. The only political party to boycott the conference was the Afrikaner Nationalist Party, although several Afrikaans editors attended.

Months before the conference I had formally applied as required by law for permission to accommodate the delegates of all races in one hotel. This had never been done before so there was no precedent, and I went through all the appropriate channels. I had to write to the Department of Indian Affairs, the Department of Coloured Affairs, the Department of Bantu Affairs and the Department of Justice so that, respectively, Indians, coloureds and blacks could be in the same hotel as whites, and the Department of Justice could give permission for liquor to be served to people of different race at one gathering. Then I had to write to the Department of Community Development for permission for a theatrical group to perform a play on white premises for a "mixed" audience . . .

All these Government departments stalled for weeks except

for the Minister of Bantu Affairs, Mr M. C. Botha, who wrote a curt letter saying he would not consider such a request nor any which might be construed as linking the name of his department to people like me. The others avoided a direct "no", possibly fearing "unfavourable publicity overseas"—they simply didn't reply. The day before the conference was to begin I had hundreds of people scheduled to arrive, many booked on flights, including members of parliament—and no official permission. There was only one thing to do: go ahead and break the law, challenging the authorities to arrest us all. In fairness to the hotel proprietor, Roy Crawford, I told him the position and warned that he could lose both his liquor and his hotel licence. Roy, a blunt-spoken man, said: "Let's go ahead. Let 'em do what they like. Fuckem."

Hours before the conference I had a visit from Captain Stoltz of the Bureau of State Security (BOSS). A stern-faced man with piercing eyes, he said: "We know what you're up to, Mr Woods. Do you think you're being wise? What purpose do you think it will serve to hold this conference?" I told him I was going ahead, that it was high time blacks and whites were allowed to meet together to discuss important national issues, and that instead of stopping such meetings the state should "open its ears and listen" to what would be said.

Stoltz surprised me by saying he had made precisely such a recommendation to his headquarters, then he went on archly: "But how will we know what is being said? My problem is now to find out what is said." I said: "Captain, if I read you right you now intend to monitor my conference, which means having Security people snooping around the Glengarriff Hotel. Now, I don't want the delegates upset or made nervous by any eavesdropping police." "But we've got to know what the speakers will say!" he exclaimed. I didn't tell him the proceedings would be published in full daily in the *Dispatch* anyway, or that a verbatim booklet of the conference would later be printed, or that all the speakers would be told this before approaching the rostrum. "I'll tell you what, captain," I said. "You supply a recording machine and we'll record the whole thing for you from beginning to end—all the formal speeches." He said: "What? Would you do that? Would you be prepared to do that for me?" I said: "Sure, on one condition—that not one police or Security man goes within miles of that hotel while the conference lasts. If you keep your pledge on that we'll record the whole thing for you." He leapt at the deal.

That evening the captain delivered a superb recording machine to be taken to the conference centre, where it was placed next to the one we had hired from Sonex Recording Studios to record the entire proceedings anyway. Both the Sonex and the BOSS machines were plugged directly into the microphones all the speakers would use. Captain Stoltz kept his word: not a single policeman showed his face near the Glengarriff Hotel throughout the conference. And he received his recordings every night—before the same material was reported in the *Dispatch* the following morning. Only one snag developed: on the first night the BOSS machine malfunctioned and missed out two speeches, but by courtesy of Sonex Recording Studios and my staff's goodwill, a grateful and embarrassed Captain Stoltz was able to retape the missing section.

One group missing from the conference was the newly-founded Black Consciousness Movement. I hadn't invited them, and even if I had done so it was unlikely they would have accepted. I knew little about them, and the little I knew I didn't like. From what I had heard about their leaders, like Steve Biko, they sounded too radical for my liking, too intolerant of people like Buthelezi and Matanzima and other black homelands leaders, the moderates with whom the moderate whites, like the Progressives, should work and consult. The conference, as I saw it, was for the moderate centre, and extremists on both sides, black and white, would have been disruptive even if they had attended.

My recording deal with Stoltz of the Bureau of State Security wasn't to be my last amusing encounter with a member of that organization. A young officer of the Bureau named Kruger occasionally played golf at the Alexander Country Club, and although locker-room and bar-room conversation tended to tail off when he approached I knew him through having been drawn in a foursome with him one Saturday. When Congressman Charles Diggs of Detroit was visiting South Africa I was invited to meet him at East London airport, and I saw Kruger of BOSS leaning against a wall in the terminal building. Diggs's plane was an hour-and-a-half late, and as time went by I saw Kruger glancing at his watch in some agitation. Eventually he approached me and said hesitantly: "Mr Woods, I am here just in case anything out of the ordinary happens. Not that that is likely, but I wonder if you would kindly do me a favour? I promised to take my kids to the drive-in tonight, and it's getting late . . ." I said: "You want me to keep an eye on things for you?" He said: "*Ag*, would you mind, Mr Woods? If anything unusual happens could you just call me later at home at this number? Man, I would appreciate it—the kids have been pestering me to see this film." I said: "Sure." And that's how I functioned as a BOSS agent for an hour. Congressman Diggs duly arrived and there was nothing "unusual" to report . . .

CHAPTER TWELVE

DURING MOST OF my time as editor of the *Dispatch* it seemed possible to function effectively against apartheid from within the system—to use elements of the system to challenge it. This situation changed at the end of 1977, but in the ten years before this I tried three different methods. One was to use what remained of normal law to challenge the Afrikaner Nationalists through the courts; another was to try to influence decisions in local politics; and a third was to attempt the same in national politics through support of the few anti-apartheid candidates who might get into the all-white parliament.

In law the only thing that could effectively be used against the Government and its supporters was to involve the law of defamation. This was common law, not statute law, and the Government hadn't yet got around to tampering with it. In their zeal to smear all opponents as Communists, subversives, agents of foreign powers and traitors to the country, they often got carried away and forgot there was still a law of defamation. The only place in which they were legally protected from being sued for defamation was parliament, but initially they overlooked this and often defamed their critics outside parliament —usually in political rallies. I told some of my editor friends that I felt we were too passive about these defamatory attacks and should start hitting back at the politicians by suing them for defamation whenever possible, but few of them knew much law and often they didn't know when they were being defamed. When they thought they were, they always went for advice to their newspapers' lawyers, and in South Africa newspaper lawyers invariably advised against lawsuits. In that way they couldn't be proved wrong, because if the editor went ahead and lost they'd be vindicated anyway, and if he didn't no one would ever know they were wrong.

Soon after being appointed editor I decided to sue every Government spokesman who defamed me outside parliament, and when I consulted a lawyer it was usually my friend

Kingsley Kingon. Ironically the defamation laws were un-intentionally made stronger by the Government because of the statutory security laws. For example, it was a statutory crime to be a Communist, so automatically it became defamatory to imply that anyone was a Communist, unless it could be proved. In the same way it was defamatory to imply that anyone was subversive, traitorous or a threat to state security. There was also the neglected law of contumelia, a remnant from Roman Law and Roman-Dutch Law, making it both a crime and a civil offence to insult anyone's sensitivities grossly without cause, even by letter or phone call or in personal conversation. Altogether I initiated more than twenty lawsuits for defama-tion or contumelia, winning them all. Generally I invoked defamation against members of the cabinet or Government officials and contumelia against the individuals who wrote me poison-pen letters. I had a form letter for contumelia, it acknow-ledged receipt of the message or phone call and threatened summons unless damages and an apology were sent by return of post. Usually the perpetrator scurried to a lawyer, who then looked up this obscure law and advised settlement. I always donated the cash proceeds from contumelia to the Institute of Race Relations or the Progressive Party, and made the per-petrator issue the cheque appropriately.

Against the big guns I had six major defamation cases. The trick was to issue Supreme Court summons in the Eastern Cape, one of the few places left in South Africa where most of the judges weren't members of the Afrikaner Broederbond and could still be counted on to judge cases strictly on their legal merits. After winning all six I noticed that members of the cabinet, when they did attack me or the *Dispatch* outside parlia-ment, began to use careful phrasing and to stop short of the point of defamation. After the sixth case, involving a member of the cabinet, I met Prime Minister Vorster at a formal banquet and he said in Afrikaans: "Well, young man, I hesitate even to greet you in case you sue me for defamation." But I didn't only sue—I was also sued occasionally, and some of the cases were big. None of them succeeded. Throughout all these cases Frank Streek backed me up and the whole board were supportive, guaranteeing all costs in case I should lose. In this way I had the best of all worlds, being able to keep defamation awards, which were tax free. Frank used to joke that they were among the perquisites of my job.

The biggest case was against the Minister of Transport, Ben Schoeman, and it cost him R7,000 in awards and legal fees. With my award I bought a grand piano. Schoeman had said in a speech to four thousand people in the Johannesburg City Hall that I was "helping long-haired Communist scum overseas" to attack apartheid in sport, and this was held to be defamatory by word-association. The other cases were routine examples of defamation through demonstrably inaccurate accusation, and the effect was to shut the more extreme Afrikaner Nationalist orators up on the subject of the "subversive press", or at least to make them more careful in phrasing their attacks. Among the men I sued was the head of the Bureau of State Security, General van den Bergh, who then retracted some vague remarks he had made about "certain editors" who "encouraged subversion". The legal principle here was that there were so few editors who could conceivably be regarded as falling into this category that there was sufficient identification for defamation.

Members of the cabinet started reserving their most vicious anti-press speeches for delivery in parliament. But at least their scope for unsubstantiated attack was narrowed, and even when they used the protection of parliament they could then be taunted and challenged to repeat their statements outside and be sued. If they declined this challenge they could be subjected to "provocative defamation"—being called liars or cowards to provoke them to sue, and thereby provide a public court test of their original allegation. In these ways it was still possible up to the mid-1970s to use remnants of the civil law to hold off some of the pressure of Government threats. The main danger from defamation by Government spokesmen was that their more extreme followers took it as a signal to harass or attack those defamed.

The biggest defamation case against me was by members of the East London City Council, who sued me for a total of 120,000 rands for alleging in a front-page editorial that they had been delinquent in rejecting an application for municipal amenities. A "hippy" group of "peace youth" or "flower-children" had applied for permission to stage a song and poetry festival at Marina Glen, a municipal park, and because the Town Clerk, an Afrikaner Nationalist named J. J. Human, apparently considered all "hippies" to be drug-purveyors and long-haired Communists, he turned it down and the city councillors allowed him to get away with it. Human had been influenced in his decision by a Minister of the Dutch Reformed Church who regarded the "peace sign" or "ban-the-bomb" emblem of the youth group as a Satanic symbol. Following my editorial attacking this decision Human convinced the councillors they had been defamed and a long Supreme Court action followed. Harold Levy, my mentor from my student days, came from Cape Town to defend me, and succeeded. When I asked what he thought of the councillors' case he replied with the story of little Abie who, asked by his teacher for an example of a four-letter word, spelt FUCM. Asked what this spelt, Abie said "Fuckem". Harold said: "That's what I think of their case", and when we won the verdict, with full costs awarded, I bought him a set of gold cufflinks on each of which was engraved the letters FUCM.

My attempt to influence local politics began with a visit to the mayor of the city, Mr David Lazarus, over the question of pass raids on blacks. These raids were carried out by municipal police, usually at night, to arrest any husband or boy-friend staying overnight in the quarters of domestic servants. Usually they had no pass, or it wasn't in order, or they had no specific permission to stay overnight in a "white" area. The worst of the raiding police was a man named Pagel, who seemed to enjoy his job. A fanatical supporter of the government, Pagel would quote the Bible to justify what he was doing, and several blacks had told the *Dispatch* that when they appealed to Pagel for mercy he would drag them to the lock-up vans saying he had to do his duty and "render unto Caesar what is Caesar's". Pagel literally broke into bedrooms and dragged men or women from their beds, from their wives or husbands, in the middle of the night to jail them under the pass laws.

I asked Mayor Lazarus to fire Pagel and stop the raids. Lazarus, a genial but ineffectual man, said he couldn't do either. I suggested that as his United Party had a majority on the Council it could surely find a way to do both, but Lazarus said that while he "deplored" the raids they were government policy and the municipality had to carry out such policy. I argued that he wasn't an official of the Government, that he was elected Mayor as a United Party candidate, and that while the United Party wasn't totally anti-apartheid it was officially opposed to apartheid excesses. Lazarus kept on smiling and saying he was sorry but his hands were tied. The best he could promise was an inquiry into Pagel's methods of applying the pass laws, and the result of this inquiry was a report, supported by the majority of the councillors, hailing Pagel as "one of our finest and most thorough officers". Another result of the inquiry was that the raids went on, and Pagel's bullying methods continued.

We on the *Dispatch* decided on a campaign to throw all the United Party councillors out of office in the municipal general election. It had to be a subtle campaign—an orthodox campaign couldn't have worked because most of the voters were so racist that they would have rallied round Pagel and the conservative majority of councillors. I called on the city's leading Afrikaner Nationalist, Robbie de Lange, who very much wanted to be Mayor of the city but was shut out because he was an Afrikaner Nationalist in a heavily English-speaking city. We did a private deal that would put him in as Mayor provided he got rid of Pagel, stopped the pass raids and agreed on a slate of candidates who were mostly liberally-inclined but not all publicly known to be such. In our campaign we emphasized the merits of the candidates as businessmen, as "new faces" who might do a better job of keeping local taxes down than their predecessors, and as younger, more vigorous men under the experienced leadership of de Lange. The campaign succeeded, and fifteen of our sixteen candidates were elected. Ex-Mayor Lazarus alone survived the landslide, finding himself the only United Party man left on the Council and no longer Mayor. De Lange moved into the City Hall and within days Pagel was fired and the pass raids stopped.

One of the candidates in our alliance was ex-policeman Donald Card, who campaigned simply by having his supporters push playing cards under doors and through letterboxes in his ward. The vote for him was heavy because grateful whites remembered how he had saved their necks from the Poqo column in the early 1960s. At first he wouldn't believe he could aspire to be a city councillor, but I talked him into it because I knew his personal popularity could unseat the ultra-conservative opponent in his ward.

When the dust had settled few people understood exactly what had happened. Even Prime Minister Vorster was fooled, naïvely sending de Lange an official message of praise for his achievement in being elected Mayor, adding that he was gratified that "our people are coming to prominence in such an English-speaking city". He didn't know the price his party colleague had paid.

One of the stars of the new council was Ruth Belonsky, who led a number of council campaigns aimed at removing apartheid signs and regulations in the city. Most of her campaigns failed because national law overruled local law, but when it didn't she won several, such as piloting through the Council a by-law integrating bus-shelters and several other amenities the central Government hadn't got around to removing from the jurisdiction of city councillors. The three best beaches in the city were reserved for whites, and blacks were allocated, by dictate of the central Government, remote and rocky beaches many miles from the city. Through her initiative the city councillors battered repeatedly at the central Government's laws of this type and gave the administration a great deal of anti-apartheid pressure they weren't used to getting from municipal councils. Ruth, Wendy and a number of other young women ran successful boycott campaigns of stores that wouldn't serve blacks or served them grudgingly, and constituted as strong a pressure group as a small minority could in a largely conservative city.

Robbie de Lange was in many ways an engaging character, and we became quite friendly. I excused him much of his racial prejudice because I liked him and because he was of an older generation and had little formal education. This friendship shocked not only the snobs of the English-speaking establishment, who looked down on Afrikaners generally and especially "working-class" or ill-educated ones, but also my liberal friends, who couldn't understand my personal regard for an Afrikaner Nationalist.

Much as I liked him, however, he knew that *Dispatch* support for him in local politics didn't mean *Dispatch* support for him in national politics. On the contrary. When he stood as an official candidate on the Afrikaner Nationalist party ticket we slammed him. During a parliamentary election, when he was picking up a lot of support because the public admired his performance as Mayor, I pulled a rough trick on him. If I had attacked him too often for backing apartheid this would have gained him votes, so instead I published an editorial the day before the election praising his abilities and saying he was too good a Mayor to send away to Cape Town as a Member of Parliament. That day many voters phoned him to say that although they had originally intended to vote for him they had now decided not to because the *Dispatch* was right—no city should lose such an able Mayor. When he lost the parliamentary election the next day he simply phoned me and said ruefully: "You bastard!"

When the general election campaign of 1973 began, Colin Eglin, leader of the Progressive Party, reminded me of a promise I had made in a moment of enthusiasm—to take leave to help him campaign in his Sea Point constituency. I did so, and joined his band of workers in Cape Town, many of whom were students or simply young people keen to oppose apartheid. The organizer was Barry Streek, Frank Streek's son, who had graduated from Rhodes University. Eglin's United Party opponent, David Graaff, was the son of the United Party leader, Sir de Villiers Graaff, and his campaign was based on crude scare-mongering—implying that if a Progressive won the area would be swamped by blacks demanding to use swimming-pools, beaches and other public amenities in Sea Point. He also used other long-established United Party methods, implying that the Progressives were soft on Communism and drugs.

Up to that point the Progressive Party had only one Member of Parliament, Helen Suzman, and we felt Sea Point was the only other seat out of more than 170 in the country which might elect a second. In the event we won Sea Point, and unexpectedly also won four other urban seats, giving Helen Suzman five Progressive colleagues in Parliament. One good thing about the election was that it signalled the beginning of the end of the United Party as the official opposition. After the Progressive victories the party won a by-election, then gained four disaffected UP members, the combined group, as the Progressive Federal Party, emerging with seventeen seats in the 1977 election to the ten seats of the United Party remnant. Although the Afrikaner Nationalists with more than a hundred seats still easily dominated Parliament, at least it meant that the official leader of the opposition, Colin Eglin, would be the first such office-holder in the all-white South African parliament to oppose apartheid.

Barry Streek, who had played a key role in the Sea Point election, seemed to me to be wasted in formal politics. He had done occasional work for newspapers, and I had been impressed with the soundness of his research and the way he wrote. I was keen to take him on to my editorial staff, particularly since during his days on the committee of the National Union of South African Students he had become well acquainted with black politics, which I began to see as a neglected sphere in South African newspapers, coverage being limited mostly to the homelands and their spokesmen, ignoring wider and more important political development among the black masses and black students. As Barry was Frank Streek's son, I realized that if I mentioned to Frank my intention to hire him he would feel he had to object, so I hired Barry first and told his father afterwards. It was almost comical to see the conflicting emotions flit across Frank's face—pleasure, consternation, doubt and regard for Barry's abilities. Barry joined us, and proved to be one of the ablest political correspondents in the country, not only breaking new ground in covering more radical black politics but winning the respect of even the conservative white politicians for his objectivity and accuracy.

The Government had cracked down heavily on English-speaking white and black students, banning eight leaders of each category. Banning was a means whereby the Government virtually house-arrested and put out of public life the more trenchant critics of the regime whom they considered not prominent enough to provoke a public or international outcry. It was done by signature of a cabinet minister, without legal proceedings or court hearings of any kind, and the banned person had no legal redress. There were many categories of banning. In one category alone, of persons who could not be quoted, there were 1,800; and as their names were gazetted publicly by order of the Minister every newspaper staff would add the appropriate names to a special set of cards which had to be referred to before certain political reports could be published, lest the paper inadvertently quoted one of them. On the *Dispatch* we called these card-indexes "the red boxes" because they were painted red for danger and kept in a prominent place in our library for quick consultation.

In all the years of the "red boxes" we were caught only once. One of our readers wrote a letter for publication, and between his posting of it and its appearance in print he was banned by Government edict. Unaware of the banning, which had not yet been gazetted, we published the letter and were prosecuted, convicted and fined. But I had faith in the Eastern Cape Supreme Court judges, most of whom were not political yes-men like many judges in other parts of the country, and we appealed against this conviction and won. After that the police redoubled their surveillance of the contents of the *Dispatch* for the slightest technicality on which to prosecute.

One morning they thought they had found one, and sent an Afrikaner police officer, who happened to have an English name, to get particulars for the prosecution. I told him I wanted my lawyer to be present and called Kingsley Kingon, who arrived in the office with a bulging briefcase and a determined look on his face. The police officer greeted him effusively: "My name is Captain Burke, Jimmy Burke—just call me Jimmy." Kingsley said: "I am Kingsley Kingon—just call me Kingsley." They beamed at each other and Captain Burke produced a folder marked "The State versus Woods". Kingsley said: "Why are you people doing this, Captain Burke?" "Please!" said Captain Burke. "Call me Jimmy." Kingsley said: "Well, Jimmy, why are you people doing this?" Captain Burke spread his hands in a shrug. "We have to apply the law, and it appears the *Dispatch* has broken the law." Then he took out his papers and asked if I would answer some questions. "Sure," I said, but Kingsley interrupted: "Maybe —it depends on the questions." Burke said: "Ah, these are just straightforward questions," and with his pen poised he asked me: "Your full names are Donald James Woods?" I started to nod, and Kingsley interrupted: "We refuse to answer that."

"But why?" asked Captain Burke. "Everyone knows that's his full name." Kingsley said: "But if we refuse to confirm it it'll put you to the trouble of proving it for the court record. Why should we do the police's work? You are putting us to trouble—why shouldn't we do the same to you?" Captain Burke smiled: "Well, if you wish to adopt that attitude . . ." Kingsley said: "We do." Then Burke asked me: "The full name of your company is East London Daily Dispatch Proprietary Limited?" Kingsley said: "We refuse to answer that. You will have to look it up in the Register of Companies." Captain Burke grew tight-lipped and asked: "You are a director of the company, Mr Woods?" Kingsley said: "No reply."

Captain Burke flushed. His pen moved down to the next question on a typed list of about twelve. He said to me: "As editor you are legally responsible for everything that appears in your newspaper, not so?" Kingsley: "We refuse to answer that." Captain Burke retorted: "I'm not asking you, I'm asking Mr Woods." Kingsley: "He's my client and I'm entitled to answer for him." "Does that mean that you refuse to answer any of these questions?" Captain Burke asked. Kingsley: "It does." Captain Burke protested: "But you haven't even heard all of them. You don't even know what I'm going to ask next." Kingsley: "Well, go ahead and read them all out, and then we'll refuse to answer them." Captain Burke threw his pen down angrily and stood up: "Now look here, Mr Kingon . . ." Kingsley held up an admonitory finger: "Uh—uh!—Kingsley!" Captain Burke swept his papers together and left in a temper.

The police never proceeded with that particular prosecution, possibly feeling it was on too trivial a point. Or maybe they were too irritated to go to the trouble of getting certified copies of my birth certificate, the register of companies and other documents to establish my full name and legal status in the case.

Few editors could have had as much backing from a manager as I had from Frank Streek. Not only did I have complete freedom to define and express the paper's policy, but editorial department administration was totally autonomous. Once he and I had agreed on the annual budget it was over to the rest of us to handle all expenditure for the year. Each editorial sub-department had its own budget, and it was left to the discretion of individual departmental heads to decide how to spend the money within that budget. It was the fullest practical system of delegation we could devise.

The only clashes Frank and I ever had were over salary increases for editorial staff. Every year I proposed increases for them, and every year Frank would object to the size of the rises. We would then argue over the merits of the individuals concerned, but he always agreed with what I wanted in the end. He realized it meant a lot to have the journalists well-paid, and that the money was available—we were a very profitable newspaper, and we carried no staff deadwood. Frank also agreed, when he saw how much it meant to me, to make the company a signatory of the union agreement with the South African Society of Journalists. He was strongly opposed to this, because it meant paying at least the union rate and he didn't want to be tied to a union rate for journalists, but my argument was that signing the agreement would be a guarantee to our staff of at least the minimum going rate in any year. We argued over this question for a long time, and eventually he only agreed when I threatened to resign.

Much as I liked and admired Frank, I found him parsimoniously resistant to salary increases, and he tended to be highly subjective about irrelevant considerations, like resisting an increase for someone he thought had slighted him. After years of tense negotiations at budget time I came to dread these annual confrontations, but in all other respects I couldn't have had a better boss. One of his weaknesses was human relations. He seemed unable to communicate well with most people, and was actually disliked by most of the printing and advertising staff. Editorial staff were also wary of him, but accepted him because I was a friend of his and had an obvious regard for him.

As the years went by I found myself increasingly protecting him from the anger or resentment of executives throughout the company, and often mediated to avert a major clash between him and one of them. Part of his problem seemed to be frustration over the company power-structure. In effect he was the head, taking all the major financial decisions and risks, but Denis Ross-Thompson showed no sign of retiring, and, while leaving all the decision-making to Frank, Ross-Thompson remained Chairman, Managing Director and chief Crewe

Trustee, which meant that although he chose not to exercise total power he retained it.

It was a strange situation, particularly since Frank paid himself more than double what Ross-Thompson drew as a salary, a huge amount, although none of us on the Board minded that. As far as I was concerned he was worth it, and I didn't care what he drew as long as the staff were well paid. Terry Briceland and Peter Eastwood felt the same way, and in the early 1970s none of us was concerned about our own rather static salaries. We accepted Frank's target figure for us, and when Peter started mentioning that our salaries weren't in fact moving up year by year as projected Terry and I thought little of it, believing Frank would look after us when he judged the time ripe. But increasingly Peter became restive—not only over the salary question but over Frank's growing tendency to act dictatorially on company decisions. Peter felt Frank was starting to regard his own judgement as infallible, and thought some of his one-man decisions on company investment were unwise. Although he tried in his quiet way to communicate this it never got through, and Peter grew uneasy about the company's future. I tried to talk him out of his unease because I had a blind faith in Frank's financial brain, and when I made no headway with Peter I arranged for the two of them to meet to thrash it out. But, bright as they were in financial matters, they were both bad communicators and the relationship deteriorated.

At this point Peter told Terry and me that he was leaving, and that since he would no longer be working for the *Dispatch* he saw no point in staying in South Africa and would emigrate to Australia. We tried to dissuade him, but his mind was made up. His departure was a loss to us all, although Terry and I continued to believe he had been alarmist about Frank. The fact that both Terry and I were drifting into deep water financially over our houses—I considerably more than Terry because of my building extravagance—was still not a major concern to us.

Then strains started developing between Terry and Frank, and, although my own relationship with Frank continued to be a good one, I noticed that since Peter's departure he seemed increasingly intolerant of anyone's shortcomings, real or fancied. I tried to talk him out of these moods and to get us all back to the friendly atmosphere we had enjoyed for so many years, but he seemed set against most of the key people in the company except me. Then one morning Denis Ross-Thompson announced that he intended to retire at the end of the financial year, and Frank seemed to take on a new lease of life. Overnight he became his old ebullient self, and we spent many a coffee-break in his office talking about how he would lead the company when he finally assumed total authority. During this time his relationship with Terry improved, and for some months it was like the good days again.

Wendy and I had become friendly with Rob and Hildur Amato, who started a non-racial theatre group, and through them we met for the first time blacks who spoke as social equals and with whom we became friendly. It was exciting to see racial barriers broken down, even within a small circle like a theatre group. To get round the law their plays were staged on private property and no admission charge was made, playgoers contributing to a "voluntary collection" which hadn't been legislated against in the race laws. I decided to try to achieve in chess, cricket and rugby what Rob was doing in theatre. I had joined the East London Chess Club several years before, and started developing my own game to try to achieve a national rating. There were no black members, and when I proposed that membership should be open to all races only one member, an elderly Afrikaner, objected. Elected to the committee, I started bringing black chess players to the club, and when the old man objected the committee told him he was welcome to leave the club if he didn't like it. Several other players didn't like it, in fact, but tolerated it rather than lose their chess.

I knew that multinational companies operating in the area were under pressure from their head offices overseas to promote black welfare and were given budgeted allowances to do this, so I went to all of them, collecting money to be made available to the chess club provided it was fully integrated. This amounted to four thousand rands, and it made us the best-equipped and most solvent chess club in the country—and also the first fully-integrated one because we were able to subsidize travel on club nights for black members living in distant town-

234

ships. From then on our club evenings were exciting. With more than fifty keen players we organized formal tournaments and got a new competitive edge going which stimulated the existing members and attracted new ones. The only holdout at first was the old Afrikaner, who stayed away rather than enter a room with "all those Kaffirs". But weeks later he started coming "just to watch". Then I noticed him watching the games of some of the stronger black players. One evening he asked a black player after a tournament game which the latter had won: "Why did you sacrifice your knight there?" Within minutes they were playing a friendly game, and that night at the club was one of my happiest. To me it seemed a microcosm of what the whole country could become—a non-racial society discovering all the exciting potential for so long stifled by the narrowness of apartheid.

Heartened by the success of the chess club integration, in which we contravened the apartheid laws regularly, gradually gaining public acceptance by printing pictures of tournament play, I decided to try the same approach to integrate club cricket. Working with Kemal Casoojee, who headed the local chapter of the non-racial South African Cricket Board of Control, or SACBOC, I became involved with black cricketers in the area. There was a lot of talent, and Kemal and I formed the provocatively named Rainbow Cricket Club, selecting such good players that on playing merit we were able to apply for first-league status. This threw the local white cricket administrators into a panic. Our star team had three blacks, two Indians, three coloureds and three whites, and the white cricket authorities refused our application on the grounds that multiracial cricket was illegal. Now began a long campaign to try to persuade them to break the law, and for more than a year they refused. I became the only white member of the non-racial national body, and was appointed to the seventeen-man national council of SACBOC. In the power-saddle was the all-white South African Cricket Association, or SACA. It was SACA that had run all major cricket in South Africa for nearly a century including international games and tours, while SACBOC was regarded by the Government as near-subversive. SACBOC held one powerful card—the support of the international cricket bodies of England, Australia, New

Zealand, India, Pakistan and the West Indies. This meant the international cricket powers would not allow South Africa back into international cricket until SACBOC was satisfied there was no longer apartheid in the game.

We in SACBOC wouldn't give this go-ahead until SACA abolished apartheid not only in teams but at grounds and in public facilities, from club level up through state level to international level. The Government wouldn't allow SACA to do this and SACA wouldn't defy the Government—something we felt they could get away with because their white cricket stars were national heroes. While the Afrikaner Nationalist government might turn a blind eye to an integrated chess club, rather than suffer adverse publicity overseas for closing it, a mass-following sport like cricket was something else. It concerned the country's entire "way of life". In those years I also became involved with the rugby body trying to do in rugby what SACBOC aimed to do in cricket. This was the non-racial South African Rugby Union, and its task was the hardest because rugby was almost a religion with South African whites, especially Afrikaners.

One day, while flying from East London to Cape Town, I met the new Minister of Sport, Dr Piet Koornhof, on the plane. It was widely believed that Koornhof had been appointed to the Sports Ministry in order to engineer cosmetic changes on the surface of South African sport to try to get the country back into international sport. He believed that if the black sports organizations were content to co-operate with a gradual programme for open sport he could get whites to approve it over a period of years—provided there was the pay-off of a return to international sports recognition. I next met Dr Koornhof at a formal dinner which Wendy and I attended in Cape Town, and knowing that I was the only white member of the SACBOC council he invited me to come to his house over the weekend to discuss how I might be able to bridge the gap between the SACBOC diehards and his department. I said I would be glad to help but didn't see any point in such a discussion unless he and I had the same goal—the removal of every trace of apartheid from sport. To my surprise Dr Koornhof said: "Then we must talk, because we share that goal."

The following morning Wendy and I arrived at the Koornhof

ministerial residence in Rondebosch, and the Minister and I talked for some hours, because it transpired that there was indeed common ground between us, and the talk was frank to the point of bluntness. I told him I wanted sports apartheid ended because it destroyed vitally-needed points of inter-racial contact which could break down race prejudice and lead to racial peace. I told him I saw elimination of sports apartheid as only one aspect of the fight against general apartheid. He said he wanted sports apartheid eliminated for different reasons. He felt that while South Africa remained excluded from international sport this constituted a political pressure point against the whole Afrikaner Nationalist regime and the main body of political apartheid. While he agreed that non-racial sport would help build useful bridges between South Africa's alienated communities, and that this was a good thing in itself for the sake of racial peace, he saw it mainly as a means of buying time for his government's general policies. In short, I wanted to end sports apartheid in order to *hasten* the breakdown of general apartheid, while he wanted to end sports apartheid in order to *prolong* general apartheid. While these two aims were poles apart, we had at least an identical immediate goal—to end sports apartheid. But for Dr Koornhof this was easier said than done. He was bound by his party's caucus and congress resolutions as well as by the prejudices and fears of his cabinet colleagues. He also had to take account of his party's grass-roots supporters.

I rather liked Koornhof, feeling that he had sensitivities on the race question that none of his cabinet colleagues had. I told him that I saw his main problem as being the media, particularly the print media. He was nervous of announcing any change in sports apartheid because this would make banner headlines in the newspapers and scare his rural party members out of their wits. The answer was therefore to gain the co-operation of the press, to talk to all the editors in private, tell them what he was up to, and ask them to de-sensationalize headlines and reports of sports integration. Television and radio, being state-controlled, would do what he told them, and so, presumably, would the pro-government Afrikaans press. But I believed the anti-government press would also co-operate on this issue, and told him so.

Koornhof seemed surprised. "Would they really co-operate?" he asked. "I'm sure we all would," I said. "We've been telling your government for years to dismantle apartheid, including sports apartheid, and if you now begin to do it we'll be only too glad to make it easier for you." "But wouldn't they just use it as a stick to beat the Government with—anything to embarrass us among our followers?" he asked. "No, I don't believe so," I replied. "Try it and see. I'm certain the response will be positive." We agreed it would be better for me to organize the briefing, to allay press suspicion that this was a Governmental pressure exercise. So I telephoned all the editors during the next few weeks, and set up a lunch in Cape Town at which Koornhof agreed to come clean about his intentions. All the editors representing Afrikaans and English-language newspapers attended, and Koornhof spoke, fielding all the questions that followed. I also spoke, urging those editors who felt as strongly as I did against apartheid to grab this opportunity of helping the Government in at least one area of our national life, sport, to do what we wanted them to do. All the editors agreed to co-operate, by presenting news of concessions in sports apartheid with restraint so that the Government would be encouraged to make further concessions without their alarmed followers believing the end of the world was at hand.

Koornhof asked if I'd help him further by attending a confidential meeting in his office of leaders of the white and non-racial cricket bodies to reassure the latter that he was sincere in his intentions and to help negotiate a programme towards non-racial cricket. When I walked into the room the white officials became alarmed and objected to my presence. "He's a newspaperman," they said. "The whole press is camped outside, and these talks are supposed to be confidential. We can't have a journalist in here." Koornhof assured them I was present at his invitation, but they weren't mollified by this. At this point one of the SACBOC delegates, my friend Kemal Casoojee, stood up to say that if the white officials would not consent to my presence at the meeting the black delegates would walk out. This threw the white officials into a flurry, and after whispered consultations they agreed to have me there.

It was an extraordinary meeting. Around the long table

were all the leading cricket administrators of South Africa—
black, white, coloured and Indian—and Koornhof sought a
consensus. In brief, what he wanted was this: an unofficial
Australian cricket team was prepared to tour South Africa on
condition that none of their South African opponent teams was
segregated. There had to be at least two "non-white" players
in every team they played. The Government wanted the
prestige of an Australian team visit, SACA wanted the revenue
and the status-recognition of it as well, but SACBOC refused
to let its black players be used for such tokenism, insisting that
all club, State and nationally representative teams should be
integrated first before they would consent. Koornhof promised
that if the Australian tour was completed without incident he
would guarantee cricket integration at all levels. SACBOC
said he should guarantee this *before* they consented to the tour,
and that they felt their players were being used as pawns merely
to gain South Africa international cricket respectability.
Koornhof protested that he needed the tour as a means of
persuading his party of the international benefits of internal
integration of cricket. The tour would be a coup for him, a
feather in his cap, which he could use as leverage for the
remaining concessions.

I said I felt there was validity to both points of view. We
were being offered a deal. I suggested we put the Minister to
the test—give him his coup, okay the tour, on condition that
within six months no barriers remained to prevent integration
of cricket clubs and teams. Koornhof startled everyone by saying vigorously: "Gentlemen, you've got no reason to trust me.
As far as you're concerned I'm one of those Afrikaner Nationalist bastards who've been buggering you around for years. But
now we've all got a chance to achieve something. I ask you to
trust me now. If we don't trust each other and come to this
agreement we're going to fuck the whole thing up!" There was
a gasp of surprise around the table, especially from the Natal
Indian Moslems, then a general roar of laughter. The ice was
broken and the deal struck. The meeting asked me to draft
a statement for the Minister to release to the press and I
reflected that this was the second time I had written a
public statement for an Afrikaner Nationalist—first Vorster,
now Koornhof. I slipped out by the back way, the others

emerged to meet the press and the Minister released his statement.

Kemal and I had a private celebration back in East London. I had told Koornhof about our Rainbow Cricket Club and he had said: "Yes, man, go ahead and tell the white officials that although it's against the law we'll turn a blind eye to it. I can't say it publicly but tell them I say it privately—that provided there's no fuss and no big bloody headlines screaming all over the place they can just go ahead." But the white officials of the Border Cricket Association were too scared to take a chance. Their president, Leigh Warren, dug in his heels. "It's all very well for Koornhof to say this privately and unofficially," he said. "But *we* have to break the laws, not him. If the police here prosecute us it is *our* cricket clubs that lose their liquor licences." I flew to Johannesburg and told Koornhof that Warren and the other white officials wouldn't go ahead without permission from him in writing. Koornhof was alarmed. "Hell, man, I can't put that officially. I can't give you a letter telling them officially to break my Government's laws." I said: "Well, they won't do a thing without your written permission." Dr Koornhof looked unhappy. "What about an informal message on the back of a cigarette packet?" I asked him. "That isn't official, but it's in writing, isn't it?" I said. "*Ja*, I suppose so," he replied. I pulled out a packet of cigarettes, and on the cardboard back of it scrawled out a message to "L. Warren, Border Cricket Union" certifying that it was in order to admit the Rainbow Cricket Club to the Border League, then held it out to Dr Koornhof. He smiled and signed. When I got back to East London Kemal said he wanted it recorded in the SAC-BOC minutes that cricket in the Eastern Cape had been integrated on the back of my cigarette packet.

We became the first region in the country to stage a non-racial league cricket game. Kemal and I were tense as the teams arrived, because the local police and populace didn't know about the cigarette packet deal, and in the *Dispatch* a restrained preview of the match had been published without stress on its non-racial nature. However, anyone could realize by the team-names—Njokweni and Mbatani were unmistakably African names and Pillay was an unmistakably Indian name—that it was no ordinary match. A bigger crowd than usual turned up to see the strange sight on one of our big-league cricket grounds of black, coloured and Indian players in one team-huddle out in the middle.

Afterwards, an official of the Department of Sport came to see me and pointed out that the Rainbow team's participation in the league was illegal. I reached into my pocket and pulled out the cigarette box signed by Koornhof. His eyes widened with astonishment. "Jesus!" he exclaimed, taking it from me to examine the ministerial signature more closely. "We have nothing about this from our Department," he said, nonplussed. "Well, phone your Minister," I said. "Or if you prefer to cause less embarrassment all round, phone his secretary, Mr Beyers Hoek, who was present when this was signed." He phoned Hoek, who mumbled some departmental jargon about "elements of the policy being under review", and advised the local East London office to "assist Mr Woods and the other cricket officials" pending further explanations from the Minister himself. The official told me this in tones of awe, after which our team felt able to arrive at designated grounds to fulfil their fixtures without risking arrest.

While we were taking advantage of these under-publicized concessions to establish as much precedent as possible, Koornhof was making as much of his side of the bargain as he could —claiming credit in his party caucus for securing the Australian tour and for the fact that it was completed without incident. Heartened by the deal, he began to wonder if we mightn't do in rugby what we had done in cricket, and asked me to approach the non-racial South African Rugby Union officials who were refusing to talk to him. It was arranged that I should organize a private "summit" meeting of rugby officials of both black and white associations with this hope in view.

But at this stage a young white rugby star of Eastern Province, Dan Watson, decided to defy the official laws and applied to join a black rugby club in Port Elizabeth. The club, Kwaru, welcomed him, but after playing one game for them Watson began to be subjected to threats by police and Government officials. He was told he was breaking no fewer than six laws, and would be prosecuted if he did it again. It was pointed out that even entering the black area of the town to get to the club was illegal, and added to the official warnings were telephone threats, anonymous letters and even a campaign by whites to boycott the Watson family's clothing shop.

The Watson story became a public controversy, with banner headlines in the papers, and it was discussed in the cabinet. Other cabinet ministers put pressure on Koornhof to act, and he went on television to warn Watson that anyone "defying the law was risking severe punishment". I phoned Koornhof, and said that in view of his statement he could expect no further co-operation from me on the rugby or cricket issues. Koornhof, however, assured me that nothing would happen to Watson. "For Chrissake, I had to make that statement," he said. "But nothing will happen, I promise you. Don't judge me by what I *say*, only by what I *do*." I wondered if he realized my telephone was tapped by the Security Police, and what they must have thought of the discussions they could overhear between a member of their party's cabinet and me.

That our telephone was tapped there was no doubt. At a function for patrons of the East London Museum, an outdoor barbecue one evening in the grounds of the museum, Wendy and I became aware of a middle-aged man joining us on a tree-stump. He seemed either diffident or nervous, and when he finally spoke we realized why. Speaking slightly above a whisper, he told us he was a technician at the city's central telephone exchange, and that he had often tried to pluck up the courage to warn us that our home telephone was not only tapped by the Security Police but that it had been connected by direct line to Security Police headquarters. There, apparently, it was listened to by a relay of officers on duty, and when they had to go out every conversation on our home phone was recorded by a voice-activated tape-recorder. Our informant said the connection was checked every week by a senior Security Police officer. Obviously the Security Police automatically had on tape all the anonymous calls we received. There was one caller who spoke in Afrikaans-accented English, and his tone was always one of barely suppressed rage. "Is that Woods the white renegade?" he would say. "Yes, is that the yellow bastard?" I'd say. "You're a white renegade," he'd say. "You're a yellow bastard," I'd say. "White renegade!" "Yellow bastard!" Not a high level of discussion.

CHAPTER THIRTEEN

DENIS ROSS-THOMPSON's retirement day dawned and Frank was officially installed as Managing Director, Chairman and successor-designate as chief Crewe Trustee. Denis, now in his seventies, moved out of his large office overlooking the ocean and Frank moved in. The first morning we had our usual coffee-break in his new office and talked about the many years he had waited for this and reminisced about all the crises and mini-crises we'd had during the past ten years—including the day he had risked his job for me. There was a disquieting moment as I got up to return to my office. Frank developed a cold expression on his face and suddenly said: "Now that I'm completely in charge people are going to have to jump around here. I've been too tolerant for too long." I said: "Ah, don't get carried away, Frank. You might become intolerable!" He laughed, went through the motions of aiming a slow punch at my jaw and did a kind of capering dance around the sacrosanct office that got me laughing again.

A few weeks later it was annual salary-revision time, and as we fixed the appointment for what we called our "yearly clash" Frank said he would first like to revise my own salary— he had noticed I hadn't ever made recommendations about it, but I must surely be heading for financial trouble. I replied that I had been concerned but hadn't discussed it with him because he had said he would adjust my salary when he saw fit in terms of the income targets he had envisaged several years before. He assured me that I had been right to leave it to him, and that the time had come to get me out of the trouble I was in. As he was now head of the company I needn't worry about our "annual clash" any more—from now on I could deal direct on staff salaries with the new financial director, Ian Kaye-Eddie, and meanwhile he and Ian were working on a plan to adjust my salary and fringe benefits to get me "solvent" again. I took the salary list to Ian Kaye-Eddie and we went through each individual case. When I was finished he said: "I'm afraid the answer is no." Nonplussed, I asked: "No to what?" "There won't be any general staff increases this year," he replied. I said: "You mean no merit increases? You can't mean general increases, because we're automatically obliged to meet the mandatory increases under the agreement with the South African Society of Journalists." Iam looked puzzled. "Well, I don't know about that," he said. "I think Frank wants to drop it." I asked what he meant, and he said Frank wanted to withdraw the *Dispatch* from the agreement with the journalists' union. "I'm sure you've misunderstood him," I said. "Frank knows I would resign if he did that."

Ian Kaye-Eddie looked a bit out of his depth on the issue, so I went on: "Well, I'd better clear this up with Frank before we talk about merit increases." I phoned Frank and told him I didn't think Ian had the full background on the salary issue and that we'd better discuss it first. Frank agreed, and joked that I obviously missed our annual confrontation since I seemed to prefer dealing with him rather than Ian. A few days later he called me up to his office, where I found him and Ian Kaye-Eddie both smiling broadly. He told me that he and Ian had considered my salary position and had found a formula to bail me out of trouble. It involved a large increase not only in my salary but also in my tax-free entertainment allowance; in addition the company would pay my home phone bills because my house phone was used mostly for *Dispatch* business. The combination of these benefits would enable my income to exceed my expenditure by a safe margin. I thanked them both, and when Ian had gone I thanked Frank again and told him what a relief it was, and how I had been starting to feel desperate about the high interest charges on my overdraft. As we walked down to the car park together Frank said: "You should never feel desperate while I'm around. You can always come to me for help of any kind." To my surprise, tears came into his eyes and he got into his car quickly and drove away. I stopped on the way home to get a bottle of champagne, and as Wendy and I celebrated I told her the good news. Knowing Frank, she was as surprised as I had been at his sudden show of emotion.

After the weekend I arrived at the office on the Monday to collect my staff salary review list for the meeting with Frank. I bounded into his office exuberantly, and had barely settled into the chair in front of his desk when he said: "I've got a rough task to perform now, and it's not going to be easy for me. You and I have come to a parting of the ways. You'll have to go." I heard the words but didn't take them in at first. What told me he wasn't joking was the look on his face. He said: "I did a lot of thinking over the weekend. It was the worst weekend of my life. I dug in the garden and thought it all out. You'll have to go." Some instinct told me to be as passive as possible outwardly; inwardly I was completely shattered. "Why the change from Friday evening?" I asked. "I had a rethink," he said, telling me how he had had second thoughts about the plan he and Ian Kaye-Eddie had worked out. I said: "Then that whole plan of Friday is now off? I'm not getting the increase? What do you expect me to do?" He answered: "You'll have to go insolvent. It'll be rough, but you've been heading for it. I think your father must have spoilt you with money when you were a kid, or something." He returned to how he'd rethought the plan over the weekend. He'd agonized over it and come to the conclusion that it wouldn't work because the receiver of revenue wouldn't allow the tax-free benefits. He had then discussed it again with Ian Kaye-Eddie, who had also said it wouldn't work. Confused by this but wanting to get out of his office for a while to think things out, I got up to go. He said: "On personal grounds you realize this puts me through the wringer. But you'll survive—it'll do you good to battle your way out of this." "You mean I've got to get another job and leave here," I replied. "When do you want me to go?" "Now," he said. "As soon as possible." I felt a surge of anger and exclaimed, "What do you mean—now? Do you think I can find a job and arrange to move my entire family overnight?" He smiled strangely: "I knew you'd try and hang on for a time." "I don't want to work here another day knowing how you feel," I replied, "but surely I should be given a reasonable chance to find another job, at least a couple of months." "Of course," he reassured me. "Of course I don't expect you to go immediately. But start looking around as soon as you can." He told me to sit down and relax for a while, adding: "I know what a shock this is for you."

He talked for a while about which newspapers he thought would give me a job. "Who will succeed me?" I asked. "Surely

245

George Farr?" Frank looked angry. "None of that crowd down there," he snapped. "I want a more management-orientated editor now." I had a sudden suspicion and asked: "Of course before I go we can settle the staff salary question, surely? The SASJ agreement . . ." He looked at me with a kind of contemptuous hostility which shocked me. "I'm dropping that. I'm cancelling it—getting us out of that nonsense from now on." I said: "I advise you to pay those increases, honour the SASJ agreement and appoint George as editor." "That has nothing to do with you now," he replied irritably. "That's no longer your concern." "But it is," I told him. "As a director . . ." He said: "An insolvent can't be a company director. It's against the law. Naturally you'll have to resign as a director too. I know your attitude to the SASJ agreement. You made it plain you'd resign if I cancelled it. Well, you've threatened me once too often with that. You've held a gun at my head over it. You talked me out of ditching Terry, too, you protected him from me."

I walked to the door. "Well, Frank, I'm grateful for all you've done for me in the past." He came to the door to see me out. "Ah, don't be sentimental," he said, smiling. "I won't," I promised.

I was surprised to find it was only lunchtime—it was as if the whole day had gone by. I drove to the seafront and parked there, thinking it all out. I tried to see things from Frank Streek's point of view—that I was simply too extravagant for the company's good, and that even if he bailed me out of financial trouble now I might well get back into it later, to the company's embarrassment; that I was already well paid as an editor, and that if he gave me the increases and fringe benefits he had spoken of earlier this could attract the unwelcome attentions of the receiver of revenue at a time when the *Dispatch* was already under harsh scrutiny from State revenue officials for political reasons. On the face of things there could be validity in all these points, although his own income was so enormous and he himself had so many fringe benefits allowed by the revenue department that it was hard for me to believe these were his real reasons for wanting to get rid of me.

What seemed a more likely scenario, as I thought it all through, was the following: Streek, now freed from previous constraints on his authority, felt he could make a lot more money for and out of the *Dispatch*. One way to save money was on salaries, and one way to save on salaries was to cancel the SASJ agreement. But to do that he needed my compliance, and to bid for this he had first subjected me to the pressure of financial ruin, then offered me the prospect of salvation from this—if I turned a blind eye to his cancellation of the agreement. Then during the weekend he had realized I wouldn't play along with his plan to drop the union agreement, and that he could bring in a more amenable editor (a "management-orientated" editor) at half my salary, and kill several birds with one stone.

Whichever of the two explanations was the truth, I was so shocked by his sudden hostility to me, to George Farr and the editorial staff, and so angered by his talk of cancelling the union agreement on salaries, that there could be no question of tamely accepting dismissal.

After work I called at Terry's house and told him the story. We were close friends, and there was no need for us to discuss whether we were together in the coming clash. We spent several hours discussing how to pull off a coup against Streek. In theory it was well-nigh impossible. He had been installed as chief executive, and over the years had gathered in a personal shareholding amounting to ten per cent of the company. Furthermore, he was held in high regard by the man who controlled most of the voting shares of the company, Denis Ross-Thompson. Among the directors, we knew George Farr and Len Beacom would support us, and that the rest of the staff would rally to us—but how and when to strike? We decided to say nothing to any staff member until Streek was overseas on a trip he was scheduled to take within a few days. Then, when we were properly organized, we would summon him back for an appropriate boardroom confrontation.

Streek flew off on the Saturday morning, and Terry, Len, George and I held a meeting that afternoon in a curiously festive mood. Although we had little reason at that stage to feel confident we were exhilarated at the approaching showdown, and felt that with time to prepare thoroughly we would stand at least an even chance of offsetting the advantages Streek held. One point on which we all agreed was that the main principle in a coup was to win. Half-success was no good, Marquess of Queensberry rules were out and there could be no compromise. We were agreed that if necessary we'd lead all departments of the company out on strike rather than have Streek back.

The first thing was to canvass the support of our senior staff to be sure we could deal from a position of strength. Security was important, because we needed all the time we could get to organize without showing our hand. Then we would confront Denis Ross-Thompson with a united rejection of Streek and compel a showdown. We spent the weekend drafting outlines of the documents we should need and, on the Monday, I asked Roger Omond whether the senior editorial executives would be solidly with me in a confrontation with Streek. Roger gave a grin of sheer delight. He said: "If you don't yet know that your staff would follow you through flame and fire you'll find it out now. There won't be one hanging back." I told him a signed document of support would be valuable, and by the next day I was in possession of it. Addressed to Denis Ross-Thompson, it said that the undersigned editorial executives understood there was a boardroom clash in prospect between the editor and the managing director, and that in effect if this resulted in the editor's resignation it would result in theirs as well. The memorandum was signed by every senior editorial executive, including deputy chief sub-editor Robin Ross-Thompson, Denis Ross-Thompson's son and heir.

All of us on the Board, except Ian Kaye-Eddie, handed this memorandum to Denis Ross-Thompson, together with another memorandum signed by ourselves to the effect that Streek no longer had our confidence, that we were no longer prepared to work with him, and that he was unacceptable not only to us but to all the staff as well. Ross-Thompson was astonished, and asked whether resentment of Streek was so widespread. We suggested he should make his own random sampling of staff opinion on the matter, and he did so over the next few days, interviewing key employees he had known for a long time. After this sampling he was shocked at the deep and widespread hatred and fear of Streek, and fired off a letter to him—a letter which had Streek back from overseas on the next plane.

At a formal meeting in the boardroom Ian Kaye-Eddie was also informed of these developments, and the news clearly came as a shock to him. We knew by now that every department was prepared to back us with strike action if necessary, but this we kept in reserve as a last resort. On his return Streek approached many of the company's senior staff in all departments for support, but not one would endorse him. I realized for the first time to what extent I had been his protection from staff resentment.

We had our board confrontation after he had put his case to Denis Ross-Thompson for several hours in private, but when we were all face to face it was obvious that no compromise was possible, and Streek cooked his own goose with some tasteless remarks which turned Ross-Thompson finally against him. He was retired from the company immediately, with a generous pension which at his request I negotiated with him on behalf of the Board.

Suddenly there was a new atmosphere in the *Dispatch* building. Morale soared, productivity improved, profits climbed, and the journalists' agreed salary scales were not only met but exceeded. I was still surprised that I had been so unaware of the extent to which Streek's presence had been oppressive to so many members of the staff. Simply because I hadn't been conscious of him for years as an unreasonable figure, simply because he had never withheld money from my department and my journalists hadn't been as wary of him as several other departments, I had been prejudiced in his favour because of his sterling support of me for so many years.

While getting rid of Streek solved a lot of problems for many people on the *Dispatch*, it didn't solve my income problems or Terry's. We could hardly ask the board to implement for us increases that for years had existed only as an intent in Streek's head. But fortunately my income was augmented by the launching in six newspapers of a nationally-syndicated column by me, an idea encouraged by the editor of the *Rand Daily Mail*, Raymond Louw. The column developed a high readership and appeared every week in the *Rand Daily Mail*, the *Cape Times*, the *Natal Witness*, the Bloemfontein *Friend*, the Kimberley *Advertiser* and the *Daily Dispatch*.

CHAPTER FOURTEEN

In 1973 I was made an honorary vice-president of NUSAS, the National Union of South African Students. This was a liberal body of English-speaking students often harassed by the government for campaigning against apartheid, and latterly it was also coming under attack from radical black students who saw liberalism as an inadequate response to the whole apartheid structure of South Africa. A group of the radical black students, led by Stephen Biko and others, had broken away from NUSAS several years before to found the blacks-only South African Students Organization—SASO. SASO was a manifestation of the Black Consciousness movement then developing in South Africa. After three centuries of trying various responses to white oppression, including war, passive resistance, pleading, negotiations and politics in co-operation with white liberals, blacks were turning increasingly to a new and more militant approach in which they functioned alone— as blacks led by blacks.

Young leaders like Steve Biko, Barney Pityana, Abraham Tiro and Harry Nengwekhulu were spearheading this new militancy, and my first response to "black consciousness" was that it was retrogressive. I saw it initially as racist, and as reprehensible in its direction as the "white consciousness" of the Afrikaner Nationalists. While I could understand why Black Consciousness had developed, I couldn't condone it— in fact, I attacked it in editorials and in speeches to black students at Fort Hare University. I urged the students to stay loyal to NUSAS and its white students who had undergone banning, imprisonment and harassment for the anti-apartheid cause, and my appeal was supported by most of them. After one such speech several hundred students supported continued loyalty to NUSAS and only a handful of about ten spoke for SASO. I noticed, however, that the SASO minority were the most articulate speakers and had the strongest personalities, but their appeal sounded too narrow and race-conscious to secure the following of most of the black students at that time.

That was the position then, but it was to change radically over the next few years, and by 1976 the majority of black students were strong supporters of SASO and the black consciousness movement generally.

During the early days of SASO various friends of Steve Biko had urged me to meet him. Men like Father David Russell told me he was a remarkable personality and that I didn't understand what he and his movement were really all about. But after decades of being involved in opposing apartheid, which placed undue emphasis on white skin, I had no interest in any movement which seemed to place undue emphasis on black skin. I dismissed Biko and the others as a group of extremists who were doing precisely what the Afrikaner Nationalists wanted them to do—emphasizing race differences and polarizing politics into racial divisions.

Steve Biko was then living in King William's Town, banned by the Government and restricted from public speaking, from being quoted, from leaving the area and from being in the company of more than one person at a time. He was irritated by my editorial attacks, and decided we should meet, so that he could explain his movement to me and remove what he saw as my gross misunderstanding of it. So he sent Dr Mamphela Ramphele to see me in my office to arrange a meeting with him. By the name Ramphele I knew that his emissary would be black, and this in itself was interesting, because black doctors were rare in South Africa. For some reason I expected a grey-haired Uncle Tom figure to walk deferentially into my office, and was unprepared for the attractive young black woman in blue jeans and a white sweater who strode aggressively into the office and introduced herself in rather a loud voice as Dr Ramphele. She had a challenging attitude, and was soon castigating me about my failure to understand Black Consciousness. Standing in front of my desk with her hands on her hips, she railed against "newspapers like yours which are always giving publicity to the wrong people". She said newspapers always covered homelands politics, which most blacks rejected, but never explained the importance of authentic black politics. "Why do you give the headlines to sellouts like Buthelezi and Matanzima?" she demanded. "Why don't you get to know the real black leaders? When are you coming to talk to Steve Biko? You know he is banned and can't come to you, so why don't you go to him?"

We had a long discussion about black politics, I explaining that because the mass-supported liberation movements, the African National Congress and the Pan-Africanist Congress, were banned, no newspaper could publish anything construed as promotional about them, but that if I could get more material about the Black Consciousness movement the *Dispatch* would certainly give full news coverage to it in spite of our editorial disapproval. "But why do you disapprove of Black Consciousness?" she said. I told her about my aversion to racial emphasis of any kind, and she gave a sort of howl of protest. "You've got the whole thing wrong, man! We're not racist. We're just insisting on being ourselves. You must come and talk to Steve, he'll explain the whole thing." Before she left she asked for coverage of the opening of Zanempilo Clinic, built by the Black Consciousness movement for rural blacks who couldn't get into urban hospitals. The clinic was part of Biko's Black Community Programmes, which included literacy classes, home industries, clothes manufacture and other enterprises designed to give practical effect to black self-reliance. The coverage was arranged, and so was the appointment to meet Steve Biko.

I drove to King William's Town to meet him. He was at the offices of the Black Community Programme, on the site of a former church made available by the Anglicans at the instigation of Father Russell. Biko was tall and well-built, with pleasant features, but his expression was reserved and there was a certain tension as we met. I had never met a banned person, and wasn't too sure of the extent of the restrictions. Although I had often written editorials condemning banning and all the other Afrikaner Nationalist devices for punishing critics without legal process, I had had the inevitable subconscious reservations one has about political victims in an authoritarian society. Intellectually you defend their right to open trial, but you have sneaking suspicions or doubts about what they might have done. It is an insidious but real by-product of the repressive society.

I challenged Biko about the attacks he and his followers made on the white liberal position, and said I saw no need to apologize for having been born white, and that we liberals had a right to resent being associated with apartheid policies which we opposed. He was amused at this challenge. He conceded that liberals couldn't be blamed for apartheid, but said blacks had to discover themselves first and realize their own political power before they could join with white allies against apartheid. We had a long discussion about this, in which he gave an articulate and impressive discourse on the full range of the subject—so much so that I began to see the extent of my misunderstanding of what he and his colleagues were about. Although I couldn't agree entirely with his thesis, I emerged from that meeting with a fuller perception not only of Black Consciousness but of blackness in South Africa in all its implications. Biko had remarkable gifts of communication. He conveyed ideas and concepts even beyond his eloquent words, and I could see why he had such dedicated admirers. In fact, I became one of them that day, and the longer I knew him the more my admiration grew. We often met after that, and it was through Steve Biko that I gained a clearer understanding not only of the realities of black politics in South Africa but of the Third World viewpoint generally.

He invited the whole family up to the Zanempilo Clinic, where Wendy and I and the children spent a Sunday with Steve and about a dozen of his friends. Wendy and I soon realized we were being looked over and were "on trial" in the eyes of the group, but we must have passed muster because in spite of our conservative views we were often invited back and became friendly with them all. Wendy and I had never met blacks like these in South Africa. They had a confidence and a bearing that blacks in the country generally hadn't. Somehow they had survived the cradle-to-grave apartheid conditioning that leaves its mark on most blacks. As our friendship with Steve grew, with his wife Ntsiki, and with Mamphela and other members of the group, we began to live in two worlds. One was the white suburban world and the other was the radically different Biko world where Security Police harassment, jailing and physical danger were a part of everyday existence. In the white world you talked of who had dined with whom, and in the black world of who had been arrested or searched that week.

I had decided from our first meeting to assign reporters to the "Black Consciousness beat", black reporters, and asked Steve to find me an able columnist to put the group's viewpoint on our forum page, where we regularly published all the political viewpoints permitted by law. Steve sent me a columnist, Mapetla Mohapi, who wrote the column I had envisaged. He did it well for several weeks, and during this time an initial reserve on his part melted and his friendly personality emerged. Then Mapetla was banned, and the security police started harassing him and his family. He and his wife Nohle were a handsome couple. Nohle had a special beauty, and while she was not "political" she was personally supportive of him, with the particular strength people needed when official harassment reached right into the home. They were hounded out of their small shack in the township, and from the time of Mapetla's banning they found it impossible to get any kind of home assigned to them by the authorities. Friends helped with temporary accommodation, but the strictures on a banned person made this difficult for all concerned.

In 1976 Defence Minister P. W. Botha, later to become Prime Minister, prevailed on the cabinet to commit South African troops to the Angolan civil war. On the advice of America's Central Intelligence Agency and, it was rumoured, with the encouragement of US Secretary of State Henry Kissinger, Botha became convinced that of the three liberation movements contending for power in Angola after the Portuguese withdrawal the least desirable and the most socialist, from South Africa's point of view, was Agostinho Neto's MPLA. So he sent the South African army in to help Holden Roberto's FNLA and Jonas Savimbi's UNITA forces. I asked Steve Biko what he thought of it all. "Neto is Africa's man," he said. "He's the one we in the Black Consciousness movement support, and he is the one who will win." When Neto sought to counter the South African invasion by appealing for and getting Cuban troops, Steve predicted: "Now when he wins the West will say it was only because of the Cubans. They'll call Neto a puppet of the Communist powers."

The South African Government denied any military involvement in Angola, and issued a strict prohibition under the

Defence Act against publication in any newspaper in the country of reports of any South African troop involvement in Angola. It was an absurd situation—newspapers all over the world were publishing stories of South African troops in Angola, yet no newspaper in South Africa was allowed to print a word about it. In my syndicated column I wrote a satirical piece about a horseback invasion of Angola by a Boer War-type general easily identified as P. W. Botha. It was an attempt to tell the people that their sons were fighting a war in a foreign land without their knowledge or approval. I waited for an angry response from P. W. Botha but none came, so I concluded with relief that the article hadn't been brought to his attention.

Some weeks later all editors were invited to Botha's office for a confidential briefing. I seated myself at the far end of the table furthest from Botha, and he gave a long address in which he admitted that South Africa was involved in Angola. An army general then gave a military briefing which indicated that the war was going against Neto and would soon be brought to a close. It reminded me of a briefing given by an American general in Washington when I was on a State Department-sponsored visit there in 1967, in which the North Vietnamese were said to be in retreat and the progress of the Vietnam war was described as satisfactory. Several editors asked Botha questions, to which he replied calmly, but when Raymond Louw pressed him closely with his questions Botha suddenly began a tirade against me for the satirical article on Angola. His voice rising, he became near-hysterical as he accused me of ridiculing him in order to lower the morale of South African troops and thus to "help South Africa's enemies and encourage Marxist terrorists". It had long been known that Botha was a highly excitable man often given to ungovernable bursts of rage. In Parliament on the day Dr Verwoerd had been stabbed to death he had pointed a quivering finger at Helen Suzman and shrieked: "You are to blame! People like you encourage our enemies!" In Botha's view it seemed axiomatic that anyone who opposed apartheid was "an enemy of South Africa". His last high-pitched threat to me as I left his office after the Angola briefing was: "Just you wait, Mr Woods! I'm after you! Wait until the parliamentary session! I'm going to fix you then!" Like other Afrikaner Nationalist leaders, he was reserving his most vicious attacks on individuals for the protective sessions of parliament when they could safely defame anyone without fear of legal action.

He seemed to blame Raymond Louw for publishing the article on Angola, and was threatening the *Rand Daily Mail* with dire consequences. I felt I should clear the record for Louw's sake, and went to see Botha. His aide said he was especially incensed because I had made a lighthearted reference in the article to Botha's award from President Bongo of Gabon. Gabon, a mini-state to the north, had wanted an airfield, and, as no African state allowed South African planes to land en route to Europe, Botha had offered to build one for Gabon if his planes could use it too. The eccentric President Bongo had accepted the deal, and on its completion had presented Botha with some official medal which Botha wore constantly in his lapel. In his office he was in calm contrast to his near-hysteria of our previous encounter, and accepted that Louw had been outside the country when the *Mail* had published my article. Then he said that, though he had been angry about the article, he had been hurt more than anything else. He added plaintively: "Mr Woods, my medal from President Bongo may be a *joke* to *you*—but it means a *great deal* to *me*. I know my enemies laugh behind my back about my wearing it, I know they say it's the only medal I've ever won because I was never in the army." Perhaps it was because he had never seen active service that he relished the military trappings of his ministry, opening a firearms factory and an airport named after himself within months. He saw no humour in a report of P. W. Botha opening the P. W. Botha Munitions Works or the P. W. Botha Airport at George, Cape Province.

We editors were invited regularly to "briefings" by his military, but they were less briefings than brainwashing sessions or public relations exercises. We'd be wined, dined, red-carpeted, squired by generals and admirals and shown their war maps after much ritual of signing the Official Secrets Act register, swearing not to disclose vital information. Their maps were naïve, consisting of broad red arrows aimed at South Africa from Angola, Zambia, Mozambique and the ocean—all bearing the hammer-and-sickle emblem. To Botha and his military any black guerilla movement was "Communist" or "Marxist", and his obvious hope through these briefings was to make us feel we were privy to the nation's defence.

I kept Steve Biko informed of my dealings with cabinet ministers like Botha, as with Koornhof on the sports issue. He was interested in Koornhof, and felt he was at least one member of the cabinet who had decent basic instincts—"But of course he is an Afrikaner Nationalist nevertheless, and therefore a captive of the system". His interest in personal anecdotes about members of the cabinet was because these shed light on their characters. He was especially interested in my meetings and discussions with Kruger, the Minister under whose powers he was banned.

I had first met Kruger at a party at the British Embassy in Pretoria, before he was made a Minister. He had been full of jokes throughout the evening, and had gone out of his way to be pleasant. It must have been before Vorster's chilling of attitude towards me, because Kruger had said: "The Prime Minister was talking about you the other day—said you seemed a nice sort of chap and what a pity your politics were so left of centre!" My answer had been that "left of centre" to an Afrikaner Nationalist meant conservative in normal terms, and Kruger had chuckled readily at this response. A year or so later I had met him and his wife at a formal civic luncheon, and my impression was that as a person he seemed eager to please and to be liked. Telling Steve all this, it struck me that now Kruger was Minister in charge of banned people he might be amenable to an approach by me to lift the ban on Steve either wholly or partially. I put the idea to Steve and he felt it was worth a try, although he saw little hope of any change, because "these Ministers function according to Security Police recommendations anyway".

I wrote to Kruger asking for an interview. Steve's words about Ministers being influenced by Security Police recommendations had set me thinking. The highest-ranking Security Police officer in the country was General Hendrik van den Bergh, head of the Bureau of State Security, who had a high regard for my friend Donald Card stemming from their days together in the Security Police. Moreover, I knew that General van den Bergh had said he would be interested to meet me when I was next in Pretoria because he found my column "interesting but provocative". So I also wrote to him for an appointment. But in the meantime something happened which was to give my interviews with them a new dimension.

Steve and his friends had reconditioned the old church in King William's Town and had partitioned the inside into offices. Through careful budgeting they had equipped the offices with essential furnishings and with three typewriters and a copying-machine. Working until late at night they finished painting the inside, and the whole place was ready for the following morning. But when they arrived it was a shambles. The furniture had been slashed, tables had been broken, the typewriters were smashed and the copying-machine stolen. We ran a front-page banner-headlined story in the *Dispatch* and a front-page editorial calling on the police to track down the vandals, and that night I had a phone call from a black man I knew, who said he had been in the Leopold Street area during the night of the vandalism, and had seen Warrant Officer Gerhardus Hattingh and two other Security Police in the vicinity of the wrecked offices. He wanted me to know this but couldn't make the statement or give his name publicly because he was afraid.

Neither Steve nor I was surprised at what he said. Hattingh was the chief Security Police bully of young blacks in King William's Town, and they had suspected him of previous acts of vandalism. A middle-aged man, he was regarded by the younger Security Police men as a "tough guy"; his nickname was "Seksie"—the Afrikaans word for "Section", short for Section-leader.

I asked Don Card to go with me to the wrecked offices, and we found Steve and the others repairing what they could. Many of their records were missing, and Steve was installing a filing cabinet with a double-lock system which he said was guaranteed against being broken into. "That?" said Card. "I'll open that within a minute!" Steve gave him a challenging look, then double-locked the metal cabinet and stood back. Card started pounding the cabinet at strategic points above the locks, then jerking at the draw-handles while rocking the entire cabinet up and down. In less than a minute he had all the drawers open, to Steve's stupefaction. It was the only time I ever saw him lost for words. Card told him what sort of cabinet he should get and what other security precautions to take. He also suggested that someone should sleep in the offices every night. On the way back to East London I asked him: "Don, you were in the Security Police with Hattingh—what was he like? Is he the sort of chap who'd do such a thing as smash up that office?" Card laughed mirthlessly. "Ten years ago Hattingh boasted to me, when I was in the Security Police with him, how he had smashed a car belonging to Alan Paton. Paton and his wife were on holiday, and stayed overnight at the Hogsback Inn near Alice. He was then the leader of the Liberal Party, and Seksie Hattingh was tailing him everywhere. Paton parked his car outside the hotel and he and his wife went inside. Hattingh waited until they were asleep, then used a big stone to smash the windshield and the rear window. Someone heard the noise and started walking out on to the verandah, and Hattingh ran. When he told me about it I said Jesus, Seksie, are you mad? But he just laughed and said that'll fix the liberal bastard Paton—smashing his new car. The only thing he worried about was that he had been seen running away—but nothing ever happened. Paton reported it to the police but they did nothing. *Ja*, smashing up those offices is just the sort of thing Hattingh might do." Steve and his friends had no doubt at all that Hattingh was the chief culprit. They knew his ways better than anyone. But they had no direct evidence, and were intrigued to hear of my informant's statement. Steve, with remarkable perception, said: "Of course, there would be no possibility of your informant coming forward publicly if he were, say, a black policeman or an informer working with Hattingh . . ."

I wrote an editorial saying the police should take all fingerprints in the wrecked offices to remove any suspicions blacks might have that the Security Police were involved, but to nobody's surprise the police found they had no leads in the case, and that was the situation as I travelled to Pretoria to see General van den Bergh and Minister Kruger.

Van den Bergh had been a close friend of Premier Vorster since the days they were both interned for subversive activities by the Smuts Government during World War II. Vorster had asked him to inaugurate and head the Bureau of State Security as an over-riding co-ordinator of all state security, including the existing Security Police or Special Branch. He was regarded as the second most powerful man in the country after Vorster.

I arrived at the BOSS headquarters building and was received by two men and escorted up to the General's floor. There another man was waiting, and he took me into a reception office where I waited while the General's secretary told him I had arrived. He came through from an inner office into an outer one, where he shook hands and we sat down to talk. He was an unusually tall man—his Afrikaans nickname was "*Lang Hendrik*"—with an alert expression and a pleasant, smiling manner. Although his English was good he chose to speak mostly in Afrikaans, so I did the same. After a number of jokes about my being a "fiery liberalist", he began to speak about international pressures on South Africa and his own role in foreign policy—obviously proud of the latter and of the trust Vorster reposed in him. He also spoke about how the Afrikaans poet Breyten Breytenbach had been arrested recently for conspiring to organize subversive resistance to apartheid through an organization called Okhela, and said he knew precisely how this was funded and by whom.

I spoke about the Government's habit of labelling critics of apartheid Communists, and asked whether this was done in total cynicism, or whether it was simply ignorance on the part of Afrikaner Nationalist Members of Parliament. He said with surprising candour that it was the latter, adding that many politicians didn't know what Communism was. As to those blacks who were Communists he said, even more surprisingly: "What would we do in their place, Meneer Woods? Can one blame them? They see themselves as oppressed by us just as we Afrikaners saw ourselves as oppressed by the British. Then the Communists offer them help to fight us, help in money and guns. What would we do? We can't close our eyes to the facts. We have to offer them something better than the Communists can."

I replied that it seemed to me his perception of these issues was not shared by the politicians. He said: "Well, they are politicians. They have to function in the realm of practical politics. How could they admit such things and keep their votes in the rural areas? Look, I'll tell you a secret. John

260

Vorster himself made a speech in Parliament calling Nelson Mandela Communist, and I said to him afterwards: 'John, you were wrong to say that, Mandela is not a Communist. Here are the files and here are the facts!' But of course he couldn't go back and say in public that he had been wrong. So that must stay a secret. Mr Woods, if you ever tell that to anyone then you and I will be enemies. And I'm not a good enemy to have, isn't that true?" He laughed jovially. Then he stopped laughing and said: "Of course you people use this word BOSS although you know damn well it is not Bureau *of* State Security but Bureau *for* State Security—but I suppose you couldn't resist it, hey?" I pointed out his Government's habit of choosing unfortunate titles in such matters, more recently the suggested Parliamentary Internal Security Commission, or PISCOM, and he looked pensive. "*Ja*, what sounds okay in Afrikaans doesn't always sound okay in English, does it?" An obvious example was the Bantu Affairs Department, which was BAD.

I raised the question of Steve Biko, speaking at some length about him and making the point that instead of persecuting black leaders the Government should rather be negotiating with them or at least making an effort to understand them. Van den Bergh said "many attitudes of the past" dictated Security Police attitudes of the present, and it couldn't be denied that there had been "serious shortcomings" in previous methods, but that he was hopeful of "better attitudes" in the future. "Now that General Mike Geldenhuys has been put in charge of the Security Police, I believe there will be an improvement," he said. I wasn't clear what he meant, and said that I hoped he was referring to methods and behaviour towards blacks. He nodded slightly, and I continued that if he meant this I could tell him of a recent case, and recounted how the offices of the Black Community Programme in Leopold Street had been vandalized, and why Warrant Officer Hattingh was suspected of being the chief culprit. I told him all I knew except the identity of my informant and he shook his head over the story, saying the matter would be looked into. I said that obviously this could only be done unofficially, since there was no available evidence against Hattingh, because my informant would not come forward to make a statement. "I'll have a word with Mike Geldenhuys about this," he said. "Mike is a very good man. He was one of my boys from the beginning, and I have a high regard for him."

I said I would be seeing Police Minister Kruger the following day and would mention the matter to him as well. Van den Bergh nodded, and said something about appreciating the "responsible" way in which I had mentioned the matter privately, at a high level, instead of "going into print". I told him I was more concerned with getting such bullying actions against blacks stopped than with a "sensational story". I didn't add that the main reason it didn't make a story in the *Dispatch* was lack of usable evidence . . .

I got up to go, asking Van den Bergh to consider a recommendation favouring some relief in Steve Biko's banning orders, and he said that although he didn't handle such matters any more he would bear in mind what I had said and see what could be done.

Then I returned to Johannesburg, and on the following day, a Saturday, I travelled from Johannesburg to Pretoria for my 2 p.m. appointment at Kruger's house. His secretary had explained that this was the only time he could spare from his busy schedule, and that it was by special favour to me that he would see me at his home during the weekend. Like most senior cabinet ministers he lived in the suburb of Bryntirion, and I was able to see several of the official residences of the ministers as I walked in the sunny weather of a Transvaal winter's day to his house.

I was about ten minutes early, and sat on a garden bench to wait. The grounds were big—several acres of lawns and flowerbeds—and I wondered how many gardeners were needed to tend them. When Kruger greeted me I noticed he was considerably overweight compared with his pre-ministerial days. He had grown jowly and corpulent. He was informally dressed and wore carpet slippers, slacks and an open-necked shirt. I said I was surprised to see no security guards around the place as I had simply walked through the front gate unchallenged, and he laughed: "You may not see them, but they're there." He showed me into his study and offered me a drink. He was in a good mood and was bubbling over with anecdotes. "Oh, how we caught Breyten Breytenbach was a treat," he said. Speaking English throughout, he described how Vorster—he referred to him as "the PM"—had been at a cocktail party when he, Kruger, had whispered the news to him, and how Vorster's eyes had twinkled with pleasure. Vorster had asked him to keep the news from the gathering "so that he could enjoy it all on his own first" before announcing it with relish to the assembled company.

Then he spoke of how students of the University of Pretoria had demonstrated in his favour outside his office after students of the largely English-speaking Witwatersrand University had demonstrated against jail without trial. "And you know, they were such decent kids, the Pretoria University kids," he said. "They had short hair, not this long hair the others had, and they looked neat and clean—really decent youngsters. I was proud of them". Having my own views of the little gauleiters-to-be of Pretoria University I busied myself with my whisky, judging the time not to be opportune for joining issue with him on the subject.

He spoke of what a busy week he had had, and I remarked how much I appreciated his sacrificing time for me on a Saturday afternoon. "That's okay. That's okay. Have another drink, help yourself," he said expansively. "Well, what did you want to see me about?" I said I had come to talk about Steve Biko in hopes that he, Kruger, might lift or relax the banning orders on him. His reaction was strange. He put both hands to his head and lifted his slippered feet high off the floor in a gesture of exaggerated consternation. "Oooooo!" he said in a high-pitched sort of wail. "My god, Steve Biko! He's all tied up in knots. I know all about Mr Biko!" He then said that Steve was "the most dangerous man in the country", but when I asked what made him say that he didn't reply. He just sipped his whisky and looked ahead, smiling to himself and shaking his head as if contemplating private information he couldn't divulge.

I asked him again what Steve had done that was "dangerous", and why, if he had done any such thing, he had not been prosecuted in court. He spoke of Steve's founding of SASO and mentioned something about "this black power business". I pointed out that SASO was neither banned nor illegal, and that Steve had never been convicted of any crime. I told him Steve was a close friend of mine, that I had grown to admire him and to know him well, and that he was no extremist. "Steve is one of the most moderate men I've ever met," I said, deliberately using the name "Steve" to offset his formal use of "Biko", which seemed so depersonalizing in that setting. How "sad" it was, I went on, that people like Kruger never met people like Steve; even though Steve was uncompromisingly opposed to apartheid it would make more sense to allow him to function openly as a leader, since the Government had no acknowledged black leaders to negotiate with if the younger blacks turned to violence in the townships. "You can't negotiate with leaderless mobs," I said, adding with unconscious prophecy several months before Soweto violence broke out that I thought black frustration in the townships was near boiling point. I also spoke of the many security laws the Government had available to use against Steve if he should be caught advocating violence or subversion, and repeated that the government was making a "tragic mistake" in persecuting black leaders instead of negotiating with them for a peaceful future in South Africa.

He thought for a while, then said he would look into "the Biko file" again and review the situation. "But I can't promise anything," he said. "I can give you no undertakings." I told him I had discussed the matter with General van den Bergh the day before, and had also told the General about the bullying methods of Security Police officers in the Eastern Cape. Kruger replied that "his" Security Police did "a damn fine job in difficult circumstances", to which I replied that a number of his Security Police were vicious criminals who were deeply hated by blacks. I mentioned in particular Warrant Officer Hattingh and told Kruger the same story I had told Van den Bergh, repeating the same request for an unofficial cautionary word to curb Hattingh's excesses. Kruger replied that if the report were true it wasn't the kind of behaviour he wanted in the Security Police. I said that even if it wasn't true, the right words from headquarters would have a salutory effect on any Security Police who might otherwise believe their brutality was "patriotic". I had heard reports by blacks of alleged torture by a Captain Spyker van Wyk of Cape Town and a Colonel Swanepoel of Johannesburg, but my main concern was the Eastern Cape and the reputed excesses of Warrant Officer Hattingh.

264

Kruger gave me to understand that he would look into these matters and I stood up to leave, but he pressed me to stay, talking at length about security threats facing the country and praising the Security Police. When at last I got up to go I asked if he would let me visit Robben Island to see Nelson Mandela. He laughed. "How could I do that? Every damn journalist in the country would want to go." "But I asked first," I said. "Well, I let Helen Suzman go, but then she's a Member of Parliament. Why should I let you go?" I replied: "Oh, because I'll write a history of South Africa one day, and you may come off slightly better if you let me go to Robben Island now." He laughed: "Blackmail! Threats! *Ag*, anyway old Nelson's finished now. Spent force. Overweight—he's past it." He stopped, and exclaimed: "You know, I love getting Helen to lose her temper in Parliament. It's so easy. I just get up and say something linking her to Communism and she goes mad—you know?"

When we got outside and he saw I had no car he insisted on driving me back to my hotel. "It's not far," he said. "And look, the dogs want a ride." Two small dogs were capering at his feet, and as we got into the car they bounded into the back seat, standing up on their forepaws to lick his ears and neck as he drove. I thanked him for his hospitality, and his kindness in driving me back. Maybe it was the whisky, but I had the thought that surely this man in his carpet slippers with two small dogs sniffling at his neck in the family car wouldn't heartlessly reject my appeal against Steve's ban or fail to do something to curb the Hattinghs in his Security Police. However, on my way back to Johannesburg the effect of his hospitable charm wore off somewhat as I thought of his remarks about Helen Suzman, because I suddenly remembered Helen's story of some years before about how this same Kruger, then a young cross-bencher MP, had had the habit while she was speaking of hissing at her: "Yiddisher Mama! Yiddisher Mama!"

In the event my efforts at personal diplomacy were in vain. Kruger wrote a stiffly formal letter to say that after reviewing the Biko file he "could not see his way clear to lifting the restrictions". Shortly after that he actually added further restrictions, including a ban on Steve's work for the Black

Community Programmes. I said: "My god, Steve, it looks as if my visit made things worse for you!" But he laughed and answered: "They were probably going to do it anyway. I expected them to stop my BCP work. Look, it was worth a try."

I had left Pretoria that Saturday afternoon, returning direct to Johannesburg. The following day I had flown back to East London. On the Monday morning I was visited at my house by Colonel van der Merwe of the local branch of the Security Police. A swarthy, thin-lipped man wearing dark glasses, he announced: "General Geldenhuys has instructed me to take a full statement from you regarding your complaint against Warrant Officer Gerhardus Hattingh of King William's Town." I said: "Wow! That's fast action. I'm impressed. General Geldenhuys isn't wasting any time."

Warning-bells rang in my mind. My response sounded positive, but mentally I was guarded, because General Geldenhuys's fast follow-up could mean one of two things—either he was taking swift action to reprimand Hattingh or he was setting me up to be punished for raising the matter. I decided to act as though I assumed the former, as I showed Colonel van der Merwe into the house. He produced papers from his brief-case and took out a pen, then laid these aside to make an effort at small talk. I wondered why he kept his dark glasses on indoors. Once or twice he tried a sociable smile, but the rest of his face never joined in, and the artificial smile beneath the dark glasses made him look sinister. After some stilted efforts at conversation he took up his papers again and asked me to help him draw up a formal statement about the Hattingh affair. With what I hoped was a naïvely puzzled expression I said: "A formal statement? There must be some mistake. My discussions with General van den Bergh and Minister Kruger were informal and unofficial. The whole basis of the matter was that no formal evidence could be produced against Hattingh because the witness is scared of reprisals."

"Oh yes, of course," said Colonel van der Merwe, somewhat put out. "But you see, General Geldenhuys really wants to act on the matter, and he only wants something from you in writing."

I suddenly thought of an idea—an idea that could turn

Geldenhuys's possible trap for me into one for himself. If he was planning to use Section 83 of the Criminal Procedures Act against me—getting me to make a sworn statement to a police officer about a crime with a view to prosecuting me for refusing to disclose the name of a possible witness to that crime—I could turn the tables on him by getting the Hattingh affair ventilated in open court. It would involve putting my neck in the noose of Section 83, but it could result in a double noose for Geldenhuys and Hattingh. "Okay, Colonel," I said. "But this is an important matter. I want to put a lot of care into the statement, and to give as many details as possible." The Colonel's eyes gleamed behind his tinted glasses. "Yes, yes, make it as full as possible," he said.

We arranged that I would bring the statement to his office the following morning. As I saw him out I decided to test the Colonel's own attitude to the Hattingh affair. Casually, as I walked him to the gate, I said: "Why do bastards like Hattingh do these stupid things? What do they think they're achieving? I think you people are very wise to act quickly to stamp this sort of thing out, because . . . ." Colonel van der Merwe became flushed and agitated. His jaw muscles tensed beneath his dark glasses. "No, I don't know what you mean, Mr Woods. We only know Warrant Officer Hattingh to be a good Security Police officer," he said with ill-suppressed anger. "What?" I exclaimed. "A bloody criminal like Hattingh? How can a thug like that be a good police officer? After what he did in Leopold Street how can you say that, Colonel?" Colonel van der Merwe's already dark face became darker and little muscles started working around his thin lips. "Who is your witness? What is his name?" he burst out. "Well, that's what I can't tell you at this stage," I said. "But I explained all that to General van den Bergh and Minister Kruger."

Colonel van der Merwe made an obvious attempt to calm down as he climbed into his car, and said in a restrained tone: "Well, Mr Woods, if you put as much detail as you can into your statement we will then be able to pursue the matter." "Okay," I answered. "I'm impressed with the speed of General Geldenhuys's response. Tell him I welcome his obvious keenness to take action." Colonel van der Merwe didn't know how to take this, or how to react to the possible irony of the remark.

He must have concluded that I was either naïve or impudent, because after opening his mouth to reply he closed it again and drove away.

I spent most of the afternoon drawing up the statement, weighing every word before getting the final draft typed by my secretary. We made two copies, putting one in the office safe and one in her filing-cabinet. The statement was, on the face of it, a bland repetition of what I had told Van den Bergh and Kruger about Hattingh's alleged involvement in the Leopold Street break-in, but two-thirds of the way down, buried in a long paragraph, was a booby-trap: it was a one-sentence reference, worded like an afterthought, relating to Hattingh's destruction of Alan Paton's car. If, as I suspected, General Geldenhuys tried to get me to convert the statement, which I had clearly headed "Memorandum", into a sworn declaration, then the booby-trap sentence would become part of the court record as well. And while my witness to the Leopold Street affair would probably persist in refusing to testify, the Paton incident could well yield up the witness who had been on the verandah of the Hogsback Inn to nail Hattingh for smashing Alan Paton's car ten years before. Hattingh wasn't safe from the latter rap—in South Africa the law required a twenty-year lapse before immunity from prosecution in such cases. But I guessed General Geldenhuys didn't know much law, and would be so keen to nail me on the Leopold Street allegation that he would fail to realize the implication of the Hogsback booby-trap.

To receive my "memorandum" Colonel van der Merwe had to come to my office together with a notorious Security Police officer, Captain Schoeman. Steve and his friends had told me about Schoeman. A pale, nervous young man who often wore a raincoat, he was sadistically cruel in his "interrogations" of blacks, and when he came into my office with Colonel van der Merwe I looked him over with particular interest. "So *you* are Captain Schoeman," I said. "I've heard a lot about *you*." This appeared to disconcert Captain Schoeman. He had several facial tics, one about the eyes and one on the side of his mouth. He blinked a great deal, but never looked me in the eye and hardly spoke at all. It was van der Merwe who said: "Oh, and what have you heard about Captain Schoeman?" He said this in a tone of jocose raillery, but I merely replied: "Oh, we needn't go into that on this occasion. At the moment I'm more interested in your Mr Hattingh." Colonel van der Merwe read over the prepared "memorandum", then said it would be transmitted to General Geldenhuys and they left.

Several days later I was summoned to headquarters in the suburb of Cambridge. Although the Security Police section was located upstairs in the general police building, it had extra bars on the windows and an iron-barred grille which had to be unlocked at the top of the stairs for us to pass through, then re-locked after us. It was like going into a jail. Colonel van der Merwe welcomed me with uncharacteristic joviality and served me with coffee, then thanked me for my memorandum and said that General Geldenhuys was grateful for my "co-operation". I noticed the memorandum lying on his desk as he handed me the sugar-basin and the milk-jug. He chatted a bit about police rugby matters as we drank coffee, then put his cup down and picked up the memorandum. Here it comes, I thought to myself. Either they've seen through my booby-trap and decided to stonewall the whole thing, or van der Merwe will ask me to convert it into a sworn statement.

The Colonel, holding the memorandum in his fingers as if he were barely conscious of it as he talked, said with what he obviously thought was the smoothness of a vacuum-cleaner salesman: "Oh, Mr Woods, General Geldenhuys did say I should mention to you that it would be more helpful if this was a proper affidavit. You know, if you could just make it a sworn statement on oath it would strengthen his hand in pursuing the matter." Inwardly I was nervous and amused at the same time, scarcely believing this was really happening. Were they *that* naïve? Or did they know things I didn't know? Was *I* being the naïve one? Outwardly I remained "innocent", simply saying: "You mean to sort of make it more official, a bit more solid, sort of?" The Colonel said: "*Ja*, that's it. I mean, you have made a true statement here, so I take it you wouldn't mind swearing on oath that it is true." I realized at this point that they were being the naïve ones, and agreed to attest the document.

Colonel van der Merwe suddenly dropped his sociable man-ner, picked up a rubber stamp and stamped it at the foot of the memorandum, then stood abruptly, glared right into my eyes and barked: "Do-you-swear-that-the-contents-of-this-document - are - the - truth - the - whole - truth - and - nothing - but - the - truth - to - the - best - of - your - knowledge - and - belief - so-help-you-God?" He raised his right hand and I raised mine saying: "I so swear". His lips were quivering as he went through the recital, but his hand was steadier than mine as we both signed the attestation. I knew as I wrote my signature that I was getting into deep waters, but had an instinctive feeling that the Security Police wouldn't come through the matter unscathed. Gone, now, was all pretence at sociability; there was no more small talk and no more joviality. The Colonel was stiffly official as he saw me to the door and out of the locked grille at the head of the stairs.

As I left I couldn't resist saying: "I don't suppose you people are thinking of using Section 83 against me, hey, Colonel?", and I laughed, as if it were a nervous joke. The blood rushed to his face, but he recovered to say in a kind of monotone: "I've no idea what action General Geldenhuys proposes to take."

I was summoned to police headquarters several days later to be confronted by Criminal Investigation Department officers with my sworn statement. Geldenhuys's ponderous tactics were clear; I had now made a sworn statement to a police officer alleging knowledge of a crime, and the police could therefore threaten to imprison me under Section 83 of the Criminal Procedures Act if I refused to reveal to them the name of a material witness to the crime, my confidential informant. They obviously wanted his identity, but it seemed they were determined to go through the charade of claiming to seek it under the pretext of prosecuting Hattingh. Moreover, I knew that they knew that I would refuse to disclose the name of my source—and they knew that I knew that they knew.

And so the farce was acted out. I was taken to a downstairs office and interrogated by two colonels. One acted the bully, shouting and threatening, while the other acted the nice guy, appealing for my co-operation. The one in the tough guy role was a Colonel van den Heever, and he wore an expression of angry contempt throughout the interrogation. The other was a Colonel Williams, a stout, quiet-spoken man—English-speaking, a rarity in the police force. Colonel Williams remained seated throughout, but Colonel van den Heever stayed on his feet, pacing about irritably as he snarled at me that I had better give them the information they wanted or I would land in "a lot of trouble". He was clearly the superior officer.

He began by telling me the Hattingh case was no longer a Security Police matter but had been handed over to the ordinary police as a routine criminal investigation. I said my understanding had been that the matter would be handled unofficially within the Security Police, but he interrupted me: "No, there's nothing unofficial about it now. You have made a very serious allegation against a police officer—" I interrupted him: "No, there's no police officer involved—I don't regard Security thugs like Hattingh as police officers." Colonel Williams snorted a startled laugh and Colonel van den Heever glared at him, then at me, and said: "This is not a joking matter, Mr Woods. You are going to jail if you don't tell us the name of your informant."

"Well, I'll never do that, because I don't have his permission to disclose it," I said. "Then you'll go to jail," he said. He raised his voice and jabbed his finger at me. "You'll go inside! We'll put you in jail in Fort Glamorgan!" I felt a surge of irritation, and said as impudently as I could: "Fort Glamorgan Jail? What's the accommodation like there?" He banged his palm on the desk furiously: "You think it's a joke? You're going inside!" I pointedly addressed myself to Colonel Williams: "Tell me, are there any single cells? I wouldn't like to share a cell with a criminal like Hattingh." Colonel Williams flushed and looked down at his papers as Colonel van den Heever again shouted: "You'll go *inside* if you don't tell us the man's name!" I said: "You mean ve have *vays* to make you talk."

Williams obviously felt he wasn't supporting his chief loyally enough, because he took over the talking, sounding very solemn and official. "Actually, Mr Woods, I don't think you appreciate the seriousness of the situation you're in. You see, if you refuse to tell us the man's name we'll have to issue criminal summons against you and bring you to court, and then if you refuse in court to tell the magistrate this man's identity you'll be sent to jail, as Colonel van den Heever says," he concluded with a deferential look at his superior, who was now standing at a table in the corner of the room, turning over the pages of that morning's newspaper. I said to Colonel Williams in a lowered tone, but just loud enough for Van den Heever to hear: "I see that Colonel van den Heever is a *Dispatch* reader." Williams was taken by surprise, because I had leant towards him as if to tell him something confidential, and he was in some doubt about how to respond, when Colonel van den Heever returned to take over the questioning.

He paced noisily to the window, clumping his shoes, and wheeled about to face me, with his elbow on the windowsill. "We've got orders right from the top to go all the way with you over this matter. The orders come right from the top." I asked: "You mean from your Police Minister? From Kruger himself? That's very interesting." "No, I didn't say that," he replied. I went on: "So it's not from Kruger?" He said: "No, I didn't say that either. I didn't mention a name." "But you said orders from the top," I exclaimed, "and the top of your department is Kruger." He said: "I didn't give a name, but I repeat that we have orders right from the top, from high places, to get you on this one." "Good," I told him. "I'll quote you in tomorrow's *Dispatch*." Colonel van den Heever suddenly looked agitated: "You can't do that. I told you that unofficially." "No," I replied, "you said there's nothing unofficial about this matter." "Besides," he went on, "it is now *sub judice*." "No, Colonel, it's not *sub judice*. It only becomes *sub judice* once a summons is issued. You don't know your law, Colonel. And besides, if you're going to use Section 83 you have to put two questions to me, not one. Two crimes are alleged, not one." To my secret delight Colonel Williams broke in at this point with: "Yes, I have a note about that here. We have to ask you the identity of the other informant as well—over the Paton case." Colonel Williams was unknowingly strengthening my booby-trap.

Colonel van den Heever, glad to get away from the subject of whether his remarks could be quoted in the newspaper, turned to the Paton case and asked the name of the informant concerned. "Again, I can't tell you," I said. "As in the Leopold Street case, my informant relies on me to protect his identity. That is not only a journalistic ethic but a moral issue as well. That is why I made it plain to Minister Kruger, General van den Bergh, General Geldenhuys and Colonel van der Merwe that no formal action could be taken against Hattingh for lack of available evidence, and that the matter should therefore be handled unofficially within the department." Colonel van den Heever said: "Well, it's too late for that now."

Throughout these exchanges I had a curious feeling of detachment from their threats. It was an irrational feeling that I was safe from them—not from the actuality of going to jail, but from being intimidated by them. If it was an illusion it was at least a comforting one. This strange feeling of immunity must have showed, because both Colonels seemed to perceive that their two-pronged approach wasn't being effectively intimidatory, and after a number of exchanges they formally put the demand to me to disclose the identities of (a) my informant in regard to the Leopold Street break-in and (b) my informant in regard to the damaging of Alan Paton's car. I formally refused to disclose either name, whereupon van den Heever snapped that I had five days in which to seek both informants' permission, failing which the police would "take action" against me.

For all my bravado and feelings of immunity until then, I experienced some real pangs of fear as I got back into my car outside the police station, and my hands were shaking. I could see no possibility of my informants giving me permission to endanger them by disclosing their identities to the police, and this meant I would certainly be going to jail. And the snag about jail under Section 83 was that sentence was open-ended. While the initial sentence might be for only three months, at the completion of that time the procedure would be to put the question to me again, and to keep jailing me every time I refused to answer. Also, in spite of my determination not to give way to the police, I knew I wouldn't relish the role I was inexorably heading for once it became reality—I liked luxury too much to adjust well to life in a prison cell.

Wanting to know exactly what I was in for, I asked my secretary to get copies of all the relevant prison regulations, and I also went to Fort Glamorgan Jail to inspect the accommodation. The warden was stupefied when I telephoned to make this appointment, and when I arrived in his office he was defensive about his facilities. I asked if I could be put into a single cell, but he said the jail was so crowded that there were no

273

single cells "even in the white section". Prisoners slept three to a cell, he explained. I asked him what sort of work I'd be doing, and he told me it depended on the duty supervisors—it would be either in the prison garden or in the kitchen. We were both conscious of the incongruity of the situation as he served me tea in his office, and I could imagine him thinking how unusual it was for the prospective convicts to make inquiries about the cells, rather like the inquiries of a prospective hotel guest.

Fort Glamorgan Jail was a grim place. Constructed round the oldest building in the city—a garrison barracks for the frontier forces first sent to the area in the earlier part of the last century—it was bleak and forbidding. But at least now I had a mental picture of the adjustments I would have to make, and the place wouldn't be too much of a shock when the time came. The warden kept steering the conversation away from my impending incumbency there and talking instead about the forthcoming concert by the prison service brass band, which he hoped "Mrs Woods as well" would be able to attend. That week in my syndicated column I described my predicament to readers in a piece headed "The Ballad of Fort Glamorgan". I played for time in extending the police deadline by giving Colonel Williams the impression that my informants might permit their names to be disclosed, and bought a couple of weeks during which I hoped the Hogsback verandah witness to the Paton car incident might come to light. This seemed the only way for my booby-trap to work. It was a slim hope, but it was something.

Meanwhile I was being summoned repeatedly to the police building for further questioning by Colonels van den Heever and Williams. My frequent visits were known to all the police, and I was interested in the attitude of the younger ones as they passed me in the corridor. Possibly because of their dislike of the political wing of the force, or perhaps because of my known patronage of their police rugby club, the younger policemen were surreptitiously friendly. They would wink as they walked past, or whisper "Good luck, Mr Woods", or simply give a friendly nod.

Eventually the two colonels must have realized I was stalling and had no intention of disclosing the names they wanted, because Colonel Williams arrived at my office to serve the summons to court. When Donald Card learnt of this he said: "I'm not letting you go to jail—you must tell them I was the one who told you about Hattingh and Paton's car." I exclaimed: "Are you crazy? That would make the Security Police and the Government your enemies for life!" "No," he replied. "I bet if you tell them I'm prepared to give evidence they'll get such a scare they'll drop the whole thing." I disagreed, saying that he had recounted the Hattingh incident to me in confidence and that I had kept his part of the account carefully from the police throughout. We argued about it, and then he declared: "Look, if you don't go up and give them my name right now I'm going to pick up that phone and tell them myself!" I was moved. Card was risking a great deal to keep me out of jail. Although he seemed confident the matter would end there, I knew how they'd resent him for it. I thought, too, if that didn't stop them, disclosure of his name would be the perfect detonator for my booby-trap for Geldenhuys, Kruger and all the Security Police—former Security Police Officer Card testifying that Security Police Officer Hattingh had boasted to him of smashing up Alan Paton's car . . . It was sensational. I wouldn't need the verandah witness to come forward after all.

It was with relish that I entered the police building to confront Colonels Williams and van den Heever with this devastating disclosure, and I watched their faces carefully as I said: "I'm glad to be able to tell you that my informant in the matter of Hattingh's damaging of Alan Paton's car has now given me permission to reveal his identity to you, and to inform you that he is prepared to give the fullest evidence in prosecution of Hattingh." Colonel Williams fumbled excitedly for his pen to write the name down. I said: "The name is City Councillor Donald John Card, formerly Warrant Officer of the Security Police."

Colonel Williams gaped, then flushed, then went absolutely white, writing nothing with his poised pen. Colonel van den Heever made rapid chewing motions with his jaws. Neither said a word and there was a long silence. Then they looked at each other, van den Heever nodded unhappily, and Williams wrote down the details as I repeated them to him. I couldn't resist adding: "You'd better tell Hattingh he'll be sharing a cell at Fort Glamorgan. I understand they're a bit crowded there."

Leaving the colonels, who still looked stunned at the disclosure of Card's name, I went to Card's office and gave him an account of the Colonels' reaction. Card laughed non-stop for several minutes. "I wish I could have seen their faces," he said. "I bet that'll be the last you'll hear about this business. Even they wouldn't be so stupid as to go ahead now on the Paton case, and they'd look bad if they dropped that one and went for you on the other one."

The shock at police headquarters must have taken several days to sink in, and the wires must have buzzed to Pretoria as General Geldenhuys tried to decide what to do next. Card received a chiding visit from Colonel Williams, who asked him in hurt tones how he could take sides against a former brother-officer in the Security Police. Card left Colonel Williams in no doubt as to what he thought of Warrant Officer Hattingh, and reaffirmed that he would give evidence against him if the State proceeded against me. Williams took down his detailed statement, shaking his head at such "betrayal". In the next few days continual police pressures were brought to bear against Card to get him to withdraw his statement. First they told him his evidence would be inadmissible on the basis of hearsay testimony, but he corrected them, pointing out that it was direct evidence. Then they threatened to prosecute him under the Official Secrets Act, which forbids Security Police members to disclose anything the Minister deems to be "prejudicial to state security"—but Card simply defied them to try it. "If I'm compelled to give evidence I'll say things more harmful to the authorities than this," he said.

When they realized Card was determined, the Colonels summoned me back to police headquarters and resumed their badgering about the identity of the Leopold Street break-in. Every time I said they now had a witness against Hattingh in the one case they sidestepped this to concentrate on the other case. Repeatedly they asked me to disclose the other witness's identity and repeatedly I refused—then with a heavy sigh Colonel Williams shook his head and said I'd definitely have to go to jail. "But you've got Card's evidence on the car damage,"

I exclaimed. Williams replied that they had orders "from the top" to pursue "the other case".

I had kept Steve Biko briefed throughout all these developments, and he was pleased at the way things were going. "It'll do them a lot of harm if they send you to jail—and it'll do wonders for your credibility among blacks." I said a few short words to him about the price of such credibility, but he only laughed. In fact he was absolutely serious about the benefit of a sentence of imprisonment, because in his world of political reality it was inevitable to be sentenced to jail or detained or banned if you kept bumping up against the system, and he saw the prosecution as proof that I had graduated from comfortable academic condemnation of apartheid to inconvenient practical activism.

I didn't sleep well the night before the prosecution. The knowledge that I was going to be sentenced to imprisonment the next day coloured my thinking all the time. There was no question of escaping sentence. Section 83 made no provision for anything less than prison sentence, and there could be no acquittal or caution or suspended sentence because I was refusing to supply a name demanded by the State, a "continuing offence" under Section 83. One bizarre aspect of the matter was that I could have escaped sentence by inventing a false name for my informant, but it would have had to be given under oath in court and the Security Police would have known I had had to perjure myself to go free. This would have been too much of a moral victory for them. There was only one possibility of staying out of jail the following day—while there could be no acquittal there was the possibility of an appeal being allowed, pending which I could be granted bail.

As I lay awake I kept wondering if there was anything I had left undone that I should still do before leaving for court at nine o'clock the following morning. A major worry was our financial situation. The mortgage rate had been put up on the house, and every month saw us going deeper into debt. I worried about what would happen about this if I spent a long time in jail. I hoped the prison term wouldn't be a long one, telling myself the State would incur some adverse pressure from the American and British embassies if it jailed an editor for a long period. My own hope was that I would be sentenced to two or three months, and that the State wouldn't reimpose sentence thereafter.

Kingsley Kingon and I had prepared carefully for the hearing and I had drafted a long statement to read from the witness-stand, telling the full story of what had happened and making use of the opportunity to call attention to the allegations against notorious Security Police bullies like Hattingh, Spyker van Wyk and Colonel Swanepoel. I had alerted my fellow-editors about this statement, pointing out that it would be a unique chance to focus attention on Security Police excesses and on the fact that more than twenty untried political prisoners had died violently in Security Police custody. The fact that my statement would be made on the witness-stand would give other papers an opportunity to publish the material with impunity, material it would not be safe for newspapers to print in other circumstances.

In the event, however, not many of them made use of this opportunity. Since few of the editors had legal training, they usually took what they thought was the safer route in such matters: "When in doubt, leave it out." I thought it was a valuable opportunity missed, because, if a number of newspapers had made use of that chance of immunity to give a straight report of the challenge to General Geldenhuys, several lives might have been saved during the following two years in South Africa's political prisons. But on the morning of the trial Kingsley and I weren't sure whether I would be allowed to read the full statement. Assuming that I would, we had a copy punched out on the telex tape ready for transmission to the other newspapers, and one of our senior reporters, Peter Davis, waited in court to release this transmission within seconds of my reading it.

Wendy and I left the house for the court in some tension, and as we walked into the garage from the kitchen to drive away Evalina gave her customary loud wailing incantation calling down retribution on all my enemies—a procedure she followed whenever I had a court case. One hopeful sign was that the magistrate we drew was Oosthuysen, who was regarded as a fair-minded man. I had met him when we found ourselves at the same hotel after an international rugby match, and we had had a beer and a discussion about the game. I had also met him at a performance in his church of Handel's *Messiah*. He didn't strike one as a fanatical member of the ruling party, unlike most of the magistrates. However, his hands were tied; he would have to sentence me, and it was only a question of how long the prison term would be.

The case began and I was put into the witness-stand. The prosecutor formally put the state's demand that I should disclose the name of my informant in regard to the Leopold Street allegation against Hattingh, and I formally refused and began to read my statement of reasons. I was tense as I read, because I knew that, if the magistrate or prosecutor realized what I was doing in making use of the opportunity to open up a public attack on the Security Police and call attention to the deaths in political prisons, one of them would stop me. I realized too that the longer I was able to read the less likely either of them was to stop me with an objection. For this reason I had made my opening words as innocuous as possible, to preclude an early interruption or objection. I was able to read right through the statement and get it on the record and, as I finished it, immensely relieved at not having been stopped, it was put on the wires. I was grateful that all my fellow directors were in court, as well as a number of our friends who were sitting with Wendy. We all tensed as the moment came for me to be sentenced. I was ordered to stand and Magistrate Oosthuysen cleared his throat. For a fleeting moment I hoped the term might be less than three months. Maybe it would only be a month, or three weeks . . .

Magistrate Oosthuysen looked up, and I could hardly believe my ears as he sentenced me to six months' imprisonment. I stayed as expressionless as I could, and didn't dare look at Wendy.

Kingsley and Advocate Kroon had prepared an immediate application for appeal, but Magistrate Oosthuysen hesitated before granting it, and when they applied for bail pending the appeal he set an unprecedented condition that bail would only be granted if the notice of appeal was lodged the same day. This made us conclude that he had had some instruction from higher quarters that he should not be lenient in this case. He did, however, set a low bail figure, and as Kingsley prepared to pay this after the court adjourned Wendy and our friends and

I crowded together in relief that I wasn't to spend that night in jail. In fact, as the appeal would take several months, we really felt it was a reprieve of sorts for the immediate future.

CHAPTER FIFTEEN

FRIENDS FROM ALL over the country were supportive throughout the long legal proceedings, and Alan Paton, now in his seventies, travelled from Durban to stay with us. With characteristic courage he initiated a prosecution against Hattingh, based on Card's statement—now officially on the court record—over Hattingh's action in damaging his car. He also travelled with us all the way to Grahamstown for the appeal case in the Supreme Court, as did Harland, whose conservatism in racial matters was offset by family loyalty. Harold Levy came from Cape Town to argue my appeal in the Supreme Court, refusing to take a fee.

I didn't see how we could win the appeal, since I was still refusing to disclose the name of my informant, but the legal brain of Harold Levy was equal to the challenge. He had found a technical loophole of such deviousness that Kingsley and I laughed aloud when he told us. He based the entire appeal on a procedural matter, arguing that the Criminal Procedures Act was so worded that it required a magistrate holding a hearing under Section 83 to be the same magistrate as the one who had signed the original subpoena requiring the name to be disclosed. The state prosecutor argued vigorously against this technicality, but after some months of deliberation in adjournment Judge Kannemeyer ruled in our favour. Kruger, Geldenhuys and other Security Police chiefs were said to be enraged over this ruling and the State lodged an appeal against the appeal judgement, taking it to the central Appellate Court in Bloemfontein. This time Harold Levy travelled to Bloemfontein, and there he won again, the highest judges of review upholding his interpretation of the statute. Some people thought Kruger and Geldenhuys would leave well alone and forget the matter, but they decided to persevere with Section 83 and start the whole process all over again—this time with the right signature on the subpoena.

All these proceedings took about two years up to Harold Levy's triumph in the Appellate Court, and while it was unpleasant to have a prison sentence hanging over my head the case helped to focus attention on Security Police violence, a subject seldom ventilated in the press before then. Steve Biko approved of the entire affair, because, as he put it, there was "maximum mileage" wrung out of the case against the image of the Security Police. Hattingh, he reported, had stopped manhandling blacks in his "interrogations" and had, he believed, been ordered to be more discreet in his methods.

In a material sense the case produced one massive windfall—after my sentencing by Magistrate Oosthuysen my fellow directors told me the board had decided to rectify my financial position, to clear my mortgage and take over our house as a company house, and to increase my salary to the level projected several years before by Frank Streek. The company also paid me enough bonus to clear all obligations and emerge with a credit balance in my bank account. They said they realized the load of worry I was carrying, apart from anxiety over the prison sentence, and wished to relieve me of the one worry they had the power to remove. This was a marvellous gesture, and it took a weight off my mind. In fact, as I gratefully told them, it was worth being sentenced to six months in prison to find myself debt-free.

The background to this gesture was a selfless action by an East London businessman, Neil Venter. Formerly a key executive of the para-statal Xhosa Development Corporation, he had gone into private business several months before my case was tried, and I had hired him confidentially to try to sell my house as discreetly as possible. When he asked why and I told him my financial position, listing all assets and expenditure, he was shocked at the position. Without telling me about his decision he had gone to a lawyer named Denis Kirk, a good friend of our company, and the two of them had approached the *Dispatch* board and expressed their concern that unless the company rectified my long-frozen salary position and did something about my mortgage the political enemies of the *Dispatch* might soon have a field day gloating over my bankruptcy.

But for this benefit of being sentenced to prison there was another price to pay—redoubled vigilance for any technical contravention of the law by publication. The Security Police were now doubly determined to prosecute on the slightest pretext. They were certainly doing this to Steve Biko at the time—prosecuting him for every technical offence they could think of, from traffic offences to breaches of his banning orders—and their obvious aim was to cost the Black Consciousness movement so much in court fees that the organization would be bled of funds. Wendy and I raised at least some of Steve's court fees from friends, and one of the few benefits of his major court appearances was that he was authorized to come to East London for the hearings. To the annoyance of the Security Police he would sometimes spend the lunch-hour adjournments at our house—something they couldn't prevent without bursting in to prove that he was with more than one of us in a room —and after drawing the curtains and closing all doors and gates we would relax over a few beers. Whenever possible I had Steve photographed for publication with embassy officials from America or Britain or Scandinavia, because he believed that such pictures, while annoying to the Security Police, increased his safety and gave him a better chance of acquittal in the courts. The blacks who had the hardest time were the "unknowns"—the ones the State could safely bully without anyone finding out. This was one of the reasons why I kept directing foreign academics, politicians and television interviewers to Steve, and writing about him in overseas newspapers. One of the most important visiting politicians to see him was United States Senator Dick Clark, Chairman of the US Senate Foreign Relations Committee, and for some time after this visit the Security Police left him entirely alone, not even following him around King William's Town as they usually did.

Possibly it was in their frustration over the kind of prominence Steve was attaining that they turned their increasing anger on Wendy and me and the children. They stepped up their threatening phone calls, which usually came at about three in the morning when the younger officers were bored on night duty with nothing else to do. We received one letter threatening to harm the children. Mailed from Queenstown, it was typed and purported to come from a black extremist. Don Card took the letter, and reported several days later that it had been typed on the typewriter of Security Police Sergeant Scheepers of Queenstown, but it was pointless initiating a prosecution because the main exhibit of evidence, the typewriter, would never survive police custody.

What the Security Police didn't know was that although they had many informers planted all over, including on the *Dispatch* staff, we had one planted on them, and he was able to tell which of them was doing what from time to time. Combined with Don Card's knowledge of their individual habits, kinks and procedures, we thus had a constant stream of accurate information about the local office of the Security Police. They were frustrated by the technicality which was keeping me out of jail, and soon they lost patience. I had to go to Durban for a meeting of newspaper editors, and while I was away two members of the East London section decided to terrorize Wendy and the children. Late at night they telephoned to say they knew she was alone and that they were coming to "get" her. She phoned both Don Card and Peter Davis, who lived nearby, and they came to be with her and the children. But when nothing had happened by about 2 a.m. Don concluded it had been a hoax and went home. Peter slept in the children's room, but our eldest daughter, Jane, couldn't sleep, and between three and four in the morning both she and Wendy heard five shots being fired and a car accelerating away. They all stayed indoors, making sure the doors were locked, and next morning they found that five bullets had been fired at the front of the house and slogans had been painted on the walls. Peter Davis's car, parked in front, had bullet holes in it and some hammer-and-sickle signs painted on it with a spray-can.

Thanks to Card's detection and our informant we were able to reconstruct what had happened. Lieutenants Cilliers and Jooste of the Security Police had been off duty, but had called at the office to make the threatening calls. Then, using a borrowed car, they had waited until Card was gone, and had free-wheeled down the street to stop in front of the house. Cilliers had used a spray-can of the aerosol type to write in large letters on one wall "Biko—commy HQ" with an arrow pointing inward to the house. He had also painted hammer-and-sickle signs on the walls as well as on the car. Then he had run out of paint, because the lettering had grown faint, with spatter-marks. They had then got into the car, Cilliers driving, and Jooste had fired five shots at the house as Cilliers accelerated to get away. I returned from Durban on getting Wendy's phone call, and when I reached the house policemen were there, going through the motions of an "investigation". It was weird participating in this kind of police charade—giving statements in the knowledge that nothing would be done, both sides knowing who the culprits were and both sides knowing the matter would go no further.

After this shooting I decided it was time we were armed—like most white South Africans—the only difference being that we were arming ourselves not against blacks but against other whites. We installed a complex burglar-alarm system, criss-crossing electronic beams throughout the downstairs section so that anyone opening a door or window or moving about there would break one of the beams. This would trigger off an eight-second low-pitched warning buzzer above our bed before lighting up the whole house and setting off a loud siren. The eight-second interval was to give one of us time to get down-stairs with a gun before the intruders knew they were detected. The system worked well. It was activated at nightfall by a simple switch, but care had to be taken that the dog and cats were shut away in case they broke one of the beams. We also installed fire-extinguishers at strategic points of the house.

Now all we needed was a suitable gun, and I went to a leading gunsmith in the city, old Mr Meyers, a kindly man who had come to South Africa from London many years before. I told him I wanted to buy an Uzi, one of those small Israeli sub-machine guns, and he looked shocked. "Oh, dear me, no, my boy!" he said. "We're not allowed to import those. That would never be allowed." Then he looked conspiratorial, and went on: "But I think I can guess why you want such a weapon—and I believe I have just the thing for you." He raised his voice to call his son from the interior of the shop. "Robert!" he called and when Robert appeared Mr Meyers said: "Robert, Mr Woods here would like to acquire a [at this point he put his fingertips together] shall we say a—persuader." He pro-nounced it "persuadah". It was a fearsome-looking weapon resembling the sort of thing Patty Hearst had been pictured waving about in a bank. It was a new type of Winchester five-shot twelve-gauge single-barrel repeater shotgun. Mr Meyers explained: "We can get Mr Harrold, our technician, to tool

285

the barrel down to four and a half inches. That'll give you a *lethal* shot-spread." He gave his grandfatherly smile as he looked over the top of his glasses: "My boy, you'll be able to pick off twenty of them at a time with that weapon."

After Mr Harrold had machine-cut the barrel suitably Wendy and I went out to his house for a test-firing. It was early evening, and as he fired into the air from the hip there was a mind-numbing explosion and flame spurted a foot from the barrel. I had never been near such a noise—it was louder than a shotgun because of the short barrel. Slowly our hearing returned as Mr Harrold brandished the gun approvingly. Wendy was shaken by it, but Mr Harrold beamed. "There you are," he said. "She's a beauty!" Don Card drooled when he saw "the persuader". "Jesus, that's a beautiful gun," he said, then he added wistfully: "I wish they'd come back so that I could wait for them with *this*!"

Cilliers and Jooste were given adequate warning about the "persuader". I had to get a licence at the police station for it, and also for a ·32 Beretta automatic which Wendy wanted because she said the riot-gun was too noisy for her to practise with. Several policemen were standing round at the police station as I filled in the licence forms, and Sergeant Fiebiger checked them. "Now I must ask you the purpose for which you require the firearms," he said. "Hunting," I replied, and noticed glances being exchanged among the watching policemen as Sergeant Fiebiger wrote this down. Cilliers and Jooste probably had the message that same afternoon.

I got a carpenter in to make a special cupboard compartment for the guns, with a safety device so that the kids wouldn't have access to them. It took several weeks to finalize all these precautions, to get the guns licensed, the alarm system installed and the gun-compartment built, and before we had the guns Wendy had one more alarm. Debbie Morgan, a student at Rhodes University, was staying with her and the children while I was away on another newspaper mission, and they were in bed when the lights went out all over the house. This could mean an intruder had thrown the master-switch off, and Wendy, arming herself with a fire-extinguisher, and Debbie, holding an iron rod, went downstairs to investigate, after alerting Terry by pre-arranged phone signal. The Bricelands lived right round the corner and Terry was there almost immediately, but they found that the lights had merely tripped through a refrigerator malfunction, and after a nervous laugh they all went back to bed.

Once all our security devices were installed we felt a lot safer, and there were one or two occasions when I almost hoped our tormentors would try their luck again.

We also had intercom phones linking the rooms, and one night when we had all been in bed for some hours Evalina phoned from her cottage outside to say the police were at her door. I took the pistol and went out. It was the Bantu Affairs Police again, an officer named Nel and a young man I hadn't seen before, demanding to see Evalina's pass or "reference book". "Why at this time of night?" I asked. Nel replied: "That's when they have the boy friends here illegally." "I suggest you leave," I told him. Nel said: "We've asked this Bantu female—" I lost my temper and shouted: "*Woman*, you bastard! She's a *woman*, not a Bantu female. Do you think you're talking about animals?" Nel's companion, who was carrying a thick stick, started tapping it rhythmically against his shoe while glaring at me. He tapped it louder and louder as his stare grew more intense, until I said: "You've seen too many Clint Eastwood movies. If you tap that stick once more I'll shoot it and may hit you by mistake." I took the safety-catch off the pistol and he stopped the tapping. "What makes you think you're safe on this property?" I asked. He said: "We're allowed to come here at any time. It's our job." "Yes, but what if I shot you both, then told the court it had been dark and I thought you were burglars? Then you wouldn't be around to deny it, would you?" They left.

Such incidents were on the increase. But the worst night was the night Steve phoned, very late, to tell us Mapetla was dead. Mapetla Mohapi had been imprisoned without trial for several weeks, and had been "interrogated" in a jail in the small town of Kei Road. A couple of days before his death he had smuggled a note out to his wife, Nohle, saying he was well and in good spirits. Yet the Security Police claimed he had been found hanged with a pair of jeans, suspended from the bars in his cell. We knew from other detainees that the Security Police often tried to get people to "talk" by tightening a towel round their throats, loosening it when the victim was about to lose consciousness, then tightening and loosening it again repeatedly. We believed this was the reason so many of the detainees who had died were alleged by the Security Police to have hanged themselves. It seemed the Security Police didn't always know when to stop in using this variety of torture.

It was an awful shock when Steve telephoned the news of Mapetla's death. We spoke for a long time, then when the call was finished our phone rang again, and all we could hear on lifting it was cackling laughter. This happened several times. The Security Police on late phone duty were telling us they had heard our conversation. They did the same to Steve that night.

We drove to King William's Town the next morning, and it was remarkable to see how Steve and the others controlled their emotions and put pressure on the police to hold a proper post-mortem. Steve knew the police would try to hurry this to complete it before the Mohapi family doctors could attend, so he phoned the police station, and with a peremptory note in his voice told the officer in charge that he had been in touch with police headquarters in Pretoria and had arranged for two doctors of Nohle Mohapi's choice to attend the post-mortem. He also added that it had been decided that it should begin at eleven rather than nine o'clock—not explaining that the "decision" was his . . .

The police officer in charge didn't question this, and Dr Ramphele and Dr Msauli were allowed, against all precedent, to attend throughout the post-mortem conducted by the State District Surgeon. Steve, a former medical student, went over and over the facts with them, and analysed technical details of the appearance of Mapetla's eyeballs, tongue and neck. The two doctors had noticed abrasions to the sides of the neck rather than under the chin, which is where they said they would have expected to find them in a case of hanging. They retained a leading Cape Town barrister, Dr Wilfrid Cooper, to represent the family at the inquest which followed. Wendy and I travelled up every day for the hearing, which was reported for the *Dispatch* by Roger Omond. Day after day we led our front page with details of the Mohapi inquest, and we filed every word to all the other newspapers in the country via the national

288

wire service—yet day after day all but two of the other papers totally ignored the story, and the two that used it played it down considerably. Wilfrid Cooper probed the Security Police explanations and alibis and their versions sounded highly unconvincing, yet the magistrate ruled that no clear evidence existed to indicate blame "on any person". Steve had expected this finding but said it didn't matter, that the important thing was to publish the evidence as we were doing, so that people could know what was going on in political prisons.

The most impressive witness at the inquest was Thenjiwe Mtintso, a reporter on the *Dispatch*. "Tenjy", as we called her, was a member of the Black Consciousness movement and had been sent to me by Steve in response to my request for a suitable person to cover the Black Consciousness beat. Tiny and pretty, she looked meek but had the heart of a lion. One day she had come into my office at the *Dispatch* looking worried, and I had said jokingly in Xhosa: "*Kuteni, mta' kwetu?*" ("What's worrying you, our child?") She said she was afraid she would soon be jailed by the Security Police, because they had intensified their surveillance of her home and were openly following her everywhere. Her mother was ill, and Tenjy was afraid she would be without money if arrested. I assured her that if that happened we would send her salary direct to her mother regardless of how long she was in jail. There was adequate precedent for this— three members of our staff had been jailed without trial at various times, and the *Dispatch* had continued paying their salaries throughout.

Tenjy was arrested two days later and jailed without trial, and it was only after months of badgering police headquarters that I was allowed to visit her. In the interview room at the jail, a tiny cubicle where we were separated by thick glass so that we would have to raise our voices for clearer recording by the bugging devices, she gave a cry when I came in. "Oh—it's *so* good to see you." She looked small and vulnerable, but well. When she was released she told me that on the first day of her imprisonment she was taken for interrogation, and that an officer had pressed a button on a machine and she heard my voice saying: "*Kuteni, mta' kwetu?*" Our entire conversation had been recorded. Tenjy warned me: "Don't talk in your office or your home—not even in your car. It's all bugged."

She was allowed out of jail to give evidence in the Mohapi inquest, and she stood in the witness stand, barely a yard away from Captain Schoeman of the Security Police, testifying about the way he and others had punched her, pulled her hair and kicked her as she lay on the floor. When the State Prosecutor tried to imply during cross-examination that she was lying about how a towel had been tightened about her neck during interrogation, and called for a towel, saying: "Show us", she did so. The courtroom fell silent as, with chilling familiarity, she demonstrated how the towel was thrown over the face from behind and the ends tightened about the throat to a point just short of unconsciousness.

It was on that day, in the courthouse in King William's Town, while Tenjy was giving evidence, that Wendy and I realized fully for the first time that there was already a state of war in South Africa between the Afrikaner Nationalists and the black resistance—a state of war few whites in the country knew about. In this war the Security Police were the frontline troops and we were among their enemies. Increasingly, they were becoming "they" and we were becoming "we". There was less and less neutral ground, and we were inexorably approaching a stage where there was none at all.

Towards the end of 1976 a serious blow was aimed against the very existence of the *Dispatch* as an independent newspaper. The Trusteeship branch of the Standard Bank decided to offer for sale the Crewe Trustholding in the *Dispatch*, and the risk to the paper was that among the willing buyers could be the pro-government Afrikaans press which would not only relish owning the profitable *Dispatch* but would like even more to change its political policy.

It seemed to a number of us in the small ranks of the liberal press at this time that the Afrikaner Nationalist Government was using public funds to boost party newspapers, not only by granting favourable printing and advertising contracts to their own papers, whose boards of directors all included cabinet ministers, but also by spending large sums of money to whittle away commercially at the liberal press. Shortly after the right-wing English-language paper *The Citizen* was launched in Johannesburg, I said in a public speech in Durban that it was obviously funded by Government money. It had so little legitimate advertising, it was so blatantly a pro-apartheid propaganda sheet, and seemed so obviously to be aimed at weaning away the *Rand Daily Mail*'s small profit margin to put it in a loss position, that no businessman in his right mind would have launched it as a normal business venture. This allegation was denied repeatedly by Government spokesmen, and only in 1979 was it finally disclosed that the Government had indeed launched the paper with public funds amounting to more than thirty million rands, as part of a massive secret propaganda effort to try to sell apartheid internally as well as internationally.

The Standard Bank's Trustee Branch, headed by a man named Schneider, risked laying the *Dispatch* open to a secret takeover by Government agencies, and this nearly happened. As Schneider saw it, there were several options open: the Argus group, South African Associated Newspapers and the Afrikaans papers would all be interested in bidding, and this would presumably have the effect of pushing the price up, to the financial advantage of the Crewe Trust beneficiaries. The Standard Bank Trustee people had gone about the scheme cleverly. They knew it would stand no chance if Terry Brice-land, George Farr, Len Beacom or I heard of it, so they convinced Denis Ross-Thompson and Ian Kaye-Eddie that it would be in the best interests of the Trust if the matter were kept confidential. They reckoned without the keen intuitional instincts of Terry, who had the nose of a witchdoctor for intrigue. One day, when about to leave for a squash game, he walked past Ian Kaye-Eddie's office and noticed Standard Bank officials there. When he raised the subject Kaye-Eddie gave a vague reply, and all Terry's alarm bells started ringing.

Terry and I confronted Ross-Thompson and he, with some embarrassment, confirmed that negotiations were going on at the instigation of the Standard Bank Trustee officials to consider offers for the Crewe shareholding. It was only when we explained all the implications of the deal that he became alarmed, and united with us to save the *Dispatch* from what was now clearly a serious threat. Terry and I caught the next available plane to Johannesburg and confronted Schneider. His scarcely disguised readiness to sell to the highest bidder, including

Afrikaner Nationalist newspaper organizations, convinced us both that we had to use as much influence as we could muster in the financial corridors of power in Johannesburg. This meant another visit to the remarkable Max Borkum—and Max pulled all the right levers. Schneider's boss was the executive head of the Standard Bank, Henri de Villiers, a conservative with apparent leanings towards the Afrikaner Nationalist Government for business if not ideological reasons, and De Villiers was backing Schneider in his negotiations. The only higher official to De Villiers in the Standard Bank hierarchy was the chairman, a man named McKenzie. Our sole hope was to get someone capable of leaning on the Standard Bank to get McKenzie to lean on De Villiers, so that he would lean on Schneider. Max caused friends in Harry Oppenheimer's Anglo-American Corporation to take action, presumably with the result that McKenzie leant on De Villiers who then leant on Schneider—and that was the end of the scheme.

It was the second time Max Borkum had helped what was left of the independent press in South Africa. In all he was to do this rescue act three times, most notably when he was instrumental in foiling a disguised takeover bid by the Government's Department of Information under Minister Connie Mulder, aimed at South African Associated Newspapers. Max stepped into the breach with a counter-offer, and it was only in 1979 that the full details emerged of how the Vorster government had used public funds to try to buy out newspapers they hadn't been able to silence completely with their network of publication laws.

CHAPTER SIXTEEN

AFTER ALL THE pressures of the previous ten years, the period shortly preceding the last months of 1977 was one of the calmest and most pleasurable for me since my appointment as editor in 1965. Suddenly it seemed there was time and money to do things I hadn't been able to do for years. I entered in the national chess championships and played in a number of other tournaments, and also got back to playing regular golf. Wendy and I had a holiday in Cape Town. One of the country's leading orchestras performed a composition of mine based on the Xhosa musical idiom, although when it was submitted to the National Symphony Orchestra I was told it couldn't be performed for political reasons because of my anti-apartheid record. Things were going particularly well on the *Dispatch*, and we had our highest circulation in 109 years of publication, with record advertising revenue and profits.

My brother Harland and I had often spoken of taking a golfing holiday overseas, and midway through 1977 the chance presented itself of a three-week tour of Britain. Hearing I was going abroad, Dr Piet Koornhof asked me to find out as discreetly as possible whether Peter Hain, Dennis Brutus, Chris de Broglio and other leaders of the anti-apartheid boycott on South African international sport would be prepared to meet him secretly to negotiate an end to the campaign. This implied a readiness on his part to meet all their demands for the dismantling of sports apartheid, and knowing the Koornhof style I realized his tactics—if he could present his fellow cabinet ministers and party caucus with a guarantee from their archenemies on the sports issue that Springbok teams could again take the international field without fear of demonstrations and disruption, he might induce them to let him pay the price for this deal by dismantling apartheid in sport.

It was a typical Koornhof move. He was taking a major risk politically, because if it leaked out that he was seeking contact with Hain and the others he could be destroyed by the rest of his party. On the other hand, the initiative seemed to me to have some exciting possibilities. Once again, as with the cricket and rugby issues, it seemed to make possible a common goal from two opposing standpoints. I, like Brutus and Hain, could be attracted by the idea that the dismantling of sports apartheid would be a major breach in the whole apartheid wall, whereas Koornhof would see it as a time-buying exercise to gain international acceptability in some measure for South Africa while preserving political apartheid.

I met Brutus, Hain, de Broglio and several other leaders of their movement in London to discuss the matter. Their initial response was suspicion. Why was I carrying messages for a cabinet minister of the hated apartheid regime? I told them the background of my involvement with Koornhof over cricket and rugby, as well as my own role in the integration of South African chess. I said that as I saw it they had nothing to lose in testing Koornhof's sincerity and ability to deliver, and that for what it was worth we in the South African Cricket Board of Control had found that he didn't promise what he couldn't deliver, and had so far kept his word in his dealings with us. They said they weren't prepared to risk alienating leaders of their movement within South Africa by dealing with Koornhof before he spoke to these others, and decided to draft a set of conditions for Koornhof to meet as a pre-requisite of any further dealings.

Soon after Harland and I arrived in England we had a cable from home to say that Mom had died. On our return home all the family gathered at Miller Mission, near Elliotdale, where her ashes were placed in Dad's grave. She had lived twenty-two years after Dad's death, and throughout that time, as before it, she was always the totally loving mother and grandmother. I couldn't imagine a more unconditional commitment than hers to those she loved. As we left Miller cemetery I tried to envisage her as a young girl galloping horses and jumping fences on the stallion that Dad had given her. There was no anguish in our grief—she had lived out a long and active life, eighty-three years, and she wasn't suited to a long decline in a hospital ward. Her great legacy to her children and grandchildren had been her communication to us all in a hundred different ways that the deepest parental love sets no demands, conditions or boundaries.

When I handed Dr Koornhof the letter from Hain and the others he pondered it at length before looking up to say: "We can meet these conditions. We can do a deal. There are certain aspects of it that will be very difficult, but I'm sure we can do it." And a few months later, when the South African Chess Federation appointed me to its official delegation for the 1977 congress of the International Chess Federation in Lucerne, Koornhof asked me to go ahead with arrangements for his meeting overseas with the anti-apartheid campaigners. The Soviet Union Chess Federation had summoned the congress to move the expulsion of the South African Chess Federation from the world body because of apartheid, and my special mandate as a delegate was to oppose such expulsion on the grounds that apartheid was rejected by the South African Chess Federation—that while it was South African government policy our Federation did not allow apartheid in its chess clubs and tournaments.

On the eve of my departure Dr Koornhof phoned to say he felt the Hain–Brutus contact was so important that if necessary I should fly from Lucerne to London to take the negotiations a stage further, and specifically to indicate that their preconditions as conveyed through me could be met. This was good news, because among the preconditions were the lifting of banning orders on black sports administrators of the non-racial South African Council of Sport, and the restoring of their passports so that they could travel freely and consult personally with the Supreme Council for Sport in Africa. Koornhof also told me that he couldn't expect the South African Chess Federation or me personally to go to all the extra expense involved, and that the chess journey was such good "cover" that he was prepared to sponsor my trip. Knowing the Federation was short of funds, I was glad to tell the executive that my journey was sponsored by "an anonymous chess fan", and they thought it was a good omen for the trip.

Then I had another call from Koornhof to ask me to come to Johannesburg a day early in order to meet General van den Bergh at Johannesburg Airport. This was intriguing—as head of the Bureau of State Security Van den Bergh was not known to be close to Dr Koornhof, and as if to allay any concern I might feel about meeting the General again Koornhof said:

"He's a good friend of mine". I wasn't concerned over our last meeting, as I had known that the Section 83 prosecution of me had not been initiated by Van den Bergh but by General Geldenhuys, with the help of Minister Kruger. Geldenhuys had been so incensed at my allegations against one of his Security Police officers that he had ordered the prosecution after clearing it with Kruger. Kruger hadn't wanted action to be taken against me but, being basically a weak man, he was afraid that if he appeared to shield an opposition journalist from Geldenhuys he would earn a black mark in the party records, so he had given the go-ahead. Van den Bergh had been called away on the Angola crisis the day after our last interview, and had returned to find the Section 83 action against me well under way.

I had no sooner checked into the hotel at Johannesburg Airport than he arrived and came straight up to my room on the fourth floor. He made small talk while I ordered the drinks. He started talking about Koornhof's sports policy, speaking entirely in English: "Piet's going too far, too quickly," he said. "He'll get into trouble with the party if he goes on at this rate, and I've asked him to slow down." I said I thought Koornhof was going too slowly in view of the hardening attitudes among the blacks on the question of sport. In my view, 1977 was the last year in which sports apartheid could be negotiated out of existence as a separate issue from general apartheid, and if the party didn't allow Koornhof more leeway within the next few months the last bus would be missed on this issue. The General smiled. "Well, of course you would think he is going too slowly. You don't know the party feelings, and I can tell you that Piet has a lot of enemies there. I'm trying to protect him, to guard him from his enemies. Piet Koornhof is a good man, and South Africa needs him in a position of influence."

I said: "You know, General, you people are so concerned with internal party considerations that you misread the bigger picture. Any day now the Black Consciousness people will form a black sports council and then you can say goodbye to Koornhof's hopes of a deal. They believe that sports apartheid must be viewed only as a part of the whole question of apartheid, and that it will only be properly solved when there is a black government running South Africa. So you see, if Koornhof's plan is to have any hope of success it must go quicker rather than slower—and the changes must be more radical than any of you seem to think, including Dr Koornhof."

Van den Bergh said that for the sake of practical politics Koornhof would have to adopt a lower profile for a time, and that our proposed meeting between him and the Hain-Brutus committee would have to be called off. That was why he was meeting me, to change the terms of the original Koornhof initiative. "There was a leak about it, anyway," he said. "One of the men present at your meeting in London telephoned a contact in Cape Town to tip him off and wreck the meeting, and so it must be called off. They were going to go in with cameras and photograph Piet there, and so on. But can you find out, anyway, whether Peter Hain would meet me instead of Piet Koornhof?" I said: "Well, I don't know. I doubt if Peter Hain would want to meet the dreaded General van den Bergh." He said: "Dreaded? Do I look dreaded to you? Do you dread me?" I said: "Sort of," and he laughed. "Well, Mr Woods, I'm still reading your column, and I still disagree with everything you stand for—except for one thing." "What's that?" I asked, intrigued. "There's one thing you and I agree on—P. W. Botha is a rubbish!" he said vehemently. I was amazed. It was incredible that this man should speak of a cabinet colleague in such terms to an "enemy" journalist. P. W. Botha was, with Mulder, one of the two most senior members of the cabinet, and was said to be in almost equal contention with Mulder for the succession to Vorster. It astonished me that such hostility could exist in a cabinet which presented a united front to the nation and to the world, and that Van den Bergh should be so outspoken to me about it. I asked him, riding my luck a bit, what the pecking order was in the cabinet, but he cagily stayed clear of the subject and mentioned only that he, Van den Bergh, had the final say over passport withdrawals of any citizen.

I asked him why the passport of Beyers Naude, head of the Christian Institute, had been taken away. "Now *there* is a great Afrikaner," I told him. "He is a credit to Afrikanerdom, while your party is giving Afrikaners a bad name all over the world. Why do you people persecute him so much?" General van den Bergh replied: "You don't know Beyers Naude as *we* know

297

Beyers Naude! That's all I'm prepared to say." I also raised again the subject of Security Police excesses, mentioning Hattingh, Spyker van Wyk and Swanepoel, but this time Van den Bergh would not be drawn.

He asked me about the strength of the Russian lobby for the forthcoming congress, and I gave a rough account of the probable line-up and said that at best we could hope to retain the support of most of the Western delegates. I told him about Koornhof's offer to sponsor the trip, but said that in view of his news about the cancellation of the Koornhof plan this might no longer be regarded as important now. "No, no, it *is* important," he said, saying that he had assumed responsibility for the sponsorship, and that a Mr Rothmann would deliver the money to me at the airways information counter. He got to his feet and wished me luck for the congress, and I said: "General, do you realize what I'm going to say at that congress? Did Dr Koornhof make it plain to you what my attitude is? I'm going to attack *all* apartheid laws and policies, and in the name of the South African Chess Federation I'm going to put as much distance between our Federation and apartheid as I can!" He said: "*Ja, natuurlik*, obviously that is what you must say to get the Western votes." "But that's not the only reason," I replied. "We in the Federation *are* against apartheid." "You don't have to tell me that," he said, nodding down from his great height. "But," I protested, "you should know what I told Dr Koornhof from the beginning—I'm doing this not only to end *sports* apartheid but to weaken *all* apartheid." He said, a little shortly: "I *know* that, man. But if the Western delegates in *any* international forum support a South African organization, that helps South Africa's name, of course."

He turned at the door: "Good luck in Switzerland—and if you can get Hain to meet me I will be grateful." He said the best place for the meeting would be Paris. "There's a French count, a friend of mine, we could meet in his house." "Why not London?" I asked. Van den Bergh laughed: "London? That's the last place I'd go for such a meeting! The British have the most efficient secret service in the world, and they would know the minute I got there!"

The next morning at the appointed time a man at the airways information desk identified himself as Mr Rothmann and handed me a sealed envelope with the compliments of the General. I put it in my inside pocket, thinking the whole thing was getting crazier and crazier, and went to meet Leonard Rietstein, one of my two fellow delegates, off the Cape Town plane. Rietstein was President of the South African Chess Federation; Bill Bowers, the other delegate, was his Vice-President and was a 'coloured' man from Cape Town. Other officials of the Federation were there, and we all went by car to lunch at the home of our "elder statesman" of South African chess, Mr J. L. A. Pfundt. While Mr Pfundt and his wife were settling us into our chairs with drinks I took out the envelope Mr Rothmann had handed me and opened it. It contained brand-new Treasury notes, and as I handed the notes to our treasurer I noticed his eyes bulging at the sight. He must have concluded that our mystery sponsor was not only a chess fan but someone with a lot of pull in the Reserve Bank. That, I thought, could be the understatement of the year, as I reflected on all the ironies of the situation. My chess colleagues would never have believed it if I'd said that Koornhof and Van den Bergh were channelling money to the South African Chess Federation so that I could (a) journey to Lucerne to attack apartheid in hopes of thwarting a Russian move to expel South Africa from world chess and (b) set up a meeting between the head of BOSS and anti-apartheid spokesmen to phase out sports apartheid. The only key to any rationality in the situation seemed to be the knee-jerk dread of the South African government of any successful Russian bid to isolate any South African organization internationally—even one condemning apartheid!

Whatever machinations Koornhof and Van den Bergh had in mind, I was determined to use the Lucerne meeting to drive home to South Africans that any degree of acceptability in a world forum for any South African organization depended on that organization's rejection of apartheid—and that ideally the more vehement such rejection was the more acceptable such a body would be internationally. The thing was to equate apartheid with international rejection, and we had a unique mandate to do that in a forum which would be covered extensively in the South African media.

Leonard Rietstein and I flew from Johannesburg to Zurich,

where we linked up with Bill Bowers and travelled on by train to Lucerne. There we were booked with the other delegations into the palatial old Schweizerhof Hotel, and as each band of delegates arrived we began our lobbying. A key bloc of delegates were the Scandinavians—the Danes, the Swedes, the Norwegians and the Icelanders—and we spent the first evening with them. They proved staunch in our support, and once they accepted that we were genuinely anti-apartheid they spearheaded our defence. All the other Western delegations rallied to us, except France and Australia, but against us we had the entire Soviet bloc and Third World delegations, who were pressing unanimously for our expulsion, and who outnumbered us.

Leonard and Bill were allowed one speech each to the congress and I was allowed two—one in presentation of our case and one to rebut the Russian case before the vote. The official opening was highly ceremonial, heralded in the great hall by a fanfare of trumpets. Seated with the Russian delegation was world champion Anatoly Karpov, who soon withdrew in dudgeon from the hall when his exiled arch-opponent, Viktor Korchnoi, marched in to sit with us in public support of our case. The Russian delegation was headed by Soviet chess chief Baturinski, and included Grandmaster Awerbach, who had the look of a Harvard professor in a western-tailored suit. Bill, Leonard and I made our speeches, Baturinski registering protest because I had been given more time than any Russian speaker, and as the long debate went on it became obvious that the vote would have little to do with the merits of our case. It was not so much a question of chess politics as of geopolitics; the non-Western countries were less interested in non-racial chess in South Africa than in chess as one more stick to beat the apartheid issue with.

Yet, as I listened to some of the speeches, I began to perceive that our case might not be all that watertight. I was especially impressed with the speech of the Nigerian delegate, who made some telling points which caused Bill Bowers and me to look at each other as if to say: "He's got something there". The Nigerian's point was that, much as he sympathized with our efforts in the South African Chess Federation to bar apartheid, South African chess could not be viewed in isolation from the general state of an apartheid society. Even if blacks were allowed into chess clubs on an an equal footing with whites, their very environment militated against *competing* on an equal footing. Coming from a politically and economically deprived ghetto, with inferior diet and education, the black was automatically at a disadvantage. "Chess is more than the wooden pieces pushed about a board," he said. "We must consider the flesh and blood of the fingers and the people who push them. We must consider the condition of the whole man—not just the chessplayer."

That night I thought long about what the Nigerian had said. It was Steve's basic viewpoint, more fully expressed, and I began to see that maybe it was the right one. Maybe such things as integrated chess clubs and cricket clubs were little more than fiddling while Rome burnt. Wasn't the Nigerian's perspective the balanced one, in its overview of the whole South African society? Anti-apartheid breakthroughs in isolated spheres had to be measured against the overwhelming weight of apartheid oppression and against such factors as the killing of people like Mapetla Mohapi. The Nigerian's speech positively undermined my belief that international isolation should be spared at least to those South African organizations strongly opposed to apartheid. In that general perspective these strivings were no longer significantly relevant; they were now too minor to be real blows against the apartheid structure. In fact, they could even be counter-productive. Why else would Koornhof and Van den Bergh want the non-apartheid South African Chess Federation to gain international approval, if not for what they saw as some sort of acknowledgement of a measure of respectability for the South African image generally?

This was how my thoughts began to crystallize on the eve of our return to South Africa. I sought out the Nigerian and spoke at length with him at the cocktail party for the delegates. A number of the Soviet-bloc delegates made a point of re-stating their case. "What you are trying to do to end apartheid is from good motives—but it is not good for the broad anti-apartheid cause." Grandmaster Awerbach gave me an autographed copy of his latest chess book, remarking: "Only a more radical solution can help the black people in your country." Good heavens, I thought, can it be that these people are actually sincere after all, and not just voting to instructions? I spoke to one after the other—the East German, the Bulgarian, the Hungarian and several others of that camp, including the Cuban delegate—and found they seemed deeply and even passionately involved with the issue. The Cuban said, with a smile: "I fought against your boys in Angola. Good boys, not bad soldiers, but too young for the job. Not trained enough."

Back in South Africa we received plaudits from the Federation and considerable press coverage for having won the support of the Western bloc at the congress, and especially that of the Scandinavians in view of their known hostility to apartheid. But I was having second thoughts the more I thought of the Nigerian's speech. After it I had decided against trying to initiate the Hain–Van den Bergh meeting. I explained this to Van den Bergh and Koornhof on my return, but both seemed so pleased at the Western support we had won that the other issue hardly seemed to matter to them any more. And that disturbed me too.

I spent a weekend at Hobeni, and went into the countryside with Harland in his van to deliver corn-maize to his customers. He tried wherever possible to deliver the bags of maize to the door of each hut. Sometimes the family would come out to chat and would allude to my prematurely grey hair, saying that as Harland's was still black he looked more like the younger brother than the older. One old woman came out of her hut with the stern nobility of Ethel Barrymore, smoking a long beaded pipe and wearing the cloth headdress. She extended her hand graciously and said: "We often think about you, Zweliyanyikima. When the big *baloni* goes overhead we wonder if you are in it."

At another kraal, just above Hobeni near the home of Headman Fudumele, I walked along the road while Harland and the men of the kraal counted off the maize-bags from the back of the truck, and met another old woman walking like a queen with her head high. "Yes," she said condescendingly, "and who are you? I know you from somewhere." I told her I was Zweliyanyikima, son of Masumpa and brother of Dumekude. She nodded: "Yes, I remember you when you were a child. You live down at e Monti (East London) don't you?" I said: "Yes." "Tell me," she went on, taking her pipe out of her mouth, "How many children do you have now?" Five, I told her. "Five!" she said. "All alive?" I said yes. "Five children, all alive!" she said. "That is a wonderful thing!"

Wendy and I went to Kimberley for parents' weekend at CBC, where our eldest son Dillon now was. It turned the clock back many years to stroll along the college grounds, to play tennis against Brother Southwell again, to hear Brother Hurley's cricket stories and enjoy the crudite wit of Brother Purcell. The Brothers seemed ageless. There was sung High Mass in the cathedral, with the college pipers and trumpeters playing the Antiphon. On the cadet field there was the traditional Retreat ceremony, with the usual army officers from Central Command—only this time the officer was Major Dempster, whom I recalled as little Dempster, a junior of several classes below me. Now he had the stout look of middle age as he took the salute from the rostrum. My heart sickened as little Dempster, the chubby-cheeked boy of grade four, 1951, warned my son and his schoolmates to aim their rifles and sharpen their bayonets to defend their fatherland to the death against the Marxist menace of black Africa to the north. I thought of the hundreds of kids taking in this sort of thing as a sacred patriotic charge, and of the whole crazy twist being given in white South African Army terms to the cause of the black liberation movements who had only turned to violence because whites would neither talk with them nor listen to them.

After the parade Major Dempster shook hands with me with the respect a grade four pupil has for a matriculation senior.

Then he picked up his brown officer's gloves and cane, touched these to his cap and withdrew with his attentive aide. It was easy to regard Security Police officers like Captain Schoeman and Warrant Officer Hattingh as the enemy; not so easy to see little Dempster in that role. But he was one of them. And what was to be, for me, their total declaration of war was only weeks away.

CHAPTER SEVENTEEN

IT WAS OMINOUS the way the list of deaths in political detention was growing since Kruger had become Minister of Police. Since the death of Mapetla Mohapi, the twenty-third since jail-without-trial was introduced, there had been another seventeen in less than a year, and by August 1977 the total had reached forty-four. Most of these deaths had occurred within the short period Kruger had held office, and I was certain of the reason—it was Kruger's weakness. He was not an assertive man, not the man to risk the anger of the Security Police by demanding too close an account of their actions. They knew they could do as they liked. He was in awe of Geldenhuys and his colleagues, and felt flattered at being their ministerial boss. He would never rage at them over deaths in detention as Vorster had done after Ahmed Timol had fallen to his death from Security Police headquarters. To offset his weakness he tried to act tough and sound tough. He took a machine pistol into Parliament, and when his turn came in the debate he brandished it as an example of the sort of "Communist weapons we are capturing from the terrorists". He was obviously doing his best to pose as the iron-hard national saviour against the savage Marxist hordes. His chubby face and paunch belied this image, but he tried nevertheless. And his prisoners died— twenty-six of them in two years—because of his timidity in failing to control the thugs in the Security Police.

It was on August 18, 1977, that Steve Biko was jailed without trial for the fourth time, and in spite of the grim statistics of death in detention his family and friends weren't unduly worried. He had been imprisoned without trial three times before, and no serious harm had come to him. We were so confident that the Security Police would treat him with extra care that when I walked into my office at the *Dispatch* on the morning of Tuesday, September 13, and was told by my secretary that there were reports that Steve was dead, I laughed at the thought. She was in tears, but I told her not to worry. I said: "Steve dead? Nonsense! I know the Nats are mad—but even they aren't so mad as to let him die of *anything* in detention."

But this didn't mean he might not be ill, so I phoned his family—and heard the sickening confirmation that he was dead.

Within those shocked seconds South Africa became a different place for me, and when I called Wendy she had a similar reaction. For both of us the Nats were now the mortal enemy who had committed the ultimate outrage. She said: "I'm beyond feeling scared of them. There's nothing worse they can do."

Newspapers in South Africa and overseas wanted our reactions to the tragedy as close friends of Steve's, and still in shock, still barely able to believe he was dead, we wrote these articles. Then I worked with Glyn Williams and John Horlor on a front-page layout with a large colour portrait of Steve in black mourning borders. Late that night, unable to sleep, I had a vivid mental picture of him alive and sitting in the room with us, as if he were talking animatedly with a typical expression of vivacity.

The next day Kruger implied that Steve had died of hunger strike, but I knew this couldn't be true because he had once said he would never take or endanger his own life in detention, and that if he were to die in jail, and it was claimed he had hanged or suffocated or starved himself or cut his wrists, I was to know it was a lie. I set off to say this in speeches around the country and to challenge Kruger's hunger strike story. Wendy spoke at Rhodes University and I spoke at Cape Town, Natal and Witwatersrand universities.

The Transvaal congress of the Afrikaner Nationalist Party was on at the time, and Kruger joined in the frivolous reception delegates gave at the news of Steve's death. Kruger, basking in the tough-guy image he adopted for the applauding delegates, said: "Biko's death leaves me cold". A delegate from Springs named Christoffel Venter stood up to commend Kruger as a "democratic Minister" who was "so democratic" that he allowed prisoners "the democratic right to starve to death". Kruger, enjoying the attention of the giggling delegates, said: "Mr Venter is right. That is very democratic." Later he became even more jocular. "Of course one feels sorry about any

305

death—I suppose I would feel sorry about my own."

Aided by a tip-off from sources close to persons who had attended the post-mortem examination of Steve's body, I put a public challenge to Kruger—if pathologists established that he had died of malnutrition or any other effect of a hunger strike, I would resign my job and go out of journalism, provided Kruger gave a public undertaking that if pathologists found that death was due to police violence *he* would resign *his* job and go out of politics. Kruger declined the challenge. In fact, he started backing away from his hunger-strike story from that moment. He made several appearances on television to try to make things look better for himself. He implied that Steve had been fed intravenously. Stating this, he gestured vaguely at his arm, giving a coy impression of a bewildered layman dazzled by medical mysteries. "I'm not a doctor", he said spuriously.

Then, as it became clear that none of his stories would hold up in public, he began to start conditioning the public to accept the Biko killing as a nation-saving event. He spoke of the danger to whites of Black Consciousness, misrepresenting a number of facts about the movement so as to lend it the most sinister interpretation for whites. He claimed that Steve had written pamphlets advocating violence, and although he provided no shred of evidence for these allegations the Afrikaner Nationalist press echoed his smear stories. The Cape Town Afrikaner Nationalist paper, *Die Burger*, published a front-page report headed *Bloed en Lyke Gevra in Biko Pamflet*, giving its readers the impression that Steve had authored a pamphlet calling for "blood and bodies". *Die Burger*, instead of attributing this allegation to Kruger, published it as if it were fact. I telephoned the editor and suggested he should put the matter right in his next issue by publishing on his front page, with equal prominence, that this report was not factual but only a claim by Kruger. He declined, so I told him I would have him cited before the Press Council, and when he persisted in his refusal I filed an official complaint to the Council.

This was ironic, because the Press Council was a device of the Afrikaner Nationalist Government and of papers like *Die Burger* to punish opposition newspapers such as the *Dispatch* and *Rand Daily Mail*. It prescribed a strict code, with severe penalties, and allowed any member of the government or public to make a complaint against any paper which, the complainant claimed, had published an "unbalanced" report. As pro-apartheidists thought any report about apartheid was "unbalanced" and "un-South African" if it didn't give equal play to official "explanations" by ministers, this enabled hundreds of cranks to tie us up in hours of administrative work defending ourselves before the Press Council for any number of frivolous reasons. Any crank could write to the Press Council complaining about any report, no matter how accurate, and for every such complaint we would have to file photocopies of the report complained of and prepare a defence including statements and affidavits by the reporters and sub-editors concerned. In 1977 this was a constant irritant—one of the many pressures mounting against the opposition press. Now for the first time the Press Council was to be used against a government publication. My complaint against *Die Burger* was the first by one editor against another, and they had to go through with it because their procedures were so rigidly defined. Because *Die Burger*'s report was so obviously slanted in representing allegation as fact, the Press Council had to uphold the complaint and order the paper to retract its report about the imaginary "Biko pamphlets". The pamphlets were obviously written by the Security Police to smear Steve's name; apart from anything else, the English was so bad that Steve could never have been the author.

The Security Police also circulated pamphlets against me. In an attempt to discredit me among blacks they scattered throughout the townships a pamphlet calling me a hypocrite who claimed to uphold the black cause but actually opposed it. They ended by saying my sons were in the white army fighting against black guerillas on the border—although my eldest son Dillon was only twelve years old. But blacks in the townships realized where the pamphlets had come from, and many wrote to the paper to say that the Security Police would have to try harder to deceive them into turning against me. Some sent the actual pamphlets in as well, having scrawled "rubbish" and "Security Police" across them.

All these Security Police devices were aimed at blunting the mounting criticism against Kruger, but they weren't succeeding. We got a reliable tip-off that he had received the coroner's report on Steve's post-mortem, that it revealed that Steve had died of brain damage, and that although Kruger had had this report for more than a week he had not yet ordered an inquest or corrected his "hunger-strike" story. So we published another front-page editorial asking Kruger: (a) whether he had received the coroner's report; (b) whether it indicated brain-damage; (c) how long he had had the report, and (d) when an inquest would be held.

The State-controlled broadcasting service tried again to mislead the public by including in a "news bulletin" the statement that initial investigation into the Biko death did not indicate the prosecution of any person and that the attorney-general was not opening one. This was sheer deviousness, seeking to give the impression that there had been a police investigation which had exonerated the Security Police, whereas it was normal procedure in such cases to hold an inquest before determining whom to prosecute. We clarified this to our readers in another front-page editorial, so that they should understand how they were being misled by the radio and television service.

By this time Steve's body had been returned to his family after the post-mortem, and I felt I should see it for myself before the funeral. The body was in a mortuary in King William's Town, and as I had to have a member of the family present to see it I arranged with Steve's wife, Ntsiki, to go with me. I also arranged for a staff photographer to take pictures of the body.

I had now begun to take the precaution of never travelling on my own, and as Kingsley and Terry were not at home I phoned another lawyer friend, Jan van Gend, who agreed to come with me. We had a lot of difficulty getting into the mortuary. Twice we were directed to the wrong one, and when we finally got to the right one it was securely locked and no one was on duty.

Ntsiki sat in the car with Jan while I went into a little fruit shop run by Indians and asked to use their telephone. I spent nearly an hour on the phone as I tracked down the mortuary technicians. The man with the key to the mortuary had been sent into the countryside in a hearse with a one-way radio, and it was only after many attempts that I managed to get a sympathetic employee of the hearse company to undertake to send the man back when he made his next hourly report. This employee wouldn't give his name on the phone, but concluded the conversation by saying quickly: "Keep it up, Mr Woods. Don't let anyone scare you off." He then hung up. Now we simply had to park outside the mortuary and wait. I tried to pay the Indian shopkeeper in the little store for all the phone calls but he wouldn't take any money. "We know what you're doing, Mr Woods. We want to help too."

It was dark by the time the mortician arrived, and he unlocked the door to the mortuary and led the way into the cold room as Ntsiki, Jan and I followed. I had a feeling of dread as I approached what looked like three large filing cabinets, one on top of the other. The two lower ones had bodies which were covered by sheets, except for the feet. Each body had a label attached to the foot, and on the label in the upper tray I saw the name BIKO.

In a matter-of-fact way the mortician walked to this tray to pull it out, and in the instant before he did so I realized that it was Steve's two bare feet we could see. I had my arm around Ntsiki, for my comfort as well as hers, and I said: "Look, Ntsiki, I have to make a close inspection of Steve's body, you understand why, but you must stand back or go out whenever you wish." She nodded.

I had never seen a dead body in a mortuary before. The mortician slid out the tray past us and we now stood level with Steve's chest, on his left side as he lay on his back. The head and body right down to the ankles was covered by the sheet, and the mortician made no move to lift it. I looked at him and he walked out to another room.

I raised the sheet from Steve's head, folding it back below his chest. The initial shock was appalling. This was so much not the Steve we had known. The facial expression was a travesty. His eyes were open, but they were a dull silvered film, and his normally full lips were thin, drained. His forehead looked badly swollen and marked, but whether from post-mortem surgery we couldn't know. Ntsiki leant over him sobbing quietly and whispering, "Oh, Steve! Oh, Steve!" She moved back to stand with Jan.

I lifted the sheet some more and saw the jagged scar of the post-mortem incision. There was certainly no sign of malnutrition—it was still the body of a big, heavily built man—but this was irrelevant now because by this time even Kruger had abandoned his first excuse of hunger-strike. I thought again of Kruger's remark: "Biko's death leaves me cold." It was cold in there. The chill air hit all of us standing about the body-tray.

Thinking about Kruger stiffened my resolve to start a complete inspection of Steve's head and shoulders, and I forced myself to go as close as I could and slowly, from two to three inches, to look with the utmost care at every part of his forehead and face. During this time I felt no grief, only anger and a clinical intensity of effort to be as observant a witness as I could, with a sense of the need, before his body was put underground, to record all the visual evidence possible of the injuries done to him. When I was satisfied that I had every detail of the marks on him trapped in my memory, I took Ntsiki's arm and we walked out.

Once on the pavement I was immensely relieved that this ritual was over without any breakdown on my part. I had the feeling that when the burial process began Steve's remains would belong exclusively to the black community, and although Ntsiki said Wendy and I would be regarded as family mourners, "as brother and sister", I knew it couldn't be so. Many of Steve's lieutenants from other parts of the country had resented his friendship with us and with other whites, and we had no intention of provoking further resentment by venturing too close to the central group at the funeral. Jan and I drove Ntsiki back to Leopold Street and we returned to East London. The press photographer had the film developed and we made many copies of each shot from every angle, locking one set in the *Dispatch* safe and depositing other sets in hiding places away from the building—a fortunate precaution because the Security Police were later to search for these pictures and even to search the cabin of a ship for them when one of our photographers, an American, was returning home.

That night I sat for more than an hour making sketch after sketch of the marks I had seen on Steve's forehead, especially the large swelling above the eyes, and it took me nearly forty sketches to get the effect I recalled. It didn't seem redundant to the photographs because none of them exactly showed up the swelling as I had seen it.

310

Wendy and I both dreaded the funeral. We were afraid there would be violence against us and other whites attending it, not by the mourners who knew us but by those from distant parts of the country. I went to see the local police chief, Brigadier Smal, a career policeman who wasn't a party man, and he was pleased at my offer of liaison with the planners of the funeral. He wanted no trouble, and nor did they. Led by Malusi Mpumlwana, Steve's lieutenant, they wanted all the arrangements to go off smoothly as a disciplined salute to Steve. The best way to ensure this was to keep the sight of police uniforms away from the funeral area, and Brigadier Smal agreed to this. Malusi and Wendy saw to poster designs— Malusi described what he wanted put on them—Roger Omond and Terry Briceland had the posters printed, and we published details of the ceremony, together with appeals by Black Consciousness leaders like Hlaku Rachidi for order and discipline.

We expected at least fifty thousand at the funeral, and possibly more, but at the last minute Transvaal, Western Province and Natal police stopped many busloads of mourners from Soweto, Durban and Cape Town, and in other parts of the country roadblocks prevented thousands of mourners from getting near King William's Town. Nevertheless, the local turnout was huge, at least twenty thousand, and by some miracle the fewer than a hundred whites attending were unharmed. It was touch and go occasionally, because the funeral took six hours and many of the speeches were angrily denunciatory of whites.

Wendy and I, Debbie Morgan and Wendy's brother Peter stood in the body of the huge black crowd, and occasionally we would see isolated little knots of whites like Terry and Val Briceland. During one inflammatory speech about "the white killers" I noticed an extremely tough-looking black township gangster-type with a knife-wound on his cheek staring at me from only a few feet away. Trapped by his icy stare and fearful of his thoughts, I stared back. Then, to my relief, he winked at me and nodded a greeting.

Several members of the Progressive Federal Party were there, including Helen Suzman, Zac de Beer and Alex Boraine, and diplomatic representatives from America, Britain, Germany, France, the Scandinavian countries, Holland, Canada, Australia and Brazil also attended. The diplomat among them who knew Steve best was Bruce Haigh of the Australian Embassy, a conscientious observer for his country who was more knowledgeable about political developments in South Africa than any diplomatic representative I had known since Bob Gosende of the USA.

The funeral ended and we returned to East London with considerable relief. Brigadier Smal had kept his policemen out of sight of the ceremonial environs, and this had undoubtedly contributed to the general calm, scarcely maintained though it seemed at times. For several days thereafter, however, violence simmered and erupted in various centres as young blacks gave vent to their rage over Steve's death and over the turning back of thousands of mourners. One busload of black schoolchildren, seeing two black policemen in uniform at a bus-stop, poured out of the bus and stoned them to death. Others burnt buildings and factories belonging to whites, and one white industrialist telephoned me while the windows of his factory were being smashed to scream hysterically that it was all my fault. This was a fairly common response among conservative whites whenever rioting began in South Africa. They always blamed, not the government for provoking such riots with the oppressive apartheid laws, but those liberals who had warned that this might happen if apartheid continued.

We and other friends of Steve's renewed our demands for an inquest, and because these demands were extensively reported internationally Vorster felt sufficiently pressured to order one to be held. It was to begin on November 14, 1977, in Pretoria. Not that we had hopes of a complete and proper investigation, but following Steve's own tactics over Mapetla's inquest we believed that at least some of the truth would emerge—at least enough to prove Kruger a liar and to point the finger of guilt at the Security Police culprits.

CHAPTER EIGHTEEN

In October I received an invitation to attend a conference of the African–American Institute in Williamsburg, Virginia, USA. Also invited was my friend Percy Qoboza, editor of *The World*, a Johannesburg newspaper with a large black readership. Percy and I prepared to leave for the conference, which was to last three days, and our departure was set for October 19. That morning I flew from East London to Johannesburg to catch the afternoon plane to London and then to Washington. At East London airport I was paged to take a telephone call. It was a reporter from the Johannesburg *Star*, with shattering news—all the Black Consciousness organizations and their leading officials had been banned and many had been jailed without trial, including Percy.

I went to the United States Consulate-General in Johannesburg to get my visa stamp and spoke with several senior members of the American mission who were concerned over that morning's bannings. But further bannings were now being announced—Beyers Naude, Theo Kotze, David Russell, the Christian Institute.

Bruce Haigh of the Australian Embassy drove me to the airport to catch my London flight. On the way he said: "I wonder if they'd ban you . . ." I said it seemed unlikely in view of all the other less extreme laws they could throw at me if they chose. "Nevertheless, I'm going to hang around until you're on that plane," said Bruce. We went into the lounge area and had two beers each as the minutes ticked by. "Well, Bruce," I said, "it's about time for me to go through customs and passport control, so I'd better get started. Thanks for waiting with me." He said: "It was a pleasure, mate. Looks like they're leaving you alone after all. Good on yer. All the best for a good journey." We shook hands and Bruce left.

I went up to the passport counter, cleared my passport with the official and walked through the gate into the inner lounge. A man stopped me, then I saw there were two other men with him. They were in plain clothes and the first man said: "Mr

Donald Woods? We're from the Security Police. Come with us, please." My immediate thought was that they wanted to ask me about the conference I was flying to attend, and I looked up at the wall clock, as the flight-time was approaching. "Don't worry about that—you won't be on the flight," said one of the Security Police officers. I answered lamely: "But my suitcase is on the aircraft." One of them said: "No, we've already removed it. Come with us, please." They took me to a small office only a few yards away from passport control. With each moment I was realizing that this was far more serious than being questioned about the Williamsburg conference.

"What does this mean?" I asked. "Am I being banned, or something?" One of them, taking a sheaf of papers from a briefcase, said: "Banned." I laughed, with a mixture of shock and disbelief. "Banned! Kruger's really gone mad, hasn't he?" The three stood silently, then one of them started reading the banning orders to me from the documents "in terms of the Internal Security Act", explaining that henceforth I was forbidden to write; to be quoted; to be with more than one person at a time; to speak with more than one person at a time; to communicate with any other banned person; to leave the magisterial district of East London; to enter harbour premises there; to enter printing or publishing premises of any kind; to enter any factory or school or other educational institution, and that I had to register regularly with the police at the nearest police station to my home.

At the time, as he read out the documents and explained them, I took in few of these details. My mind was still racing with the shock of being banned. I had a sensation of being confined, hampered, it felt like an assault. He finished reading, then said: "We are from Security Police Headquarters in Pretoria. We have come direct from Minister Kruger on his personal orders to take you into custody and return you immediately to your home in East London." All I could say was: "He's gone crazy today—all these bannings." One of them pointed out, I don't know why, that Kruger signed my banning orders that very afternoon, at two-thirty. "We came straight here. We knew you were on this flight." "Well, what happens now?" I asked. He said: "You've got to come with us to the Security Police office upstairs."

It felt strange re-entering the main concourse of the airport, a big hall with hundreds of people sitting and standing about, and I looked at the far exit in the hope that Bruce Haigh might not yet have left. "Your friend has gone," one of the officers said. "We waited all the time you were here with him having your drinks. We waited until he was gone." "Can I phone my wife?" I asked. He replied: "No, that's not possible." I felt a surge of anger, and seeing all the public telephone booths across the concourse I strode towards them.

The three were at my side immediately, but I didn't slow down. If they were going to stop me phoning Wendy they were going to have to wrestle with me in front of all the bystanders— something I knew they would want to avoid. "What are you doing?" the one demanded. "I'm going to phone my wife," I said. "Wait, Mr Woods," he exclaimed. I said "No, you say I can't phone her—well, I'm going to." "All right," he replied. "You can phone her, but not from these public phones. You can phone from our office upstairs." I turned and went with them back along the concourse to the elevators.

Suddenly I heard my name being called out. It was Dr Danie Craven, head of the South African Rugby Board. "Hullo, Doc," I said. "Where are you off to?" He answered: "I'm flying over for the international rugby conference and the centenary festival game." My custodians seemed uncomfortable about this chance encounter and I had the feeling they would be put out if I told Dr Craven what was happening. But I thought it would cause the old man too much distress if I told him, so I simply said: "Well, Doc, from now on if you want to see me you'll have to come to East London." He smiled a farewell and looked rather puzzled as I moved on with my three "watchdogs", but I knew he would soon learn what had happened.

I was taken into the main Security Police office at the airport. It was barred and double-locked with a grille as in the East London Security Police offices, and a fourth Security Police officer was there. He started searching through my suitcase. "What are you looking for?" I asked. "Firearms," he said, going through every item in the case. He took out two books I had packed for light reading and examined them. I smiled, because one was on rugby tactics, by Danie Craven, and the other was on cricket, by Garfield Sobers.

I reminded them that I wanted to phone my wife. "All right," said one. "There's the phone—but make it a short call. We're not supposed to allow it." My son Duncan answered the phone. Wendy wasn't there. She was working at the Progressive Federal Party election campaign office. I got the number from Duncan and called her. Wendy was shaken by the news, I could tell, although she didn't let on in the tone of her response. She had long learnt not to give Security Police eavesdroppers the satisfaction of hearing any semblance of demoralization over the telephone, and she was always decisive in a crisis. I thought at the time, while the Security Police were telling me to hurry and conclude the conversation, that her discipline reminded me of all the times we had sped to the nursing home for her to give birth. She was scared every time and never hid her fear of the pain, but once the crunch came she would always be businesslike and organized. Before I put the receiver down I said to her quickly: 'Tell Allister, John and Roger." Although my Security Police custodians couldn't know that this referred to Allister Sparks and John Ryan of the *Rand Daily Mail* and Roger Omond of the *Dispatch* and therefore meant: "Sound the alarm", they didn't like it and were growing increasingly jumpy about the call. But I did manage to tell Wendy that I was being "escorted" home overnight.

While we were walking to the lift the Security Police officers told me they had instructions direct from Kruger to convey me to East London as soon as possible, and that we should be leaving by car almost immediately. "Why by car?" I asked. "Why can't we fly?" One said: "There are no more flights available to East London tonight. They're booked up. We'd also prefer to fly, but now we have orders to take you by car." "We could get an early flight tomorrow," I protested. "We have to take you by car," the man answered.

With the call to Wendy completed I felt I could now get in a couple of jabs at my captors. "Now I know," I said. "In the past, when you banned people, I always criticized it and condemned it—but I always wondered what they might have done. But now I know, because it has happened to me, that you ban people for nothing. For no crime. You ban people for opposing you." One of them replied: "We wouldn't know about that.

That is all decided at a high level. We just carry out instructions." "You mean *Befehl ist Befehl*," I said. "What?" he asked. "What is that?" I said: "That's German for orders are orders. In Afrikaans it would be *bevel is bevel*. It's what the defence argument was at the Nuremburg Tribunals, and it failed as a defence."

One of the Security Police officers stepped forward. An elderly man with grey hair, he said: "I am Major Boshoff and this is Lieutenant Beukes. We have the responsibility of taking you by car back to East London." Absurdly, through some social reflex, we shook hands as if we were being introduced at a cocktail party.

All the conversation with me, from the time they had arrested me at passport control, had been in English. Now they had a hurried conversation among themselves in Afrikaans about the travel arrangements, the original occupant of the upstairs office urging speed because, as he said, "you should have left already, without this telephoning and delay." We went downstairs, where a car awaited us. Major Boshoff sat in the left front seat, Lieutenant Beukes drove, and I sat in the back seat. "You can sit either side, Mr Woods," said Boshoff in an avuncular manner. "Just make yourself comfortable—we have a long way to go." I replied: "I'll stay here on the left," adding: "*Ek het linkse neigings*." ("I have leftish inclinations.") Boshoff laughed, obviously relieved that I wasn't going to be "unpleasant", and commented flatteringly on my Afrikaans pronunciation. But I didn't feel like talking further and sat back alone with my thoughts. Beukes drove expertly and fast as he weaved in and out of the traffic in the Johannesburg outskirts to get clear of the city. He and Boshoff talked in low tones about their families' arrangements for the evening and during their absence. I looked at my watch and it seemed strange to see its familiar face in those circumstances.

Major Boshoff hooked his elbow over the backrest and half-turned to face me: "I knew Steve Biko, you know. Well, I met him once, in a raid on the campus at Natal University. He had a white girl with him in his room." "Did you arrest him for that?" I asked. He said: "No, that wasn't what we were after him for." After a pause he added: "He was very intelligent, I agree with you about that." I wasn't sure how seemly such a conversation about Steve was in the circumstances, and felt some anger. I said: "Yes, he was very intelligent. Killing him was not intelligent." "Well, we don't know yet what happened, do we?" he asked. I said: "Yes, we do—he died of brain damage—damage to the back of the brain caused by a blow to the forehead. It's called a contracoup injury. Ask your Minister. Kruger knows it. He's had the medical report for weeks now."

Boshoff was quiet for a while, then he asked: "Do you really think Biko was murdered?" I said: "No—not murdered in the sense of intentional killing. I believe he was beaten up by your people in Port Elizabeth and that they went too far. Well, maybe it can be called murder because in our law a person is presumed to intend the reasonable consequences of his actions." "But who do you think is responsible for that?" he said. "Kruger," I replied. "Not only did he allow it to happen, but after it had happened he tried to cover it up with lies about a hunger strike." There was silence for a time. Beukes, the driver, had spoken little, but I saw from the set of his neck that he was listening intently. I said: "You are from Security headquarters, you told me. You deal with Kruger, then?" Boshoff said: "Not directly. Not usually. But in this instance we have to report back to him once you are delivered." "Well, then, you can repeat everything to him that I've said here," I said, knowing they would anyway. "Kruger is a little man trying to be a big man. He's a weak man trying to be a strong man. He's trying to act like another Vorster." Both of them gave an involuntary little giggle at this, possibly of embarrassment. Then Boshoff said in a mild tone: "You know, Mr Woods, Biko was your friend and I understand how upset you must feel about this whole business. It's a terrible business, no matter what happened. You know? It's terrible that someone dies anyway. But I've been in the Security Police for many years, and I can honestly tell you that I've never seen any beating-up or torture like what you talk about and your people write in the press." I said: "But you don't know everything that goes on in the Security Police, do you?" "But we'd hear about it if it happened," Beukes retorted. "Who says?" I replied. "Let me tell you, this Colonel Goosen in Port Elizabeth has got a reputation for torture."

"How do you mean, a reputation?" Beukes asked, now completely drawn into the conversation. "A reputation among blacks," I said. "And so has this thug Hattingh, down in King William's Town, and so has Spyker van Wyk in Cape Town and so has Colonel Swanepoel in Johannesburg." "*Ja*, but blacks would say those things, wouldn't they?" Beukes said, still driving very fast. I replied: "I know a white man who said it too. Hugh Lewin described how Swanepoel tortured him." There was a long silence, then Boshoff said: "Well, Mr Woods, do you know what most of us in Security feel? We feel we welcome an inquest, and let the truth come out."

After a pause, Beukes asked: "Tell me, Mr Woods, because I don't know much about politics, but I've got two small children and I think about the future—tell me, if you were Mr Vorster what would you do?" I said: "To answer that would take hours." They laughed, and Beukes went on: "Well, we've got hours. We've got a long journey ahead of us, so let's talk to pass the time." I said: "Well, the first thing I would do is to announce a national convention—a full national convention attended by all the elected leaders of every race group in the country to plan a new democratic constitution and to agree on how to introduce it in careful phases and stages for maximum stability during the transition to majority rule."

This set off an hour-long discussion, largely between Beukes and me, about whether black rule would lead to destruction of the whites. Beukes felt as a father that his two children would have no future in a black-ruled country, and I tried to make the point that black rule was coming anyway and that his children's future would be more secure if it came about peacefully by negotiation rather than through violence. But he had the rigid Afrikaner Nationalist approach, the mentality that simply cannot envisage "racial mixing". I referred to his earlier statement that he "didn't know much about politics" and said: "If you don't know much about politics what are you doing in the Security Police? Do you expect me to believe you're non-political?" He answered: "No, well, of course I'm a member of my branch of the Party and I support the Party, but I really want to know what is best for South Africa's future, and I'm interested to hear your ideas." In the ensuing discussion he proved to be extremely naïve about basic Progressive Federal

Party policy and was surprised about the relative conservatism of that party's policy of qualified franchise.

I fell asleep for about an hour. When I awoke it was nearly dark, and I asked where we were. "Near Parys," said Major Boshoff. "Are you hungry, Mr Woods? We were thinking of stopping to eat." I wasn't, but said I was. I wanted to stretch my legs and was curious how and where we should eat. Arriving at Parys we went first to the police station to get petrol, then to have dinner at, of all places, the Parys Holiday Inn. Like all Holiday Inns it looked familiar and had some slogan of good-will in large lettering outside, something like "Happy birthday to Piet". The dining-room was fairly full and I had a strong urge to stand up and tell everyone in a loud voice what was happening to me. But there would have been little sympathy for a banned person—this was the Orange Free State, the hot-bed of Afrikaner Nationalism.

Boshoff and Beukes were now speaking in Afrikaans, and because it usually seemed inappropriate to speak anything but Afrikaans in the Free State I said: "*Ek is seker die enigste inge-perkte persoon in die hele Vrystaat*", ("I must surely be the only banned person in the whole Free State.") They spoke almost together: "*Nee, daar's Winnie Mandela!*" ("No, there's also Winnie Mandela!") Winnie Mandela, the wife of Nelson Mandela, had been banned and restricted to the town of Brandfort in the Free State because the State feared her influence if she were restricted to her home in Soweto. "Winnie Mandela? Yes, of course—in that case I feel honoured and privileged to share that with her." We ordered dinner and both of them, unfailingly polite, pressed me to have a drink. I had a beer, and when invited to I had another, saying: "I'm entitled to it as a taxpayer. It's my tax money paying for it." They agreed and laughed, even raising their glasses to wish me "Good luck" and "Good health".

As we got up to leave Major Boshoff looked at his watch and noted that it was eight o'clock. "Would you like to watch the television news?" he said. "They'll have your banning on it." Feeling the whole thing was getting increasingly bizarre I said I would, and the three of us went into the main lounge of the hotel. Every seat in the room was occupied with residents and other customers eagerly watching the large colour television set to hear about the day's spate of bannings and detentions. We stood near the back. The report of the bannings was the lead item in the news, the screen showing Kruger's face, and it was weird to hear my name spoken in a news broadcast in connection with the Minister's claim that he had had to act in the nation's interest for "the safety of South Africa".

We travelled on to Winburg, where they handed me over to three Security Police officers waiting for us there. Major Boshoff asked if I had anything for a sore throat and I gave him two Syndol tablets. Oddly, I felt quite sorry to see him and Beukes go. They had, at least, become fairly familiar and these others were total strangers. Boshoff and Beukes shook hands and asked if I had a final message for Kruger. "*Reg*," I said. "*Se vir hom net—Onthou die wet van Transvaal!*" ("Right, say to him simply—remember the law of Transvaal!") This was a reference to a crude Afrikaans saying whenever one has to suffer for making a blunder: "*Kak en betaal is die wet van Transvaal*" ("Shit and pay is the law of Transvaal.") Although the obvious implication was that Kruger would have to pay for his blunder in banning me, all the Security Police officers burst out laughing.

Two of my new captors were university graduates, in political science. After some miles of silence the brighter of them suddenly said: "Well, Mr Woods, we've got a long way to travel. What shall we talk about?" I answered: "Let's talk about deaths in detention. Let's talk about all the people who've died under Security Police interrogation." There was a long, tense silence. Then he asked without turning his head to look behind: "Do you mean in South Africa?" I said: "Yes, of course in South Africa—the forty-five people who've died in Security Police jails without even being charged with any crimes. Why do you ask?" "Well," he said, "what I mean is that those Baader-Meinhof people in Germany also died in jail. Do you think they really committed suicide?" I replied: "I don't know, but I'll tell you what—I live in South Africa, you live in South Africa, we are now in South Africa, so let's talk about deaths in detention in South Africa." There was no response at all to this, and we travelled for several miles before they started up the conversation again.

When we arrived at Aliwal North just across the Orange

River boundary between the Free State and the Eastern Province, my three Free State escorts handed me over to two Queenstown-based Security Police officers. The Free Staters shook hands, saying: "*Tot siens, Meneer Woods*," adding, to my amazement: "*Sterkte, hoor?*" ("Strength, hear?"). In Afrikaans this phrase is normally used among friends in adversity, and in English the nearest colloquial equivalent would be "Keep going".

I hardly spoke throughout the long journey. I was tired, so I lay down on the back seat. All the Security Police drivers had driven at frantic speed, ignoring speed limits throughout, even while going through suburbs. We arrived in Queenstown at about 4 a.m., and here I was handed over to two East London Security Police sergeants whom I had never seen, and again I barely spoke a word until we arrived in the city at about 6 a.m. It seemed there was a special dimension to being a political captive in one's own country. The closer we got to East London and the more familiar the countryside and landmarks became, the more my feelings of indignation grew. Who were these people to confine me in my own "territory"? Here was King William's Town, close to home, and now off-limits to me. There was the Transkei road, now also forbidden territory. It would be a crime for me to travel to Hobeni or Elliotdale or Umtata, or anywhere beyond the small area to which I was now restricted. Now we were entering the suburbs of East London itself. We arrived at Security Police headquarters and there, waiting for us, was Colonel van der Merwe—an ultra-stern and brusque Colonel van der Merwe, by no means the smiling Colonel van der Merwe of the police rugby club dinner who had brought his wife from the other side of the room to be introduced to me, or had sat beside me at a formal lunch in the King's Hotel on the Esplanade.

In a harshly official tone of voice, standing at his desk as I stood before it like a naughty schoolboy in the headmaster's study, he read through all the banning orders and explained each prohibition to me. He said that from now on, as a Restricted Person, I was forbidden any "social intercourse". He glared at me as I smiled at this, then explained it meant I was barred from any gathering with a "common social purpose". "You may only speak with one person at a time, not with more

322

than one. If you meet two people in a street or anywhere, you may not engage in conversation with them or with either of them until one has moved away." I asked: "How far away?" He said: "Far enough not to be part of the conversation. The onus is on you to ensure this. My men will be watching all the time to catch you breaking your ban, so you'd better be as careful as you can be." He looked at the banning documents again and went on: "For purposes of these restrictions your wife and children are regarded as one person—but not other relatives. Parents, brothers and sisters are each one person and you can only talk with one person at a time. Furthermore, you can only be in a room with one person at a time—even inside your home."

He put down the papers and glared at me again. "Mr Woods, you know very well that we know what goes on in your house. I won't say more than that, but take it as a warning. Don't think you can get away with breaking the ban even inside your house. We'll be checking up on you. My men will come into your house at any time of the day or night to see if you are breaking the ban by talking to more than one person at a time or being in a room with more than one person at a time or writing. You are forbidden from now on to write anything. You may not write anything and you may not be quoted, therefore you may not function as a journalist any more, and you mustn't try and be a writer in any other way, through diaries or letters or suchlike."

He said I was not allowed into the *Dispatch* building or into any printing or publishing premises or school premises or "non-white" areas. "What about my children's prizegivings or school plays?" I asked. "Of course you can't go to those!" he snapped. "For two reasons—that would be a gathering with a common social purpose and it would be on school premises."

"What else?" I asked. "Registering every week at the police station, every Monday before noon," he said. "You must come in to the charge office here every Monday before noon to sign a register. My men hate you, Mr Woods. Every day for years you have written things in your newspaper which have caused them to hate you. Now they will be looking for every chance to catch you breaking the law." I said there should be no talk of breaking the law; that the word "law" should only refer to rules whose contravention could be tested in courts of law and not to regulations framed by politicians to be ruled on by Security Policemen. "It is the law, whether you like it or not," he said. "I'll give you some good advice now—observe these restrictions and you'll be left alone. Break them, break one of them, and you'll land in big trouble, I promise you." "I'm not looking for trouble, Colonel," I answered. "I've never looked for trouble." "We'll see," he replied. "But if at any time you're not sure what you may do, come here and ask me, or ask the Chief Magistrate. Don't take chances!" He nodded to my two escorts and they drove me to my house.

Shortly after six o'clock on the morning of October 20 I walked into my house as a banned man—a Restricted Person. I put my case down in the entrance hall and ran up the stairway to our bedroom. With Wendy there were Roger and Mary Omond and Barry Streek. There was a lot of hugging—then we all burst into laughter at the thought that we were all breaking the ban so soon. "We're probably safer now than we'll ever be in the future," I said. "They won't expect us to break the ban in the first few hours." But Barry, who was something of an expert on bannings, spoke some words of caution. "You mustn't take chances. They'd love to catch you breaking the ban."

For the first time we locked the outside doors and drew the curtains, something we should grow accustomed to in the following months, and I positioned my chair slightly outside the room, inside the adjoining dressing-room, so that at least technically we were not all in the same room and no perjury would be necessary if we should all be charged. It was the first of many adjustments we had to make in our life-style.

The downstairs television room became my room for receiving visitors one at a time. Wendy would "screen" all visitors—and at first there were many, including journalists mostly representing the overseas media—and while I saw them singly in this room the others would sit talking with Wendy in the lounge. The downstairs television room, a sort of family room which had previously functioned as a playroom for the children, looked out on to the lawn and garden with its big msintsi trees which were now in red blossom, and it was odd to sit looking at that familiar scene in these strange new circumstances of restriction.

One of the early problems of the banning was communicating the full extent of the restrictions to the children. They were used to bringing schoolfriends home, and couldn't at first grasp that I couldn't be in a room with them if their friends were present. I, or the friend, or the children, would have to leave the room. It was even more awkward with close friends. Terry and Val Briceland could no longer call in to sit with Wendy and me over a drink. We would have to "split up" between the lounge and television room, although we often relaxed this to the extent of sitting near enough to each other in adjoining areas such as the lounge and hallway to carry on a general conversation.

Contraventions of the ban, even within the house, drew strict punishment from the State when they could be proved. A Rhodes University lecturer, Terence Beard, had been the subject of a severe ruling on this score. Beard, a banned person, was given a birthday party by his friends in Grahamstown. He stayed alone in the kitchen throughout the party and the guests stayed in the rest of the house, coming one by one into the kitchen to sit with him. Although there were at no time more than two people in the kitchen, he was prosecuted and convicted of breaking his ban on the grounds that he had taken part in a "common social purpose".

An amusing example of this restriction came when I decided to test the outer parameters of the banning orders within the first few days. I went to Colonel van der Merwe and said: "Colonel, I'm still captain of the East London Chess Club—am I no longer allowed to play chess at the club on Monday evenings?" "Certainly not," he replied. "Of course you may not attend a club or gathering of any kind." But I was ready for this, and said: "You misunderstand me, Colonel. I know I am not allowed to attend the chess club in the normal way any more, but I can make special arrangements to play my league matches in a separate room. How can that be breaking the ban if I'm with only one other person in a separate room at the club?" He frowned and puzzled the matter over, leafing through the restriction documents, then he looked up and said: "I can find no specific objection to such an arrangement—but don't drink tea or coffee while you're playing." "Don't drink tea or coffee?" I asked. "What's that all about?" "Common social purpose," he replied, looking through the documents again. "The restrictions are not only there to prevent conspiring against the State, they're also aimed at preventing any common social purpose. You can be in a separate room at your chess club if there's only your opponent present, but if you drink tea or coffee that will mean it's a common social purpose with other members elsewhere in the club, because they will also be drinking tea or coffee."

At first this seemed an odd differentiation, but apparently the legal interpretation of a common social purpose was that the purpose has to be identical, whereas chess games are not identical. To make our chess-playing a common social purpose, according to this interpretation, we would all have had to be engaged in the same game, with the same moves. Making use of this ultra-legalistic reasoning I played several league games in this fashion. Eventually, however, I stopped going to the chess club because the strain on the other members seemed too great. The artificial arrangements obviously pained a number of them, as I had their sympathy, and they found it hard to have to restrain themselves from coming to talk with me. South African citizens generally know little of the full ramifications of banning orders and are usually confused as to what they can or cannot do. Many think it is forbidden to talk to a banned person at all. The chess club members were as supportive as they could be. They approached me one at a time to speak whenever I walked away from my table to the entrance hall or rest-room, and this began to pose a new problem. It was a problem I was encountering at home as well—the problem of endless repetition. When you speak with only one person at a time your conversation becomes unbearably repetitious. People generally ask the same questions, requiring the same answers, and whereas in general conversations these are dealt with once only, twenty individual visitors in a day or thirty individual chess club members in an evening amount to about fifty identical exchanges of remarks. To the kind supporter the conversation is new and once only, but to the banned person it is tediously familiar.

Another unexpected punishment that was a by-product of banning was, ironically, considerable loss of privacy. There was a constant stream of visitors all day, to be seen one at a time, and this made it hard even to lie down and sleep for an hour. Wendy couldn't turn away people who were kind enough to go to the trouble of calling and so we felt I had to see every one of them. It was brave of them, all sorts of people and from all race groups, because the Security Police had posted an "observer" on the other side of the street, opposite our front gate, to note the licence plates of cars parked at our house and the identities of callers. Although there seemed to be many of them, we were conscious that they represented only a fraction of the general populace, particularly the white populace, most of whom were either glad I was banned or too fearful of appearing in any way to be associated with or supportive of me. Still, the callers seemed to be many because they could only be seen one at a time, and I could hardly spend less than about fifteen minutes with each. It seemed supremely ironical that the ban, designed to isolate me, was the cause now of almost total lack of privacy during the daylight hours. Many of the visitors were television, radio and press representatives of America, Britain, Australia, Canada, Germany, France and the Scandinavian countries, who had to conduct their interviews with the cameraman outside to avoid contravening the ban. Sometimes film was shot through a window or door to highlight the restrictions. Inevitably, and to our relief, the visits began to slacken off after some weeks. One of my visitors was Frank Streek, and now that our fight was over we were glad to bury the hatchet.

My fellow-directors took turns to visit and to assure me that my salary would be maintained in spite of the ban, in accordance with established *Dispatch* policy regarding staff members punished by the State without legal process. I realized how lucky I was to be employed by the *Dispatch*, as Thenjiwe Mtintso, Gordon Qumza and Owen Vanqa had been, in view of the plight of most banned people, whose banning invariably meant loss of income as well as other punishments, because generally employers in South Africa fired banned employees.

Members of the *Dispatch* staff all visited us at various times. Glyn Williams and Tom Watters often came for a game of chess, and other members of the chess club also called for occasional games in between other visits. One day within the first week three of the *Dispatch* journalists and I risked a round of golf. Whether by sheer good luck or because of the Security

Police reluctance to create an issue over something as frivolous as golf, we completed the eighteen holes without incident. Emboldened by this, and curious as to what the reaction of club members would be, I walked into the club bar and lounge. Most members melted away as if I had leprosy, and others acted as though they hadn't seen me, looking past me at an oblique angle. But some pointedly came forward to shake hands as publicly as possible. Out on the course we had joked about what our defence would be if prosecuted. We thought we could make the court proceedings farcical if we pleaded that, as hooks and slices kept us all far apart, we couldn't be said to be sharing the same fairway or any common social activity.

What helped to pass the time when the visits slackened off was the gift of a snooker table from Harland. We installed it in the poolroom, and the boys and I had hours of entertainment with it. John Horlor and his Demaprint division of the *Dispatch* brought me a table tennis set, and this too gave us much enjoyment. Don Card often came for a game of snooker, and Barry Streek and I played a lot of ping-pong.

But my main activity, started within ten days of my banning, was a book on Steve Biko.

CHAPTER NINETEEN

ALTHOUGH THE *Dispatch* directors had guaranteed the continuation of my income for the full five-year period of the ban, the idea of sitting out those years passively was unthinkable. And the idea of editing the *Dispatch* at the end of the five-year ban was also unthinkable, because it would mean accepting an appearance of press freedom that no longer existed. I was not prepared to function by favour of the Afrikaner Nationalist Government. As far as I was concerned their changing of the rules was permanent. Besides, even compliance with the ban for five years was no guarantee of any release afterwards. Such bans were usually extended, on the last day of the five-year term, for a further five years. I was a journalist, and since Steve's death an activist. I felt I had to do something journalistic and activistic, and with increasing certainty I felt I should write a book about Steve, as an affirmation of what he was and stood for. It seemed an appropriate way to use the leisure Kruger had imposed on me.

I discussed the idea with Wendy, because she would have to help get the material for the book. Originally the intention was to write it anonymously, in order to escape the severe punishment which discovery of its authorship would provoke from the State. The first thing was to assemble all Steve's writings, statements, and recorded interviews that were obtainable, and to edit them. Wendy played a key role in this. As we saw it, a vital part of the book would be Steve's remarkable evidence in the SASO-BPC trial, when he had testified brilliantly for days without being trapped by the wiles of the state prosecutors, and Wendy travelled to Johannesburg to hunt this evidence down. It wasn't easy, because there were few records of the trial available, but eventually she managed to borrow all the relevant volumes for eight hours of exhausting photocopying, packing the copies in among her clothes in the suitcase she brought back. She also attended the entire Biko inquest, making notes and collecting the record of evidence.

Meanwhile I was working on Steve's earlier articles and interviews, some of which I had in my own records. I was also writing accounts of all the conversations with him that I could recall, and personal anecdotes which were typical of his character and personality. This work had to be done entirely at night, to escape detection by the Security Police. They had threatened to come at any time of the day or night to see whether I was breaking the ban by writing, but we knew it would be easier to escape detection at night, because with the children asleep and none of their school friends around a knock at the locked door would be clearer warning that it was probably the Security Police. During the daytime the manuscript would have had to be hidden every time there was the sound of a door opening, every time one of the children came in from the garden, every time we heard somebody on the doorstep. So for more than two months I worked through most nights until dawn. The first time I did this I came up against an unforeseen problem—where to hide the manuscript? Most people would believe it to be easy to hide papers in their house, but when you are under threat of sudden search by Security Police you realize for the first time that there is no safe hiding-place anywhere. What seem at first to be the most ingenious hiding-places soon seem the most obvious.

On the first night, or rather morning, because it was getting light outside, I hid the manuscript in my study. The walls were covered with bookshelves, and I simply dropped the night's work behind a high row of books and went to bed. But in bed I started reconsidering this hiding-place, because increasingly it seemed one of the first places the Security Police would search. Under some carpet? Also too obvious. Inside the piano? No— I'd seen movies where papers hidden inside piano sound-boards were discovered. Eventually I hit on a place which, while not foolproof, would take a great deal of searching to find. We had a music alcove in the lounge with shelves of music and many records. I hid the manuscript inside the sleeve of one of these records. The one I chose was that of the speeches of Winston Churchill. This became my hiding-place for each night's production of manuscript until the whole book was finished. Every morning the completed section would be placed inside a rolled-up newspaper by a visiting friend and taken to another hiding-place in his house—right past the Security Police observer outside the house.

Much of the work in the later stages consisted of editing hundreds of thousands of words down to the bare essentials of facts in the most economical language. The only long burst of day-work was spent subbing the mass of photostat pages of SASO trial evidence Wendy had wangled out of her Johannesburg visit. I did this on a Sunday, in a locked house while she took the kids to the beach for the whole day. It was a non-stop twelve-hour sustained effort beginning at eight in the morning and ending at eight that night, and in that time I subbed and processed over two hundred thousand words. Many times that day I blessed my experience on the Cardiff *Western Mail* and the castigations of Don McNicoll at Associated Press in London. My "subbing knuckle" was bruised at the end of that marathon spell with the red pencil and my eyes were out of focus—but an entire key section of the book was now complete.

It was after I had started on the book that I had a visit from a man, Drew Court, who was a personal friend of a London publisher, and he asked if I had thought of writing a book on Steve Biko. I was guarded at first, but the opportunity seemed heaven-sent to arrange the smuggling of the manuscript out of the country section by section. After some discussion I told him I had already started such a book; that it would have to be published under a false name and substantially as written, to avoid some London re-writer sensationalizing it or producing from it a portrait of Steve that wouldn't accord with my view of him. I also wanted to know more about the publishers, and was impressed with what I heard. They were committed liberals who would preserve the politically important aspects of the book even if their retention meant that it was less marketable. This was important, because I wanted to include material about the political history of South Africa and its black leaders who had gone before Steve, material I knew most publishers would want to cut out for commercial reasons. I made arrangements with Drew for the manuscript to be sent to London in sections, some going in the personal baggage of air travellers, some in cars going across the border into Botswana, and at least one section going by ordinary air freight.

Having completed the more objective parts of the book,

taken from public and private records, I realized that its authorship could not be kept anonymous, because this would preclude any kind of personal testimony as to Steve's remarkable character. Without it he would have emerged from the book as a totally political person and no more—and he was so much more than that. I knew it meant risking considerable punishment, probably a prison sentence as well as a heavy fine, if I was caught breaking the ban in this way, but it seemed necessary, so I wrote in all the personal reminiscences and got Wendy to do some as well.

Then came another crisis of decision as I reached the last stages of the book. Having given the political background to Steve's emergence as a leader, having included personal reminiscences about him as well as his speeches, writings and testimony and the evidence that was allowed to emerge at the inquest, I felt the book was still incomplete. A further section was needed—a comprehensive indictment of the government and system which had killed Steve Biko and so many others, and a plea to international opinion for stronger action to be taken against the regime. I began the last section of the book, entitled "The Indictment", and the more I wrote, detailing the crimes against humanity by the apartheid system, the more I set out what the rest of the world community could do to help fight apartheid, the more I realized that my family and I would have to leave South Africa before the book could be published. The main reason was that I was calling in print for economic sanctions against the Pretoria regime—and this was a capital offence under the new Terrorism Act. It was classed as an act of terrorism meriting the death penalty.

Wendy and I discussed this new threat and agreed that we should call for sanctions and flee the country to reinforce this appeal. Also, of course, to escape the consequences in terms of Government rage and vengeance. For some time Wendy had been more radical than me, but Steve's death had brought my thinking level with hers. And the final factor that convinced me that sanctions was the least response which apartheid should now draw was the shockingly callous finding of the inquest magistrate. The inquest had been largely farcical anyway. Key evidence had been suppressed; Peter Jones, who should have been the main witness to the assaults on Steve in jail, was not called to testify; and Kruger was shielded from cross-examination. Yet enough had emerged from even the prepared police testimony to indicate clearly to the country and to the world that Steve had been the victim of violence at the hands of the Security Police. I had expected the magistrate to protect the police in his finding, but I had, at least, also expected him to deal with the more obvious anomalies in their testimony. The callousness and contempt with which he closed the proceedings in three brief sentences enraged me.

The book, including the final section which burnt our boats in South Africa, was completed by the middle of December 1977, and Wendy and I decided we would carefully lay plans to leave the country the following May. We reckoned it would take the publisher that long to prepare and print the book, and we felt the four-month period would give us time to siphon enough money out of our bank account to be able to re-establish ourselves overseas, and plan to salvage as many of our things as we could sneak out of the country.

But two things caused us to accelerate our escape plans drastically, and one of them was a vicious hoax by the Security Police on our five-year-old daughter Mary. It happened while Wendy was in Johannesburg, getting material for the book. My secretary, Linda Murray, brought my mail to the house, and among the envelopes was a fairly long, padded parcel. Linda opened it and found it contained two small tee-shirts. On the front of each was a picture of Steve, so the parcel seemed to be a gift for our smaller children, Gavin and Mary, by some admirer of Steve. As it was early afternoon and all the children were outside playing, I laid the shirts aside and forgot about them as I went through the rest of the mail.

That evening the children asked me to watch television with them. We had barely sat down in the television room when Mary came in excitedly with the two tee-shirts she had found. She held up the smaller of the two and started to put it on. The other children and I were engrossed in the television show when we heard a scream from Mary. With Jane's help she had taken off her own shirt and had half-pulled the tee-shirt on, and I thought at first that she was shouting in frustration because it didn't fit, or because she couldn't pull it all the way down over her face. I shushed her, but as she got the tee-shirt

333

on properly she began a series of high-pitched screams, shouting: "My eyes are burning!" Evalina rushed in from the kitchen to see what was going on, and she and Jane tried to hush Mary, whose screams persisted. I got up to go to her, thinking the dye from the picture on the tee-shirt might have stung her eyes, and as Evalina and Jane stripped the tee-shirt off her and took her to the bathroom to bathe her eyes I picked up the shirt and noticed that it had a kind of faint powder which stung the hand on contact. I smelt it, and at first it smelt like chlorine which is put in swimming-pools. Mary continued to scream with obvious pain even after her eyes had been washed.

I phoned our family doctor who said he would come as soon as possible. He bathed Mary's eyes with an oil solution which seemed to soothe her. He also gave her a sedative and she was soon asleep. By this time there were pronounced purple blotches around her eyes, on her forehead, neck and shoulders and upper body—wherever the shirt had touched her. It was even noticeable on her head when you parted her hair. I noticed that the tee-shirt itself had turned a purplish colour in patches, and couldn't be touched without irritating the skin like stinging nettles. The chlorine-type smell was now pronounced, even at a distance of several feet. Terry arrived, and I told him, saying the dye on it had got into Mary's eyes and stained her skin. But when he picked up the shirt he said immediately: "No, somebody's done this on purpose. This isn't dye, it's something sprayed on this shirt." "I'm sure it's the dye," I told him. "Smell it, it's like chlorine." Terry said adamantly: "No, I tell you somebody has done this deliberately to get at your kids!" I laughed. "Come off it, Terry, you're getting paranoid. Nobody would do such a thing to a five-year-old—they'd know such a small tee-shirt could only fit a small child."

Terry telephoned Don Card, saying nothing over the phone, and when Don arrived I told him only that Mary had had her eyes stung by the dye on a tee-shirt that had been sent to us. But when he saw the tee-shirt, handled it and smelt it, his eyes narrowed and a look of rage came over his face. "Those bastards at Security have done this!" he said. "I know this stuff. I've worked with it myself. It's used by security police—it's like mace."

334

It was later established that the substance, Ninhydrin, was a Swedish-invented acid-based powder supplied to police forces all over the world to trace fingerprints on paper. Wherever fingers had touched a sheet of paper, you had only to dust the sheet with this powder, even weeks thereafter, and within minutes the powder would have interacted with the traces of amino-acid in the skin to reveal the clear fingerprint in a purple colour. Detectives handling the powder were warned to wear gloves, because on direct contact the acid reaction was powerful and produced a burning sensation. "The bastards have gone too far, to do this to a child," Card said. "They *knew* what they were doing. They put the stuff on the inside of the shirt, that's why it wasn't noticeable on the outside. It was only when Mary put it on that it reacted to her skin." With a sick feeling I realized Card was right. The reaction had continued even after the shirt was torn off Mary, so that what had been a perfectly white tee-shirt now looked as if it had been dipped unevenly in purple ink.

Terry phoned for a staff photographer. "We've got to get pictures," he said. Don telephoned the police. "We must report it," he said. "They probably won't help, but we've got to go through the channels. I'll tell you what, though—I'm going to find out exactly which of them did this thing."

Fortunately the doctor was able to assure me that Mary wouldn't suffer any lasting effects. "It didn't actually get into her eyes," he said. "As she pulled the shirt over her head the material got near enough to them to burn or sting, but she'll be all right." Don confirmed this. "The purple blotches wear off after a day or two. It's not dangerous. But it is very painful."

The photographer arrived, took a picture of Mary sleeping while Jane stroked her forehead, and went to put the picture out on the wires while a reporter did the story. Then the police arrived, under an English-speaking sergeant called Eric Magnus. He took a statement, in such detail and with such an expression of purpose that I gained the impression he was genuinely keen to track down the culprit. In fact, over the next few days his zeal in following up all the available leads was such that he was taken off the case on orders from headquarters, and later transferred to another police region far from East London. He was replaced on the case by two Afrikaner

335

Nationalist detectives, and that was the end of any real attempt to pursue the matter officially. But while Magnus was still on the case he managed to establish that the parcel containing the tee-shirts had been mailed in Natal, by a man called Holmes, and I then remembered that Holmes, whom I knew, had telephoned me some weeks before to say he was producing tee-shirts with Steve's picture on them and would send me two. Obviously the parcel had been intercepted and the Ninhydrin sprayed on before delivery to my house. This information about the mailing of the shirts enabled Card to deduce what had happened. He knew that my mail was intercepted every day and scrutinized at Security Police headquarters before being returned for delivery to me. It seemed clear to him that when the Security Police had opened the parcel containing the children's tee-shirts and seen the picture of Steve Biko on each, they had sprayed the insides of both shirts with Ninhydrin powder.

To prove that mail interception was a daily routine, Card showed me five letters he was mailing to me from different mailboxes in various suburbs. He coated all five letters with silver nitrate, and in the sealing flaps of two of them he put potassium permanganate. "Three of these will be delivered to you—all a day late," he said. "The other two won't be delivered, because when their long-spouted steaming kettle heats the potassium permanganate crystals the whole envelope will be discoloured in purple stains and they'll be too embarrassed to deliver them because it will be obvious they were tampered with. But they will handle all the letters inside, and will therefore touch the silver nitrate—and that will turn their fingers black for two weeks."

My sons were fascinated by this claim, especially when Card allowed Duncan to touch the white powder of silver nitrate with his fingertips and noticed a couple of hours later that his fingertips had turned an indelible black. "You can't scrub it off," Don Card laughed. "It only wears out when the skin-layer wears off." He mailed all five letters, then said confidently: "Within two days I'll visit the Security Police offices and see who has black hands!"

That night Kingsley Kingon telephoned to invite me "for a game of chess" at his house. This meant I should go there without asking questions. At his house was a man sitting in a back room. He had come to Kingsley's house knowing that Kingsley was my lawyer, and had asked Kingsley to arrange a secret meeting with me on "an urgent matter". It was an extraordinary meeting. The man trembled with emotion—which I later realized was mingled fear and anger—as he said what he had to say, in essence the following: "Mr Woods, I'd rather you didn't know my name. I am an employee of the postal service. I am a supporter of the Government. I don't like you and I don't like your views. To me you are a danger to our country and a danger to the white man. But I don't like people who attack children, and I have to tell you who did that thing to your child. I remember the arrival of that parcel from Natal. It was an unusual shape. It was taken away with all your other mail to the Security Police offices in Cambridge by Warrant Officer Jan Marais and Warrant Officer Van Schalkwyk. These two officers call for your mail every day at 2 p.m. and return it in the late afternoon. But that parcel was returned by them the following day when they called for the next batch. I'm telling you this because of what they've done to your child. I've got children too and I had to tell you. But for God's sake don't bring me into this and don't find out my name. I still support the Government. I'm still against you and your ideas. But these bastards of the Security Police are going too far when they bring children into their activities."

The next thing was to tell Don Card of this development. "Right," he said. "Now I know whose hands to inspect!" The next day Kingsley went to the sorting department of the post office at 2 p.m. to make some spurious inquiry about postal delivery. Van Schalkwyk and Marais, not noticing him, arrived at the counter and were promptly handed a batch of mail which Kingsley noticed was addressed to "D. J. Woods, 61, Chamberlain Road, Vincent, East London". Talking casually to one another they put this mail in a briefcase and left. Downstairs a *Dispatch* photographer with a telefoto lens photographed both men emerging with the case. The following morning Don Card shadowed the unsuspecting Marais into a supermarket, and saw that his hands had the black blotches of silver nitrate.

All these facts were communicated to the police but, predictably, nothing was done. Card explained to them that sworn statements from postal staff could establish that Marais and

Van Schalkwyk had intercepted the parcel, and how this could be done without revealing the identity of any who told what they knew, but no such affidavits were ever sought. There was something weird about the constant visits to the house by the police "investigators". They would go over and over the statements, going through the motions, yet they knew that we knew that they would take the matter no further. We wondered why they even bothered to go through the motions.

One day, however, they made a major blunder. No doubt trying to show they were at least doing something, they produced the two missing letters Card had mailed to me, blotched purple by potassium permanganate. Wendy phoned Don Card, who arrived while they were there and asked where they obtained the letters. "From the post office," said the police detective. "You bloody liars!" Card shouted. "Those came from the Security Police. I mailed them myself. Look on the inside—you'll find they come from the SPCC. That's the Society for Prevention of Cruelty to Children—and that's me!" The policeman's face was a study. "You hypocrites!" said Card. "There's all the proof you need that Marais and Van Schalkwyk did this. You know damn well who did it. Give me police powers for one hour and I'll have this case settled. Ask them why they have silver nitrate on their hands. Question all the postal workers properly. I was in the police for years. You people make me ashamed of the police force!" I intervened and suggested an interview with Brigadier Smal, but the only change in the police tactics was to change the "investigating officers" yet again. The new batch also stalled the investigation, sending the tee-shirts to Pretoria for "chemical analysis", after which they were never seen again. Police Minister Kruger later said in the South African Parliament that police investigations of the incident had cleared the Security Police . . .

The tee-shirt attack on Mary started me thinking we shouldn't wait until the following May before making our escape. Elsewhere in the country there were attacks by Security Police or their fringe elements on families of banned people, and this series of attacks was to culminate in two shootings. One was a shotgun blast through the front door of Fatima Meer in Durban, which wounded a guest in the house. Subsequently, there was the killing of Rick Turner, who had been banned for several years. Rick, who was living with his two small daughters, went to answer a knock at his front door and was shot dead by an unidentified gunman.

Another thing that made us speed up our escape plans was that when Wendy came back from Steve's inquest she told me that the Security Police had been following her, and we both felt that our family wouldn't be left alone. And we knew too that even the non-political police were no protection against their Security colleagues.

The final straw was the result of the sudden general election called by Vorster. Although we placed no great importance on South African elections, because the vote was reserved to whites and therefore to only a fifth of the population, and because even among whites the vote was loaded in favour of Afrikaner Nationalist areas, we still hoped the election would reflect at least some marginal expression of disgust by a significant section of the whites over the killing of Steve and other detainees and over the bannings and detentions. But when the whites flocked overwhelmingly to Vorster's banner of racism and national chauvinism we lost our final traces of doubt about the decision to leave.

All the talks Wendy and I had about it were in the middle of the lawn, for fear of bugging. We confided our intention to our publisher's friend, Drew Court, who applauded the decision, saying it would also give the book more impact and obviate the need to suppress certain sections of it. He left for Botswana to try to charter a light plane. Our idea was to slip past our Security Police watcher by taking off over the back fence early one morning to meet the plane at Morgan Bay, a remote spot on the coast with a rudimentary airfield, and try to fly from there direct to Botswana. Botswana was the safest haven to head for because it was outside South Africa. While Lesotho was closer, it was entirely surrounded by South African territory which would still have to be traversed—even by air. But the Botswana plan failed because Drew wasn't able to charter a suitable light plane with that sort of range.

Then, by a lucky coincidence, we had a visit from a friend from upcountry, Robin Walker, and one of the first things he said to me was: "You're crazy if you don't skip the country—and I'll be mad as hell if you don't let me help you." We introduced Robin to Drew, and after discussing the merits of various routes and methods of escape we hit on the following plan.

According to the maps, the nearest obscure border was in the Telle Bridge area of Lesotho, only a few hundred miles away. Robin said that if Drew could help me get near this border, he would wait five miles up the road to Maseru on the Lesotho side to drive me to the capital. Crossing the Telle River appeared to pose no problem—it was said to be only a few yards wide, and that it could be waded without difficulty. The idea was for Drew to drop me several miles from the best river crossing-point—which, however, was uncomfortably close to the border post—and for me to wade across, give the border post a wide berth by striking out over the Lesotho hills and then reach the road about three miles beyond the border, walking until I reached Robin's waiting car.

Because of frequent police road-blocks on the route we should have to take, Drew planned to borrow two cars and two walkie-talkie radios with their own frequency so that he could go ahead in the first car, probing for road blocks ahead of the second car which I would drive, suitably disguised. The only snag was that I should have to hitch-hike a considerable distance to the point where these two cars would be available: we should be travelling by night, and Drew wanted to use cars with up-country licence-plates, because cars travelling so far away at that hour with East London licence-plates might arouse suspicion. For the initial stage of the journey I should have to make my own way, but this posed no problem—the East London–Queenstown road was one of the best in South Africa for hitch-hikers.

We went over and over the plan, because Robin had to return to Natal the next morning to prepare for his journey to Lesotho, which he would have to make immediately on receipt of an agreed telephone "code" call from Drew. He would then have to be at his post along the Telle–Maseru road at 3 a.m. on the second morning after the call.

Wendy's task was to smuggle me out of the city limits of East London on the eve of this rendezvous, then give me twelve hours' start before setting off with the children to "visit her parents in Umtata". She was to get to their house well before

10 a.m., which meant leaving East London with the children at about 6 a.m. In Umtata she was to wait for a telephone call from me from Maseru at precisely 10 a.m. If this call didn't come by 10 a.m. she was to know I had been caught and was to go back home claiming to know nothing of my whereabouts. But if the call came through on time she was to drive to the border with the children and cross into Lesotho as tourists before the Security Police discovered I was absent from my house. Our fear was that if the Security Police discovered I was missing they would close all border posts to Wendy and the children to hold them hostage against my surrender. We also planned to buy me that twelve hours' start by giving the Security Police the impression that I was asleep in the house—that I was sleeping late while Wendy was taking the children to the beach for the day. Satisfied as to all the basic details of the general plan, we parted from Drew and Robin. The idea was that on getting a "coded" call from Wendy, Drew would alert Robin, and would then wait for me at an agreed point near the highway northward with the two cars in a field on his cousin's farm.

As Christmas of 1977 approached we debated whether to make our "break-out" on Christmas Eve. We wanted to choose a time when we thought the Security Police would be drinking and off guard. Several times Wendy nearly made the "code" call to Drew and once he telephoned to chat inconsequentially —obviously to see whether we'd make use of his call to utter the agreed words. But some instinct prevented us from choosing Christmas Eve. One of the reasons was that I wanted more time to make some arrangements designed to lull the Security Police into complacency—such as making phone calls to arrange a meeting with a journalist at my house in February, and chatting to Harland about a visit from him also in the new year. We knew our decision was only days, perhaps hours, away, but had to keep up the appearance of sounding as if we would still be at home. Wendy also had to deceive the music society because she had been asked to give a piano recital during January and couldn't tell the committee we wouldn't be in the country by then. She felt bad about this, but their posters and advertisements announcing her performance served our purpose well, and I kept telling her they would understand later.

One snag was that we couldn't get our money out of the bank in any quantity. By this time we had quite a lot of money saved, but dared not draw any large cheques. The bank had made Wendy wait at the teller's counter when she withdrew cash a few days after my banning; the teller had gone into an inner office before paying the money out, and it seemed to us that the Security Police had some sort of understanding with the Standard Bank that any movement in our account had to be made known to them before payment. So we knew we'd have to leave virtually all our money and possessions behind, and that these would probably be confiscated by the State. Wendy did, however, manage to amass about eight hundred rands in cash from separate withdrawals, and this was all we felt it safe to "salvage".

We reached our decision about the timing of our escape only two days beforehand. On Wednesday, December 28, we had an instinctive feeling that there was little time left, and set New Year's Eve as the best time. Drew was alerted, he warned Robin, and Wendy and I began our last-minute preparations.

CHAPTER TWENTY

DEPARTURE WAS SET for 6 p.m., and by lunchtime everything needed for the escape journey was ready. A late elaboration of disguise was to dress as a priest, because the detailed map of the border area showed St Teresa's Catholic Mission near the crossing-point, and if police stopped me I could say I was heading for the mission. I had a dark suit, so all that was needed was a dark shirt-front and white priest's collar, which was easy for Wendy to make. Black hair-dye was bought matter-of-factly at a cosmetics counter. I had a fake passport which showed me as a black-haired priest, in case I should be challenged for identification at a roadblock. It couldn't have been used at any major border-post, but the region I should be travelling through was a backwater, and for identification purposes it would do.

The period between lunchtime and four-thirty passed with agonizing slowness. I played the piano distractedly, then went to the billiard-table to practise some shots. I should have felt desperately tired, because I had had little sleep the night before, Wendy and I both being keyed up at the thought that this would probably be my last night in our house—and her second-last. We had agreed that on the last afternoon I should stick to my usual habits, and one of these on a Thursday was a game of chess with Tom Watters at his house at about four-thirty. Wendy and I had tea at four o'clock and chatted tensely until a quarter past, then I left for my chess game. Tom had the board all set up, and Ellen had a Scots tea waiting. The game with Tom was surrealistic—here I sat with my closest chess friend and I couldn't tell him this would be our last game as I was running away to leave the country and go into exile.

Tom usually beat me. A remorseless theorist who devoured the chess textbooks as soon as each one was published, he played a scrupulously orthodox game and spent long periods in analysis. Somehow I had to end this game within an hour, so I launched a wild sacrificial attack which Tom countered so correctly that he soon had me in desperate trouble. In a sudden mood of superstition, I developed the fear that if I lost this game everything would go wrong, and I was beginning to imagine all the things that *could* go wrong, when Tom uncharacteristically blundered away a rook and gave me my win. He saw me to the door, sourly assailing himself for his mistake, and said: "Well—see you next week for my revenge."

Arriving back at the house I drove the Mercedes into the garage, closing the doors to make the Security Police watcher think I was staying all night. Wendy confirmed this impression by telling Val Briceland over our bugged phone that I was tired and would be going to bed early and sleeping late the next morning while she took the kids to the beach for the day.

In the bathroom she wet my hair thoroughly and sloshed on the jet-black dye. I said: "The dye is now cast," but she was too tense to react. Then I had to sit for half-an-hour while the dye "took". I changed into what I called my "going-away" outfit —dark suit, black socks and shoes, black silk shirt-front and Roman collar. Wendy dried my hair with a hair-dryer and combed it differently from my usual way, slicking it down. When I saw my face in the mirror I was astonished at the change. I hadn't realized what a difference dyed hair could make to a face. I looked like a black-haired stranger, especially without my glasses on.

And so we left, and came to the highway where I was to be a hitch-hiker. I was well-prepared for this role. If my driver was English-speaking I would pose as an Afrikaner, as few English-speaking South Africans spoke Afrikaans comfortably, and that would cut conversation down to a minimum. If my lift-giver was an Afrikaner I would pose as an Australian. At this stage my priest's outfit was hidden by my black overcoat, with the collar turned up.

I had no difficulty getting lifts as far as the rendezvous point with Drew. Although I didn't need to draw too heavily on my two extra identities, the knowledge that I could at any time turn on the performance, so to speak, helped take the edge off my nervousness as a hitch-hiker. My final lift-giver was a big, thickset man in a safari suit who spoke little and hardly nodded goodbye as I got out. It was drizzling as I walked through the wet grass to the rendezvous. When I got there I had a moment of pure panic. There was no sign of a car, let alone two. Here I was out in the veld breaking my restrictions wide open, and all alone. I wondered if I could possibly have misunderstood the arrangement in my nervousness. It hardly seemed possible. We had gone over and over it with a sketch map and all the natural features seemed right.

Suddenly, from under a stand of trees, a pair of headlights flicked on and off once and I saw two cars parked there. As I drew closer Drew waved. He whispered excitedly as we compared notes, then explained the workings of the two-way radio. It seemed simple to operate, but I was still nervous that it would be picked up by police cars, and Drew became quite annoyed, assuring me that it couldn't because it had its own frequency.

The arrangement was that he would drive several miles ahead of me so that we wouldn't appear to be travelling together and he would be able to give me warning of any roadblock. At a warning I was to pull off the road, get out of my car and hide until he came back to park behind me to indicate the coast was clear. Shining his torch on the radio equipment, Drew caught sight of my appearance for the first time and was taken aback at how different I looked. "I look even more different," I said, pulling aside my coat to show my priest outfit. He was impressed. "It's about the best cover you could get!" he exclaimed. "Come on, let's get started!"

He led the way cautiously to the junction with the highway as we tested the radio, then tore ahead to establish his lead. After some miles punctuated only by his radioed: "All clear so far" every few minutes, I began to feel less tense, although I never felt other than scared. There was the constant thought that at any moment, at any turn in the road, vehicles and lights would flag us down for a police inspection in spite of Drew's vigilance. This fear grew worse when the radio failed and I could get no response from Drew until I came suddenly upon his tail-lights. He was waiting for me, cursing the failing radio, and he fiddled about with his set until it crackled into life again. But his words were faint and often indistinct, and our discussions became increasingly difficult. He believed reception would improve as we reached higher ground, but meanwhile it was often more unnerving to hear indistinct words than nothing, because they might mean he was trying to warn of a roadblock.

Then I had a bad scare. On the outskirts of the village of Cathcart my car stalled and I couldn't restart it. The battery was stone dead. Drew, after waiting anxiously on the other side of the village, came back to see what was wrong, and when I told him he smiled, went to the trunk and, amazingly, took out a brand-new battery. He told me that he had meant to switch the batteries before we left, but there hadn't been time. So he had decided to bring the new one along "just in case". We were installing it when out of the mist came the profile of a police van. I felt sick with fear as the van with the familiar wire-mesh sides drew to a stop next to us. "Need any help?" said a voice in English. It wasn't the police—just a farmer with a caged police-type van. We told him that all was well with us, and had the new battery connected up so fast that we drove away at almost the same time as he pulled away in the opposite direction with a friendly wave.

Fortunately, as we reached higher ground our two-way radio reception did improve a lot, and we were soon conversing with absolute clarity. Then we fell into a long silence and drove for more than an hour with no more exchanges than Drew's regular reports that all was clear ahead, and my acknowledgements.

We entered Queenstown and drove through the brightly-lit streets with no alarms. But on the other side we had another scare. A police van appeared behind me—a real one this time —and showed no inclination to pass. After several miles with this ominous escort I radioed Drew and told him about it. "Okay," said Drew. "Slow right down and get him to pass you. If he won't pass you then wait until you're around a corner and accelerate like hell." I slowed down and my heart hammered as the police van slowed down too—but eventually he passed and for some miles he stayed between our two cars. In fact we conversed right over his head by radio until Drew felt it was safe for me to pass him and both cars could steadily draw away. This we did, and finally lost sight of his headlights far behind.

The next scare came in Jamestown, the small town where Premier Vorster was born. It was now about midnight, and as I pulled up at a traffic light in the town a police van drew alongside and stopped right beside me. I was no more than four feet away from the policemen in it, and we looked at each other. I forced myself to look away deliberately, as if bored, and when the light changed they turned to the left and drove away as I went straight on.

We came at last to a remote branch road off the main north highway, cutting across a section of the north-western Transkei for the last two hours of driving towards the Telle Bridge area. Because of its remoteness and less frequent usage the dirt road felt safer to me, yet in another way more dangerous because, being among the few cars using the road, we were more conspicuous. We were going along fast on this dirt road when my car had a blow-out. I radioed Drew, who decided to make use of the unavoidable delay by refuelling as well. Each car had been carrying a large supply of gasoline in the trunk in defiance of South Africa's strict fuel-rationing laws, and we started filling both tanks up from these extra canisters. With the wheel changed and the tanks refilled, we drove on. During the next stretch of road, which seemed endless because it was through desolate country, we passed only three cars. We had now been driving for eight hours.

Wendy, after getting me clear of the town, had returned to the house to project a rented film for the children, and as they watched it she packed the barest minimum of clothing they would all need for their own journey. We had told the two eldest, Jane and Dillon, what was happening, but couldn't risk an indiscreet comment by the smaller ones. Early the next morning Wendy loaded the cases and got the children into the car, driving them "towards the beach" but in reality turning east to head for Umtata, a hundred and fifty miles away, "to see Grandpa and Grandma". She nearly didn't make it to Umtata by ten o'clock, as the car developed distributor trouble and barely crawled along the last fifty miles.

During the early hours of that morning I was having problems of my own. We arrived in the Telle Bridge area an hour later than the schedule Drew and I had worked out with Robin, which meant I would have to do some fast hiking over the hills to reach the rendezvous in time. On top of that, we found that after days of continuous rain in the area the Telle River was in flood, and the tiny stream was now a broad

347

torrent. It was no longer a case of wading across but of a swim through floodwater in the dark. Drew and I found the going heavy even to reach the river bank. The rain had turned the arid river basin into a kind of marshy series of deep gulches each of which took a long time to cross.

When we got to the actual bank the crossing-point seemed too turbulent. Unburdened, I could have swum the river, but I was carrying a heavy bag which contained the duplicate typescript of the book. We realized I should have to find a better crossing-point, and that the search for one might take another hour. I thought of the increasing danger Drew was in the longer he delayed his return, and told him to leave me there. But he refused point blank and we had quite an argument about it.

We tried to retrace our steps across a gulch to find a better crossing-point, still arguing over whether he should stay or go, and with awful suddenness a very bright light hit us from nowhere. In the movies searchlights seem to move towards fugitives with considerate slowness, approaching them deliberately and giving them plenty of time to lie flat—but here the beam hit us immediately and seemed to light up the whole surrounding world. We dived to the ground, I aided by a thump in the back from Drew which winded me slightly and sent my face into the sand.

The beam seemed to hold us for a long time. I was impressed with its intensity, because in its light I could see the individual hairs on my wrist. But the "searchlight" was only a pair of powerful headlights from a car travelling the riverside road and trapping us in its beam for probably only a few seconds before it took the curve and was gone. The driver, watching the road, would not have seen us in the distance. But the light *had* been intense, and only one make of car we knew had such bright lights. "Bloody Mercedes!" muttered Drew as we got to our feet. The scare was useful to me because it underlined the danger he was in. "Look," I said, "I'll certainly get across that river, I promise. I'm safe already, being so close. But you must get out of this area fast!" We had left one of the cars back on the road many miles before, and now I waved him away in "mine". We said goodbye and he called: "See you one day in London!"

I looked for houses of local blacks, confident they would help me to find the best crossing-point over the flooded river, and by a remarkable coincidence was directed to the house of a man I had known ten years before when I had interceded for him with his employer, who had wanted to fire him for belonging to a banned organization. It was now nearly four o'clock in the morning, and when Tami Vundla sleepily opened his door he didn't recognize me. When I told him who I was he flung his arms round me and cried: "My friend! You are escaping! God has sent you to me to help you!" He made coffee in the tiny kitchen of his shack as we talked, then led me down towards the river bank to the best crossing-point.

The river here was narrower, and I could wade and swim it without much difficulty. I thought that if I left my coat and jacket with Tami, threw my shoes across with the socks in them and put my glasses inside my buttoned shirt I could make it across fairly easily. But the snag was my bag. I couldn't swim while carrying it, and it was too heavy to hurl across. I picked it up and swung it to feel how far it might be thrown, and the bottom panel gave way. Part of my manuscript bulged through, and the Beretta, which had been underneath the manuscript, dropped on to my ankle-bone. It was painful, and I jumped around swearing.

Tami, who had carried the bag part of the way, laughed and said: "You'd never throw that across, it's too heavy. What is it full of—guns?" I said: "It's got only one gun to carry, but lots of words. For all I know the copy is already safely in London, but I don't want to take chances with the section I have here. It's a book I've written about Steve." Tami said excitedly: "A book about Steve!" He took off his leather belt, wrapping it round the bag and buckling it tightly. "This *must* get out with you!"

Then another thought struck me. "Tami, how far are we from Telle Bridge?" "*Awu!* From the bridge? We are quite far —about nine miles. Why?" I explained about the rendezvous, realizing I would never link up with Robin in time to telephone Wendy from Maseru at ten o'clock if I crossed nine miles from the bridge, then still had to climb over a couple of mountains as well as several miles of road on the other side. It was already nearly six o'clock in the morning, and I was beginning to feel desperate. The other bank seemed so close, but what use

349

would that be if Wendy and the kids turned back to East London as arranged if the call didn't come through?

Then I had a bold idea. "Tami," I said, "do you know anyone you can trust who has a car?" He smiled: "I trust *me*, and *I* have a car. It's a terrible old car, but it works." "Can you drive me to near the bridge?" He said: "Yes, of course, but you can't swim over there." "That's okay," I replied. "I'm going to bluff my way past those border guards. I have a fake passport, and if I can get past them it'll save two hours on the other side. "*Awu!*" he said. "*Masiqube! Let's ride!*" He laughed delightedly, stamping the ground with his foot and going into a sort of Xhosa litany at the thought of the Government's reaction when I got out: "Vorster is going to shit himself! Kruger is going to shit himself! Botha is going to shit himself!"

We got into his battered old car, and he drove along the dirt road like a racing driver. It felt as if we were shaking to pieces, but he got me there and warmly wished me luck as we embraced farewell. "You'll make it," he said. "You'll make it and they'll shit themselves. *Mayibuye i Afrika!*" ("Rise again Africa!") "*Mayibuye!*" I answered, and walked towards the gate.

It was six-thirty, the sun was just up, and I was afraid that even if I got across promptly I was unlikely to make contact with Robin in time to reach Maseru and phone Wendy. Once across I had a five-mile walk to find him—if he was still there four hours after our rendezvous time. I reached the big diamond-mesh gate of the border post and saw no sign of life. It was padlocked, and I rattled it for a full five minutes before a sleepy-eyed black police constable walked up on the other side of it. "Greetings, Reverend," he said respectfully. "Greetings," I said. "Why is this gate locked?" "We only open at seven, *Mfundisi*," he replied. "We are not allowed to open before." "But I have to say early Mass at Qthing," I exclaimed. "Can't you open it a little earlier today?" "I'm not allowed to, Reverend. And even if I could, the senior officials at the post only come on duty at seven." So there was a frustrating half-hour wait.

I was fretting that by now the Security Police might have discovered my whereabouts and my route, and might even now be in pursuit and about to appear over the hill along the road to the big gates where I waited with my bag held together by Tami's belt. A few minutes later I was looking at the approach road when I saw a vehicle come over the brow of the hill, travelling very fast. An awful fear hit me in the pit of the stomach as the shape of the vehicle developed into that of a police van—a Land Rover type, the characteristic light grey in colour. I looked round and at the river bank down below the bridge with the wild thought of running for it, dumping the bag in the mud and swimming—but it was crazy, because if they knew I was on the run they would certainly have closed the frontier to Wendy and the children already, and getting out without them had no point at all.

My only hope, as the vehicle got closer and closer, sending up a huge aftertrail of dust, was that they might not be police. But who else could they be? I could make out two figures as the vehicle started braking to a halt directly in front of me in a shower of gravel, dust and clods of mud. Then I thought I must be going crazy, because the front seat passenger had the face of a dog. Then I saw that it *was* a dog. A big brown dog. And the driver was black. He had Lesotho licence plates and he wore a knitted cap. Blackness meant safety.

"*Awu!* Not open yet!" the driver got out and said exasperatedly at the gate. "*Awu!* Sorry, Father! I didn't notice you were a Father at first." Taking a chance on the fact that Lesotho was heavily Catholic, I said: "Yes, I am impatient too! I have to say Mass over in Qthing and I'm already late." "What is the time, then, Father? My watch says seven o'clock." I said: "No, I'm afraid it's only ten to."

So we chatted as we waited out the ten minutes, I trying not too obviously to be sneaking looks up the approach road. "How is it you are walking?" he asked. "Oh, a friend brought me this far, and other friends are meeting me across the border." "Well," he replied. "Why don't you get in here with me and I can at least drive you over to them and we can go through the checkpoints together? I am well known here as I pass through often. I am a Government servant in Lesotho, an inspector of postal services." I offered up a silent prayer of thanks and climbed in next to him, his dog reluctantly yielding me the front seat as it flopped into the back and glared at me. I felt a lot safer as an accredited passenger than as a pedestrian priest. My

351

benefactor introduced himself as Moses, which I thought an appropriate name in the circumstances, but I was so tense that I never took in his second name.

Still we waited for the gates to be opened and still they stayed shut.

At five past seven the constable sauntered up to the gate, and with agonizing slowness unlocked the big padlock, fumbling at it intolerably and snarling the lock-chains before finally untangling them to open up. Moses revved up as the constable fumbled away, and the vehicle shot forward as soon as there was enough space between the opened gates to let us through. "Sorry, but I know you're also in a hurry," said Moses. I smiled in what I hoped was a benign and priestly way.

Then we were at the counter, Moses ushering me respectfully forward: "You go first, Father." He greeted the officials, whom he seemed to know, and added by explanation: "Father's late to say Mass in Qthing." The official barely looked at my "passport", but sleepily shoved the form towards me. I filled it in with a brisk air of conscientiousness. By now all three officials were turning their attention to Moses's request for quick process in view of his own lateness, and there was much stamping of both our papers. Suddenly it was all over, and we were clambering into the vehicle as the constable raised the boom for us to go through to the Lesotho officials on the other side of the bridge.

We rumbled over the bridge, up to the middle of it, along to the far end of it, over the last of the water below and up to the Lesotho post on the other side. Here Moses dominated all the conversation in a rapid flow of Sotho, and, although the Lesotho officials scrutinized my papers less perfunctorily than their counterparts on the other side had, I was again waved through first and stood on Lesotho soil.

It was a marvellous moment, and I did a brief dance of jubilation.

I had composed myself into a more priestly mien by the time Moses came out. "Now, Father, I can't take you to Qthing, but I could take you part of the way to Maseru." "Well, if you could just get me five miles up the road to where my friends are waiting, Moses," I asked. "But on what road?" he said, looking puzzled. "On the Maseru road," I said. "But there are several roads to Maseru," he explained. "Your friends could be on any one of them." This was a new one on me. "Isn't there a main one? A tarred one?" Moses laughed: "Father, you won't see much tar in Lesotho. We're a poor little country. There's no main road. Just some roads. All dirt roads."

"Well, which road were you planning to take?" I asked. "One of the smaller ones, because I have to inspect a building in a little village away from the main roads." I said: "Oh, well, let's go your way," realizing that linking up with Robin was now a near impossibility. "I hope there'll be a telephone," I said after the first few bumpy miles. Moses laughed again. "No telephone, Father. It's a very small village."

Then I saw a car parked by the side of the road. The driver was asleep. His head looked like Robin's head, the licence plate was the right one. Moses had inadvertently stumbled on the needle in the haystack. When I later learnt that Robin was also on the "wrong" road and didn't know where he was, I understood the dimensions of the coincidence. I told Moses he had found my friend, thanked him for his kindness and wrung his hand. He drove away with a cheerful: "Goodbye, Father! Good luck!"

I approached the sleeping Robin and rapped on the door. He glanced up listlessly. I raised my hand in benediction and said: "Bless you, my son." He looked dazed, obviously not recognizing me. I then said: "Wake up, you sleepy bastard!" Robin burst into a shout: "By Christ! By Christ!" He had given up after driving along several roads during the night and searching in gulches and ditches by torchlight. Early morning though it was, he broke open a six-pack of beer and we had quite a celebration as I urged him to break all speed records to Maseru. "We've got to get there by ten o'clock!" I pleaded.

Our teeth nearly shook out of our heads as he hurled the car over the appalling road at speeds which frightened me but which were necessary if the call to Wendy was to go through on time. We tore into Maseru at ten minutes to ten. No rally driver could have done better. I grabbed a passing pedestrian. "Quick," I said, "which is nearer—the American Embassy or the British Embassy?" He said the British were only a block away, reminding me proudly that in Commonwealth countries embassies are called High Commissions. At the High Commission I asked to see the High Commissioner urgently and was told: "The High Commissioner is away, but the Acting High Commissioner will see you." The Acting High Commissioner, Jim Moffatt, greeted me politely, recognized my name and readily assured me of the succour and assistance of Her Majesty's representatives in Lesotho.

"Do come in," he said, then added, incredibly, "Would you care for a cup of tea?" I laughed rather hysterically at this, then said: "Thank you, sir, but could I first use your phone for an urgent call?" He said: "Most certainly," and within seconds, right on the stroke of ten o'clock, I was speaking to Wendy to say, "Come on over—quick as you can."

By nightfall Wendy and the children were across the border, and we were all safe in Lesotho before the South African Security Police were even aware that I was no longer in my house.

Owing to the heavy rainfall in Lesotho for several days many of the roads were impassable, and Wendy and the children had to spend the night in a village near the border before joining me in Maseru in time to celebrate New Year's Day. She had had a tense time with a South African passport official who, fortunately, was in a state of severe distraction because he had given up smoking that morning. In consequence he hardly took note of names and dates for passport purposes—a good thing, since she was so nervous that she garbled the dates of several of the children's birthdays on the form she was filling in. She made full use of the man's preoccupation with his withdrawal-symptoms, kept him discussing his non-smoking problem and recommended a brand of tranquillizer which he wrote down. He stamped her and the children's documents, and when she left his desk he was still in an agony of uncertainty about how he was going to cope with life without tobacco.

Having had car trouble reaching Umtata, she and the children had to be driven to the Lesotho border by her father, Harold Bruce, who saw them safely across. By this time the Lesotho officials at the border had been alerted by their Government, and they were expecting Wendy and the children.

Immediately on my arrival Jim Moffatt had communicated with London and with the Lesotho Government, which immediately granted us political asylum. The Lesotho officials were good to us. From the moment we were within their borders they assigned armed police guards to protect us and the children from possible attempts by the South African Security Police to pursue us and take us back. In the past there had been several attempts at abducting refugees from South Africa, and the Lesotho authorities weren't taking any chances with our safety. When we were all reunited in Maseru at the home of Jim and Pam Moffatt, who provided hospitality and friendship far beyond the call of official duty, it was a moving sight for me to see the black Security Police of Lesotho guarding my white children against the possibility of attack by the white Security Police of South Africa. Several members of the Lesotho cabinet, including the Prime Minister, Chief Leabua Jonathan, went out of their way to welcome us as "white Africans", and to assure us of sanctuary.

The children seemed to be enjoying the adventure of the whole experience, and were adjusting to it with remarkable composure. Wendy related how, when it was safe for her to tell the smaller ones that they weren't returning home, Gavin had responded: "Aw, why didn't you say so earlier? I would have brought my skateboard."

Reporters in Maseru soon learned of our arrival, and the first the South African Security Police knew of our escape was when the midday radio news was broadcast of our presence in Lesotho. Reporters from Johannesburg started phoning us, and I had to face the question of how I had crossed the border. Drew and Tami had asked me to put out a "smokescreen" story to protect them by drawing attention as far as possible away from anything to do with their roles or the Telle Bridge area, so when a Johannesburg newspaper concluded that I had swum the Telle River I did not contradict this, beyond pointing out that the Telle is a small river usually fordable without swimming. The newspapers seized avidly on this, and before long I was being credited with an epic swim through raging floodwaters—into which one magazine even inserted crocodiles, in spite of my denial to the reporter concerned that there were any crocodiles within hundreds of miles of the Telle . . .

One good consequence of the reports of my mythical swim was that the story threw the Security Police off the right scent for several weeks, until my helpers' various tracks were well

355

covered. By the time the police started looking at transit records over the Telle Bridge border post these records were so obscure that they never got near the right story. They interrogated several people but were obviously wide of the mark, because by that time both Robin and Drew were overseas, and they never went near Tami Vundla or found any traces of his involvement.

One of my first concerns in Maseru had been to make arrangements for our flight out of Lesotho. Only charter services flew out of the country, and all three light aircraft had been grounded for several days because of the severe weather. Two of the planes needed servicing, and therefore only one would be available to fly us out—if the weather let up. Day after day went by with no sign of improvement, and with each day the danger grew that the South African government would prevent our flight over their territory. The delay was giving them time to formulate a response, and was nullifying our original advantage of surprise. Among the journalists who had come to Maseru to cover the story was a representative of the Government publication, *The Citizen*, and he told us that it had been decided in Pretoria to block the flight, to refuse transit to the charter plane and to force it down with jets if we ignored this veto.

Jim Moffatt took me to see the head of the charter company, Mr McElrea, a Canadian, and his chief pilot, a New Zealander named Richie de Montauk. I could sense that in spite of Pretoria's threats these men wanted to help us. They agreed with my view that the longer we waited the harder it would be to defy Pretoria's ban on overflying. I felt we had to take the chance—and the sooner the better. It *was* quite a chance, because the flight from Lesotho over South African territory to Botswana took two hours and twenty minutes. Lesotho charter planes were required by South Africa to land in Bloemfontein or Johannesburg in transit, and we would have to ignore this requirement or risk having the plane impounded and all of us arrested. The pilot took no part in the discussion. A taciturn man, he simply puffed on his pipe and listened. Eventually Mr McElrea came to a decision and said: "I say let's take the chance—what do you say, Richie?" Richie merely nodded and puffed away on his pipe. The plan was to take off the next morning and hope the weather wouldn't be impossible.

Next day we said fond farewells to Jim and Pam Moffatt, who had been so kind to us. The plane looked tiny as we climbed aboard. It was a nine-seater Britten–Norman Islander, and I only hoped we would have no mechanical failure which would force us to land in South African territory. A group of journalists gathered at the airport to watch us take off. Wendy's brother Peter was among them, and within a year he would follow us by the same route. Also there to see us off was John Ryan.

As we were boarding, Mr McElrea had a signal from the South African control tower in Bloemfontein demanding that he should disclose the names of his passengers. By this time the South African Government had ordered that all flights out of Maseru had to be monitored by Bloemfontein, and ours was to be the first flight in five days. The Lesotho Government had made the gesture of assigning an official to travel with us as an escort, although the Prime Minister, Chief Jonathan, told me: "I don't know if it will help, but it's the best we can offer." When the Bloemfontein control tower insistently demanded that the identities of all passengers should be disclosed, Mr McElrea "failed to hear" the signal. Eventually, after persistent questioning, he responded that the plane contained his pilot, an official of the Lesotho Government, and "seven holders of United Nations passports". The UN office in Maseru had issued us with refugee passports, special travel documents provided for political fugitives. Mr McElrea then gave final instructions to Richie as he warmed up the engines. "Whatever happens, don't land in South African territory," he said. "You're to land either in Botswana or back here." Richie nodded, shut his door and taxied to the take-off mark.

Beside Richie sat the Lesotho Government official. I sat behind Richie, with Dillon on my right, then came Jane, Gavin and Duncan, and in the last two seats Wendy and Mary. It seemed a small space to hold us all—a couple of square yards in this fragile little aircraft—but it represented a chance to get away, and as far as I was concerned the sooner we were in the air the better.

The little plane sped down the runway, our friends on the ground waved, and we were in the air. The sky was cloudy,

357

light rain was falling, and we bumped about as we gained altitude. Maseru being right on the Lesotho–South African border, within minutes of take-off we were over South African territory.

I wondered how serious the threat was to force us down. One of Wendy's last comments to a reporter who raised the subject of danger in the sky was: "If we're shot down just say we died of hunger strike!" As a journalist I knew I'd be given a good hearing if we got out—but the first priority was to make it to Botswana to be finally clear of apartheid territory. Unlike Wendy, who later told me she was beyond feeling any fear at that stage, I was tense and fearful throughout our flight. My mind surged with prayers I hadn't said since my convent days in early childhood. This seemed no time for sophistication or for intellectual rejection of what Elizabeth Browning would have called my "lost saints". I called them all into action—particularly the specialist, St Christopher. I suppose I didn't close my eyes for a moment during that flight. I was searching every section of the skies above us, ahead, to the left, to the right and below. I tapped Richie on the shoulder: "Hey, Richie—what'll you do if jets try to force us down?" Richie took his pipe out of his mouth and said in ripe New Zealand tones: "I'll go down to below five hundred feet and see what they can do that close to the ground!" It seemed a comforting reply, but had nothing to do with reality. Jets could do almost anything under five hundred feet. But maybe it was the casual way he resumed puffing on his pipe that reassured me more than his words. It was only later that I realized he was putting on a front, to encourage us, and that he also was tense and apprehensive during the flight.

Much of the way we were in thick cloud, and this seemed to offer the illusion of protection. The cloud would then part, and through a hole we'd see the brown fields of the Free State. Time passed with agonizing slowness. I had to stop looking at my watch because it seemed to immobilize the minute hand . . . After it felt as if we had been travelling an hour I found we had been going barely fifteen minutes, and it was like that throughout the long flight. Every minute dragged, and there were one hundred and forty of them to endure, second by second. There was virtually no conversation in the cabin. The engine-noise was loud, the Lesotho Government man concentrated on his book—or at least gave that impression—and I didn't want to distract Richie with talk. From time to time Dillon asked a question, and Duncan and Gavin occasionally had one of their puppylike scuffles, but Jane lay back with her eyes shut and Mary slept most of the way on Wendy's lap. Wendy appeared either to doze or to stare blankly ahead, and I thought how much more physically courageous she was than I. I knew she wasn't going through my brand of prayerful tension; she had a far more fatalistic approach.

Eventually the long, slow flight drew to a close. I was estimating by my watch that we should be crossing into Botswana to land soon at the capital, Gaberone, which is barely a dozen miles from the border, when we flew out of a steep cliff of dense cloud into brilliant sunshine and Richie pointed ahead. "Gaberone!" he yelled. "We're going in to land!" The little plane's nose dipped, we lined up poised above the landing strip, then settled softly in a perfect landing. I leant forward and clapped Richie on the shoulders with both hands. "Good on yer, Rich!" I yelled. He smiled around his pipe.

As we climbed out of the tiny plane I felt a pang of affection for it. Its propellers, still slowing down as we alighted, seemed so small. Reporters and onlookers lined the fence beside the airfield as we were welcomed by the British High Commissioner in Botswana, Fred Turner, and his wife Muriel, who had been phoned by Jim Moffatt.

From Gaberone we flew to Francistown and on to Lusaka, in Zambia, where President Kaunda welcomed us as guests of that state and had us to dinner in State House. Black magnanimity seemed a comforting contrast to the white viciousness which had subjected Mary to the tee-shirt incident, and that thought was in my mind as President Kaunda led us in to dinner. He brought a radio to the table so that we could hear the international news bulletins—and one of them told how Security Police had come to our house and impounded all our belongings, confiscating everything, including our savings in the bank, our furniture and clothes.

At State House we gave the last of several press conferences that had been held in Zambia, then took leave of the President and left under presidential motorcade escort for the airport for our final flight to London. At the airport we were welcomed by Caledonian Airways and shown to the first-class cabin, courtesy of the line. At dawn we landed for refuelling in Tunisia, then had our last look at Africa as we took off for London on the final stage of our journey.

As the plane came in to land at Gatwick I warned the children to behave because there would be reporters waiting. "How many reporters, Daddy?" asked Dillon. "Oh, several, I suppose," I said. "From different papers, and probably a few photographers." We weren't prepared for the scale of our welcome. As we came down the aircraft steps we saw a sea of journalists as reporters and photographers surged forward. It was staggering. It was also encouraging, because it meant a chance to get major exposure for advocating an intensification of the international anti-apartheid campaign. The black people of Southern Africa had been grossly under-represented in the Western lobbies, where so many millions of rands were spent by the apartheid embassies to buy propaganda points which their victims had neither the money nor the image to counter. I decided to make use of every opportunity to help redress that balance; to take every chance offered to spread the truth about South Africa. Apartheid wasn't only a policy of repression against the blacks of South Africa; it was an affront to all humanity, and therefore logically the concern of all humanity, and I would do whatever I could to help raise awareness of that fact.

As we walked from the aircraft into the crowded terminal, I felt full of hope and a new perception. For so long, in the war between the apartheid "they" and the anti-apartheid "us", it had been "they" who had monopolized the political power and the media support. But in this wider perspective of a whole world full of people, it suddenly seemed that "they" were now in the weaker position. There were so many more of "us" now.

In fact, most of humanity.

EPILOGUE

OUR DEPARTURE FROM South Africa didn't end our sense of involvement with the country, and we continued to keep in touch with friends there by various means. It did, however, have a direct effect on the lives of some people, enemies as well as friends.

Warrant Officers Marais and Van Schalkwyk were punished for embarrassing the Government over the tee-shirt incident. Both were transferred to minor posts by Minister Kruger, before the same thing happened to him. Donald Card was ousted from his job by his employers for taking our part over the tee-shirt and shooting incidents. He successfully founded his own firm and became Mayor of East London in 1980. Some of our friends were interrogated by the Security Police shortly after our escape, but were released unharmed because they had known nothing of our plans, and our close relatives, being "non-political", weren't molested in any way. My deputy, George Farr, took over the *Dispatch* editorship.

Shortly after our arrival in London I received a warning from the South African Security Police that I wasn't to think I was "beyond their reach", and that in particular I was on no account to make any speeches for the anti-apartheid movement abroad. This made me all the more determined to do everything I could to further the fight against apartheid, and after the book on Steve Biko was published a mass of speaking engagements took me literally round the world. Always in my mind was the thought that the sooner the international community could be persuaded to adopt strong economic and diplomatic action to end apartheid, the more lives could be saved on both sides in the developing South African crisis.

The irony has been that the South African Government's ban on me, which sought to stop me from writing, to confine me to my home and to prevent me from communicating publicly, has in fact caused me to write more than ever and to communicate with a greater mass of people than ever would have been possible had I been left alone. It has seemed, in the circumstances, an appropriate response to such a ban.

During the two years since our escape South Africa has been much in the news—Premier Vorster resigned in disgrace, Dr Mulder was fired and General van den Bergh was replaced as head of the Bureau of State Security, which was reorganized and renamed. The Muldergate scandal—a series of admissions that the Vorster government had for years been spending millions to undermine opposition newspapers commercially, bribe legislators in foreign capitals, buy favourable reports from Western journalists and run "dirty tricks" squads to smear opponents of apartheid—was essentially the manifestation of a power-struggle in the high councils of the Afrikaner Nationalists in which P. W. Botha emerged as the victor over Mulder to succeed Vorster as Prime Minister.

His apparent "liberalization" of policy was not a softening of basic apartheid but the result of an agreement among the new party leaders to try to repair some of the damage done to their international image in 1977 and 1978, and to improve race relations within the country. This agreement was aimed at altering the *tactics* of apartheid in order to reinforce the *strategy* of it—to put a better face on it externally and to buy time to consolidate white control further over the black majority.

The new image-builders decided on several steps to seek a better press overseas. The Biko family were paid a substantial sum not in acknowledgement of guilt but to prevent adverse publicity in a civil hearing, and some superficial concessions were made in sports apartheid so that people overseas would be given the impression that basic apartheid was being eroded. To ensure that spokesmen of the anti-apartheid South African Council on Sport couldn't put their case overseas their passports continued to be impounded and their bans maintained, while inside the country integrated sport at club level continued to be the token exception rather than the general rule.

But the essence of apartheid still remained: the retention of effective political and economic power in white hands. That alone will be the core of the coming conflict in South Africa. What the blacks want is the vote—universal adult suffrage expressed as "one-man-one-vote"—and *nothing* less. The Afrikaner Nationalists could scrap literally hundreds of apartheid laws without touching this core, and by doing so could possibly buy time—but not a lasting peace. On the contrary, delay in confronting the core of contention will lead only to a further build-up on both sides for the final conflict. The wallpaper covers the cracks temporarily, but the cracks continue to widen.

While the Botha government is considering minor concessions the black resistance movements are proceeding with the training and arming of tens of thousands of guerillas in various African countries, and, as the southward march of the wresting of control from white rule—in Kenya, Angola, Zaire, Zambia, Malawi and Mozambique—has gradually reached the doorstep of South Africa in Zimbabwe, the African National Congress and the Pan-Africanist Congress have been stepping up their preparations for the final showdown.

Whites in South Africa know little about these developments, nor of the scale of the threat being prepared for them. Since the banning of the Black Consciousness Movement in 1977, which meant that all the significant black militant groups within the country were driven underground, the whites have increasingly mistaken the tip of the iceberg of black militancy for the whole mass of it. New laws have further eroded what has been left of press freedom, and during 1978 and 1979 governmental and societal pressures against journalists and publications further inhibited even the few anti-apartheid newspapers, so that editorial reflection and criticism of racial policy has become increasingly less blunt and more circumspect. The new Police Act effectively forbids any South African newspaper to expose or criticize police misdeeds too forthrightly, and the reports we published about the police at the time of the Biko killing in 1977 could not have been published since 1979.

Aiding the process of illusion is the widely held belief among white South Africans that the major black challenge to them is from black spokesmen, including a couple of homelands leaders, who function legally within the still-permitted limits of the system and may be expected at a later stage to help create a black middle-class and participate in a compromise settlement as a buffer against the militants. There is no wide awareness among white South Africans that the real challengers are training in bush camps across the border, or that the 1980s will see the final confrontation with white rule on the continent of Africa.

Following the huge election success of Robert Mugabe's party in March 1980, which finally changed Rhodesia into Zimbabwe, the South African government leaders have had to take a new look at their own situation, and there have been immediate signs of ferment within the Afrikaner Nationalist leadership, with the relatively liberal Botha faction contending with the right-wing Treurnight faction. But it wasn't conceivable that even the Botha faction could go far enough to meet real black aspirations.

To achieve the near-miracle of averting tragic civil war, the Afrikaner Nationalist leaders would have to free all political prisoners, enable the black liberation movements to participate freely and fairly in legitimate elections based on one-man-one-vote, and demonstrate a willingness to abide by the result. There is no evidence to suggest, however, that the grassroots Afrikaner Nationalist power-base would permit government leaders to go this far.

By 1980 the harsh reality for South African whites, whether they realize it or not, is that the key political organization whose decisions will have the greatest bearing on the fate of the country is no longer the Afrikaner Nationalist Party but the African National Congress. Whether alone or in concert with allied movements, or even in union with all the black liberation elements, the nucleus and following of the ANC, the most senior of all the liberation movements historically, is as crucial a determinant in the South African situation as the Patriotic Front in Zimbabwe, the Frelimo in Mozambique and all the other mainstream liberation movements throughout Africa.

Only two things can be said with certainty about the developing war in South Africa—that the whites will lose, and that the more fiercely they fight the more comprehensively they will lose.

INDEX

by

Michael Gordon

FOR THE BEST IN PAPERBACKS, LOOK FOR THE 🐧

In every corner of the world, on every subject under the sun, Penguin represents quality and variety – the very best in publishing today.

For complete information about books available from Penguin – including Pelicans, Puffins, Peregrines and Penguin Classics – and how to order them, write to us at the appropriate address below. Please note that for copyright reasons the selection of books varies from country to country.

Donald Woods in Penguin

SOUTH AFRICAN DISPATCHES

Donald Woods's columns in the *Daily Dispatch*, syndicated all over South Africa, lacerated the pretensions and absurdities of his government with razor-sharp wit and incisive analysis. Woods lambasts the double-talk of Pik and P. W. Botha, official committees and the pussyfooting preachers who tried to be 'non-political'; he pleads for Mandela's release, tells the story of Kissinger and the crocodile, exposes the scandalous deaths in detention, and celebrates the rebels such as Father Mac. Woods is often a master of high-spirited and revealing satire, but the death of his close friend Steve Biko, inspired the series of darker, far more impassioned pieces which led to his arrest; they rank among the classics of committed journalism.

BIKO

'Courageous and passionate ... Mr Woods's brave attack on the shabby and ultimately murderous expedients of a society dominated by fear and greed should serve as both an inspiration and a warning' – Christopher Hampton in the *Sunday Times*

Founder of the Black Consciousness Movement, Steve Biko was a natural target for the South African authorities. On 18 August 1977 Steve Biko was arrested, interrogated and beaten. On 12 September he was dead. Donald Woods was a friend of Steve Biko's and went into exile in order to write his testimony about the life and work of a remarkable man.